Innovations and Emerging Technologies for the Prosperity and Quality of Life

Edited by Małgorzata Runiewicz-Wardyn

Innovations and Emerging Technologies for the Prosperity and Quality of Life

The Case of Poland

PWN

Cover and title page design:
Piotr Fedorczyk

Cover photograph:
kentoh /Fotolia

Project editor:
Dorota Siudowska-Mieszkowska

Editorial coordinator:
Renata Ziółkowska

Copy editor:
Bogna Piotrowska

Production coordinator
Mariola Iwona Keppel

Typeset by
ALINEA

Copyright © by Wydawnictwo Naukowe PWN SA
Warszawa 2016

ISBN 978-83-01-18952-5

First edition

Wydawnictwo Naukowe PWN SA
02-460 Warszawa, ul. Gottlieba Daimlera 2
tel 22 69 54 321, fax 22 69 54 288
infoline 801 33 33 88
e-mail: pwn@pwn.com.pl
www.pwn.pl

Printed and bound by OSDW Azymut Sp. z o.o.

Contents

Preface

Since the late 20th century we have witnessed a major acceleration of scientific and technological advance. The advent of the Internet as a result of a long term development process in the field of information and communication technologies in the mid-90's completely changed the innovation paradigm, making possible the reconfiguration of the process of disruptive innovation: a large new base of generic technologies was made available through a model that favoured new views and approaches, heavy user feedback and involvement and new methodologies for rapid prototyping and product / process initiation.

The nature of the new innovation process is very important, in the sense that it has set up and is being fed by new creative platforms where a lot of converging technologies meet, and in the process they generate new models for introducing new concepts and paradigms in an endless reconfiguration continuum. A major characteristic of these new platforms is that they do not necessarily need completely new technologies to run and produce their effects: the power of the platform approach resides in the self-organizing profile of open technologies and services that create new opportunities in driving forward convergence, which is the major model for disruptive new approaches in product / process generation. ICT emerged as a powerful enabler for global convergence, creating new devices and new services through an ever-progressing combination of features, generic technologies and scientific domains. New areas have emerged in biotechnology, medicine, chemistry, drug conception and production heavily impacted by ICT (in silico modes are overwhelmingly overtaking in vitro preparation in most of the aforementioned fields). New services have emerged for the citizen, that has now become the epicentre of a major remote access revolution covering information, banking, work, travel, leisure, and increasingly healthcare, security and communication.

The digital revolution has now entered a new phase with emphasis on data and analytics, promising to modify completely the production chain (industry 4.0, 3-D Printing, big data for cities management) as we knew it. A second wave of new and disruptive technologies has hit the market and makes already a huge impact on reconfiguring the technological offer available to modern economies.

Yet, conditions for the deployment and uptake of these technologies (and scientific breakthroughs) are not ideal; some countries are simply too far away from being able to follow the new achievements of the knowledge economy. Differences in knowledge and innovation capabilities are potentially big, and Europe is no exception in this respect. The knowledge economy has a price, and the more a country fails to adjust to the speed and depth of such technological change, the greater the risk of its being marginalized and left out of the world game. The knowledge economy has changed dramatically the way countries integrate the global financial environment, creating harsh conditions in terms of competitiveness, growth and jobs, as several countries have difficulties in positioning themselves within the new global value chains.

It is precisely in this context that the added value of research and innovation can make a difference for countries under similar threats. More specifically, European countries that by definition adhere to the European social model of a social market economy, have no other alternative for regaining competitive advantage and repositioning themselves in the global economy. The real problem then for countries is how to maximize the quality of their research and innovation investment and design an effective strategy for setting up an efficient research and innovation ecosystem that is able to translate within reasonable timing these investments into tangible economic and social benefits.

Despite years of serious actions by the European Union using multiple funding streams and technical assistance (such as the Framework Programme for Research and Innovation, the Competitiveness and Innovation Framework Programme, the European Structural and Investment Funds and more recently the financial engineering tools introduced by the European Investment Bank), a huge innovation divide persists in Europe . Due to a host of structural reasons most countries of Central and Eastern Europe, as well as countries (and regions) in the South of Europe, present significant disparities in terms of research and innovation performance.

To fight against these disparities, Europe has a full array of programmes and tools that try to address the root causes of the problem, namely stimulate excellence in research and innovation communities, link better business, academia and government in innovation-driven partnerships, and cultivate competitiveness through research and innovation strategies for Smart Specialization (RIS3) at national and regional levels. Smart Specialization (a place-based growth strategy based on knowledge assets as priority drivers for economic development) is now earmarked in the new Cohesion Policy regulations as the pre-condition for any kind of support the ERDF would allocate to EU Member States for research and innovation investment (ex-ante conditionality). RIS3 points to an integrated strategy at local level for deep economic transformation, using new alternative routes for identifying investment priorities: Europe can only compete in global markets through knowledge investment, trying to outsmart its global partners with new ideas. This however is not possible without an integrated strategy to identify the best growth opportunities and drivers for economic change at national and regional levels. Such a strategy should be always bottom-up, involving a full participatory process of all living economic forces in a country or region, in particular all four parts of the so-called Quadruple Helix (academia, industry, government and civil society).

The European Commission has been fully supportive towards Member States' efforts for building RIS3 either at regional or national level. A RIS3 Platform has been established in the context of the Joint Research Institute (JRC), Institute for Prospective Technological Studies (IPTS) in Seville (Spain), where a dedicated team of officials and experts have been shouldering the initiatives of the MS and regions, through dedicated workshops, analytical tools, databases and guides, and a fully-fledged website. The website features also an online database open to all interested parties (Eye@RIS3), covering the declared thematic priorities and orientations of the registered countries and regions in the database. This is an important tool that allows a better knowledge of peer priorities and a deeper understanding of trends in the European regional landscape.

With the process of planning almost completed at European level in terms of cohesion policy programming (2014-20), the attention of policy makers turns now to the challenge of implementation that calls even more forcefully for synergies and interactions with Horizon 2020, for which the European Commission published a thorough guide last year (2014). Horizon 2020 has no actions on capacity building in terms of cohesion policy, but has an important part on upgrading research and innovation performance for countries and regions that underperform. Part IV (Spreading excellence and widening participation) focuses thus on new Centres of Excellence (Teaming), extensive networking for upgrading quality and performance of involved institutions (Twinning) and an innovative action for bringing excellence in underperforming research institutions (European Research Area Chairs, or ERA Chairs). These activities are complemented through support to COST, the oldest intergovernmental cooperation framework in science, technology and innovation that has now an increased interest for the same group of underperforming countries.

This book is about the importance of knowledge and innovation for building competitive advantage in countries that need to reposition themselves at world level and gain an edge in the global economy. It focuses on Poland, one of the most dynamic European economies, engaged in a transition process. The European programmes and actions are well placed to support such efforts by offering opportunities and investment for a dynamic transformation: this is our global challenge for this young 21st century that unfolds.

Dr Dimitri CORPAKIS
Head of Unit RTD.B.5, Spreading excellence
and widening participation
Directorate for the Innovation Union and the ERA
Directorate General for Research and Innovation
European Commission

Introduction

Emerging technologies, such as information technology, educational technologies, biotechnology, create the potential for greater efficiency, new business opportunities and economic growth. Therefore these technologies constitute an important strategic element defining the future of European Union (EU) in the 21st century.

The increased interest in emerging technologies and innovations not only is a result of the deepening knowledge regarding it and the complexity of the topic, but also reflects an appreciation of the important role they play in determining the economic welfare and quality of life in the EU. The European competitive advantage on global scene as well as its improvements in the quality of life is determined by the capacity of EU regions, communities and individuals to transform these advanced technologies into socio-economic benefits. Numerous political declarations and theoretical concepts emphasize their significance, but provide rather weak evidence of their role in the empirical studies. The emergence of these new technologies, and their increasing convergence present both opportunities and challenges, which should be investigated by researchers and further on considered by policy makers.

The following study discusses firstly, the role of emerging technologies and innovations in building economic prosperity and quality of life in Poland and the EU, and secondly point to the major present and future challenges related to these technologies on national, regional and individual levels.

The book contains seven chapters. The first chapter opens the discussion on the drivers and socio-economic challenges, such as sustainability in relation with 21st century innovations and technological advances. The second chapter emphasizes the key role of private firms and clusters for the development and adoption of these technological advances and gives some possible policy actions to boost private R&D investments and innovative climate. The third chapter takes up the role of latest developments and innovations in meeting the challenges of environmental sustainability. The recent report of the 2030 Water Resource Group predicts that the worldwide water supply-to-demand gap is likely to reach approximately 40% by 2030 unless significant efficiency gains can be made. It further on predicts that by the year 2050, around 60% of the world's population could experience severe water shortages. In the EU, water scarcity and droughts already affect one third of the EU territory across different latitudes. The same chapter outlines some of the challenges and suggests some exploitable technological solutions in this field.

The fourth chapter discusses the important role played by the entrepreneurial culture, geographical proximity and social capital networking in enhancing innovations and building competitive advantage of regions and communities. The ageing of the population presents vast societal challenges to ensuring that our infrastructures can support the needs of older people, enabling them to live healthy, independent, and productive lives. Technological change helps mitigate demographic challenges. Chapter five discusses the role of ICT for independent living and elderly care.

Technology advances enable public sector innovations and therefore improve quality and efficiency in public services. Therefore, chapter sixth discusses the improvements of the quality of life in Poland through smart regulations and an innovative tax return system. The importance of a sound tax return system should not be viewed only through the budgetary needs – it has important implications in terms of the allocation of economic resources. It affects key economic decisions, such as investment into physical and human capital as well as the decisions to engage in entrepreneurial and innovation activities. Therefore, the proper design of revenue systems represents a key determinant of growth performance and overall standard of living.

Finally, chapter seven presents valuable views on the current state and future prospects of clinical research industry in Poland – the country that remains the largest clinical trials market in the Central Eastern European region.

Chapter I

Innovations and Technological Advances – Drivers and Challenges Related to the 21st Century

Lech W. Zacher

Innovations for Socially Creating a Sustainable Future (conditions, necessary transformations, probable results)

1. Introduction

> "From today's critical perspectives, however, and from the long view encompassed in this study, it seems clear that progress is neither inevitable nor necessarily sustainable."
>
> J. E. McClellan III, H. Dorn (2006) *Science and Technology in World History*, 2nd ed., Baltimore, MD, The Johns Hopkins Univ. Press

Our thinking on development and the future needs re-invention. Past experiences and traditional concepts and theories cannot explain a new socio-economic and environmental reality. The world is on the move, transformations are ongoing, and change is a main feature nowadays. An interpretation of this new changing reality requires new approaches, new cognitive methods, and a new language as well. So innovations of various type are badly needed if we want to understand the ongoing civilizational transformations worldwide and to build capacities to their rational and advantageous co-shaping.

2. Changing intellectual mindsets and Weltanschauung

The socio-economic developmental narrative and its participants are not immune to magical thinking, popular misconceptions, ideological assumptions, politics, interest-driven convictions, or even stupidity, not to mention errors and ignorance. So messages sent to decision-makers often happen to be confusing, ambiguous, and less than valuable for practice. Thus, it is important to check our mindsets especially in an era of great transformations (to recall Polanyi's term).

Instead of criticizing traditional concepts, theories, and practical patterns (e.g. in economic policy), it seems more useful to highlight new ideas and theoretical developments often based on empirical studies. A deeply modified intellectual, as well scientific, mindset is required under the new radically changing economic, social, and environmental realities (see e.g. Naisbitt 1990, 2006). Imagination (see e.g. Weber 2005) and reflexivity (e.g. Giddens 1990) should be reinforced. Cognition of the world's structures, mechanisms, and driving forces should also be a matter of mass social imagination as they are necessary in the accepting of governments' visions and policies on national and global levels. It is especially important in democratic countries where participatory demands of citizens are treated seriously and realized with the help of ICTs. Moreover, in mentally approaching these challenges, for our mindsets it is necessary to accept the idea of shared responsibility activities. Building a sustainable future is a concern of governments, businesses, and civil societies, which will include the participation of – to be more specific – systems designers, operators, planners, managers, educators, individuals in their multiple roles, e.g. as parents, local activists, consumers, NGOs' members etc. So general strategies for sustainability should be appropriately tailored to socio-organizational entities and coordinated as much as possible. Sustainability is a collective challenge and collective responsibility.

Coping intellectually with increasing complexity and accompanying diversity requires removing traditional convictions that the developmental processes tend to lean to, such as simplification, imitation, similarity, and universalization. These views were to a great extent a sign of domination of the Western economic power, culture, science, and media. So the past experiences of the West (in technological or economic policies or social behaviour) cannot be fully applied in other cultures, ideologies, religions, or political regimes. Huntington's "clash of civilization" proves true.

Diversity in material living worldwide fructifies with the plurality of worldviews, lifestyles, visions of the future, and the ability to develop a trajectory to sustainability. Multiculturalism should not be a "uniting" idea and practice, but a way to respecting differences and looking for agreeable consensus through participatory procedures. Relationships among people of the world cannot rely on imposition and power. The present reconfigurations of the world and the emergence and influence of non-Western centres of development should be reflected in our thinking (see Zacher, 2013). Sustainability must be an intercultural idea and activity.

New economics of development (recently called economics of moderation) is needed that is not universal but multioptional, responding to existing differences (and conflicts of interests worldwide) and trying through the networking of intellectual, political and economic actions to coordinate all efforts as much as possible between governments, diplomacy, international institutions and organizations, international NGOs, etc. However, innovativeness in this area should not emphasize the universalism but point up the differences; even in science and technology activity (see Indian and African manifestos – bibl.). The former comfortable (and wishful) assumption concerning world stability should be contested and rejected. The end of the Cold War, the fall of the Soviet Union, the rise of globalization and world trade, and the increased networking and cooperation have not saved the present development from much dangerous domestic and international instability (caused e.g. by Russia or by Jihadists). They may generate an international economic crisis, a new arms race (good for science and business, bad for taxpayers), new nationalisms, and ideological and religious clashes. Globalization, international cooperation, and trade can be slowed down and limited. Such a situation seems structural in its nature, and suggests the new approaches in the economics are needed, especially in the modern unstable world.

To deal with the aforementioned challenges (there are many more) it is necessary to invent and apply widely (e.g. in mainstream economics and sociology) new appropriate approaches and methods. Historically, the progress of science took place by multiplying new directions of research, new sub-disciplines, and new institutions. Paradoxically, it led to increasing specialization and fragmentation of research. This unintended "procedural" reductionism allowed for better understanding of "microcosm" but not of "macrocosm". Already a few decades ago, systems thinkers (e.g. E. Laszlo) and cyberneticians suggested a holistic and systemic approach with a wider use of modelling and simulations (made easier by the aid of computers). There were calls for inter- and trans-disciplinary approaches and research (even a post-disciplinary era was announced – see e.g. Zacher, 2006). However, science was (and is) institutionalized structurally, organizationally, and often personally. Networking – thanks to ICTs – does not automatically result in a successful cooperation. New proposals are emerging that are connected with such concepts as Computational Social Science and Big Data, and the use of supercomputers can help.

Innovations – intellectual, organizational, and institutional – are badly needed to overcome traditional approaches that are not currently fitting into a rapidly changing reality. Traditionally produced and often historically biased knowledge also has some generational dimension (Zacher, 2009). New generations of scientists born and formatted as "digital natives" may have less respect for old traditions and are more comfortable with new, not only technical competences. However so called "old knowledge" is still widespread and strong in education, in people's minds and not rarely in science institutions as well. Deside-ologization can be postulated in many scientific areas and investigations. For example, the ideology of unlimited exponential growth should be debated in terms of systems analysis, which evidently shows that the Earth as a closed system (without inputs from outside) is not able to assure living space, water, food, mineral resources, and a sound environment to an ever growing population (see Meadows, 2004). Ideologists believe (in a really religious manner) that it will be possible. Discussions on the limits to growth – spatial, physical, environmental, financial, etc. – are often not rational. Unlimited growth requires abundant resources that are not available. Moreover, it can be cynically stated that thanks to the underdevelopment (poverty, epidemics, short life expectancy, ethnic and religious wars) of the majority of the human population the world is still in a kind of stable equilibrium. This is sustainability mainly for the rich and dominating. To change this situation a holistic and systemic approach is fundamental in theory, politics, and actions. This is sustainability science which tries to address all of the issues, innovations included, connected with contemporary conditions, contexts, and challenges of the present complex, diverse, and endangered world.

To change a mind's intellectual baggage and also mainstream Weltanschauung in science and innovation areas, especially in a perspective of global science and technology policy, requires not only a prospective but also a retrospective approach. Colonialism vanished just about half a century ago. That is why some authors use the term a postcolonial globalizing world (Harding, 2011), reflecting that not only did Western scientists exploit non-Westerners but also that the imperial powers generally treated science (and technology) as a means of domination and dependence. Postcolonial transformations are often considered as inadequate. Scientific and technological institutions and practices still discriminate against the non-Western world by being rather insensitive to the non-Western scientific world; moreover, some neocolonial practices exist and brain drain is in progress. So demanding from the less advanced countries (more than a half of the human population) their participation in a drive to sustainability needs not only finances and innovations but also new thinking. Non-Western practices and knowledge, also local and indigenous, may be quite enriching for achieving sustainability on a local level and in relation with the technologically advanced world.

There are some recommendations for the present science and technology policies in less advanced countries. They are articulated in the two above quoted manifestos (http://www.set-dev.eu/) concerning India and Africa. Their policies should focus more on developing their own science and technology that best serves Indian and African agendas, not necessarily following the global North and West which have rather different research histories, possibilities, and goals. It is worthwhile to recall E. F. Schumacher, with his deep understanding of technological differences, who postulated so called intermediate and then appropriate technology (Gamser, 1988). The Western mainstream was not receptive to such novelties, nonetheless Schumacher and then his son tried to produce such technologies and install them in LDCs almost half a century ago. It seems practical and fruitful in the long term to set joint scientific and technological centres to educate and prepare new elites (also Western) to appreciate understanding differences and common challenges in realizing sustainability goals.

Sustainability can also be treated as a whole humanity project, which needs massive engagement, negotiations, cooperative solutions, and joint actions. This unprecedented challenge, unknown in history, requires two developments: a women's revolution and democratization. The first means an introduction of more than a half of the human population (i.e. women) into processes of development and sustainability building. It will generate costs, investment, and workplaces (ICTs can help to organize more possibilities of distant learning and working), but advantages may hopefully be immense. However, such an undertaking is basically connected with a great cultural transformation of patriarchally formed societies. Such a cultural innovation will have an inclusive power in every part of the world. The diffusion of this innovation (begun in the 19th century) has a processual character that is gradual though fundamental. Would male religious, political, and business leaders, all men in power, give up their dominating position? In any case, it would be a long term process of change.

Democratization is a political innovation well known for ages, however practised in less than half of the planet. Democracy, especially participatory, means sharing the power (in contrast to an electorate democracy that gives power to representatives who theoretically represent society) and assumes information, transparency, deliberation, negotiations, and a desire for consensus and cooperative solutions. The public is often neglected by political structures and business decision-makers. It seems, however, that in the times of increasing complexity, diversity, and uncertainty the social inclusion in visioning, policy elaboration, and business functioning can be advantageous in assuring legitimation and acceptance. In the areas of innovations, research, science, and technology there are growing participatory demands and more and more experiments and practices performed (see e.g. Zacher, 2011). Policies of knowledge production and use are crucial for sustainability, especially in the future perspective.

So the new risks, dangers, challenges, and opportunities require profound changes in our mindsets and Weltanschauung (term popularized by Mannheim) – it can be called "epistemic modernization" (term coined by D. Hess: in Harding, 2011). Old type scientific paradigms (e.g. in economics or sociology) are ineffective in the face of new challenges connected with sustainability goals.

Change of approaches, theories, and paradigms is needed now because of the reality we live in has evolved into a rather virtual reality. Cyberspace and its rich contents have become an additional social space. It is a fully technological innovation and technological "object" (or system). For some it is just a subsequent product of research and technology. For others it is a milestone innovation transforming almost everything – societies, individuals, economies, wars, human communications, etc. Moreover, it radically divides human living space into two parts – the real and the virtual. This is another case of world hybridization. There are many new questions: how to function in these two worlds? Does cyberspace have (or should have or can have) its own network logic? What do diffusions between these two worlds mean? How will human activities in this hybridity be separated or networked?

Cyberspace is an informational virtual world "inhabited" by internauts (already billions) mostly representing the younger generations; however, the Net has almost everything, good and bad, and what was invented in the real exists in the virtual. The old world – material, "heavy", hard, and traditional – wants to control its "baby", but the baby – according to what is written in the Cyberspace Manifesto (by J. P. Barlow) – demands autonomy, separation, independence, and freedom. So are they parallel worlds? Or does the old world (also its power?) dominate and regulate the new one (by force?, economically?)? How many activities in the real world are transferred to the new space (to make business, to use it, to conquer it, offering mutual advantages)? Does it function by various relations or unity, integration or systemic functioning? Perhaps a "border" between the two worlds will not be so sharp – more and more traditional activities are being informatized and digitized, and new generations will soon consist mostly of "digital natives". Will old world branches (e.g. industrial) and activities be conducted and operated by such natives? Where will the power be?

Any way that innovations can make some better order, including sustainability goals, is impatiently expected. Until now the two worlds were treated separately in what can be illustrated by exemplary titles of respected books and articles: information vs industrial economy/society; digital vs predigital economy/society; virtual vs traditional economy/society, etc. Perhaps in the long run some self-evolution of the hybrid world will be a solution or another option that might include conflict and clash or some type of negotiated co-shaping formula as a possibility as well. The situation is extremely difficult since the processes described above are new, embryonic, and multitrajectory. Social, political, and cultural innovations can further help in developments in science, technology, law, management, and politics. Inertia, evolutionary spontaneity, or "the invisible hand of the market" do not guarantee a desirable sustainable future. First, we should deal intellectually and in scientific discourse with these new "unfinished" problems. Fortunately, the literature of the subject has recently increased (see e.g. Castells, 2004), but with a rather more descriptive than innovative and policy-oriented bent. Information, networking, digitization, and virtualization create not only a new technological base for societies and individuals, but, having immense performative power, also change everything, including the world societies and individuals.

3. Transformations needed (a processual model)

Matching our mindsets and Weltanschauung to the present and prospective challenges generates in many spaces more or less fundamental transformations. Usually these transformations take time, hence they start a shift to a new but not fully imagined nor planned future. Because of their importance it may be worthwhile to treat them as a kind of paradigm where they left the past and opened the way to the future. A conceptual framework (or a processual model) of the transformations leading to the sustainable future(s) are presented in Figure 1.

Figure 1 shows the passage toward many sustainable futures (plural indicates that a set of the futures contains multiple options and failures; moreover the sustainable ones can differ depending on the parameters) as a process which started from bifurcations and – in spite of many contextual difficulties – produced various transformations, which in turn can to a significant extent be controlled and steered. However, some changes may not be easy to recognize and master. Human agency has some performative power – institutional, organizational, collective, and individual – to overcome the inertia of development, path dependence, old vested interests, blind market forces, cultural obsoleteness, and global instabilities. There are many positive factors and mechanisms which can be used, if the sustainable future is to be achieved. It would be utopian to think that all regions, countries, organizations, and individuals will agree and undertake proper decisions and actions that will be effective and successful on the way to sustainability. Probably it is enough to accumulate a kind of "critical mass" of theories, research, strategies and policies, regulations, responsibilities, structures, undertakings, actions, and patterns of behaviour to step on a sustainability trajectory. Moreover, it seems that the world has already obtained such a point (or is close to it). Progressively developing such "mass", humankind (and its organizational entities as societies) can significantly reduce the risks and danger connected with the current, but rather irrational and irresponsible, model of unsustainable growth.

Strong leaders (politicians, international activists, business people, concerned scientists, local engaged citizens, media representatives, internauts, etc.) are necessary to make a vision of sustainability a reality and to do it on time (i.a. before the coming crisis). Sol-

PROCESS

RESULTS

BIFURCATIONS
- factors
- structures
- institutions
- agencies

- seeds of change:
  discoveries

  CHANGE

  CHANGE

  inventions

  (embryos)

  (advanced)

  innovations

- driving forces
- dynamism
  – barriers
  – inertia
  – path dependence

TRANSFORMATIONS

Fabric of change:

- strategies
- policies
- actions
- behaviours
- coordination
- co-shaping
- internal and external influences
- synergy

Futures

Multiple options:
- various proportions of factors
- mechanisms
- obstacles, positive and negative effects
- costs and time horizons

Sustainability

Sustainability:

- orientation
- trajectory
- advances

Factors embeddedment:

- market forces (free or controlled)
- interests (vested, conservative or progressive, future-oriented)
- power (adaptive or proactive, reform-oriented)
- culture (traditional or capable of change and innovation)
- global context (turbulent or stability, networking and cooperation)

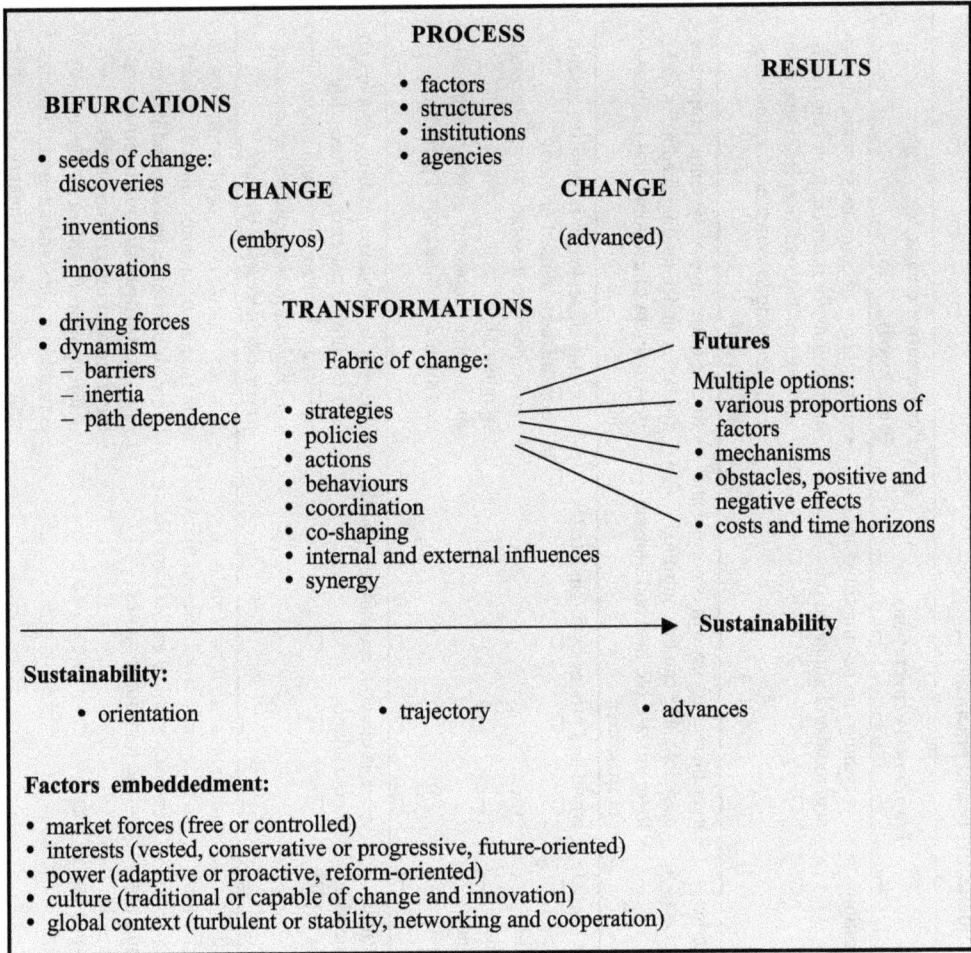

Figure 1. Transformations toward sustainable futures (a processual model)

idarity, cooperation, rationality, and trust across borders – religious, ideological, political – can contribute to attaining this goal. Will human values prevail and prevent humanity from a deep global crisis (see e.g. Zacher, 2013)? Nobody knows, but survival is at stake, so this may also impose proper reactions and actions. There are many challenges, but more and more means of effective response are becoming available (see Table 1).

Table 1 shows on one side several important characteristics of our times and their impacts, both positive and detrimental, and on the other side traditional approaches confronted with new approaches and performative means (unordered) are presented. The first ones are in fact innovations of various kinds or a call for innovations that are able to respond to the challenges we face. Their enumeration is just exemplary; it merely presents areas demanding innovations and selected means to produce and introduce them.

Table 1. Selected challenges to be responded to intellectually and practically

Types of challenge	Impacts	Traditional expectations	Performative means (unordered)
COMPLEXITY	• difficult recognition and separation of development processes • interferences • multidimensionality	• everything can be simplified and separated and impacted on	• using theory of complex systems, recommendations for practice; to develop new approaches and statistics, Big Data, also early warning systems; new institutions are needed
UPSCALING	• big projects globalization, Internet – scale of functioning and of impacts unknown before • feedback loops networking	• ever increasing growth is normal and desirable, and can be controlled • there are still old firm and transparent structures	• to take advantage of systemic properties for better understanding feedbacks and development of economy and its functioning
SYSTEMIZATION	• some factors and mechanisms started to function as system (feedbacks) • make all plans, policies, actions of governments, businesses and people risky as to processes and as results, strengthening resilience and flexibility of systems	• world and processes fragmented	• economy of scale can be positive asset if reorganized and used properly • can be positive to some extent, especially in human life • too much of economy of scale is unhealthy and should be limited and prevented
ACCELERATION	• new technologies, esp. ICTs stimulate pace of info and communication: also transportation and pace of life	• speed is effect of technology, people should adapt	• diversity is good, stimulating, people can enjoy multiple patterns, cultures, lifestyles, important for democracy and citizen activism; negotiations should be basic means to come to necessary consent
DIVERSITY	• differences in growth, standard of living, technologies used, cultures remain and will be increasing; • plurality of ideologies, religions, policies etc. growing (thanks to media and the Internet), multiculturality and lifestyles	• imitation, similar patterns, and universalization will prevail thanks to world technical and cultural leaders and traditional values	• in many aspects is effect of normal evolution (social, economic, cultural); reflects some global trends and contradictions of interests (domestic and international) • there are also integration processes (economic, political), alliances, agreements, networking; for some integration means centralization and domination of strongest partners

Types of challenge	Impacts	Traditional expectations	Performative means (unordered)
DISINTEGRA-TION	• traditional spatial, economic, social and cultural entities and structures fall apart; particularism and nationalism grow • new position of metropolis • glocalization	• there are some counter-processes, countries should conserve their values, heritage, culture, customs etc.	• can be downscaled by forecasting, by careful planning, by preparing buffers, new theories • needed, computer simulations can show possible futures and people's preferences (Big Data)
UNCER-TAINTY	• results of actions not certain • strategies and activities should have proper (costly) buffers, surprises can be negative	• can be diminished and controlled by state, regulations, social evaluation and norms	• should be controlled and limited by stability measures (in politics, law regulation and enforcement), chaos theory should be used, also Black Swan and Fragility concepts of Taleb
UNPREDICT-ABILITY	• unexpected situations, barriers • costs • risks	• predictability very limited, there are some deterministic processes (connected with technology and economic trends); important is religion, law, morality as orienting points	• multioptionality, simulations, approximation approach in decision-making, organizational and political flexibility can help, also management
CHAOTICS	• processes not regular, random spontaneous emergencies	• should be fought with; conservative solutions	• theories of change, transformations, revolutions and crisisology should be intellectually adapted and practically exploited (e.g. transition management, policies
FUZZINESS	• "borders" of structures, institutions' responsibility and processes are not distinct and changing • liquid modernity (Bauman)	• preferred and new governance needed • should be limited by more effective bureaucracy, transparency, firm organization, central control and detailed regulations and adaptive behaviour	of change and radical reforms, anticrisis policy); conflict resolution and negotiatory practices to be performed, crisis management developed, early warning systems and various monitorings needed; flexibility and buffers (e.g. financial) can help to take advantage of positive effects and limit detrimental ones
NON-LINE-ARITY	• jumps, revolutions and crises occurred • irregular processes • catastrophes	• revolutions not good since break petrified order	

23

4. Science, technology, innovations: contexts of citizens' engagement

Sustainability is a multi-field, multi-activity, transborder, and complex task that requires continuous streams of innovations: scientific, technological, economic, social, ecological, cultural and so forth. Discoveries and inventions are a basis of a new knowledge and innovations. In other words – this is science which is a main source of technological progress, social and economic reforms, and other improvements. Innovative activity does not depend solely on R & D expenditures, government policies, and business strategies (not to mention market demand for new solutions and new technologies). Flows of innovations are a result of science–society relations. These relations are notoriously under changing boundary conditions. Generally, it is expected that innovations are a foundation for future prosperity. At a time of economic crisis as now experienced, innovative activity is perceived as a means to get out of the crisis (see Report: Science in Society, 2013). One can explicitly add one more "responsibility" of science and technology: innovations should be sustainability-oriented.

Discourse around science and technology in the EU redefined the programme line of R & D Framework Programme 7 from Science and Society to Science in Society. This transformation emphasizes the integration of both techno-scientific and societal development. Innovations are praised with a new label of the EU strategy: "Innovation Union 2020". On the national and sectorial levels innovation creation and application strategies should be contextualized. Society is involved in its values, attitudes, customs, fears, behaviours, consciousness, and imagination. All this gives, or does not give, innovation a performative power, and also its embeddedness. More and more technological artefacts produced not only change our surroundings, which are becoming increasingly artificial. This transforms societies and men themselves. The technological world produces, thanks to our social and individual experiences, a technological age (Williams, 2014: 466). Technology becomes overwhelming, pervasive, and influential. It is used in virtually all human activities, requiring and determining many people's behaviours and playing a dominant role for technological creativity and technology-driven goals. It is a fundamental "redirection of human energies and desires toward inquiry into and manipulation of the material world for all sorts of utilitarian and nonutilitarian purposes" (Williams, 2014: 466). It is good for innovativeness to have such a positive grounding. However, the big differences and gaps between individuals and societies should not be forgotten. But to some extent, the innovativeness may be imitated and induced, while the present networking makes it possible to transfer knowledge, technology, and skills worldwide.

In a perspective of sustainability, with its generational concern, reflexivity is an important attitude. Sustainability is, in fact, about the future and about the long-term consequences of the present generation's behaviour (modes of production, consumption, lifestyles, etc.). According to evolutionists only mature societies have begun to think about the consequences of their choices and their impacts. Moreover, not all human actions are deliberated, planned, and rational. Purposive actions may not be rational as well. Rational behaviour may be, for example, reactive, adaptive, proactive, and creative. In each case a different type of innovation is needed and would be proper. But innovations are even more required in situations of social inaction, inertia, errors in decisions, irrationality, stupidity in politics, and poor management. Global uncertainty and market spontaneity are subsequently difficult challenges for innovation efforts and policies. Domination of technological innovations, without other accompanying – and from a necessary systems view – types of innovations, produces a kind of disequilibrium. Innovations' compatibility and interconnections may create a synergy in developmental processes and efforts serving the sustainability future. The aforementioned challenges and barriers can determine areas and directions of innovative activities for governments, businesses, and citizens (civil society in other words).

Prospective thinking is an important innovation because it is overcoming social (scientific as well) scepticism related to the future prognoses. However, for example, in economics the forecasting is well grounded. Imagined futures (Beckert, 2013) and social expectations (e.g. Brown, Michael, 2003) may influence policy and business behaviour, and consumers may shape technology and innovation (Pollock, Williams, 2010). Societal engagement is basic (which proves foresight). Active participation in producing knowledge about the economic future should have a form of network communication and coproduction of predictions by forecasters and their network of various representatives of economic science, business, politics, and government. It is called epistemic participation (Reichmann, 2013), which "conceptualizes the relationship between researchers and a highly reflexive and communicative object". Producing knowledge about the future is not a guess about but rather inventing and co-shaping the future (see e.g. Zacher, 2010). Well-known objections – from Popper to Taleb – are not really applicable in understanding future thinking, which can be valuable for political decision-making, giving it an innovative impetus. The warning function of forecasts challenges optimistic expectations and policies, e.g. in natural resources and demography (e.g. reports of the Club of Rome and other reports forecasting various "limits to growth", and biotech risks – Tutton, 2011).

So reporting the above cases and experiments has to encourage citizens to engage – innovatively – in knowledge production and in science and technology outputs and their impacts. Participatory engagement distinguishes anticipation from prediction (made solely by experts). Anticipatory thinking introduced to policy and strategic planning is dedicated to reducing or eliminating ex ante negative side effects of science and technology. It is intellectually connected with Toffler's idea of "anticipatory democracy" (Bezold, 1978). Anticipatory thinking, as endorsed by the evaluation of innovation outcomes, is an innovation itself, which is still important and needed. Since 1970 it has been integrated into concepts, theories, and procedures of technology assessment, social impact assessment, or impact assessment. Evaluating probable negative side effects of introduced technologies into practice is still a very innovative way of gauging citizens' engagement. Participation produces vital knowledge on people's imaginings of the future, on their expectations and fears, and on their thinking about a distribution of good and bad fruits of new technologies. Technology assessment invented in the US is now more vivid in Western Europe (mostly in Germany – see Grunwald, 2000) and almost unknown in Eastern Europe. However, even in less advanced countries such issues as technology transfer, technological FDI, new large constructions, and energy installations generate social unrest and protests. "Anticipatory governance" can be a good method of engagement and participation of citizens in decisions on ambivalent effects of new technologies (on anticipatory governance see – Guston, 2013). Nowadays people start to think more on technology outcomes, especially possibly detrimental ecologically, than on its development per se. Citizens' engagement may influence design and applications, which can alert scientists, investors, legislators, and communities to the eventual negative and often long-term effects of technology. This can also promote a new culture connected with new revolutionary technologies as, for example, bio- and nanotech and social robotics (Šabanovič, 2014) and lead to a broader social learning process oriented toward sustainability. Such actions require instruments to be elaborated and exploited to influence governance of public–private partnerships in genomics (Hanssen, Gremmen, 2012).

It goes without saying that the perception of the measuring and role of science and innovation in society is shaped to a great extent by media. Scientific journalism requires two special skills: a solid scientific knowledge and an ability to present it properly by not simplifying the information unnecessarily (which often damages messages). Public common sense knowledge and implicated public opinion are vital not only for the legitimization of public policy in the science and technology area, but they can influence even private investors. More importantly, from an innovation perspective, they may also reinforce social interest in active participation in innovation activities. It is not only public discourse on science and technology policies and activities and their consequences that are at stake, but also a possibility of co-shaping innovations, e.g. by cooperating with companies (see e.g. Ornetzeder, Rohracher, 2006), and engaging in citizen science. Such engagement provides opportunities for citizens to be involved in research conduct and to gain scientific knowledge, and also allows citizens to reflect on science production and applications, not to mention developing positive attitudes toward science and technology (see e.g. Crall *et al.*, 2012; Finke, 2014). The use of lay people is often criticized, nevertheless for problems of community relevance it seems proper. More and more refined instruments for public involvement are invented and used (e.g. societal interface group – Hanssen, Gremmen, 2012).

So media are able to ensure public communication on science and technology and help in the public's understanding. However, scientists often criticize the media for a simplification of problems, for poor framing of complex issues, and for confusing information preferences of media and public ones (Rivenburgh, 2014; Boczkowski, Mitchelstein, 2013) for biased stands dictated by sponsors, lobbyists, politicians, etc.

New technologies, for example bio- and nano-, are a subject of discourse also in new media. The social web platform can be an example (Veltri, 2012). The Internet upscales enormous possibilities of communication, transfers of knowledge, expressions of social attitudes, and participation in innovative activities. However, this kind of performativity has not been fully explored yet. Its potential seems great, especially in communication, including scientific communication. There were once hopes that the Internet's enabling of transborder exchanges of information, knowledge, innovations, good practices, networking, and cooperation would give chances to bridge the digital divide. At present there is some skepticism regarding this. Even digitization may not ensure peripheries a kind of digital universalism (Say Chan, 2013). So conflicting situations can emerge that are harmful for stability and sustainability (not solely in the ecological sense). Innovations, i.e. political, to ameliorate divisions are needed. Citizens should be aware of such challenges.

To be aware and well oriented in sustainability discourse and in innovation problems people should possess some level of science literacy enabling their rational and active engagement. An educational background as a rule is not sufficient as some "research practices" are necessary. Science literacy comprises a decent level of scientific understanding of vocabulary and language, process, impacts, and numeracy skills (i.e. to understand statistic – probabilities, risk assessment – see von Roten, de Roten, 2013; Sol Hart, 2013). Societal scientific literacy is vital for the emergence and building of knowledge-based societies as a subsequent form after information societies' formation. Science (or scientific) literacy is often connected with citizen science. There are cases of citizen science training programmes on participant attitudes, behaviour, and science literacy (see Crall *et al.*, 2012). Such programs contribute to informal science education, where participants show increases in social capital (i.e. political participation in deliberations and debates, growing networks, community connections and communication). Additionally, there are sound elements of democratization and of modernizing culture. They raise the level of science communication (see Kawamoto *et al.*, 2011) and show that innovation is a social process based on communication, criticism, skepticism, deliberation, negotiations, and acceptance. Citizen science and scientific literacy constitute an important element of the social learning process and facilitate the inclusion of public concerns and needs in scientific research and development.

Scientific literacy is also valuable in preventing the social production of ignorance (e.g. in debate on GMOs, nuclear energy, bio- and nanotechnologies, and energy technologies, such as wind energy – see Hirsh, Sovacool, 2013). Not infrequently knowledge and ignorance overlap. Scientific literacy may help to separate them and allow citizens to be more critical and skeptical of media reporting on innovations or political press conferences, while a social acceptance of technological decisions is sought.

Cognitive, political, and business biases and interests make scientific and technological innovations vulnerable and easy to manipulate. Behind innovations are big money, competitive advantage, monopolistic position, political success, international connections, etc. So in many cases, especially emotionally and politically sensitive ones, there are various counteractions performed by journalists, scientists, NGOs, and politicians, both national and local communities – financed by businesses. Such counteractions involve ordering sceptical or negative expertise, media campaigns, political lobbying in parliaments, creating special scientific units, and encouraging NGOs and local communities to engage in various manifestations and protests. It is called "denial industry" and is well recognized (see e.g. Dunlap, McCright, 2011). "Organized scepticism" means manipulation of data (e.g. on climate warming, GMOs, biomedical research), attacks in the media, over-politicization of debates, biased persuasion, personal disqualification, and so forth. It is detrimental to an image of science, technology, and innovations in society, showing decisions in these areas as ethically "dirty games". But they may actually be "pure games" that are objective, honest, respecting public interest, and friendly to environment and sustainability ideas, strategies, and policies. Democratization efforts in this areas lose ground, and sense; deliberations and negotiations should not be based on "scientific" products of skepticism, denial, ignorance, and manipulation. Good choices and decisions require verified data, and, as a rule, as little as possible biased experts and shareholders engaged in their particular interests.

People should trust science, in its credibility, and in epistemic and moral authority of science (O'Brien, 2013). Scientific authority, in a policy context, is important in the processes of advising and expertizing. The appreciation of scientists, advisors, and experts elicit public support for decisions. The more knowledgeable a society, the better its communication with decision-makers and the better choices in controversial issues. Innovative ideas, connected with citizens' participation in science and technology, are a subject of discussion in the STS (Science, Technology, Society) academic community. An active scientific citizenry, which extensively uses deliberative democratic decision-making, is considered an important republican value and ideal. The distance between real participation and a normative model is called the "democratic deficit." There are different ways to diminish it (see Mejlgaard, Stares, 2012), which opens space for innovations.

The numerous difficult problems discussed above can be solved by innovations – political, social, organizational, and managerial – to avoid biased solutions. There is also a structural bias, i.e. over-economization of science and technology policy, which causes a general underestimation of societal stakeholders (see Berman, 2014). So many "additional" redirecting innovations and reforms are needed to maximize advantages of science and technology for sustainability.

5. Final reflections, remarks, and conclusions

In the previous chapters, the discussion was focused on transformations – triggered and stimulated performatively – through innovations leading to sustainability. Areas, sectors, directions of actions were indicated. This exemplary overview provides a list of such innovations: some already existing and available, some just emerging, some not verified and diffused, and some only forecasted and badly needed. Existing contexts and necessary conditions (and necessary accompanying conditions – what was always underlined by systems analysis as e.g. R. L. Ackoff) were considered, also policies, actions, and behaviour oriented towards a sustainable future of world, countries, and people. Usually breakthrough technologies (innovations) are highlighted. Throughout this paper more attention is paid to social, political, and cultural aspects of the way to sustainability. There is a growing awareness in academia and government of a "socialization" of innovations via public engagement, involvement, and participation in decisions on science, technology, and innovations. This observation is valid for advanced and democratic countries which are aware of the risk, dangers, and challenges of unsustainable pattern of development.

The point of view of societal roles and activity innovations can be associated with such areas/actions as:

- education, research, innovation, knowledge production, citizen literacy, educational and research institutions, NGOs, joint projects, media, promoting scientific and technological culture, and popularization, etc.;
- citizen science: engagement in research, citizens/experts, functioning in the Internet, in relations with business (as critics and improvers), community-based research; public common sense building; creating positive attitudes, marketing supporters;
- participation: engagement, involvement, shared responsibility, participation in decision processes, in democratization and social learning process; role as stakeholders, communicating problems and opinions; science literacy contributes to informal science education;
- co-shaping innovations: evaluating ambivalent effects of new technologies, their outcomes, distribution of costs and effects, introducing long-term (generational) issues; influencing politics and legislators.

So citizens and their groups and associations can contribute – via their innovative efforts – to knowledge production, and innovation; to developing relations between government, business and civil society; to evaluating effects of innovations (especially social and environmental) in the long run.

From the point of view of necessary and desirable innovations leading to sustainability, they can be formed in a few exemplary areas:

- in mentality, worldview, research approaches and methodologies, cultures, education, media coverage of sustainability (especially vital in R&D sector, education, media);
- innovations in public understanding of science and technology and their transformative role (especially important in less advanced countries, and paradoxically in leading ones producing cutting-edge technologies);
- innovations in citizens' engagement, involvement and participation (fundamental for democratic development and for democratizing innovation – see von Hippel, 2005);
- efforts and activities to make citizens active in future thinking (long-term visioning, foresight, forecasting, scenarios) and evaluative processes and procedures (e.g. technology assessment, social impact assessment, environmental impact assessment).

All of these areas and kinds of innovative activities can be profiled towards sustainability; together, they create a culture of innovativeness desirable both for innovations per se and for sustainability that contain oriented goals and social choices, actions, and practices ("good environmental practices" included). Innovative society is a term sometimes used to describe a society where innovative attitudes and activities are massive and common. Sustainability can be then treated as a normative guiding principle.

References

Becker, H. A., Vanclay, F. (eds.) (2003), *The International Handbook of Social Impact Assessment. Conceptual and Methodological Advances*, Cheltenham, UK and Northampton, MA: Edward Elgar.

Beckert, J. (2013), *Imagined futures: Fictional expectations in the economy*, "Theory and Society", 42(3): 219–240.

Berman, E. P. (2014), *Not Just Neoliberalism: Economization in US Science and Technology Policy*, "Science, Technology & Human Values", Vol. 39(3): 397–431.

Bezold, C. (1978), *Anticipatory Democracy – People in the Politics of the Future*, New York, Vintage Books.

Blankensteijn, M. *et al*. (2014), *Contested science – Public controversies about science and policy*, Den Haag, Rathenau Institute.

Boczkowski, P. J., Mitchelstein, E. (2013), *The News Gap – When the Information Preferences of the Media and the Public Diverge*, Cambridge: The MIT Press.

Brown, N., Michael, M. (2003), *A sociology of expectation: Retrospecting prospects and prospecting retrospects*, "Technology Analysis & Strategic Management", 15(1): 3–18.

Castells, M. (ed.) (2004), *The Network Society*, Cheltenham – Northampton, MA: Edward Elgar.

Crettaz von Roten, F., de Roten, Y. (2013), *Statistics in science and in society: From a state-of-the-art to a new research agenda*, "Public Understanding of Science", 22(7), October: 768–784.

Disco, N., Kranakis, E. (eds.) (2013), *Cosmopolitan Commons: Sharing Resources and Risks across Borders*, Cambridge, MA: The MIT Press.

Dragojlovic, N., Einsiedel, E. (2012), *Playing God or just unnatural? Religious beliefs and approval of synthetic biology*, "Public Understanding of Science", 22(7): 869–885.

Dunlap, R. E., Van Liere, K. D. (1978), *The new environmental paradigm: A proposed measuring instrument and preliminary results*, "Journal of Environmental Education", 9(1): 10–19.

Dunlap, R. E., McCright, A. M. (2011), *Organized Climate Change Denial*, in: J. S. Dryzek *et al*. (eds.), *Oxford Handbooks on Climate Change and Society*, Oxford, Oxford University Press.

Foucault, M. (2007), *Security, Territory, Population*, New York: Picador.

Gamser, M. S. (1988), *Mobilizing Appropriate Technology*, London: Intermediate Technology Publications.

Gibbons, M. *et al*. (1994), *The new production of knowledge. The dynamics of science and research in contemporary societies*, Sage.

Giddens, A. (1990), *The Consequences of Modernity*, London, Polity Press.

Grunwald, A. (2000), *Technik für Geselschaft von morgen*, Frankfurt – New York, Campus Verlag.

Guston, D. H. (2013), *Understanding "anticipatory governance"*, "Social Studies of Science", Vol. 44(2): 218–242.

Hanssen, L., Gremmen, B. (2012), *Influencing governance of a public–private partnership in plant genomics: The societal interface group as a new instrument for public involvement*, "Public Understanding of Science", 22(6): 718–729.

Harding, S. (ed.) (2011), *The Postcolonial Science and Technology Studies Reader*, Durham, NC: Duke University Press.

Hippel, E. von (2005), *Democratizing innovation*, Cambridge, MA: The MIT Press.

Hirsh, R. F., Sovacool, B. K. (2013), *Wind Turbines and Invisible Technology: Unarticulated Reasons for Local Opposition to Wind Energy*, "Technology and Culture", Vol. 54, No. 4, October: 705–734.

Huntington, S. P. (1996), *The Clash of Civilizations and the Remaking of World Order*, New York: Simon & Schuster.

Jordan, R. C. *et al.* (2011), *Knowledge gain and behavioral change in citizen-science programs,* "Conservation Biology", 25, 6: 1148–1154.

Kahnemann, D. (2002), *Maps of Bounded Rationality,* http://nobelprize.org/nobel_prozes/economics/laureates/2002/kahnemann-lectura.pdf:24.07.2012.

Kawamoto, S., Nakayama, M., Saijo, M. (2011), *A survey of scientific literacy to provide a foundation for designing science communication in Japan,* "Public Understanding of Science", 22(6): 674–690.

Kehrbaum, T. (2009), *Innovation als Sozialer Prozess. The Grounded Theory als Methodologie und Praxis der Innovationsforschung,* Wiesbaden: VS Verlag.

Kleinman, D. L., Suryanarayanan, S. (2012), *Dying Bees and the Social Production of Ignorance,* "Science, Technology & Human Values", 38(4): 492–517.

Knowledge Swaraj (2013), *An Indian Manifesto on Science and Technology,* http://www.set-dev. eu/(acces April 13, 2013).

Kostakis, V. *et al.* (2013), *Peer Production and Desktop Manufacturing: The Case of the Helix T Wind Turbine Project,* "Science, Technology & Human Values", Vol. 38(6): 773–800.

McClellan III, J. E., Dorn, H. (2006), *Science and Technology in World History,* 2nd ed., Baltimore, MD: The Johns Hopkins University Press.

Meadows, D. *et al.* (2004), *Limits to Growth – The Thirty-Years Update,* White River Junction, VT: Chelsea Green.

Mejlgaard, N., Stares, S. (2012), *Performed and preferred participation in science and technology across Europe: Exploring an alternative idea of "democratic deficit",* "Public Understanding of Science", 22(6): 660–673.

Naisbitt, J., Aburdene, P. (1990), *Megatrends 2000,* New York, William Morrow.

Naisbitt, J. (2006*), Mind Set!,* New York, Collins.

O'Brian, T. L. (2013), *Scientific authority in policy contexts: Public attitudes about environmental scientists, medical researchers, and economics,* "Public Understanding of Science", 22(7), October: 799–816.

Ornetzeder, M., Rohracher, H. (2006), *User-led innovations and participation processes: lessons from sustainable energy technologies,* Energy Policy, 34: 138–150.

Ornetzeder, M., Rohracher, H. (2011), *Nutzerinnovation und Nachhaltigkeit: Soziale und technische Innovationen als zivilgesellschaftliches Engagement,* in: Beck G., Kropp C. (eds.), Gesellschaft innovativ – Wer sind die akteure? Wiesbaden: VS Verlag.

Pernick, R., Wilder, C. (2007), *The Clean Tech Revolution: The Next Big Growth and Investment Opportunity,* New York: HarperCollins.

Reichmann, W. (2013), *Epistemic participation: How to produce knowledge about the economic future,* "Social Studies of Science", 43(6): 852–877.

Rivenburgh, N. K. (2011), *Media framing of complex issues: The case of endangered languages,* "Public Understanding of Science", 22(6): 704–717.

Šabanović, S. (2014), *Inventing Japan's 'robotics culture': The repeated assembly of science, technology, and culture in social robotics,* "Social Studies of Science", 44(3): 342–367.

Say Chan, A. (2013), *Networking Peripheries: Technological Futures and the Myth of Digital Universalism,* Cambridge, MA: The MIT Press.

Schulz, M. S. (2015), *Future moves: Forward-oriented studies of culture, society, and technology,* "Current Sociology", Vol. 63, No. 2, March: 129–139.

Science in Society: caring for our futures in turbulent times (June 2013), Strasbourg, European Science Foundation.

Shelley, T. (2008), *Nanotechnology: New Promises, New Dangers,* "The Journal of Industrial Ecology", Vol. 12, No. 3: 491–492.

Simonis, G. (ed.) (2013), *Konzepte und Verfahren der Technikfolgenabschätzung, Wiesbaden*: Springer.

Sol Hart, P. (2013), *The role of numeracy in moderating the influence of statistic in climate change messages*, " Public Understanding of Science", 22(7), October: 785–798.

Steinfeldt, M. *et al.* (2008), *Nanotechnologies, Hazards and Resource Efficiency: A Three-Tiered Approach to Assessing the Implications of Nanotechnology and Influencing its Development*, "The Journal of Industrial Ecology", Vol. 12(3): 493–494.

Stiglitz, J. E., Sen, A., Fitoussi, J.-P. (2010), *Mismeasuring Our Lives: Why GDP Doesn't Add Up*, New York: The New Press.

Taleb, N. N. (2007), *The Black Swan: The Impact of the Highly Improbable*, New York: Random House.

The African Manifesto for Science, Technology and Innovations – http://www.set-dev.eu/(access April 13, 2013).

Theodore, L., Kunz, R. G. (2008), *Nanotechnology: Environmental Implications and Solutions*, "The Journal of Industrial Ecology", Vol. 12, 40, 3: 490–491.

Tutton, R. (2011), *Promising pessimism: Reading the futures to be avoided in biotech*, "Social Studies of Science", 41(3): 411–429.

Weber, M., Hemmelskamp, J. (eds.) (2005), *Towards Environmental Innovation System*, Berlin – Heidelberg – New York: Springer.

Williams, R. (2014), *Our Technological Age, from the Inside Out*, "Technology and Culture", Vol. 55, April: 461–476.

Zacher, L. W. (2006), *Co-existence of sciences (from mono to post-disciplinarity)*, "Teorie védy/ Theory of Science", vol. XV/XXV/III/2006, No. 3, p. 123–148.

Zacher, L. W. (2009), *Generational Transformations of Societies and of Scientific Communities: The Coming Challenges*, in: Kugel, S.A. (ed.), *The Problems of Scientists and Scientific Groups Activity*, St. Petersburg: Science, p. 16–31.

Zacher, L. W. (2010), *The Future as a Space, Where Knowledge, Imagination and Interests Clash*, in: Zalewska, D. (ed.), *Limits of Knowing the Future*, Wrocław: Ed. OPSIS, p. 47–74.

Zacher, L. W. (2012), *Toward Democratization of Science and Technology Spheres. Some Opportunities and Problems*, in: Bammé, A. *et al.* (ed.), *Yearbook 2011 of the IAS-STS*, München – Wien: Profil, p. 165–187.

Zacher, L. W. (2012*), Society, Market and Technology Nexus as Contexts of ICT Policies and Applications: Some Issues and Reflexions*, "International Journal of Information – Communication Technologies and Human Development", July – September, 2012, Vol. 4, No. 3, p. 32–42.

Zacher, L. W. (2013), *Human and Societal Potentials for Transcending the Crisis of Civilization*, in: Targowski, A., Celiński, M. J. (eds.), *Spirituality and Civilization Sustainability in the 21st Century*, New York: Nova Science Publishers, p. 59–96.

Zacher, L. W. (2015), *Digital Future(s)*, in: *Encyclopedia of Information Science and Technology*, 3rd ed., Hershey, PA, IGI Global: 3735–3744.

Janusz E. Dmochowski

Poland, 21st Century Technologies: Challenges and Solutions for the Global Society

1. Science-based vision, forecasting versus science fiction

At the end of the 20th century it was customary to speculate on what human life would look like in the next millennium. Many authors attempted to provide visions of the future based on their own experience, analysis of the current status of science and technology and subjective opinions. Some of these publications must be qualified as science fiction, close to the novels of Jules Verne or H.G. Wells in the late 19th and early 20th centuries. Some could be regarded as quasi-scientific. The essays of Professor Freeman J. Dyson from the Institute for Advanced Study, Princeton, USA, won an award of the American Physical Society and appeared in a book form under the title *The Sun, the Genome & the Internet: Tools of Scientific Revolutions*. Professor Dyson described his vision as a model. If we were to refer to a vision as a theory, it would have to be a structure constructed of logics and mathematics, and subjected to experimental verification. The theory is usually useless as there are too many parameters affecting the real processes and science is unpredictable, yielding new discoveries or new ideas or inventions. On the other hand the model is more useful, since by definition it takes into account only a limited number of facts and factors of the real world. However, the model does not yield exact predictions and describes just the direction, the approximate place we are heading to.

Such visions, though very interesting, could not be regarded sufficient for planning or taking decisions regarding directions in which real science, technology, and economy should evolve. Consequently, the author's studies turned into search for other sources for analyzing science, technology and economy, which would provide more complete documentation of the issue. The search for such sources started with the review of the reports of national government agencies, such as: *Physics and the future of technology*, UK Foresight Programme; *Advanced technologies: a chance for Poland's development*, a report of the Polish Government Centre for Strategic Studies; *Transformation of Science in Poland*, the series of publications published by the Polish State Committee for Scientific Research, as well as the series of monographs: *The Knowledge-Based Economy: The Global Challenges of the 21st Century, The European Challenges of the 21st Century, Poland's Challenges of the 21st Century*. The last one refers to the reports edited by Professor A. Kukliński. Among OECD publications one appeared especially important: *21st Century Technologies – Promises and Perils of a Dynamic Future*. This monograph formed a part of the preparations for EXPO 2000, the World Exposition in Hannover (Germany) – the OECD Forum for the Future. Furthermore, *People, Nature and Technology: Sustainable Societies in the 21st Century*, and the conference *21st Century Technologies: Balancing Economic, Social and Environmental Goals* both aimed to build a comprehensive foundation for assessing the critical choices likely to face citizens and decision-makers in the next century. To provide a glimpse into a global scale of reported projects one can quote Joseph F. Coates of Coates & Jarratt, Inc., United States: "In a three-year project, Coates & Jarratt, Inc. collected all of the forecasts in all of the areas of science, engineering and technology that could be found, from around the world. These were analyzed in a systematic way, and 41 reports running to about 4000 pages were produced. Later, in the second phase of the project, we produced our own forecast for the year 2025, which has now been published as a book... *2025: Scenarios of US and Global Society Reshaped by Science and Technology* by Joseph F. Coates *et al.*, 1997".

2. The vision of the future at the beginning of the 21st Century

An analysis of the aforementioned sources yielded the conclusion that the next few decades of the development of the global economy could be described as a Knowledge-Based Economy, and the nearest future as a Fifth Schumpeter wave. This description originates in the ideas promoted by the Austrian economist Joseph Schumpeter, who at the beginning of the 20th century argued that the development of the economy in industrial era is cyclic. He attributed these cycles to innovations: new technologies introduced into the economy resulting in the so called "creative destruction". The introduction of new technology results in the crisis: the old industries are destructed and new innovative technologies flourish, replacing the old ones, and giving the economy a new direction, new dynamics. Here are some of the most important technologies which resulted in such waves: utilization of hydro-energy in metallurgy and textile manufacture in the 18th century; utilization of steam energy for railway transport, in industrial machines and steel production in the 19th century; electrical energy, chemicals, and the internal combustion engine in the early 20th century; invention of transistors which gave rise to contemporary semiconductor electronics, petrochemical industry, and the emergence of avionic industry in the mid-20th century; and Internet, mobile and satellite telecommunication, advanced computer systems, and new media from the 1990s on, which triggered the last, fifth wave. Consecutive breakthroughs are related to globally introduced innovations. These innovations should be distinguished from new ideas or inventions, from which these innovations originate. It takes several years or decades to transform a new idea or invention into globally available innovative technology.

3. Innovations and emerging technologies: basic definitions

For the sake of clarity, it is worth at this point to define the notion of innovation, which is sometimes identified with a new or emerging technology. The experience of the last decades points towards the evolution of the notion of innovation. New interpretation of the processes of creation and diffusion of innovations is necessary. The notion of innovation has changed dramatically and is not understood any more as a philosophy of a single act of creation, but rather as complicated social mechanisms, facilitating the emergence of new products and production processes. Simultaneously, the old linear model of science and technology used for explaining the process of creating innovations should be replaced with an interactive model of innovations. The old model, based on institutionalized division of scientific disciplines – with problems defined and processed by scientists and researchers, mostly academic, within the area of their interests – is to be supplemented or replaced by the model driven by trans-disciplinary applications, without rigid institutional structures, performed by teams of researchers, engineers, practitioners working towards finding solutions in real conditions. The notion of technology can be described as practice – the way we do things around here. In Polish, this definition refers to "the method of doing something, elaborated scientifically or experimentally" and seems to be apt and useful in different contexts of science and economy. On the other hand, the word "method" refers to the kind of tool, and that tool can be either physical (hardware) or non-physical (software). Instrumental, utilitarian character of technology is emphasized in OECD reports. One can find statements that the very existence of technology, its feasibility, is not important per se. It is rather the introduction and application of the new technology that is nowadays a subject of social, economic, political or ethical issues, due to its possible negative implications.

4. The overview of the future technologies of the fifth wave

Having in mind the above mentioned circumstances, the following section aims to overview the major groups of the future technologies of the fifth wave. This overview has been prepared based on the OECD-published monograph on "21st Century Technologies. Promises and Perils of a Dynamic Future" (Paris 1998). Furthermore, the author has filtered the information through his own scientific and research experience in physics and engineering, in particularly in the field of semiconductors, lasers, solid state physics, electronics and optoelectronics.[1] The author has also conducted independent studies in problems related to the energy sector. The latter have led the author to a better understanding of the rather

---

[1] The author has been affiliated to various academic and research institutions in Poland (the Institute of Physics of the Polish Academy of Sciences), and abroad, while visiting the Johannes Kepler University in Linz, Austria, serving as Visiting Research Fellow at the Imperial College of Science, Technology and Medicine in London, UK, also exploring science and technology at the Graduate School of Management KAIST in Seoul, Republic of Korea. He has been also a lecturer at the Białystok University of Technology, the Kielce University of Technology, and the Electrotechnical Institute in Warsaw.

recent Fukushima nuclear accident[2] and consequences of this accident for future developments in the energy sector. Today one should raise the question what happened then, whether it would have been possible to predict such hazard as well as whether nuclear power could be made significantly safer in the future? The answers to these questions would make it possible to find proper solutions for Poland or any other country with similar problems.

The most important future technologies could be grouped in the following areas:

- computing and telecommunication technologies
- genetics
- brain technologies
- new materials (miniaturization and smart composites)
- energy
- transport
- tools and systems of environment protection.

The first two areas – "computing and telecommunication technologies" and "genetics" – should facilitate the technical base for many innovations, such as developments in computer and genetic informatics. They should provide new capabilities and new information necessary to progress in understanding and applying new hardware and software tools to advance biology, medicine, agriculture, telecommunication, design, etc.

Computing and telecommunication technologies

Extrapolation of the existing trends of developments in the *computing and information technologies (ICT)*, in particular in the hardware related to semiconductor electronics, integrated circuits, microprocessors and memories (mostly built with silicon technology) commonly described as Moore's law, gave us hope that we can proceed within observed rules for the next few decades. So far this process follows observed earlier trends.

The process of "miniaturization" in the field of ICT is related to vast efforts to develop new technologies which would allow placing more and more transistors on a single silicon chip. This, on the other hand, requires development of new optical technologies described in semiconductor industry as photolithography, allowing for the use of new light sources with shorter wavelengths of the light emitted. It requires development and application of lasers and other light sources, like synchrotrons, in blue, ultraviolet or even X-ray (Roentgen) wavelength range of the electromagnetic spectrum. It is important to remember that these new light sources are not candles or lamps any more. They are rather similar to accelerators we know from particle physics and therefore require multi-billion dollars/euro investments. So, there are only few big players in the business, who can afford such investments. And ultimately the idea of the transistor reaching the limits of miniaturization at atomic level is not very far off the reality.

---

[2] In March 2011 accident at Japan's Fukushima Daiichi Nuclear Power Station. The large quantity of radioactive material released has caused significant human suffering and rendered large stretches of land uninhabitable. http://carnegieendowment.org/files/fukushima.pdf.

The announcements that progress in computing might be achieved with utilizing processes on molecular level, so called quantum computing, has still not gone beyond scientific laboratory stage. However novel ideas, like spintronics, electronics using magnetic properties of matter, in particular electrons, attracted much attention recently, also with a contribution by Polish scientists, e.g. Tomasz Dietl of the PAS Institute of Physics. It is worth mentioning the entering of new competitor into electronics – graphene. This single-layer, 2D carbon earned the 2010 Nobel prize for Andre Geim and Konstantin Novoselov "for groundbreaking experiments regarding the two-dimensional material graphene". There are speculations that this material will replace silicon in next generation electronics, considering its promising physical properties, low-dimensionality, flexibility, mechanical strength, etc. Major development programmes have been initiated in EU and globally, and Polish scientists are in the forefront of technological competition with promising patented demonstrations (GRAPHENE Shop, Nano Carbon).

A major breakthrough has been achieved in the field of optical memories. Envisaged introduction of blue laser diodes, based on gallium nitride technology, resulted in a new generation of optical discs – blue-ray technology. Unfortunately, the high quality blue diode lasers, made on Polish substrates developed at UNIPRESS, have not reached the industrial potential of mass production necessary for blue-ray devices, due to the shortcomings of high pressure technology, which precludes the production of low cost, large size substrates. But there is still hope: new ideas born in Warsaw and commercialized by Ammono may yet increase the Polish share of the market. Further progress in optical memory devices, predicted to use bulk materials, 3D, or multilayer technology, as compared with contemporary flat, 2D, single-layer memories, as well as those using multi-chromatic light sources are still a matter of the future.

The progress in development of the Internet, in terms of its scope, accessibility and the impact on the global society (by utilizing advances in optical fibre technology, ultra-fast opto-electronic devices, satellite communication technologies and mobile telecommunication technologies) as well as the appearance of new generations of smart phones and tablets – should be regarded as one of the most important innovations of our times. The development of the software for these devices, and the role of Polish programmers in the business is worth noticing. The software applications, like Facebook, Twitter, e-shopping, internet payments, etc., definitely shape our everyday life. The predicted role of linear infrastructure, such as electric grids or pipelines, in the growth of the Internet network seems to be overestimated, but the future development of smart grids might increase the interrelations between networks.

The other future developments, such as voice recognition and voice command execution, the further possibility to enhance the interaction of humans with computers, are on the way to be implemented. Contemporary smart phones already have such applications in operation. Software for real-time translations is still under development, but on-line translators and voice generators have already changed our life and made speechless people talk again. The most famous case is artificial voice of ALS-suffering Professor Stephen Hawking[3]. The recent developments in constructing devices to communicate with the dis-

---

[3] http://www.wired.co.uk/magazine/archive/2015/01/features/giving-hawking-a-voice.

abled, who lost their voice or are paralyzed, even with people regarded until recently as mentally unable to communicate, are waiting for implementation for all who need such devices. One can say that these emerging technologies are recently among the greatest achievements of humanity. The Polish contribution – System SENSOR[4] – to the advancement of the such technologies merits recognition.

The future developments of bio-sensors with interface to the computer or mobile phone able to provide medical information to remote medical services or to emergency rescue teams is likely to be in operation soon and the notion of e-medicine is likely to become reality.

Professor Dyson (1999) suggested that global accessibility of the Internet may change human habits and make "the Internet end the intellectual and economic isolation of rural populations… enriching villages all over the world and halting the migration from villages to megacities". The Internet can be the tool to reverse the process of marginalization of rural areas, providing e-jobs, e-shops, e-medicine, e-entertainment. Such innovations, however, can be a challenge to the traditional local businesses providing goods door-to-door. Furthermore, Internet and other communication technologies change our live styles and work environment. New technologies empower governments and companies to secretly track, analyze and record virtually every detail about our lives. The syndrome of the Big Brother spying might be an obstacle preventing people from using such technologies in business. Furthermore, the perils or threats from the innovations introduced for the sake of improving safety, the surveillance tools, cameras, microphones, satellites, drones, etc. These are everywhere and can monitor everyone. We have less and less privacy. But with certain limitations it can be accepted as a price for feeling safe. There is also a danger of treating the human being as a cell in the multi-cell organism.

On the other hand activity observed on social media, especially by people who are physically immobile, or impaired in mobility, is stunning and really hopeful. This is a *signum temporis*: they are escaping the black hole of disability and marginalization, and jumping over the walls, which impair their equal participation in society.

Genetics

Progress in biological, medical and agriculture sciences, especially in genetics and genetic engineering, is the most controversial area of research and development which may produce promising, but also potentially dangerous results. Projects, such as exploring the genetic code of humans, genome, preceded or accompanied by similar research on plants and animals, and the attempts to immediately commercialize acquired results as well as the genetically modified food, animals and human cloning, may be regarded as revolutionary, but with consequences that are difficult to predict. Such projects may help early diagnostics and treatment of genetic disorders. Many of diseases were found as gene-related only recently and described as rare. Genetics and bioengineering promise production of new generations of drugs, stem cells or even organs to be used in modern therapies. Trans-dis-

---

[4] http://www.systemsensor.pl.

ciplinary projects in biophysics, biochemistry, biotechnology, nanotechnology, microelectronics, and neuroinformatics aim at building biosensors interfaced with human organism for diagnostics or even coupled with the human nerve system for controlling or stimulating the operation of the human body, restore the operation of failed neuromuscular systems, or heal the broken spinal cord. As was recently demonstrated in Poland[5], it may be possible to cure a patient with the broken spinal cord or to use exoskeletons for rehabilitation of patients with impaired mobility after stroke or accidents.

The revolution in food production has already commenced. American farmers have introduced dozens of genetically modified plants and in 1997 sowed them into more than 10 million hectares of land. Producers and biotechnological companies argue that the plants are safe, more resistant to plant diseases, parasites and insects. And more resistant to pesticides, so fighting weeds becomes more efficient. GMOs are advertised as more efficient in production, better in taste, nicer to look at, and easier to store for longer periods.

In the European Union there is still no consensus on genetically modified organisms (GMO). For a long time European authorities have not licensed GMO to be used for food production. Since 1999 any use of GMO has been put under control and producers using GMO for food production have been requested to label their products with the adequate information. There are discussions on possible long-term effects of introducing GMO into the food chain and into the environment, since the consequences for the health of animals and humans are not known and the tools for controlling safety of food might not be adequate. There is a danger of appearance of new, so far unknown diseases. The outbreak of mad cow disease, BSE, in UK in 1989, and evidence of possible transmission of the disease to humans, resulting in Creutzfeld-Jakob disease, became a real warning. BSE has a long incubation period, about 2.5 to 8 years. In humans, it is known as new variant Creutzfeld-Jakob disease, vCJD or nvCJD, and by October 2009 it had killed 177 people in the UK, and 44 elsewhere[6]. The origin of the disease itself remains unknown. The infectious agent in BSE is believed to be a specific type of misfolded protein called a prion. Prions are not destroyed even if the beef or material containing them is cooked or heat-treated. Prion proteins carry the disease between individuals and cause deterioration of the brain. Research in 2008 suggested that mad cow disease also is caused by a genetic mutation within a gene called the prion protein gene[7].

Recent reports on the health status of US society may be described as obesity epidemic: approximately 80% of the population over 25 years of age is overweight[8]. This suggests that US citizens suffer from the lifestyle, nutrition habits and food quality. There is still controversy as to whether introduction of GMOs into environment can irreversibly violate our fragile equilibrium.

---

[5] A man who was completely paralyzed from the waist down can walk again. The Polish surgeons used nerve-supporting cells from the nose to provide pathways along which the broken tissue was able to grow. https://www.theguardian.com/science/2014/oct/21/paralysed-darek-fidyka-pioneering-surgery.

[6] http://www.foodsafetynews.com/2014/06/4th-mad-cow-fatality-in-u-s-since-2004-investigated-in-texas/#.Vuv4zJJ3B1k.

[7] https://www.sciencedaily.com/releases/2008/09/080912075208.htm.

[8] http://www.ncbi.nlm.nih.gov/pmc/articles/PMC3033553/.

Brain technologies

Research on human brain, its structures, functions and the way it operates has been pointed out to be very important and promising for 21st century innovations. The outcome has been envisaged to be useful in creating systems of artificial intelligence, in understanding the way we learn and think, and in providing grounds for hope as regards unravelling the mechanisms and causes of mental diseases. Progress towards treating some common mental diseases was recognized by the 2000 Nobel Prize to Arvid Carlsson, Paul Greengard and Eric Kandel (in the field of Physiology or Medicine) "for their discoveries concerning signal transduction in the nervous system"[9]. Hopes for treating schizophrenia and depression with new drugs introduced into practice are still waiting to be fulfilled. Alzheimer disease, SM, ALS-MND still remain enigmas with unknown etiology. The knowledge of the physical mechanisms and materials requirements underlying semiconducting devices operation in computer systems convince that medicine is still on the way to understand physical mechanisms of malfunctions of neurons and neuronal network constituting the human brain or generally nervous system.

New materials (miniaturization and "smart composites")

The achievements of material sciences, available technologies on molecular and atomic level should facilitate, in a not too distant future, the production of materials with any desired characteristics or properties. Such hypothesis could have been substantiated at the beginning of the millennium, though the progress in particular projects and programmes is not as dynamic as expected. The example of high temperature superconductors can be put forward, and the lack of understanding of the physical mechanism of the observed phenomena seems to be the main reason. One can know how to produce certain materials, but doesn't know of what and why. The latter knowledge is necessary to succeed.

Nanotechnology provides us with the tools to create atomic layer-by-layer deposition of the materials e.g. Molecular Beam Epitaxy[10]. Nowadays one can produce objects with atomic dimensions manipulating with single atoms, molecules, creating quantum objects: quantum wells, quantum wires, quantum dots. These objects can provide computer logics operating on a single atom, a single electron, but also on electronic states of an artificial atom – a quantum dot. These structures are at the heart of contemporary transistors, light emitting diodes, laser diodes, light detectors, solar cells, also different sensors, biosensors etc.

Furthermore, traditional material science evolves under environmental pressure. For example, many Western governments implement the regulations for the consumer products that should conform to 3R requirements: recycling, reclamation, remanufacturing. As a result of the environmental pressures, new branches of future material technologies emerge, e.g. biomimetics. Biomimetics, which relates to the development of materials similar to or imitating natural products (which are much more complex, more efficient than anything we can produce technologically), may be one of the new directions of the material revolution.

---

[9] http://www.nobelprize.org/nobel_prizes/medicine/laureates/2000/press.html.
[10] http://www.britannica.com/technology/molecular-beam-epitaxy.

Energy

The history of the way humanity produces energy can be summarized with a simplified scheme of advances in energy production, depending on the utilized sources of energy: wind=>hydro=>coal=>oil=>natural gas=> nuclear=>renewables. The practice of the last century was almost entirely extensive exploitation of fossil fuels: coal, oil and gas. This practice exploited and continues to exploit resources originating from organic matter that has decomposed under the intense pressure and heat of the Earth's crust. Humanity burns these fuels at an unprecedented pace, as compared to the time necessary to produce them by natural processes. At the end of the 20th century man first realized that this practice may result in observed changes in the climate, following the globally observed rise in temperatures. The emission of flue gases from burning fossil fuels was seen by the scientific community as the main factor of climate change: the greenhouse effect of gases emitted into the atmosphere, in particular emission of the main by-product of burning fossil fuels – carbon dioxide, CO_2. Scientific studies organized and coordinated by the Intergovernmental Panel on Climate Change (IPCC), working under the auspices of the United Nations Organization, have confirmed, with almost 100% probability, that the human factor and gas emissions are responsible for the observed phenomena (www.ipcc.ch). This was recognized by the Norwegian Nobel Committee, which awarded the 2007 Nobel Peace Prize to IPCC and Al Gore, "for their efforts to build up and disseminate greater knowledge about man-made climate change, and to lay the foundations for the measures that are needed to counteract such change"[11]. The conclusions of the IPCC reports support the long-lasting efforts to elaborate global policy to counteract the dangerous changes in the human environment. Energy-related issues are at the heart of these efforts. The global energy policy of the future desperately seeks possibilities of diversifying sources of energy with progressively increasing share of renewable energy sources to replace fossil fuels.

In the first decade of the 21st century there was also a kind of consensus on the necessity to increase the share of nuclear energy, which, after a half century of development, was regarded as a matured, reliable and non-emitting source of energy. In fact, nuclear energy was considered to be the only alternative to fossil fuels regarding required stability, predictability, and desired amount of energy produced. The problems of safety and economy, and the issue of radioactive waste processing and storage were considered to be solvable in due time. The renewables, modern wind technologies or solar energy plants, photovoltaic or thermal, were regarded unstable (in case of a large share of energy systems having problems with accommodating temporal overproduction or compensating for stoppages in production). The technology of storing energy and stabilizing the system was not in place as far as the amount of energy to be stored was concerned. Large-scale hydro-projects remained controversial regarding environmental and social issues.

Our thinking on the global solution of the energy problems was subjected to a severe test in the wake of the Tohoku earthquake and tsunami on 11 March 2011, which resulted

---

[11] http://www.nobelprize.org/nobel_prizes/peace/laureates/2007/.

in the damage of the Fukushima Daiichi nuclear power plant[12]. This accident was finally evaluated as the most severe nuclear accident in history. The extent of damage included the meltdown of three reactors, explosions of hydrogen, destruction of the housing of the reactors and the spent fuel storage, the huge amounts of radioactive emissions to the environment, social-economic implications, the evacuation of the surrounding settlements within the radius of 80 km from the plant, and many other reactions. The Fukushima disaster appeared to be a test of many aspects: the preparedness of a modern industrialized country for severe accidents as well as its ability to cope with the post-crisis situation. The decommissioning of the destroyed nuclear plant will last for decades. Therefore, it is not possible even to estimate what the overall economic, social and technological cost will be.

The nuclear disaster had far-reaching repercussions. The Prime Minister of Japan, Naoto Kan, an engineer, graduate of the Tokyo Institute of Technology, who in his capacity was involved in efforts to respond to the earthquake, tsunami and Fukushima disaster, said: "There is no other disaster that would affect 50 million people – maybe a war"; "The cause of this catastrophe is, of course, the earthquake and the tsunami but, additionally, the fact that we were not prepared"; "We did not anticipate such a huge natural disaster could happen"[13]. He also noted that "there is only one way to eliminate such accidents, which is to get rid of all nuclear power plants". These conclusions, though drastic, are not unreasonable. The Fukushima disaster triggered worldwide discussion on truth and lies, hidden secrets and misinformation of the nuclear industry. New nuclear reactors had a hidden military purpose (during the cold war). The operation of these installations was kept secret and out of economy. Presently, the information on the functioning of such installations reveals that almost all types of nuclear reactors, which are in use for generating electricity, have suffered a major failure or accident. For example, the Windscale fire of 10 October 1957 in Britain, where its graphite-moderated reactor caught fire and caused radioactive contamination of the surrounding area. The upgrading of the reactor design and replacing air (as a cooling agent) with CO_2 in the UK Magnox reactors has not gained much interest elsewhere. RBMK – graphite-moderated, water-cooled reactor designed in the Soviet Union – proved unstable at low power, and went out of control, causing an explosion and meltdown of the reactor on 26 April 1986[14]. The accident is known as the Chernobyl disaster, now Ukraine. This type of reactor is regarded as the most dangerous among all in use in the nuclear power industry. Ignalina NPP was decommissioned after the fall of the Berlin wall and Lithuania's joining the EU. There are still such reactors in operation in Russia, with some improvements in the design, also known as MKER: in Kursk, Leningrad-St. Petersburg and Smolensk. The Chernobyl disaster had been preceded by a major breakdown in US Three Mile Island (TMI) NPP on 28 March 1979. The PWR, Pressurized Water Reactor, water-moderated, water-cooled, US-designed facility, melted down on loosing the coolant – LOCA – Loss of Coolant Accident – with subsequent release

---

[12] http://www.psr.org/environment-and-health/environmental-health-policy-institute/responses/costs-and-consequences-of-fukushima.html?referrer=https://www.google.be/.
[13] http://www.scientificamerican.com/article/nuclear-power-odyssey-of-naoto-kan-former-japan-prime-minister-during-fukushima/?print=true.
[14] http://www.nrc.gov/reading-rm/doc-collections/fact-sheets/chernobyl-bg.html.

of unknown amounts of radioactive gases and radioactive iodine into the environment. It was the worst accident in the history of US commercial nuclear power plants; and the first decommissioned destroyed reactor. Cleanup started in August 1979, and officially ended in December 1993, with a total cleanup cost of about $1 billion[15]. The accident also had a major social impact. The Hollywood movie *The China Syndrome* attracted much attention and the TMI accident enhanced the credibility of anti-nuclear groups, who had predicted an accident, and triggered protests around the world. It was an impulse to slow down or even withdraw from new investments in nuclear power in the US. Many similar reactors on order were cancelled: in total, 51 US nuclear reactors were cancelled in 1980–1984. The two decades after Chernobyl allowed the nuclear power industry to recover and design new generations of reactors with declared improved safety. This calm period violently ended with the Fukushima disaster. In its aftermath many facts, swept under the carpet for many years, came to light. The public gained new information on the nuclear industry and came to realize that operating nuclear reactors are not the only danger. In fact the Fukushima disaster showed the destructive power of switched off reactors. The very physics of nuclear fuel, starting with Maria Skłodowska-Curie and discovery of radioactive nuclides like polonium and radium, prove that the products of nuclear fission of uranium are much more radioactive than uranium itself. This is the reason why nuclear fuel keeps burning even if the chain reaction is stopped. The nuclear reactor once started cannot be switched off completely, and it keeps working on about 5–10% of full capacity after the chain reaction has been quenched. If the energy released is not taken out of the reactor, as in the case of Fukushima (with major LOCA in place), the reactor destroys itself within several hours. The energy released by slowly burning fuel accumulates. The latter results in the increase of the pressure and temperature in the reactor. Next, the cooling water evaporates and nuclear fuel melts down. Further chemical reactions produce hydrogen out of water, and finally hydrogen comes into an explosive reaction with oxygen. As a result it causes an explosion such as in the recent case of Fukushima.

The loss-of-coolant LOCA is thus as dangerous in the case of reactor itself as for the storage basin, each containing several loads of spent fuel removed from the reactor. Such an accident happened in the Soviet Union, now Russia. The huge explosion on 29 September 1957 in the Mayak reprocessing plant near Ozyorsk city in the Urals, was named Kyshtym disaster, since Ozyorsk was a classified city, not marked on maps. The accident had been kept secret for years by the then Soviet authorities[16]. The information on the disaster in possession of CIA was also classified to avoid panic or adverse social reaction regarding similar installations in USA. The very existence of such installations was equally not known to general public in France.

The Fukushima disaster demonstrated that the very basic assumption underlying the design of nuclear reactor – in the wake of accident one can turn off the reactor, and, in the worst case, one can abandon the reactor since it is contained in the safety shield – is not true. If the system of cooling the reactor ceases to operate or is destroyed, the energy

---

[15] https://prezi.com/fzialwk9fbgu/nuclear-power-plant/.

[16] http://mentalfloss.com/article/71026/kyshtym-disaster-largest-nuclear-disaster-youve-never-heard.

released by the nuclear fuel, even without chain reaction, will accumulate inside the shield, finally erupting like a volcano. And this volcano will be radioactive. The stronger shield we build, the stronger eruption we can expect.

The tsunami wave after Fukushima disaster travelled around the globe. This resulted in the decision on definitive quenching of nuclear power in Germany, in worldwide screening of all existing and planned nuclear installations regarding safety procedures, in delaying or abolishing planned investments. Trust in the safety of nuclear power even for new generations of reactors disappeared, or at least diminished. The new generation French-German European Pressure Reactor, EPR, a first prototype under construction in Olkiluoto, subjected to Finnish safety rules rocketed in cost and time. The project started in 2005 and was originally scheduled for 4 years and 3.7 billion euro. It is expected to last at least 13 years and the final cost is estimated to more than double the original (roughly 8 billion euro)[17].

The nuclear power definitely lost momentum and two important players in the world technology market, Japan and Germany, declared change of priorities: search for alternatives, renewables or any other solutions. It is difficult to estimate consequences of Fukushima for ambitious long-term plans of India to develop its own nuclear programme to utilize thorium instead of uranium as a nuclear fuel. Those in favour of this idea put forward arguments about differences in the physics of uranium and thorium fission, and claim that the thorium fuel cycle is safer than the uranium cycle, however the process of engineering might face similar or different problems.

As long as the basic concepts of nuclear power remain unchanged, one cannot expect any revolutionary inventions. The history of nuclear power demonstrates that more ambitious designs, more sophisticated or utilizing more expensive materials, like Canadian-designed heavy water-moderated reactor, CANDU, play an important role in the development of the industry, but cannot compete with simpler designs. The recent swing of authorities in Finland to choose Russian VVER technology instead of the sophisticated EPR design, and the decision of the United Arab Emirates to choose Korean consortium to build a nuclear plant with Korean APR-1400 reactors rather than opting for Areva EPR or US competitors, point into this direction. China remains a big market, currently globally the biggest investor – almost one third of NPP under construction are located in China – and a future important player in nuclear power. It tests almost all existing technologies and develops its own domestic industry, demonstrating absorptive capacity and innovative potential, and thus prepares to become a global player. The Chinese CAP-1400 reactor, with design based on the US Westinghouse AP-1000, is to be deployed in large numbers across the country[18]. The long-lasting problem of storing, reprocessing or utilizing the spent fuel, as well as technical problems underlying decommissioning of closed plants, will require concerted efforts for decades or even centuries. The accommodation of the very cost of these activities into the budget of the nuclear industry is necessary for fair play economic competition in the energy market.

---

[17] http://www.eurosolar.de/en/index.php/arguments-mainmenu-108/info-papers-mainmenu-14/157-the-costs-of-nuclear-energy.

[18] http://www.world-nuclear-news.org/NN-Preparations-continue-for-initial-CAP1400-units-2704155.html.

The Fukushima lesson for Poland is not to hurry to build nuclear power plants. At the moment "the wait and see" might be a good policy. Of course, one should monitor developments and prepare the infrastructure: technical, legislative, human resources, etc., to be able to enter into any project which will deal with nuclear-related energy. Something new, more suitable for Poland, should appear from the last energy crisis. One of them is looking for the new developments, new ideas or new inventions customized especially for Polish conditions. The nuclear fusion energy projects still remain in the domain of the future, and the future of renewables remains to be bright. The photovoltaic technology is progressing with the electronic pace. Technologies of production, storage and usage of hydrogen are under development. Solar energy might be utilized directly for heating using solar panels. Vacuum technology provides for utilization of solar energy even in very cold places. The hybrid PV-heat panels have been considered. Bio-fuels might be regarded as complementary to photovoltaics, providing locally energy, fuel for transport, especially for agriculture. Therefore, the wise policy should use the low-quality soils for energetic crops as well as utilize the waste from food production for bio-fuel production, including bio-gas.

Furthermore, the hydro-energy should be re-invented with emerging technologies de-coupled from water retention or big reservoirs. Water retention can also be re-invented, especially in mountain regions. Small and micro-hydro in large quantity might supplement big hydro. Artificial snow production and snow storage might be an example of new water technology. New ideas to prevent big fires of forests and bushes and use the saved biomass as a fuel are envisaged.

Finally, the geothermal energy might become a black horse of the energetic race. The energy flux from the Earth core towards the surface is much smaller than the energy flux coming to the Earth from the Sun. Any progress in the utilization of the energy produced in the Earth interior and released in the form of volcanic activity or just irradiated into the space energy, instead of fossil fuels will be beneficial. Countries with volcanic activity already utilize hot waters for heating or SPA's and Island and Philippines generate one third of electricity from geothermal plants. The extracting of heat from the Earth became a matured technology with demonstrated feasibility to be an effective heat source for residential heating and hot water production. The heat pump is a kind of heat amplifier or heat transistor since it uses one unit of electric energy to transfer 4–5 units of thermal energy from the low-temperature source to the high-temperature heat sink or receiver. Hot water production by heat pumps requires only 20–25% energy needed to heat water directly in ordinary electric boilers. The utilization of new agents like CO_2 in the construction of heat pumps is known to improve the performance. CO_2 is also less harmful than fluorocarbons when released to the environment. The development of big, industrial grade heat pumps might open new areas of application. The generation of CO_2 industry might be a driving force for wider introduction of carbon capture and storage, CCS, technologies and transformation of fossil carbon industry. The prospects of geothermal energy in Poland are bright. The geothermal potential is demonstrated in such regions as Mszczonów, Pyrzyce, Geotermia Podhale or utilization of hot thermal waters in Bukowina, Bańska Niżna, Białka Tatrzańska, Lądek Zdrój, Uniejów, Mszczonów and Toruń.

The minimization of energy consumption, introduction of new energy-saving technologies in industry, housing and transport, and the decoupling of economic growth from energy demand would be a very important factor in energy policy in the next few decades. The future will be shaped by ideas how to change a consument into a prosument (a combination of producer and consumer), passive or active housing or local communities, which for new technologies of energy management require smart grids and small or micro energy generation using local energy resources, all these initiatives subjected to strict rules regarding environment protection.

Transport

The future transport technologies will aim at the construction of more efficient, less energy-consuming vehicles and more environment friendly transport concepts. A renaissance or rejuvenation of rail transport is expected, with fast rail of 200–300 km/h competing with air transport on middle distances in passenger traffic, and with sea transport on long distances, including for example Euro-Asian rail projects. The development of ultra-high speed rail systems using MAGLEV magnetic levitation, has been predicted in the latest reports which find it feasible that trains will travel at up to 500 km/hour. Some talk of even more exotic ideas of vacuum tube capsules exceeding 1000 km/hour speed. New technologies for public city transport will use new fuels and new engine concepts, including compressed natural gas CNG, liquid natural gas LNG internal combustion engines, hybrid, combustion engine + electric engine, drives and electric, powered by batteries or fuel cells. The latter will utilize natural gas or hydrogen for producing electricity on board. Pilot projects are underway worldwide, with hydrogen technology tested e.g. in Berlin, and CNG, LNG, hybrid or electric vehicles in operation in Warsaw. The satellite telecommunication systems will be in operation, GPS, Galileo, to monitor and eventually control or manage the traffic. The introduction of biofuels, eco-diesel or bio-diesel is underway, which will benefit rural communities. In Poland, the project recently lost momentum, with objections from car producers. The argument of the latter is that such fuels are more suitable for old diesel engines than the new ones. Toyota's recent presentation of its Mirai – the first commercial electric car powered by fuel cell supplied with compressed hydrogen – demonstrates progress in the automotive industry following the successful launching of the gasoline-electric hybrid Prius model. Toyota will give away thousands of patents for its fuel-cell cars in an effort to encourage other automakers to follow suit. The future depends on whether car manufacturers can bring down the prices, as well as on a wide enough network of filling stations, which need to be built. Toyota expects it will take 10 to 20 years for the Mirai to reach sales in the range of tens of thousands of vehicles a year. Toyota faced a similar scenario with its gasoline-electric hybrid, the Prius, which is now a big money earner.

Tools and systems of environment protection

There is a kind of consensus that the environment protection of the future, or sustainable development, requires this field to be part of the economy; it should be built into the whole system, rather than remaining outside, and protect nature against humans. All emerging technologies should be subjected to this rule. The recently observed boom in using artificial snow might be a very important example of such sustainable activity. The life cycle of materials and energy demand should be planned all along: starting from planning, through production or building, to end-of-life re-manufacturing, recycling, and utilization. Monitoring of waste production should be introduced for all kinds of waste: solid, liquid, gaseous, chemical, radioactive, industrial, residential, medical and so on. Minimization of wastes should lead to waste-free economy as the ultimate goal. Waste utilization or collection at the source, to avoid its introduction into the environment, should be the first step in this direction. Environment protection, or sustainable development, requires globally introduced planning, including environmental impact assessment of any new technology, any investment or development project. Pro-ecological and pro-health educational campaigns should be part of the system. Environment protection is a global task. There are no political borders if we look to the Earth from space, and pollutions are not susceptible to orders to stop on the border. Sustainable development requires a change of philosophy of economic growth. Philosophy of competition or even economic war – keeping secret the planned developments, research, data and information protection, restrictions in illegal use of intellectual and industrial property – should be replaced by philosophy of cooperation, exchange of important information, even free access to information, and promotion of the best practices in the interest of all. This is not an easy task. The change in overall philosophy could even be called cooperation for peace, as such common human problem solving also means breaking down prejudice and divisions, and putting more effort towards fair distribution of goods. After all, this is what it is all about when we talk about quality of life.

5. Closing remarks

One can ask which of the new technologies or innovations can provide the best solutions to achieve the quality of life? Is the free market model able to steer the economy to the desired goal – the improved standards of living for all? What kind of "state intervention" and "international linkages" will be needed to determine the optimal trajectory? How to transform industrial society towards a "new society" – able to better balance one's time to work and learn with the time for leisure and recreation? What means have to be applied to improve public health and reduce the cost of medical treatment? How to change the educational systems and tailor it to the needs of lifelong learning? How to overcome social divisions, the problem of poverty, unemployment, marginalization, exclusion of individuals, social groups or entire nations or groups of nations from human achievements, while not destroying the values that we all represent?

One hopes that the forces of reason, peace and solidarity prevail and allow for the development of humanity without exposing it to disasters and for a continuous development. One way is to understand and appreciate the vast knowledge and wisdom gained by the humanity through the experience – by trial and error. Also the knowledge embedded in the traditional ways of farming, traditional recipes how to use gifts of nature, respect the wisdom that has been passed through generations in families and communities.

References

21st Century Technologies – Promises and Perils of a Dynamic Future, OECD, 1998.

Dakowski, M. (2001), *Perspektywy energetyki: słońce, hydraty, wodór*, "Rurociągi", 4/2001.

Dakowski, M., Wiąckowski, S. (2005), *O energetyce dla użytkowników oraz sceptyków*, Warszawa.

Dmochowski, J. (1998), *Opracowanie technologii warstw epitaksjalnych GaN i badanie ich foto-przewodnictwa*, MSE thesis, Warsaw University of Technology, Warszawa.

Dmochowski, J. (1998), *Studium uwarunkowań i kierunków zagospodarowania przestrzennego m.st. Warszawy*, Warszawa.

Dmochowski, J. (2002), *Technologie 21-go wieku – obietnice i niebezpieczeństwa dynamicznej przyszłości*, Institute of Electron Technology, Warszawa.

Dmochowski, J. E (2003*), 21st Century Technologies: the challenges and solutions for Future Society*, "Telecommunication XXI", 3rd International Conference for Students and Young Scientists, Kielce-Wólka Mianowska.

Dmochowski, J. E. (2006), *ARKA – Active House Polish Expression of Interest for EU FP7 Specific Programme*, "Ideas".

Dmochowski, J. E. (2006), *Dom przyszłości (House of the Future). ENERGIA ODNAWIALNA: Innowacyjne idee i technologie dla budownictwa*. Pierwsza Międzynarodowa Konferencja Energii Słonecznej i Budownictwa Ekologicznego SOLINA 2006, "Zeszyty Naukowe Politechniki Rzeszowskiej. Budownictwo i Inżynieria Środowiska", z. 40, 99–104.

Dmochowski, J. E (2008), *Summary of World's Café round table on scenarios of climatic change: Round table on CLIMATE CHANGE, FORESTS and TOURISM*. COST Strategic Workshop "Global Change and Sustainable Development in Mountain Regions", Innsbruck, Austria, 7–9 April.

Dmochowski, J. E. (2008), *Nowe metody gospodarowania CO$_2$*.

Dmochowski, J. E. (2011), *Koncepcja Rozwoju Instytutu Badawczego, Institute of Innovative Technologies EMAG*, Katowice.

Dmochowski, J. E. (2011), *Contribution JRC-EC, MNiSW, PAN Conference. Scientific Support to a Competitive European Low Carbon Economy: Energy, Transport, and Emerging Technologies*, 7 July 2011.

Dmochowski, J. E. (2013), *Carbon Capture and Storage: CO$_2$ – waste or asset?* Abstract. BIT's 2nd Annual International Symposium of CLEAN COAL TECHNOLOGY (CCT), 26–28 September 2013, Xi'an China. 2013 EURO ASIA ECONOMIC FORUM.

Dyson, Freeman J., (1999), T*he Sun, the Genome & the Internet: Tools of Scientific Revolutions*, Oxford University Press Inc. *Słońce, Genom, Internet – Narzędzia rewolucji naukowej*, WN PWN, Warszawa.

Froggatt, A., Mitchell, C., Managi, Shunsuke (2012), *Reset or Restart? The Impact of Fukushima on the Japanese and German Energy Sectors*, Chatham House.

Gibbons, M., in: M. Gibbons *et al.* (1994), *The new production of knowledge. The dynamics of science and research in contemporary societies*, Sage.

Herman, M. A., Sitter, H. (1989), *Molecular Beam Epitaxy*, Springer.

Kim, Linsu (1997), *Imitation to Innovation: The Dynamics of Korea's Technological Learning*, Harvard Business Press.

Kossut, M. (2001), *W głąb mózgu*, "Wiedza i Życie" 3/2001.

Kukliński, A. (ed.) (1991), *Transformation of Science in Poland*, Vol. 1, State Committee for Scientific Research, Warszawa.

Kukliński, A. (ed.) (1992), *Society, Science, Government,* Vol. 2, State Committee for Scientific Research, Warszawa.

Kukliński, A. (ed.) (1995), *Nauka-Technologia-Gospodarka: wzajemne powiązania i globalne tendencje rozwoju,* KBN, Warszawa.

Kukliński, A., Orlowski, W. M. (eds.) (2000), *The Knowledge-Based Economy: The Global Challenges of the 21st Century*, Vol.4, State Committee for Scientific Research, Warszawa.

Kukliński, A. (ed.) (2001), T*he Knowledge-Based Economy: The European Challenges of the 21st Century,* Vol.5, State Committee for Scientific Research, Warszawa.

Kukliński, A. (ed.) (2001), *Gospodarka oparta na wiedzy: wyzwania dla Polski XXI wieku*, KBN, Warszawa.

Miodek, J. (2000), *Inny słownik języka polskiego PWN*, "Wiedza i Życie" 6/2001.

Ney, B. (2002), *Zaawansowane techniki szansą cywilizacyjnego rozwoju Polski*, "Przegląd Techniczny" 8/2002.

Physics and the future of technology, "Physics World", June 2001.

Sokołowski, J., Zimny, J., Kozłowski, R. H. (2005), *Polska XXI wieku – Nowa wizja i strategia rozwoju*, Łomianki.

Strategia rozwoju Warszawy do 2010 roku, Warszawa.

Technology and Economy. The Key Relationship, OECD, 1992.

Joanna Żyra, Viktor Shevchuk

ICT, Innovations, Regional Growth and Wages in Poland

1. Introduction

It is commonly asserted that since the mid-1990s the ICT revolution has rapidly spread across nations and transformed the way people communicate, work, and live (Vu 2011, pp. 357–373). Danish White Paper on regional states assumes that innovation is one of the four incentives in regional growth policy, next to human capital, entrepreneurship and welfare service (Cornett 2006). To the same extent, enormous effects of long-term economic growth on the advances made in production and use of information and communication technology (ICT) during the past decades should not be underestimated (Van Ark 2002, pp. 1–14). Beside the aggregate supply factors, the ICT revolution is considered a tool of fostering improvement in labour skills, consumer sophistication, and an increased level of broad-based education (Quah 2002). ICT is considered a tool for creating possibilities for economic development leapfrogging in developing countries, i.e. bypassing some of the processes of accumulation of human capabilities and fixed investment in order to narrow the gaps in productivity and output that separate industrialized and developing countries (Steinmueller 2001, pp. 193–201). Recent developments in ICT, such as social networks, smart phones, apps stores, e-readers and cloud computing, have a potential to provide an extra boost to the world economy, recovering from the financial crisis of 2008–2009.

The aim of our study is to assess empirically how the ICT and innovations affect the rate of regional growth in Poland. It is presumed that a higher level of ICT penetration is favourable for either innovations or economic growth. Although economic growth should correlate with higher wages and well-being, implementation of ICT and innovations could lead to a decrease in demand for labour and/or to an increase in the supply of it, which used to be associated with stagnating wages.

Using annual data from the 16 Polish voivodships between 2008 and 2012, our main results could be summarized in the following way: (i) almost all ICT components are positively correlated with indicators of innovative activities; (ii) as expected, innovations accelerate economic growth; (iii) however, an increase in the number of innovative firms or expenditure on innovations per worker lead to a weaker wage growth, while general expenditure (in percent of regional product) is neutral with respect to wage dynamics.

2. Important links between ICT, innovations and regional growth

As stated by Cornett (2006), regional growth is not an exogenous or independent phenomenon, as it relies on the ability to stimulate entrepreneurship and on the capacity to innovate at regional and local level. In the short run, innovation and knowledge creation allow for the process of regional adaptation to industrial change as a response to changes in the competitive environment. Furthermore, they create preconditions for successful restructuring of the economic base in a longer perspective. It is important to note that innovation is different from pure invention, involving successful implementation of a new product, service, or process, which for most activities entails their commercial success (Gordon and McCann 2005, pp. 523–543). Innovations could be simply due to factor allocation changes within existing functional production relationships, or to changes in the production functions, involving either or both price and non-price quality competition. The sources of innovations are identified across a wide range of factors, such as behaviour of the entrepreneur, industrial environment, the nature of the individual firm within an evolutionary, behavioural, and organizational context, processes of inter-firm competition, learning, and imitation, specific features of particular industrial sectors, geographical areas and time periods. Although innovation used to be associated with developing brand new, advanced solutions for sophisticated and well-off customers, through exploitation of the most recent advances in knowledge, with the use of highly educated labour in R&D intensive companies, in a broader perspective, innovation is an attempt to try out new or improved products, processes or ways to perform most if not all economic activities (Fagerberg et al. 2009). Regardless of the nature, sources, and impacts, on the basis of the arguments presented above there are three common identifiable features of all innovation: (i) newness, (ii) improvement, and (iii) overcoming uncertainty (Gordon and McCann 2005, pp. 523–543).

Empirical studies confirm the importance of innovation in economic growth on the national level (Bottazzi and Peri 2004; LeBel 2008, pp. 334–347; Wu 2010), on the regional level (Quatraro 2009, pp. 1001–1022), and on the firm-level (Gordhuys and Veugelers 2012, pp. 516–529). An empirical investigation of 102 European regions in the period 1990–2002 indicates that higher innovation performance contributes to per capita income growth and that social capital affects this growth indirectly by fostering innovation (Akçomak and ter Weel 2009, pp. 544–567).

Although the importance of innovation for economic growth is fairly well understood, there is substantial ambiguity with respect to its impact on a nation's economic well-being. For European regions, it has been acknowledged that a region can rely on both internal and external sources of innovation. However, the socio-economic conditions needed to maximize the innovation potential of each region are necessarily internal, as regional spillovers do not have any substantial impact on local economic performance (Rodriguez-Pose and Crescenzi 2008, pp. 51–67). Britain's experience suggests that failure in generating large payoffs from technological development are explained by structural weaknesses in the commercialization environment (Nicholas 2014, pp. 181–204). As argued by Reinert (2006), coupling innovation and social cohesion could be helpful in the creation of an innovation-based Europe, though both "innovations" and "social cohesion" used to be alien elements in the equilibrium of standard textbook economics.

Archibugi and Filipetti (2011, pp. 1153–1182) argue that the economic crisis of autumn 2008 had a negative impact on innovative investment in almost all EU countries, but the catch-up countries are the most affected. The resulting investment slump in such countries as Greece, Bulgaria, Lithuania, Latvia, Romania, Hungary etc. leads to an increasing divergence in investment activities. In Poland, the difference between the share of firms increasing their innovation investments and the decreasing ones rose to 25%. Consequently, growing disparities in innovative capabilities may also lead to divergence in income and well-being.

Though the slowdown of economic growth across the OECD area since 2000 has substantially weakened previous optimism of "a new economy" adherents that the marginal costs of producing ICT goods and services are virtually non-existent, there are still several reasons to believe that ICT will have a longer lasting impact on the potential for economic growth through such channels as: (i) wide range of applications and large impact across the economy, (ii) complementarity to new technological and organizational innovations, (iii) ability to continue improvements over time and the falling cost of using it (Van Ark 2002, pp. 1–14). Vu (2011, pp. 357–372) discusses three channels through which ICT penetration can affect growth: (i) fostering technology diffusion and innovation; (ii) enhancing the quality of decision-making by firms and households; and (iii) increasing demand and reducing production costs, which together raise the output level. Steinmueller (2001, pp. 193–210) compares ICTs with the leading industries of the past that were responsible for industrial growth and development, such as steel, chemicals, and machinery. ICT applications are quite often complementary to efforts to improve the quality, speed and flexibility of production. ICT plays a significant role in the process of reallocation, being more likely to expand (in terms of employment) (Van Reenen *et al.* 2010). Also, ICT could affect innovation through stimulating patents, assisting product and process innovation or improving the firm-level stock of intangible capital. It is important that the main growth boost comes from ICT use, not ICT production (Oulton 2010). Communication technology increases the diffusion speed during the process of "learning by using" (Mukoyama 2005). It has been established empirically that technological spillovers are stronger in the branches with a more intensive use of ICT (Kirby and Riley 2008, pp. 619–630).

However, there might also be some negative effects of this approach. ICT-based innovations can cause decreased rather than increased competitiveness, leading to falling wages and increased downward pressures on wages and profits (Reinert 2006). The Nobel prize-winner Paul Krugman remarks that technologies could depress demand for either *low-end jobs* or *high-end jobs* (*The Economist* 2011). Alan Blinder, another American economist, argues that these are not so much differences between workers with high and low education, but between workplaces with an easily digitalized tasks (and thus endangered by foreign competition) and those where such a possibility is non-existent (Orszag 2011).

Decrease in employment and reduction in value added in certain industries and geographic areas are possible negative effects that should be mentioned. Basu *et al.* (2003, pp. 9–80) argue that the availability of cheap ICT capital is likely to be effective only if firms can deploy their other inputs in radically different and productivity-enhancing ways. Pohjola (2002) does not find any significant correlation between ICT investment and economic growth between 1985 and 1999 for a sample of 42 countries, without disparities between industrial or high-income countries in this respect. Hempell (2003) concluded that in case of German service companies ICT capital is most productive if complemented by training measures in skill-intensive firms.

There appears to be a positive economic impact on expanded broadband deployment and adoption in the USA, though it is admitted that there is the time lag for businesses to effectively exploit innovative broadband applications (Holt and Jamison 2009, pp. 575–581). Although broadband network development does not always correlate with a nation's overall wealth and economic strength, better results are achieved when it becomes a national priority (Frieden 2005, pp. 595–613).

At the beginning of the 2000s it was stated that the empirical support for a direct effect of ICT on the economic growth mainly came from the US experience, creating numerous concerns that ICT did not have the potential to raise growth by as much as such great earlier innovations as the introduction of electricity or the combustion engine (van Ark 2002, pp. 1–14). On the surface, this assumption is supported by the fact that a gap between the levels of US and EU output per worker increased from 1.8% in 1995 to 9.8% by 2004, being the result of stronger productivity growth in the US ICT production and market service sectors (van Ark *et al.* 2008, pp. 25–44). However, not all studies share such a viewpoint. Colecchia and Schreyer (2001) argue that despite differences between countries, the United States has not been a unique case in benefiting from the positive effects of ICT capital investment on the economic growth, nor was the United States the sole country to experience an acceleration of these effects since the beginning of the 2000s. During the second half of the 1990s, contribution of ICT rose from 0.2 to 0.3 and from 0.5 to 0.9 percentage points per year for Australia, Canada, Finland, France, Germany, Italy, Japan, the United Kingdom and the United States, depending on the country. Empirical evidence for European countries indicates that 10% increase in ICT capital is associated with 0.23% increase in firm productivity, above theory-based result at 0.16% (Van Reenen *et al.* 2010).

It is worth noting that positive ICT diffusion depends on the right framework conditions, not necessarily on the existence of an ICT producing sector. As implied by firm-level estimates for Europe, high levels of labour and product market regulation are associated with a lower productivity impact of ICT (Van Reenen *et al.* 2010). Antonelli *et al.* (2010) find evidence that the emergence of a new technological system based upon ICT depends on a process of knowledge recombination, meaning that strong cores of complementary knowledge consolidate and feed an array of coherent applications and implementations.

The recombination process has more chances for success in countries characterized by higher levels of coherence and specialization of their knowledge space. It is quite natural that these kinds of countries have experienced higher rates of increase of national multi-factor productivity growth.

Recent empirical studies are overwhelmingly in favour of positive ICT growth effects, for example, in 15 European countries, Australia, Canada, Japan and the USA (Oulton 2010). For a sample of 102 countries, the support for the hypothesis that ICT was an important source of growth in 1996–2005 was found (Vu 2011, pp. 357–372). The penetration of personal computers, mobile phones, and the Internet users had a significant causal effect on growth, with the marginal effect of the penetration of Internet users being larger than that of mobile phone users, which in turn is larger than that of personal computer users. As it could be expected, the marginal effect of the ICT penetration lessens as the penetration increases. The importance of ICT capital deepening and innovation for productivity has been established empirically for German and Dutch firms from the services sector (Hempell *et al.* 2004).

Cortés and Navarro (2010) acknowledge that the possibilities of investment in ICT in European countries have not been exploited to the extent they have been in the United States, but they explain this fact by important differences between technologically intermediate countries (Austria, Belgium, the Czech Republic, Germany, Spain, France, Ireland, Malta, Portugal, Slovenia and the United Kingdom), technologically underdeveloped countries (Bulgaria, Cyprus, Hungary, Lithuania, Latvia, Poland and Romania), and technologically advanced countries (Denmark, Estonia, Finland, Luxembourg, the Netherlands and Sweden), technologically pre-intermediate countries (Greece, Italy, Slovakia). It is suggested that technologically backward countries, mainly from Eastern Europe with lower level of GDP, should above all foster ICT in the business sector, while the countries with an intermediate or pre-intermediate level of development should focus upon the implementation and use of ICT in households.

Addressing an argument that divergence in ICT adoption is observed regardless of the income levels of countries, Erumban and de Jong (2011) suggest that the ICT adoption rate of a country is affected by the national culture. The results are robust, even when taking under consideration levels of education and income.

For the post-socialist economies, adoption, diffusion, and productive use of ICT depend on suitable infrastructure (Piatkowski 2002). Measuring the level of preparedness for harnessing the potential of ICT to accelerate the long-term economic growth and catching-up with developed countries, Slovenia scored the highest, followed by the Czech Republic and Hungary. Albania, Bosnia and Herzegovina were among the worst performers. Among the Central and Eastern European (CEE) countries, during the 1990s only in the Czech Republic and Hungary ICT production contributed more to productivity growth than the EU-15 average (Piatkowski and van Art 2005). Initially, rapid ICT investment in new plants and growth in ICT production were driven by openness and basic fundamental reforms. Later deeper structural reforms focused on product and labour market flexibility, business re-organization and investment in human capital and ICT skills set preconditions for reorientation towards more intensive use of ICT, particularly in the service sector. The study of more than 1000 Lithuanian firms provides evidence that reaction to factors fostering and restricting innovations depends on the connections between educational system and supply of know-how susceptible employees demanded by business companies (Adekola *et al.* 2008, pp. 595–611).

3. Data sources

The analysis is based on the regional data for Poland's 16 voivodships, obtained from the Polish Central Statistical Office (www.stat.gov.pl). For the purpose of our study, we use indicators which reflect the use of ICT and innovations, along with the data on the gross regional product and average wage.

ICT usage in enterprises is represented by the following indicators (in percent of the total number):

- enterprises using computers,
- enterprises using local Internet computer network (LAN),
- enterprises having access to the Internet,
- enterprises using their own website or home page to produce catalogues or price lists,
- use of the Internet in dealings with public administration,
- use of the Internet in electronic communication with public administration.

Innovation activity is measured by means of three indicators:

- average share of innovative enterprises in the total number of enterprises (in percent),
- expenditure on innovation activities in enterprises in relation to regional output (in percent),
- expenditure on innovation activities in enterprises per person economically active (in zlotys).

Regional growth rate is calculated on the basis of the gross regional product per capita (in 2000 prices), with Poland's consumer price index used as a deflator. Wage growth is considered in nominal terms. All indicators are analyzed on the annual basis. For any individual indicator, the average between 2008 and 2012 is used for the empirical analysis below.

4. ICT and innovations

As presented in Figures 1–3, ICT contributes to innovations across several measures of innovative activities. All indicators of ICT positively correlate with the average share of innovative enterprises, which ranges between 10% and 18%. The strongest positive effect is observed in the cases of using internal computer networks, having access to the Internet and using website to produce catalogues or price lists. Using electronic communication seems to have the weakest effect upon the share of innovative enterprises in total numbers.

Our results correspond to the findings of Van Reenen *et al.* (2010) which suggest that network hardware as a specialized form of tangible ICT capital is strongly associated with firm productivity. The same strong positive effect is obtained for "own-account" software, while purchased software has a weak relationship with productivity but may stimulate complementary investments.

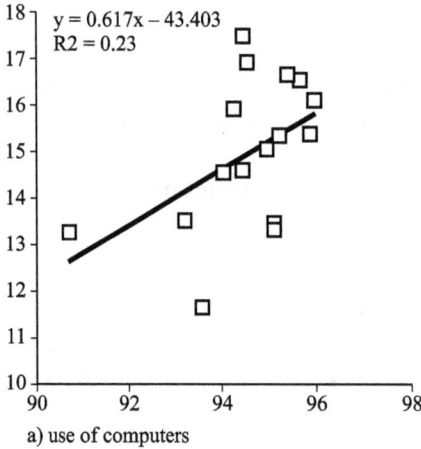

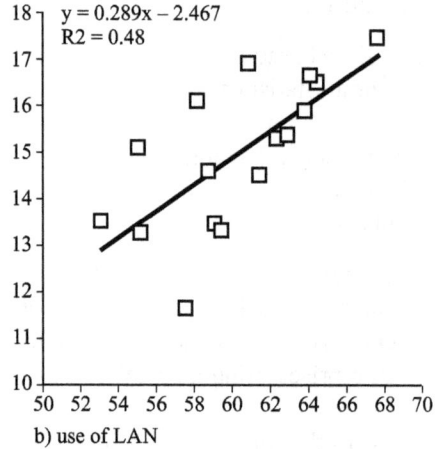

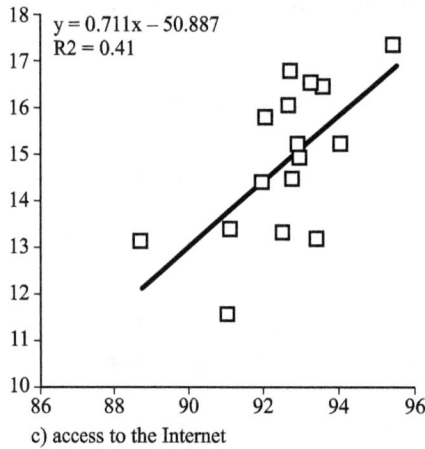

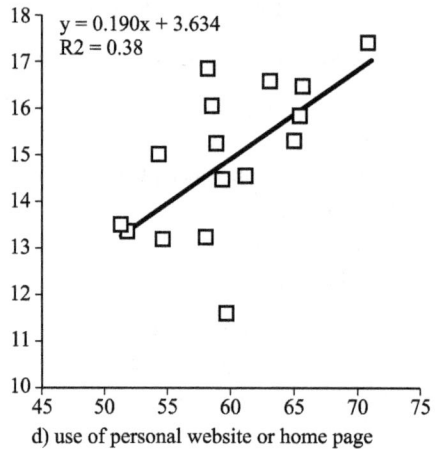

$y = 0.617x - 43.403$
$R^2 = 0.23$

a) use of computers

$y = 0.289x - 2.467$
$R^2 = 0.48$

b) use of LAN

$y = 0.711x - 50.887$
$R^2 = 0.41$

c) access to the Internet

$y = 0.190x + 3.634$
$R^2 = 0.38$

d) use of personal website or home page

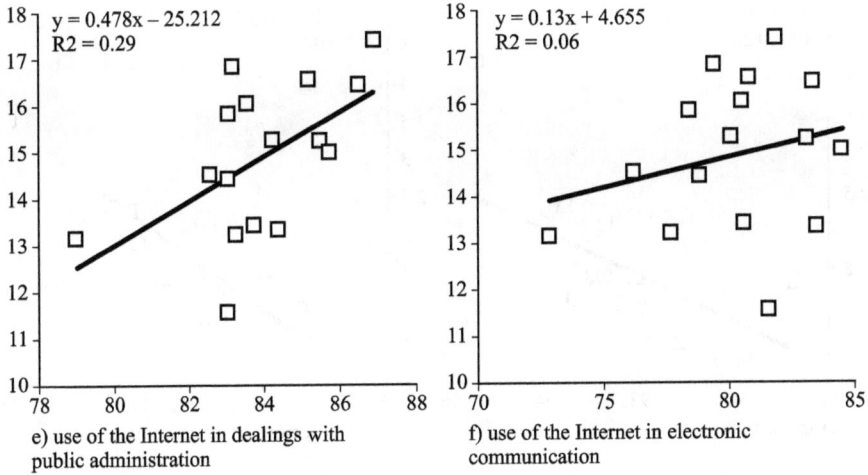

Figure 1. ICT effects on the average share of innovative enterprises
Source: Author's elaboration on the CSOP regional dataset.

Expenditure on innovative activities (in percent of regional output) seems to be independent of the frequency of using computers and electronic communications (Figure 2). Using networks is strongly correlated with expenditure on innovations, but the explanatory power is higher for the indicator of using website to produce catalogues or price lists.

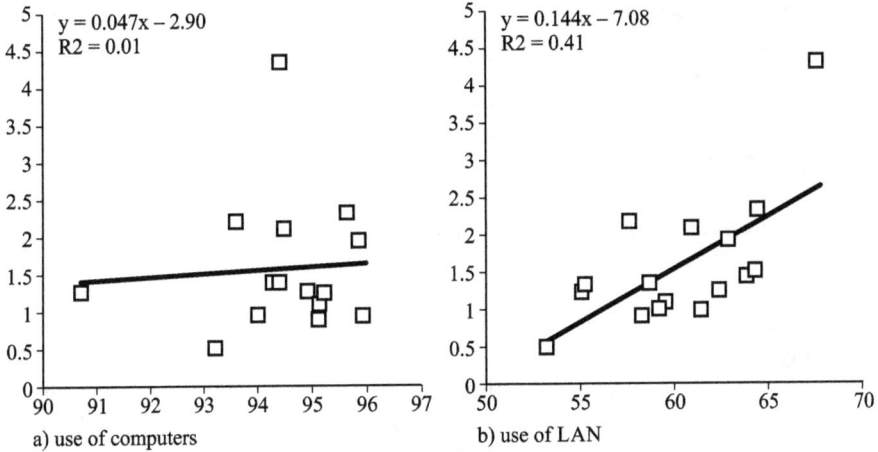

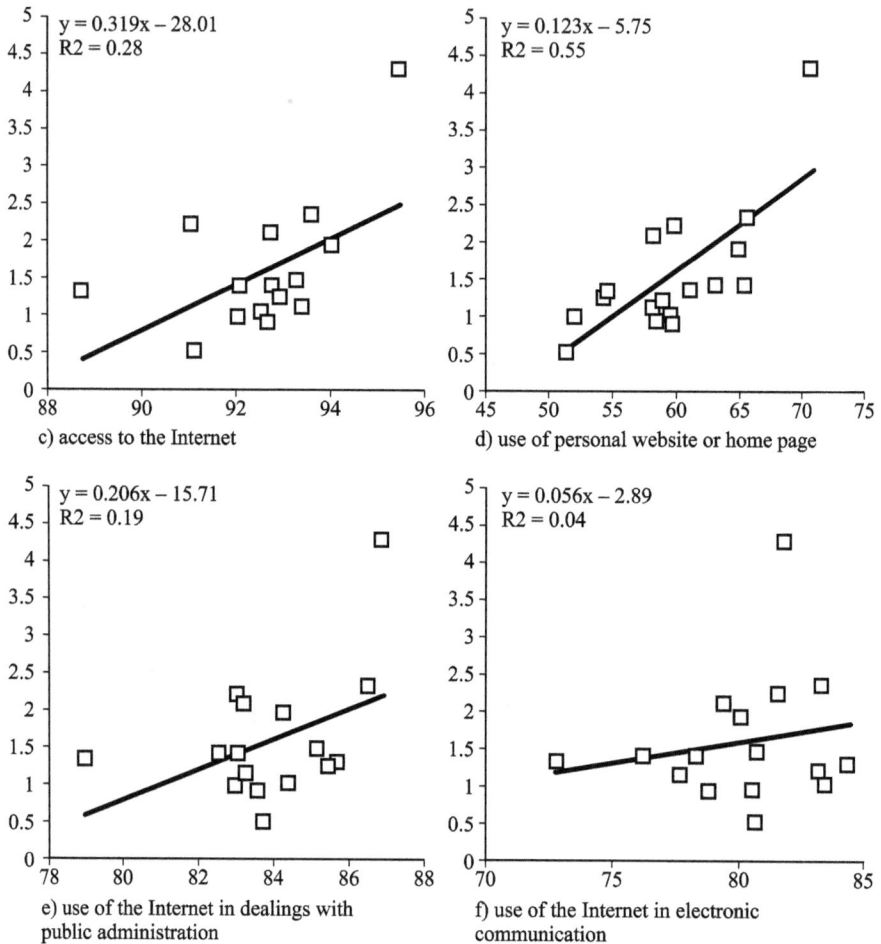

Figure 2. ICT effects of expenditure on innovation activities in enterprises in relation to output
Source: Author's elaboration on the CSOP regional dataset.

Analyzing explanatory factors behind expenditure on innovation activities per person economically active, it is clear that using networks and websites are the two most important determinants of innovation activities (Figure 3). Similar to other indicators, using computers and electronic correspondence does not play any important role in financing innovations. It means that innovation activities are stimulated by developments in the field of information technologies rather than simply investments in computer hardware.

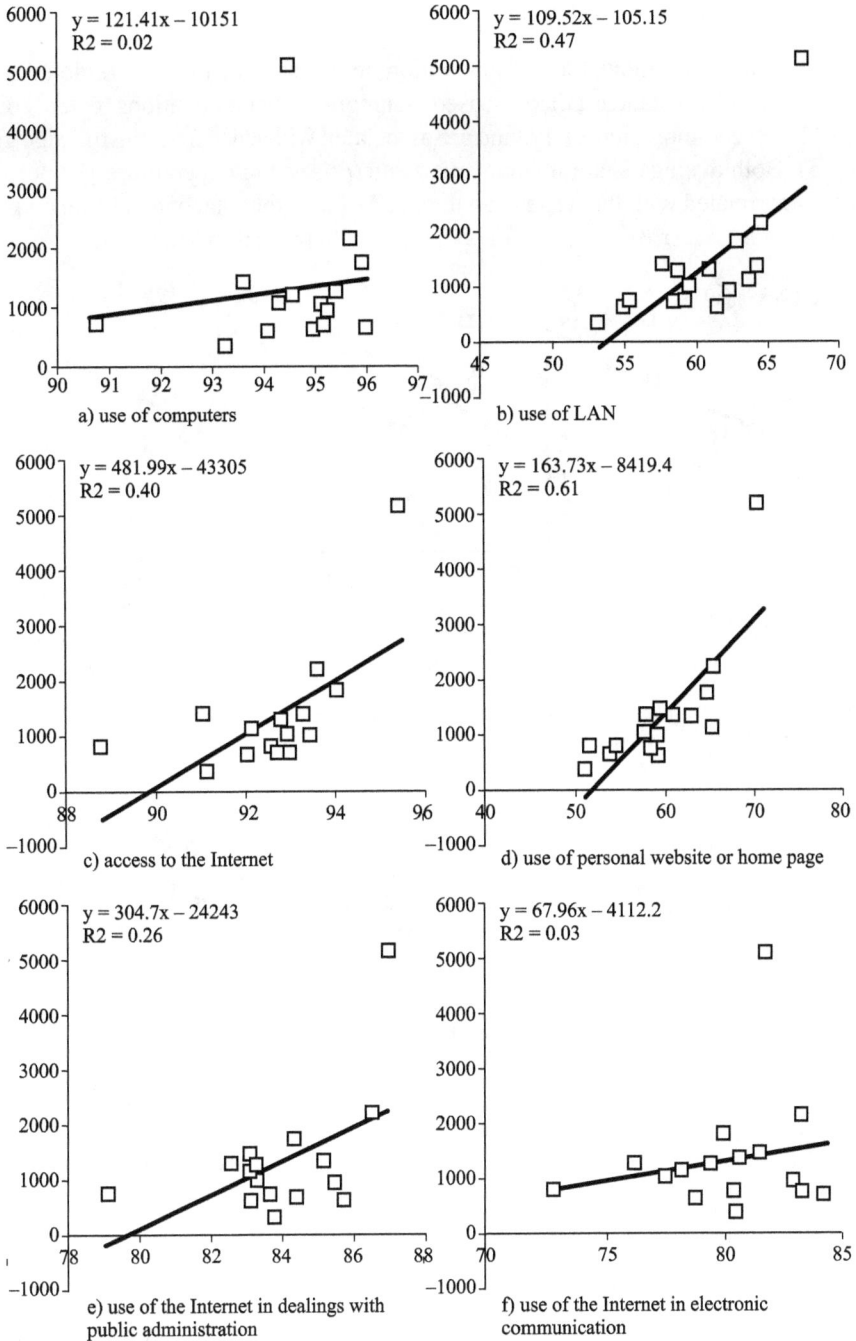

Figure 3. ICT effects of expenditure on innovation activities per person economically active
Source: Author's elaboration on the CSOP regional dataset.

5. Innovations and regional growth

As expected, all three indicators of innovation activities contribute to regional growth (Figure 4). It confirms standard theory-based assumptions that innovations foster economic growth. However, innovations in Poland are associated with a deceleration of wage growth (Figure 5). Both average share of innovative enterprises and expenditure per person are negatively correlated with the wage growth rate. As far as the total expenditure on innovative activities is concerned, it seems to be neutral with respect to wages.

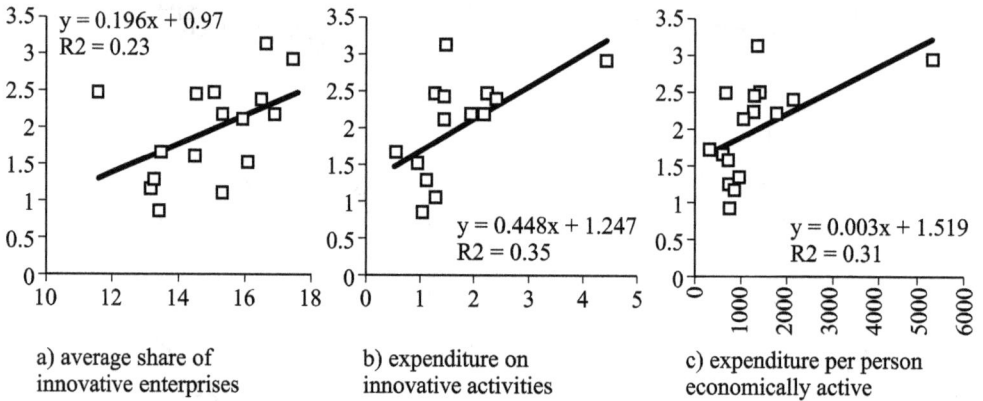

Figure 4. Innovation effects on regional output growth rate
Source: Author's elaboration on the CSOP regional dataset.

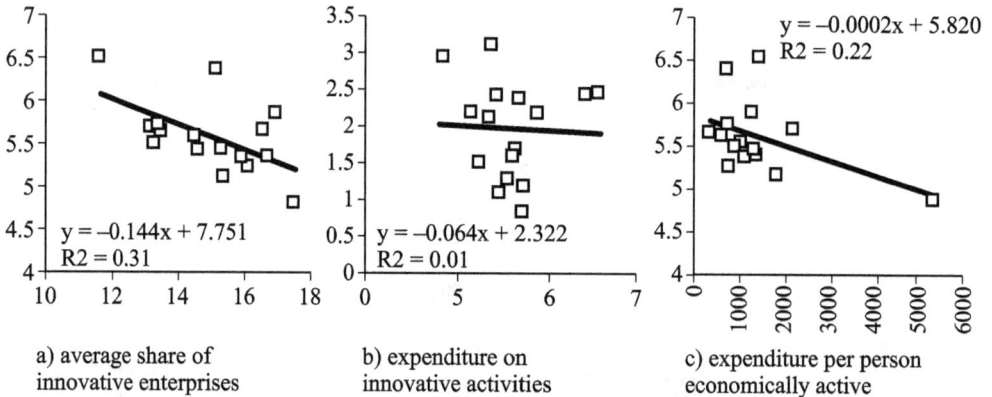

Figure 5. Innovation effects on the wage growth rate
Source: Author's elaboration on the CSOP regional dataset.

In general, our findings correspond with the results that imply possible ambiguity in the relationship between innovations and economic well-being. If ICT is an aspect of the skill-based technical change (SBTC), it leads to an increase in productivity and wages of the highly-skilled, educated workers, but at the expense of less-skilled workers. If the demand for labour is relatively weak, an increase in the supply of "excessive" labour force should exerts a downward pressure on wages. At this point it is of particular interest to consider the direct impact of ICT components on economic growth and wages across two sectors, which could potentially differ in their reaction to the SBTC effects. Assuming that non-financial enterprises employ a larger number of low-skilled workers when compared with financial firms, innovations and ICT could have different effects on financial and non-financial sectors. This aspect is considered in more detail below.

6. ICT sectoral growth and wage effects

When considering direct ICT effects on regional growth and wages, it is of particular interest to compare their impact on financial and non-financial enterprises. Figures 6 and 7 present growth and wage effects, with the results for non-financial enterprises in the left diagram and for financial firms in the right diagram. It is clear that the stimulating effect

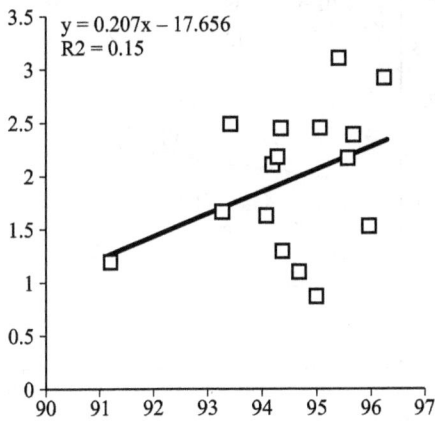

$y = 0.207x - 17.656$
$R2 = 0.15$

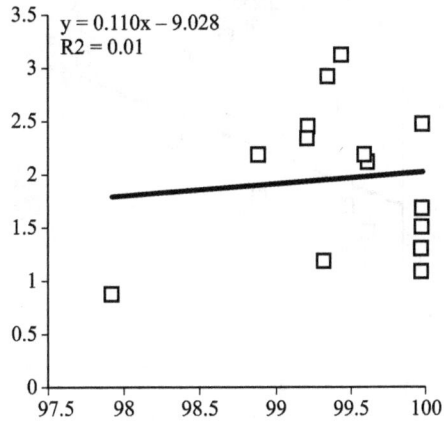

$y = 0.110x - 9.028$
$R2 = 0.01$

a) use of computers

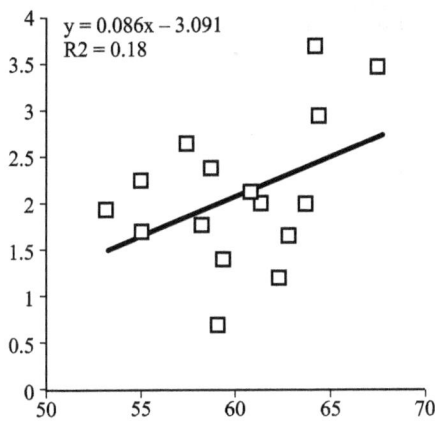

$y = 0.086x - 3.091$
$R2 = 0.18$

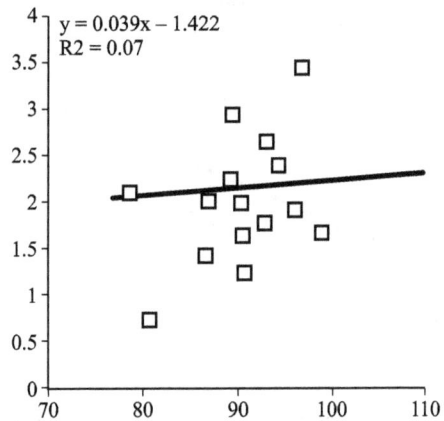

$y = 0.039x - 1.422$
$R2 = 0.07$

b) use of LAN

$y = 0.199x - 16.487$
$R2 = 0.19$

$y = 0.139x - 11.806$
$R2 = 0.10$

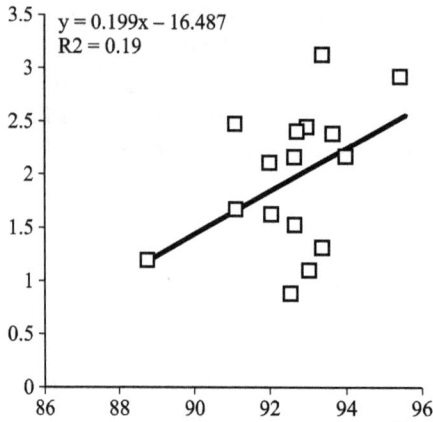

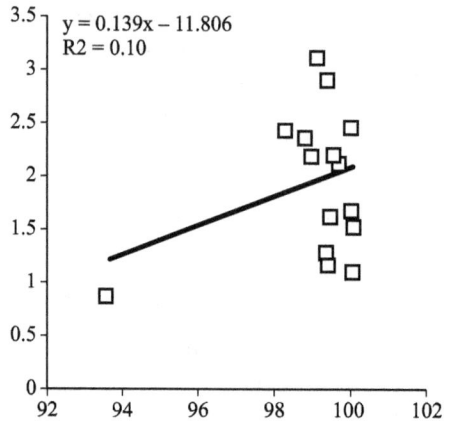

c) access to the Internet

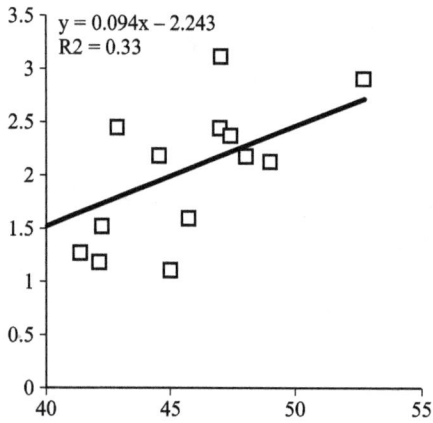

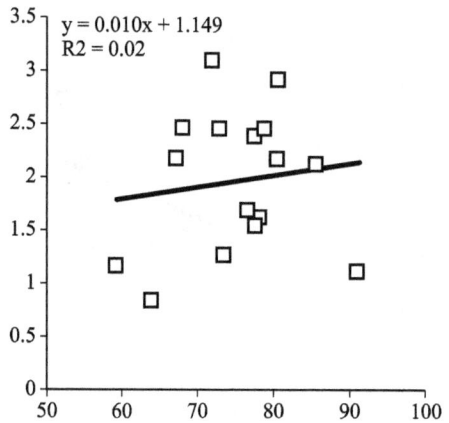

$y = 0.094x - 2.243$
$R2 = 0.33$

$y = 0.010x + 1.149$
$R2 = 0.02$

d) using a website or home page to produce catalogues or price lists

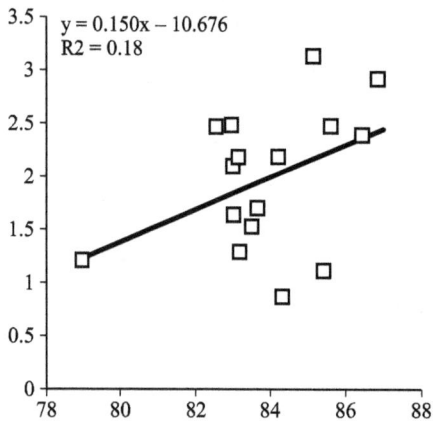

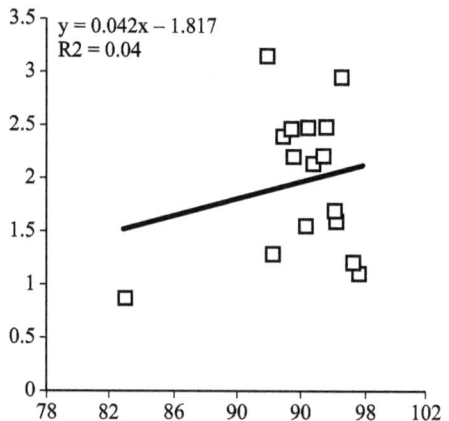

$y = 0.150x - 10.676$
$R2 = 0.18$

$y = 0.042x - 1.817$
$R2 = 0.04$

e) using the Internet in dealings with public administration

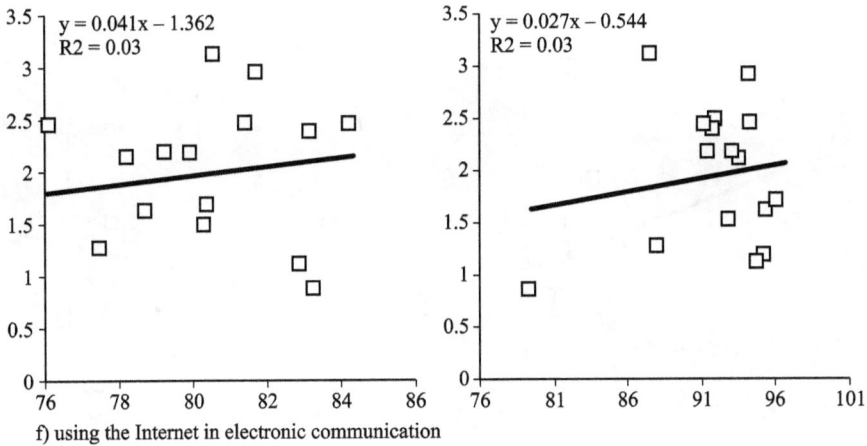

f) using the Internet in electronic communication

Figure 6. ICT sectoral effects on the regional growth

of ICT is much stronger in the non-financial sector. For the financial sector, only access to the Internet and using networks do matter to some extent. On the other hand, non-financial enterprises benefit from using computers, networks and the Internet. But the strongest positive effect is achieved in the case of using the Internet.

As mentioned by Steinmueller (2001), the emergence of the Internet technologies strengthens the potential for leapfrogging by supporting the global flow of information and the emergence of a "virtual" cyberspace domain, in which many of the constraints of time and distance have been eradicated. The Internet technologies are particularly important because they provide an unprecedented variety of new and "open" formats for the distribution of information and the establishment of inter-organizational connections.

Several differences between non-financial and financial sectors are observed with respect to the ICT effects on the wage growth (Figure 7). Using computers decreases wages in the non-financial sector, but it is just the opposite for financial enterprises. For the former, downward pressure on wages is obtained for three other indicators, namely using computer networks, access to the Internet, and using website for price and product offerings. Electronic correspondence is the only example of the ICT usage that is positively correlated with wages in the non-financial sector. As for the latter, the inverse relationship with the wage growth is obtained only for using website for price and product offerings. In all other cases, ICT seems to be neutral with respect to wages in the financial sector.

With reference to the non-financial sector, our results seem to reject the logic of SBTC adherents that new technologies have a positive effect on the demand for labour, with only minor labour supply outcomes (Machin 2004, p. 189; Machin and McNally 2007, pp. 8–9; O'Mahony et al. 2008). As for the financial sector, it is possible to argue that its employees possess necessary high skills to be able to make efficient use of modern technologies, including ICT in the first place. Also, it is not to be ruled out that workplaces in non-financial enterprises could be more easily digitalized in comparison to financial firms, where personal expertise does play a much more prominent role.

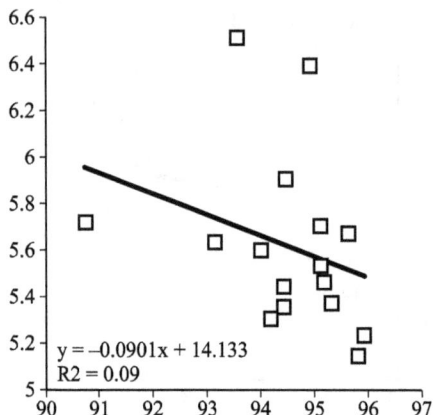

a) use of computers

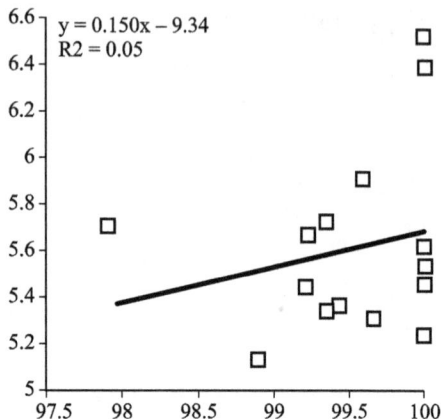

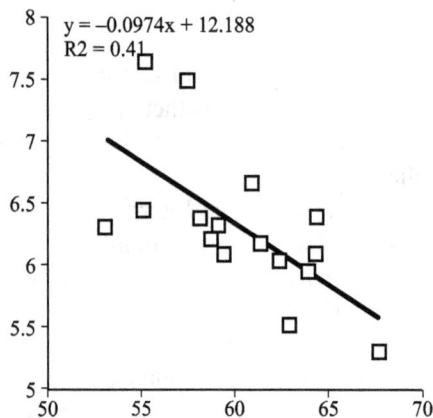

b) use of LAN

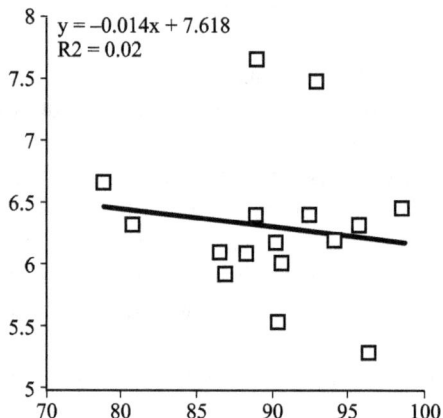

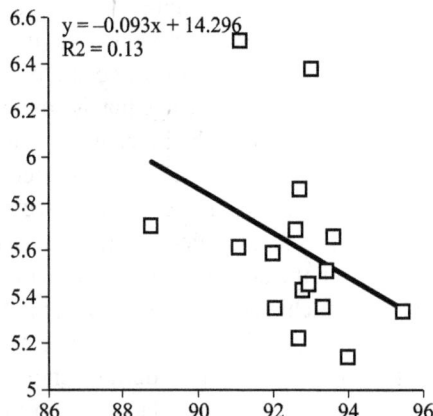

c) access to the Internet

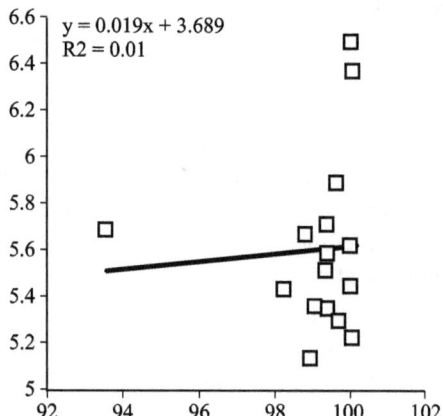

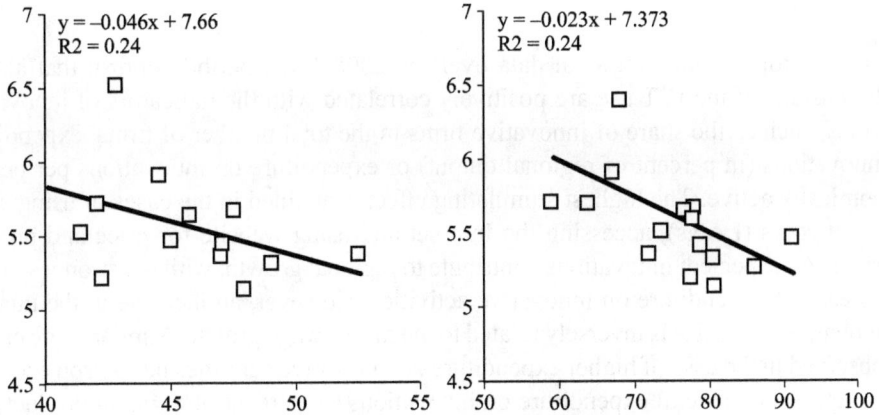

d) using a website or home page to produce catalogues or price lists

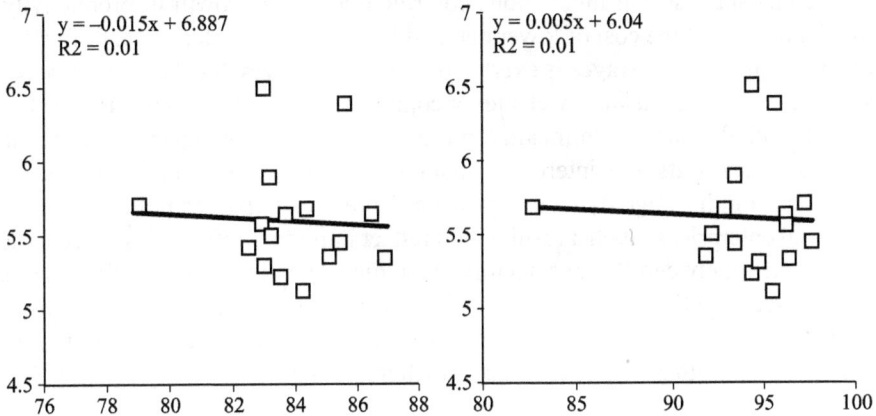

e) using the Internet in dealings with public administration

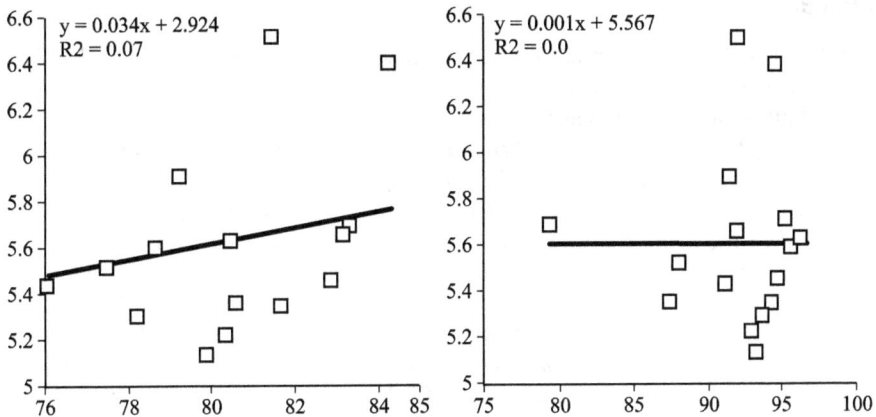

f) using the Internet in electronic communication

Figure 7. ICT sectoral effects on the wage growth rate

7. Conclusions

Our results for Poland's regional data over the 2008–2012 period confirm that almost all dimensions of the ICT use are positively correlated with the indicators of innovative activities, such as the share of innovative firms in the total number of firms, expenditure on innovations (in percent of regional output) or expenditure on innovations per person economically active. The highest stimulating effect is attained in the cases of using computer networks (LANs), accessing the Internet and using website for price and product offerings. As expected, innovations contribute to regional growth, with the strongest effect of increase of expenditure on innovative activities. However, an increase in the number of innovative enterprise is inversely related to the rate of wage growth. Similar wage effects are observed in the case of higher expenditure on innovative activities per person economically active, but general expenditure on innovations (in percent of regional product) are neutral with respect to the wage dynamics.

Our results suggest that innovations contribute to faster growth in productivity and regional output, but at the cost of lower demand for labour. Considering ICT effects, similar downward pressure on wages is exerted by using computers, local computer networks, access to the Internet and using a website for commercial activities. Only using the Internet for contacts with the public administration is associated with the higher wage growth.

Among other results, it is interesting that the use of ICT in financial firms has no significant effects on the wage dynamics, while a depressive impact is rather strong for the non-financial enterprises. Such a result could reflect important differences in technologies and employment between the two sectors. Assuming prevalence of non-financial enterprises on the regional level, there is ground for concern that a wider and more intensive use of ICT that could reflect a more general SBTC trend may lead to a combination of higher regional output growth and slower wage growth in Poland.

References

Adekola, A., Korsakienė, R., Tvaronavičienė, M. (2008), *Approach to innovative activities by Lithuanian companies in the current conditions of technological and economic development of economy*, "Baltic Journal on Sustainability", vol. 14, no. 4, pp. 595–611.

Akçomak, I., ter Weel, B. (2009), *Social capital, innovation and growth: Evidence from Europe*, "European Economic Review", vol. 53, issue 5, pp. 544–567.

Antonelli, C., Kraff, J., Quatraro, F. (2010), *Recombinant Knowledge and Growth: The Case of ICTs, Structural Change and Economic Dynamics*, Elsevier, vol. 21, issue 1, pp. 50–69.

Archibugi, D., Filipetti, A. (2011), *Is the Economic Crisis Impairing Convergence in Innovation Performance across Europe?*, "Journal of Common Market Studies", vol. 49, no. 6, pp. 1153–1182.

Basu, S., Fernald, J. G., Oulton, N., Srinivasan, S. (2003), *The Case of the Missing Productivity Growth, or Does Information Technology Explain Why Productivity Accelerated in the United States but Not in the United Kingdom?*, "NBER Macroeconomics Annual 2003", vol. 18, M. Gertler, K. Rogoff (eds.), Cambridge, Mass.: The MIT Press, pp. 9–80.

Bottazzi, L., Peri, G. (2004), *The Dynamics of R&D and Innovation in the Short Run and in the Long Run*, "CEPR Discussion Papers" No. 4479, London: Centre for Economic Policy Research.

Colecchia, A., Schreyer, P. (2001), *ICT Investment and Economic Growth in the 1990s: Is the United States a Unique Case? A Comparative Study of Nine OECD Countries*, OECD "Science, Technology and Industry Working Papers", 2001/07, Paris: OECD Publishing.

Cornett, A. P. (2006), *Aims and strategies in regional innovation and growth policy – A Danish perspective*, Paper prepared for the *International Workshop on Creativity and Smart Policy as Signposts for Innovative Development* (29–30 May, 2006, Amsterdam, Netherlands), Amsterdam: Tinbergen Institute.

Cortés, E. A., Navarro, J.-L. (2010), *Do ICT Influence Economic Growth and Human Development in European Union Countries?*, "International Advanced Economic Research". vol. 17, no.1, pp. 28–44.

Erumban, A. A., de Jong, S. (2005), *Cross-country differences in ICT adoption. A consequence of Culture?*, "Journal of World Business", vol. 41, no. 4, pp. 302–314.

Fagerberg, J., Srholec, M., Verspagen, B. (2009), *Innovation and Economic Development,* [in:] *Handbook of the Economics of Innovation*, B. Hall, N. Rosenberg (eds.), vol. 2, Amsterdam: North Holland, pp. 833–872.

Frieden, R. (2005), *Lessons from broadband development in Canada, Japan, Korea and the United States*, "Telecommunications Policy", vol. 29, no. 8, pp. 595–613.

Goedhuys, M., Veugelers, R. (2008), *Innovation strategies, process and product innovations and growth: Firm-level evidence from Brazil*, "Structural Change and Economic Dynamics", vol. 23, issue 4, pp. 516–529.

Gordon, I., McCann, P. (2005), *Innovation, agglomeration, and regional development*, "Journal of Economic Geography", vol. 5, issue 5, pp. 523–543.

Hempell, T. (2003), *Do Computers Call for Training? Firm-level Evidence on Complementarities between ICT and Human Capital Investments*, "ZEW Discussion Paper" No. 03–20, Mannheim: Centre for European Economic Research (Zentrum für Europäische Wirtschaftsforschung GmbH).

Hempell, T., van Leeuwen, G., van der Wiel, H. (2004), *ICT, Innovation and Business Performance in Services: Evidence for Germany and the Netherlands*, "ZEW Discussion Paper" No. 04–06, Mannheim: Centre for European Economic Research (Zentrum für Europäische Wirtschaftsforschung GmbH).

Holt, L., Jamison, M. (2009), *Broadband and contributions to economic growth: Lessons from the US experience*, "Telecommunications Policy", vol. 33, issues 10–11, pp. 575–581.

Kirby, S., Riley, R. (2008), *The external returns to education: UK evidence using repeated cross-sections*, "Labour Economics", vol. 15, issue 4, pp. 619–630.

LeBel, P. (2008), *The role of creative innovation in economic growth: Some international comparisons*, "Journal of Asian Economics", vol. 19, issue 4, pp. 334–347.

Machin, S. (2004), *Skill-biased technical change and educational outcomes*, [in:] *International Handbook on the Economics of Education*, G. Johnes and J. Johnes (eds.), Cheltenham, UK: Edgar Elgar, pp. 189–210.

Machin, S., McNally, S. (2007), *Tertiary Education Systems and Labour Markets*, "Tertiary Review", Paris: OECD.

Mukoyama, T. (2005), *Rosenberg's "learning by using" and technology diffusion*, "Cahier 21–2005", Montréal: Université de Montréal.

Nickolas, T. (2014), *Technology, Innovation and Economic Growth in Britain Since 1870,* "The Cambridge Economic History of Modern Britain", chapter 7, vol. 2. [in:] R. Floud, J. Humphries, P. Johnson (eds.), Cambridge: Cambridge University Press, pp. 181–204.

O'Mahony, M., Robinson, C., Vecchi, M. (2008), *The impact of ICT on the demand for skilled labour: A cross-country comparison*, "Labour Economics", vol. 15, no. 6, pp. 1435–1450.

Orszag, P. (2011), *Winds of Change Blow Away College Degree*, http://www.bloomberg.com/news/2011–11–09/winds-of-economic-change-blow-away-college-degree-peter-orszag.html.

Oulton, N. (2010), *Long Term Implications of the ICT Revolution: Applying the Lessons of Growth Theory and Growth Accounting*, "CEP Discussion Paper" No 1027, London: London School of Economics and Political Science.

Piatkowski, M. (2002), *The new economy and economic growth in transition economies: The relevance of institutional infrastructure*, "WIDER Discussion Papers" No. 2002/62, Helsinki: World Institute for Development Economics (UNU-WIDER).

Piatkowski, M., van Art, B. (2005), *ICT and Productivity Growth in Transition Economies: Two-Phase Convergence and Structural Reforms*, "TIGER Working Paper Series" No. 72, Warszawa: Centrum Badawcze Transformacji, Integracji i Globalizacji.

Pohjola, M. (2002), *New Economy in Growth and Development*, "Discussion Paper" No. 2002/67, Helsinki: World Institute for Development Economics (UNU-WIDER).

Quah, A. (2002), *Technology Dissemination and Economic Growth: Some Lessons for the New Economy*, "CEP Discussion Paper" DP0522, London:. Centre for Economic Performance, London School of Economics and Political Science.

Quatraro, F. (2009), *Innovation, structural change and productivity growth. Evidence from Italian regions, 1980–2003*, "Cambridge Journal of Economics", vol. 33, issue 5, pp. 1001–1022.

Reinert, E. (2006), *European Integration, Innovations and Uneven Economic Growth: Challenges and Problems of EU 2005*, [in:] *The Future of the Information Society in Europe: Contributions to the Debate*, Technical European Commission Report, R. Compano, C. Pascu, A. F. Bianchi, J. C. Burgelman (eds.), Brussels: European Commission; Seville: Institute for Prospective Technological Studies, pp. 111–134.

Rodriguez-Pose, A., Crescenzi R. (2008), *R&D, spillovers, innovation systems and the genesis of regional growth in Europe*, "Regional Studies", vol. 42, no. 1, pp. 51–67.

Smits, R. (2002), *Innovation studies in the 21st century: Questions from a user's perspective*, "Technological Forecasting & Social Change", vol. 69, no. 9, pp. 861–883.

Steinmueller, E. (2001), *ICTs and the possibilities for leapfrogging by developing countries*, "International Labour Review", vol. 140, no. 2, pp. 193–210.

The Economist (2011), The latest bubble?, 13 April.

Van Ark, B. (2002), *Measuring the New Economy: An International Comparative Perspective*, "Review of Income and Wealth", Series 48, no. 1, pp. 1–14.

Van Ark, B., O'Mahoney, M., Timmer, M. (2008), *The Productivity Gap Between Europe and the United States: Trends and Causes*, "Journal of Economic Perspectives", vol. 22, no. 1, pp. 25–44.

Van Reenen, J., Bloom, N., Draca, M., Kretschmer, T., Sadun, R., Overman, H., Schankerman, M. (2010), *The Economic Impact of ICT*, SMART N. 2007/0020, London: London School of Economics.

Vu, Khuong M. (2011), *ICT as a source of economic growth in the information age: Empirical evidence from the 1996–2005 period*, "Telecommunications Policy", vol. 35, issue 4, pp. 357–372.

Wu, Y. (2010), *Innovation and Economic Growth in China*, "Discussion Paper" No. 10.10, Perth: The University of Western Australia.

Małgorzata Runiewicz-Wardyn

Innovations and Emerging Technologies as Drivers of Economic Growth in the EU

1. Introduction

Innovations and technological advancements, especially in the field of high-tech, matter more and more in defining both the economic development and growth rate of a given region's GDP. High rates of innovation, especially in the high-tech sectors, are associated with high rates of productivity growth, which leads to higher growth in real wages and improvements of the standard of living. Although the direct economic weight of high-tech industries is relatively small, its impact can be significant for regional economic growth. High-tech industries have a large indirect economic impact on promoting regional growth by inducing innovations on other non-high-tech industries and sectors in the region. ICTs and their application are the prime support needed for the rapid growth and modernization of various sectors of the economy, as well as for creating entirely new industries, e.g. e-commerce. Moreover, there is evidence of significant potential for catching up and convergence in ICT-using manufacturing industries and services, particularly in the less developed EU regions.

However, analysis of trends in the high-tech industries reveals that they are not immune from problems which occur in the economy. Cyclical behaviour of high-tech industries may have an important impact on the regional GDP dynamics. The following study aims to analyze the linkages between the technological change and development of the high-tech industries and the economic growth and the catching-up process of the EU regions.

The exact impact of technological change and knowledge spillovers on regional growth is very difficult to measure, just as it is difficult to measure the process of innovation creation and diffusion with a simple linear model. The empirical evidence of the role of innovations, technological change, and economic growth suggests there are also many feedback loops and feedbacks of activity across the processes of innovation, technological change, and regional growth.

2. Patent activity and high-tech industries' life cycles

One of the generally adopted approaches towards studying the technological maturity of industries is tracking the intensity of patent applications. Several researchers, including Haupt et al. 2007; Watts and Porter, 1997; Andersen, 1999, have tried this approach. Patents embody information about technological development itself since they contain the technological know-how. Registered patents inform us about research intensity and innovativeness, and therefore the technological state of the art in the relevant field. The number of patent applications can vary at different stages of the technology life cycle. At the *emerging* and *growth* stages, the indicator of the number of patent applications is typically higher than that of all other indicators. When basic technological and market uncertainties have vanished, innovations become less radical, R&D risk decreases and the number of patent applications may increase. In the following phase of *maturity,* the number of patent applications (typically incremental innovations) remains constant. After that, when the potential for new product innovations decreases on the basis of technology, and consequently the number of annual patent applications decreases constantly, the technology's *decline* stage begins.

However, patents can only affect industry dynamics if the market adopts them. In other words, when the new technology is widely diffused and used. Within this context, adoption refers to the stage at which individuals or organizations select the technology for use. Diffusion refers to the stage at which the technology spreads to general use and application.

Based on the studies of Wunderlich and Khalil (2002) on technology diffusion and maturity analysis as applied to different industrial sectors, and biotechnology based on Utterback and Abernathy (1975) and Fisher and Pry (1971), the following section discusses the maturity of technology and its relationship to technology diffusion. The measure of technology diffusion may be expressed as a percentage and can be characterized over time by applying the Fisher-Pry equation. Two characteristics of the Fisher-Pry equation are that by measuring technology maturity through technology diffusion $- L / (1 + e^{**}(-b(t-a)))$ it firstly reveals the midpoint in time (identified as "a") at which the market achieves 50% adoption, and secondly, provides a relative quantification of the rate (known as "b") at which the technology was adopted. Based on data of the US National Academy of Engineering (NAE), data on the timeline summarizes the 20 most notable technological engineering achievements, and Wunderlich and Khalil (2002) have grouped them into industrial sectors accordingly. The technology performance parameter extracted from these timelines is the technology diffusion parameter. The timelines of these technologies enable at least a rough estimate to be made for the start of the rapid growth of each technology. The scores ranged from a 0 to 100%, based on the Fisher-Pry equation for technology diffusion. Since the GEA data is for the 20th century, an initial score was established for the year 1900 (Wunderlich and Khalil, 2002). A score of zero would indicate that the technology had not yet been conceived. For example, the start of technology for laser and fibre optics moved from a base level of zero to a score of 1.0 when Einstein established the theory of stimulated emission in 1917. More significantly, a score of 15 was assigned as the milestone indicating that rapid market growth was about to occur. It is assumed that at this point anyone who wanted to obtain the technology could get it. A classic example of a 15% score would be the rise in automobile technology in 1908, when mass production of the Model T Ford began. Then, the area between 1 and 15 was feathered, based on the early developmental milestones listed, such as the origination of mass production techniques by Ransom E. Olds in 1901. The significance of the 15-point milestone for technology diffusion is that it indicates that rapid market growth has been initiated and will carry on until it reaches another significant point of 85%, which indicates the end of rapid market growth. At this point of time, the technology is judged to have achieved widespread diffusion in a way that nearly everyone who had wanted to obtain it had done so (according to Wunderlich and Khalil, 2002). A score of 100 would indicate that a specific technology had reached complete diffusion or maturity.

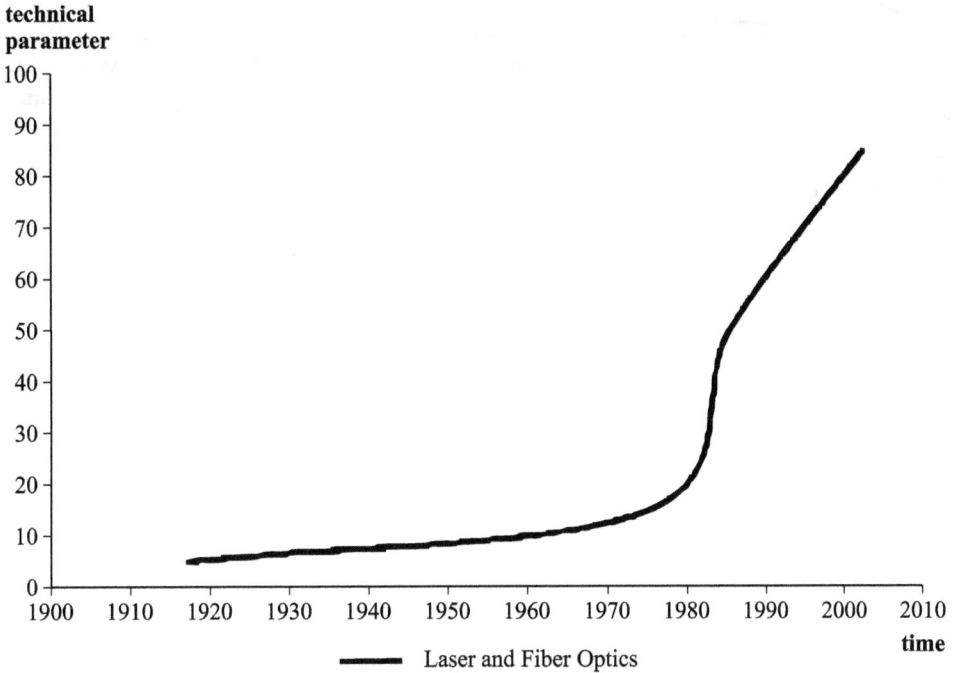

Laser and Fiber Optics

technical parameter

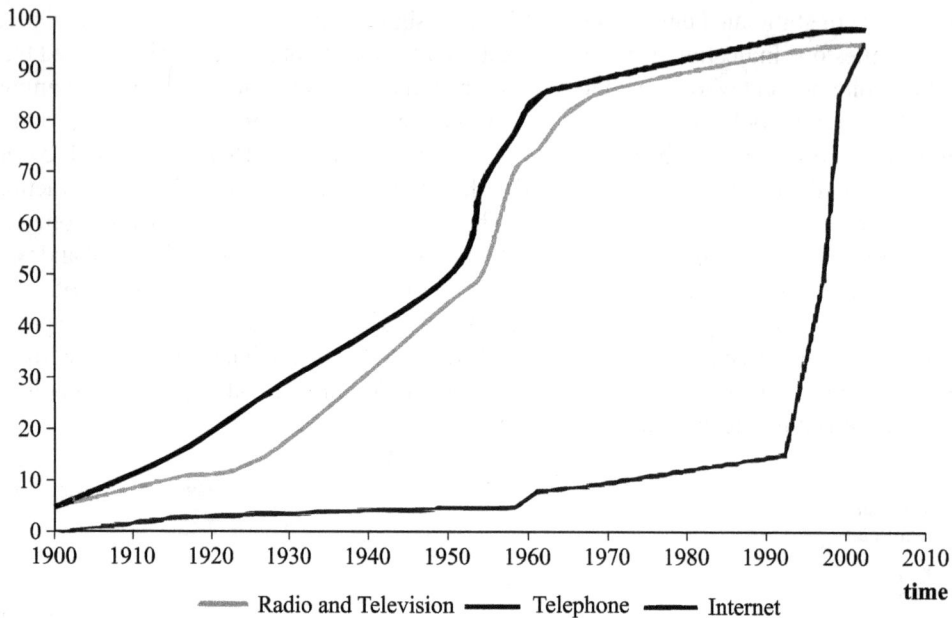

Radio and Television — Telephone — Internet

time

technical parameter

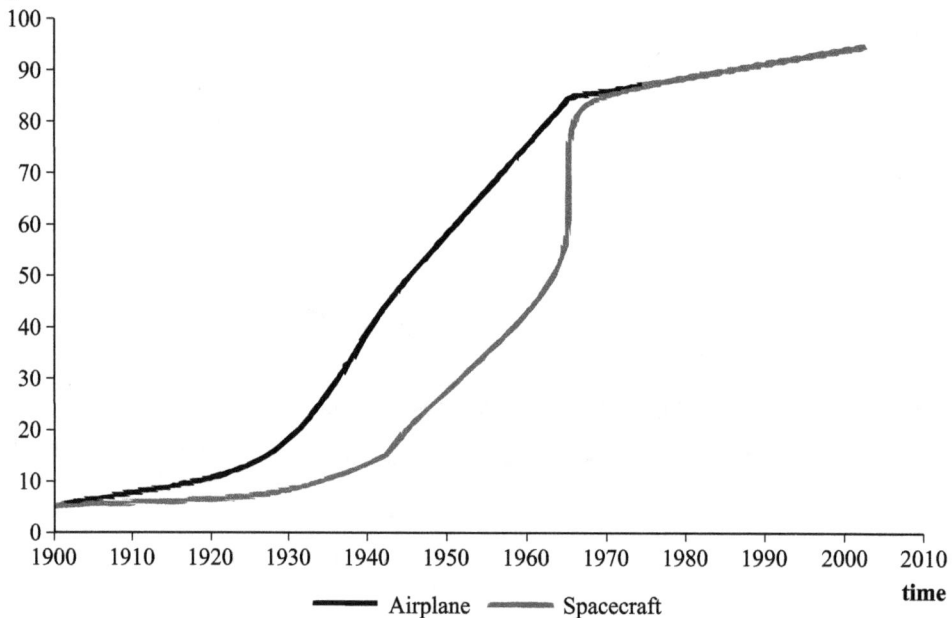

Airplane — Spacecraft

time

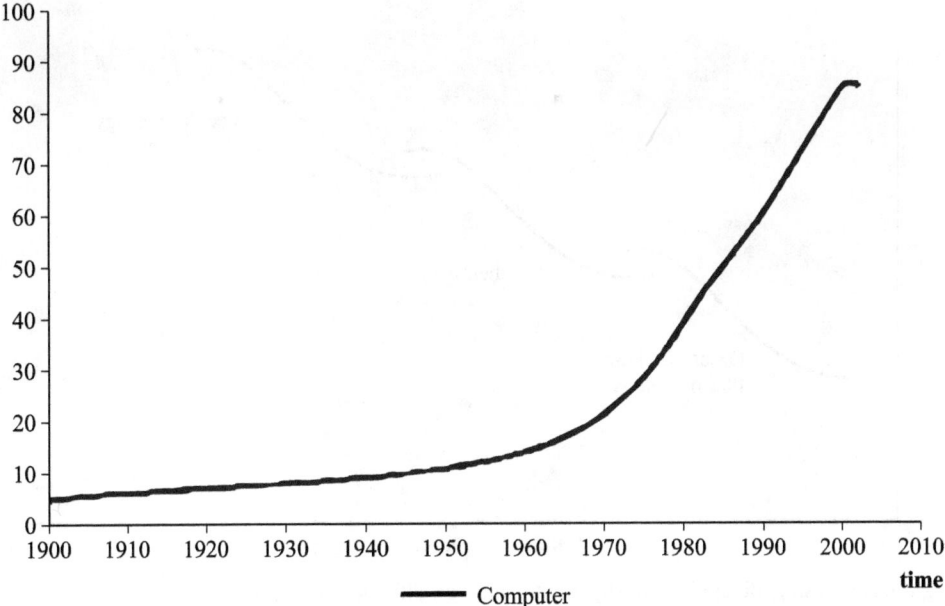

Computer

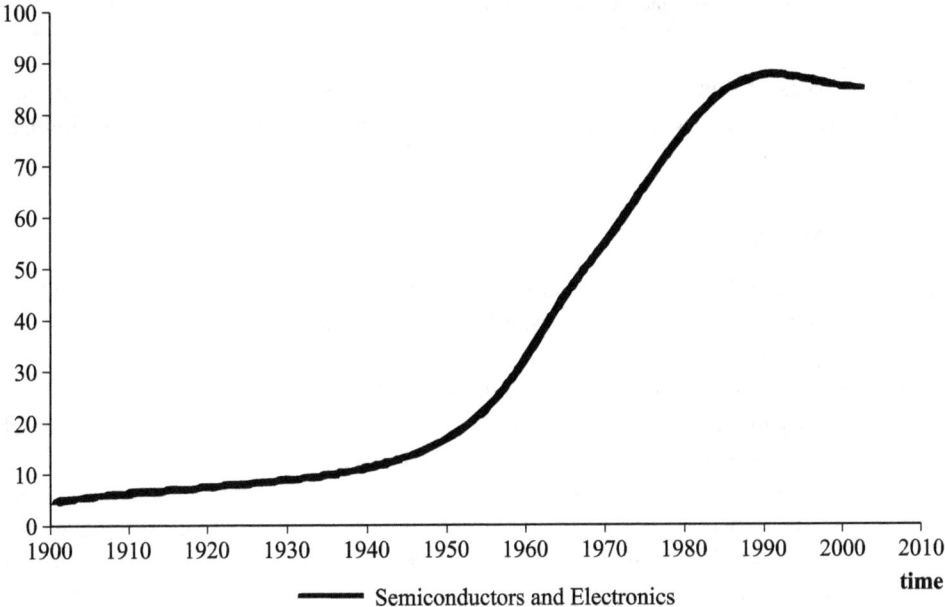

Semiconductors and Electronics

**technical
parameter**

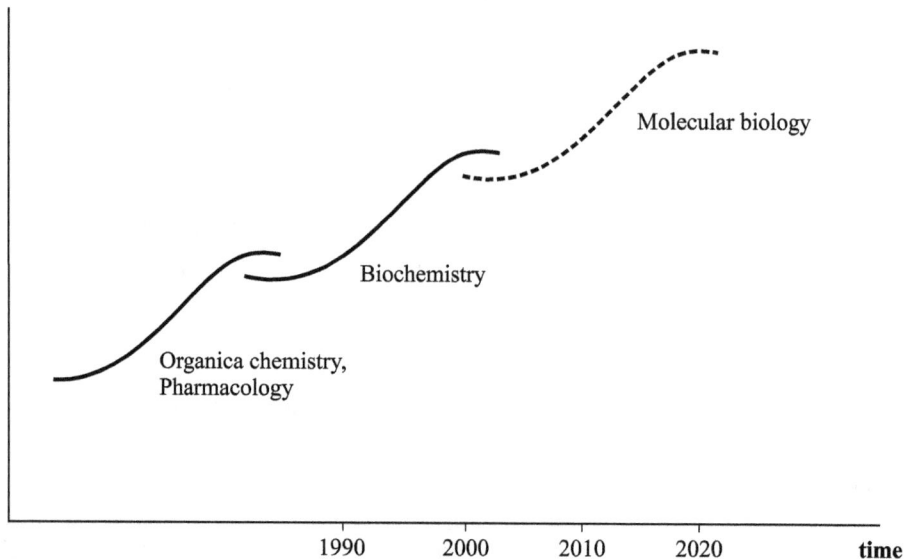

Figure 1. Industry life cycle maturity and technology diffusion in high-tech industries
Source: Own elaboration based on Wunderlich and Khalil 2002; biotechnology based on Utterback and Abernathy (1975) and Fisher and Pry (1971).
Note: Technology Life Cycle Maturity Level Score: Solid concept/idea conceived 1; rapid growth enabled 15;
peak growth: 50% diffusion 50; rapid growth slows, market-saturating 85; market saturated, technology
mature 100.

On the basis of this more selective rather than exhaustive survey, the following section discusses technological maturity of each high-tech industry as a proxy for industry
dynamics.

Aerospace industry

The results of Wunderlich and Khalil (2002) and Utterback and Abernathy (1975) (for
biotechnology industry findings) for each high-tech industry are illustrated in the Figure
above.

As shown in Figure 1, the *Aerospace industry* (both the aeroplane and spacecraft industries) is currently in the growth stage of its life cycle. In general, the industry has extremely
long product life cycles and development periods. The aerospace industry is characterized
by its renowned heavy upfront investments and exceptionally long programme lives. It normally tends to be very regulated and also requires huge stocks of existing knowledge (even
though a slow deregulation of the industry in recent decades has lowered entry barriers
into its market). As a result, the process of technological substitution and adoption of new
products and processes is very long indeed. In technical terms, the technology diffusion
for the aircraft manufacturing industry has achieved a high rate of maturity, because now

anyone who can afford the products in that market is able to obtain them without difficulty. However, because of a big lack of expertise of suppliers and users of specific technological processes, the diffusion process may be an "incomplete success or at times a failure on the part of the user to completely absorb the technologies provided by the suppliers" (Asif Rasheed, Irfan A Manarvi, 2008). Some smaller firms may be disadvantaged due to inadequate human resources, and weak organizational and R&D capacities. As a result, the dynamics of the aeroplane industry may be slow; however, it is far from its maturity stage. Because of the high investments into R&D and high cost-related activities, it seems the industry is fairly concentrated. In summary, the aerospace industry still offers the most attractive competitive opportunities with its products and services (Porter 2008) and proves that it is still in the growth phase of its life cycle. Thus, diversity and heterogeneity play a key role and may also have a significant impact on the industry's competitive advantages and further dynamics.

Furthermore, industry dynamics converge with the expansion of other industries. IT investments are becoming increasingly important. In the airline industry computers and IT in general have both become a necessity for many parts of operations and marketing (Subramanian et al., 1994; Anbil et al, 1991). Additionally, the industry has been facing a gradual deregulation of competition[1]. The recently noted consolidation in the form of mergers between companies or takeovers of failing carriers may be a part of the birth-and-death process expected to be in existence in a competitive marketplace such as the airline industry (Swan 2005).

Aeronautics is one of the EU's key high-tech sectors on the global market (Aeronautics Industries: Industry Profile 2015). In 2013, aeronautics industry provided more than 500,000 jobs and generated a turnover of EUR 140 billion. Its advantage stems from the production of civil aircraft, including helicopters, aircraft engines, parts and components.

The industry is highly concentrated, both geographically and in terms of the number of enterprises involved. The industry absorbs a sizeable share of R&D investments, which is reflected in an increasing number of patent applications. Because of the high investments into R&D and high cost-related activities, it seems the industry is fairly concentrated. The employment in the aerospace sector is particularly significant in the United Kingdom, France, Germany, Italy, Spain, Poland and Sweden.

Computer industry

The development of the *Computer industry* illustrates the traditional industry life cycle by first experiencing product innovation, then processes and services innovations, according to Cusumano, Kahl, and Suarez (2006). In the old days, when mainframe computers dominated the industry, researchers and engineers paid more attention to product or system design issues than to the process of constructing a particular piece of software or an oper-

---

[1] In a 1981 study, David Mowery and Nathan Rosenberg have argued that rapid diffusion of technological innovations in the US commercial aircraft industry to US airlines during the mid-twentieth century was due partly to actions of regulatory agencies, http://elsa.berkeley.edu/~bhhall/papers/HallKhan03%20diffusion.pdf.

ating system. Based on the Fisher-Pry score, Figure 1 shows that in the mid-1980s computer technology was at its highest growth rate (with the PC industry as its driving force). It retained its high growth rate for over two decades, mainly due to upgrades in hardware, services, and add-on products and features. By the end of 2000, the market had become very competitive and as Figure 1 suggests, the industry had entered its early period of the maturity stage. This trend could be supported by observing the present market, with many manufacturers producing a range of models, from desktop computers to notebooks, and continuing the product differentiation process which began in the growth stage.

Despite these slowing dynamics of the computer industry in highly advanced market economies such as the US and Europe, the diffusion of computing technology and its adoption around EU countries was proven to be significantly varied, depending on the region concerned. Overall, nearly seven out of ten EU households have an Internet connection (68%), roughly the proportion with access to a personal computer (72%) (Eurobarometer 2014). The results obtained in 2014 reveal a significant difference in household computer ownership between the European Union's old and new Member States: EU-15 (69%) compared to EU-12 (60%) (Eurobarometer 2014). The reasons for the slower computer adoption in the EU-12 could be associated with income levels, qualifications of human capital, investment rates, property rights protection, and a big share of agriculture in their GDP.

In sum, the computer industry shows slowing dynamics or greater stability over the past decade, but because of the diffusion of computing technology and its adoption in advanced countries, the effects of local industrial structure on industry growth may differ from country to country.

Communication industry

The *Communication industry* is one of the prime support services needed for the rapid growth and modernization of various sectors of the global economy. It has become especially important in recent years due to the enormous growth of information technology (IT) and its potential. In fact, the biggest drivers of the communication industry are the availability of broadband infrastructure and a speedy rollout of new services, which may, however, be slowed down by regulations over privacy and security issues that have been introduced. Meanwhile, ownership of a telecom licence can represent a huge barrier to entry into the communication market. In addition, solid operating skills and management experience is fairly scarce, making entry into the industry even more difficult.

Broadly, the communication industry sector is composed of three main sub-industries: radio and television, telephone, and Internet industries. Based on the finding of Fisher-Pry, technology diffusion in the telephone, radio, and television sectors is moving closer to maturity, scoring 98, 95, and 95 respectively. The results of this Fisher-Pry-based analysis of the telecommunication industry are not in coherence with general observations that have been carried out regarding the EU telecom market, and Internet technology diffusion in particular. In terms of EU experience, the development of telecommunication technology has been rapid in recent years, with IT and related services playing important roles. The telecom sector has experienced a major process of transformation in terms of growth, technological content, and market structure in the past decade through friendly policy reforms. Roughly, the EU completed the liberalization of the European telecommunications market in 1998[2]. As reported by Eurobarometer (2014) study the penetration of telephone access in EU-27[3] was over 91% by mobile phone, fixed phone, or both. Individual mobile telephone access rates are highest in Luxembourg (98%), Latvia (98%), the Czech Republic (97%), Denmark (97%) and Finland (97%), and lowest in Poland (88%), France (88%), Bulgaria (86%) and Portugal (85%) (Eurobarometer 2014).

Even if the communication industry could have been considered as an industry reaching its phase of maturity, Internet technology and the diversification of products and services of its application will continue creating new market opportunities for the telecommunication industry[4]. New Internet applications emerge and prosper in diverse fields, such as electronics, medicine, biotechnology[5], aerospace, etc., which suggests that a diversified local industrial structure could generate the biggest technological externalities for this industry.

Semiconductor industry

The *Semiconductor industry*[6] has been reporting constant growth since it came into being in the late 80s and through the 90s. Since its beginning, the semiconductor industry has continually introduced innovative products. According to Gruber, the adoption of new technologies is extremely rapid (1994). Declines in the price/performance ratio of semiconductor components have propelled their adoption in an ever-expanding array of applications (in electronics industries, telecommunications, automobiles, military systems, consumer electronics, personal communications, and home appliances (Macher *et al.*, 1999). However, Gruber (1994) points out that even though semiconductor manufacturers receive a great deal of publicity, they make their money mainly from semiconductors in their growth and maturity stages. The past decade has observed the maturing process of the semiconductor and electronics industries (based on a Fisher-Pry score for technol-

---

[2] The agreement on the timetable for full liberalization included transitional periods for certain Member States. As a result of a case-by-case assessment by the Commission, the following periods have been confirmed: Luxembourg fully liberalized its market from July 1998; Spain from December 1998, Ireland and Portugal from January 2000, and Greece from January 2001. For Member States joining the EU in 2004 and 2007, the liberalization process was completed at a later date.

[3] Including the two latest Member States, Bulgaria and Romania.

[4] The Internet has already had a strong effect on the financial services, telecoms media, and government (eGovernment services, etc.), and has an even greater impact on the coordination and integration of all manufacturing operations across different geographies, e.g. through Internet-enabled supply chains, eCommerce and eBusiness applications (Jean-Luc Gaffard and Jackie Krafft 2000).

[5] Bioinformatics is a branch of biotechnology that uses information technologies to work with biological data like DNA. http://www.careercornerstone.org/industries/sciresearch.htm.

[6] Semiconductors are classified into major product groups mainly according to their function. The largest product group is memory chips, which accounts for about one third of the total semiconductor market. The second-largest semiconductor product group are micro components, mainly microprocessors and micro-controllers. The remaining part of the semiconductor market is made up of logic devices (including application-specific integrated circuits or ASICs), analogue devices, and other parts (Gruber 1994).

ogy diffusion). The decline of the semiconductor industry is explained, firstly, by the fact that there are no immediate substitutes for semiconductor chips – therefore, current substitution is extremely low. Secondly, by the competitive nature of the marketplace and the need to acquire production experience and move down the learning curve (Gruber 1994). In fact, innovations in the semiconductor industry depend highly on the stock of existing knowledge of productive units and the process of "learning-by-doing spillovers". Learning-by-doing spillovers may also generate a string of incremental innovations and may perhaps allow firms to enter the desired markets (Bailey and Huang 2010; Malerba and Orsenigo 1994). Furthermore, as many authors emphasize, semiconductor firms focus on the improvement of quality and thus vertical product differentiation (Malerba 1985; 1992; Georghiu *et al.* 1986). The latter requires specialized human capital (scientists, engineers, developers, etc.), which is not easy to duplicate. All this suggests that the biggest technological externalites will result from the specialized local industrial structure, possibly clustered around universities and corporate R&D centres.

Biotechnology industry

Based on the theory of the innovation life cycle, the process of technological change in the *Biotechnology industry* represents technological evolutions in the biopharmaceutical industry as a whole. Biotechnology is a relatively young branch of bioscience, developed by the biopharmaceutical industry in the late 2000s. The innovation process shows that there is not just one S-curve but a succession of S-curves from organic chemistry/pharmacology to biochemistry and molecular biology (Figure 1). It can be seen that the waves of molecular biology overlap the waves of biochemistry and are about to leap upwards, according to Utterback and Abernathy (1975). Currently, scientists and researchers are attempting to exploit basic molecular research to identify new drugs, the production of which will be based on recent advances in genomics technology. Scientific breakthroughs, such as genetic engineering, the ability to create monoclonal antibodies, and the mapping of the human genome, have opened up new areas of research, and the pace of discovery in basic biomedical science has accelerated dramatically over the past few decades.

The emergence of biotechnology is changing the pharmaceutical industry in terms of requiring a convergence of science and technologies, and a multi-disciplinary approach to produce new technological discoveries (biological sciences, chemical engineering, bioprocess engineering, information technology, biorobotics). Increasing competition drives the specialization of firms in specific products; however, so far this has been somewhat limited due to the few experts in the specific biotechnology fields, e.g. cancer diseases.

Biotechnology is firmly rooted in the growth stage, with heavy reliance on science and R&D investments. Patenting has increased sharply over the past few decades[7], with biotechnology patenting applications far outpacing the general rise in patenting applications.

---

[7] Still, this is not to say that biotechnology patenting outside the OECD did not experience significant growth. In fact, in the BRIC economies, as well as a number of other Asian and Latin American "tigers", biotechnology patenting increased substantially over the same time period.

The biggest number of patents in biotechnology grew from the late 90s up to early 2000. For example, in 1977, there were only 12 biotechnology patents filed globally under the PCT. By 2009 this number had increased up to 9,339 patents (this is substantially more than a 77% increase). Almost 70% of these patents were filed by an inventor resident in either the EU-27 or US (Patent statistics, OECD 2012). However, while the biotechnology sector shows a strong growth stage, the degree of diffusion and adoption of biotechnology products and processes has been slowed down for several reasons. Although product innovations enabled by biotechnology have increased the quality and variety of goods and opened up new markets, integrating product innovations into modelling frameworks is difficult according to Pianta (2005). Furthermore, the substitution of traditional techniques for producing products with the use of biotechnology is related to the costs of transformation of existing production processes, e.g. substituting diesel extracted from petroleum with biodiesel made from feedstock or canola oil (McNiven, 2007). Moreover, in the present case of biopharmaceuticals, the demand side is largely influenced by regulations. It is strongly regulated and therefore excludes many inventions due to morality (based on Art. 53(b) of EPC). The latter may have an impact on further intensity in biotechnology. These influence the financing of new products and the degree to which markets may grow. As a result, industrial biotechnology is still in its relatively early stage of growth, and many potential products are not yet on the market.

Biotechnology industry is one of the fastest growing areas within the EU. Nevertheless, in 2012, only 512 (0.9 % of the EU-28 total) patent applications filed with the EPO were related to biotechnology inventions (Patent statistics. Eurostat 2015). The level of activity in the biotechnology industry among the EU countries depends largely on the research field. Europe's competitive edge lies mainly in healthcare applications and in industrial biotechnology, including the chemical industry. Some Member States have developed advanced biotech sectors whereas others have stayed behind (Denmark, Germany, UK). New Member States of the EU are generally the early movers in the biotechnology sector. Thus, the identification of the stage of life cycle of the biotechnology industry must be treated with necessary caution.

Laser technology industry

The *Laser technology industry* is the sector showing characteristics of an industry still in the early phases of its evolution. A huge variety of lasers has been developed since they were first invented 50 years ago (Figure 1). Laser systems prove to be a core technology, enabling many new applications, particularly in medicine. They can be available in many forms, each of them being of a different nature and having a different purpose. Laser applications are equally varied and are employed, for example, in manufacturing (e.g. welding and marking), surgery, defence (e.g. ranging and weaponry), scientific research, and development. The rich applicability of laser technologies in a wide range of disciplines suggests that their industrial cluster is very heterogeneous and diverse.

The annual number of patent applications has decreased (in 1998–2001 there were on average 50 patents per million inhabitants in the EU, whereas in 2002–2008 this number dropped to 31 patents, on average). This may indicate that the innovation system in the field of laser beam sources has reached a certain stage of maturity or that its growth is slowing down.

Similar results are presented in Figure 1, which illustrates the Fischer and Pry score for the laser and photonics industry and shows that the rapid growth of both industries slows down as the market for their applications becomes saturated (85). The dynamics of innovation and diffusion processes could be infringed by several factors. The first is related to the complexity of the technology. Each application for laser technology can be thought of as a technological opportunity requiring a range of different patentable inventions that are combined in a functioning product. In another words, a product using laser technology will usually also embody some patents relating to different technological areas outside of optics (Graevenitz et al., 2011). Finally, laser technology industry experiences long technology cycles, so the process of substitution and adoption may take longer, too.

3. Patent applications and high-tech exports from the EU

Over the period 2002 to 2007, patent applications in the EU manufacturing sector increased almost continuously until the global economic and financial crisis began to be felt in 2008. After peaking in 2006, EU patent applications in the manufacturing sector fell by 7.2 % between 2007 and 2010. This was more than for total EU patent applications, which declined by 4.5 % over the same period.

Taking a more detailed view of the manufacturing sector, the trend at EU level is to a large extent mirrored in the individual sectors as outlined in Figure 2. Of the five largest EU manufacturing subsectors, the pharmaceuticals sector has been hit the hardest, with patent applications dropping by more than 15.4 % between 2007 and 2010. This was followed by the television and radio transmitters sector (−9.0 %). All of the remaining sectors – basic chemicals; office machinery and computers; and motor vehicles, trailers and semi-trailers – have been hit to a lesser degree (varying between −3.0 % and −5.9 %). During that period, industrial patents as a share of total patent applications also declined gradually, from 47.7 % in 2007 to 46.3 % in 2010.

Employment in knowledge-intensive activities and the contribution of medium and high-tech product exports to the trade balance have been the main drivers of the countries' strong growth performance.

4. Business cycles and high-tech employment in the EU

Although the direct economic weight of high-tech industries is relatively small, its impact can be significant for regional economic growth. High-tech industries have a large indirect economic impact on promoting regional growth by inducing innovations on other non-high-tech industries and sectors in the region. ICTs and their application are the prime support needed for the rapid growth and modernization of various sectors of the economy, as well as for creating entirely new industries, e.g. e-commerce. Moreover, there is evidence of significant potential for catching up and convergence in ICT-using manufacturing industries and services, particularly in the EU-10 regions, which have been undergoing

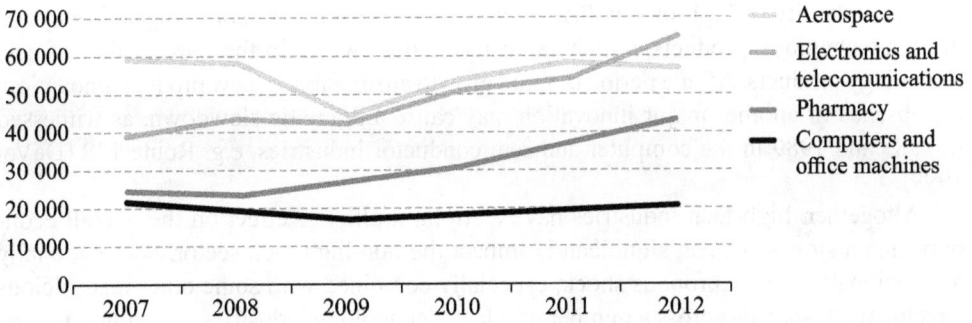

Figure 2. High-tech exports outside of EU-27, by high-tech group of products, EU-27, 2007–12 (EUR million)
Source: based on Eurostat data.

a privatization and restructuring process in their manufacturing and service sectors (van Ark and Piatkowski, 2004; Kołodko and Piatkowski, 2002).

Furthermore, the effects of any new technology introduced on a certain scale extend beyond factories and research centres, influencing the broader scale of social and economic aspects by increasing the standard of living (Eurobarometer, 2005). For example, the aerospace technology's greatest contribution – apart from flying – is in satellite communication that delivers information on environmental and security issues; laser technology enabled the shift in storage capacity from vinyl to CDs and DVDs, whereas potential benefits of biotechnology include solving food shortages, improvements in medicine, agriculture, environmental management, etc.[8] These advantages may surpass the rather low impact of biotechnology on labour productivity and cost reductions (Freeman, 2003; Nusser *et al.*, 2007; Hopkins *et al.*, 2007). Another issue that arises from technological advancement is the safety and ethics of the research and its applications, e.g. risk of genetic engineering accidents in biotechnology or privacy invasion related to the ICT industry. These issues are important and deserve to be mentioned in this book. What is significant from the perspective and purpose of this book is that regions' specialization and participation in global high-tech value chains increase their vulnerability to economic fluctuations (demand shifts and shocks). This is especially true in the case of regions where high-tech industries account for a large share of economic output. Their economies could be more vulnerable to a high-tech contraction (Lasselle, Aloi, and McMillan, 2000). Moreover, since high-tech industries trigger growth in demand for a variety of other high-tech industries and service sectors, as was discussed in the previous section, a synchronous shock in one high-tech sector spreads across a number of related technology industries, e.g. in the computer and semiconductor industries (DeVol, 1999). For example, a general downturn in the computer industry in the mid-1990s led to a decline in the demand for semiconductor technology products; as a result, producers responded with lower prices and job cuts (Hart, 1986).

---

[8] Biotechnology Industry Organization (BIO). "Biotechnology in Perspective", Washington, D.C.: Biotechnology Industry Organization, 1990.

The volatility of high-tech industries may be the result of a shortening of life cycles in high-technology products, which can cause major swings in the introduction of new technology products. After a period of rapid growth attributable to new product innovation, the absence of another major innovation may cause a dramatic slowdown, as witnessed in 1985 and 1989 in the computer and semiconductor industries, e.g. Route 128 (DeVol 1999).

Altogether, high-tech industries have a strong multiplier effect on the overall economy, and a slowdown can significantly impact the non-high-tech sector, both nationally and regionally. If synchronous shock, especially combined with some other inauspicious development, spreads across a number of related technology industries, an economy-wide recession may occur.

One approach to analyzing the behaviour of high-tech industries over the business cycle is to compare the relative dynamics of the high-tech industry and knowledge-intensive service sectors to the overall economic GDP dynamics and total industry and service sector employment trends. Figures 3 and 4 show that for all EU regions high-tech industry employment seems to be inherently volatile. The changes in high-tech industry employment are even more pronounced for the EU-10 Member States regions, which may introduce risks for the regions that have developed high-tech clusters.

Until the year 2000, the growth of the high-tech market was relatively fast; in 2001 the growth rate declined as a result of the global ICT downturn, but in 2002 it rose again. Figure 4 shows there is a delayed effect of high-tech downturn on the EU-10 regions' employment. The highest employment drop in high-tech manufacturing was observed in 2002, when most of the EU-15 had already entered the recovery stage.

The recent global financial crisis brought an economic cooling to markets throughout the world. As a result, the demand for total manufacturing and high-tech products and services in the EU area decreased. Due to large cuts in investment expenditure, both by companies and households, these industries, overall, had been deeply affected by this crisis, which resulted in large overcapacity (for instance in electronic components) and a decline in profits. It is interesting that the scale of the impact of recent economic crisis on ICT manufacturing employment was less profound than the downturn in 2002–2003. The study on the longer-term trends in this sector suggests that the ICT sector has become less employment-intensive, which means there is greater pressure on skills requirements to cover broader ground and have greater flexibility (Runiewicz-Wardyn, 2006). Similar pressures have been observed in other high-tech industries (e.g. semiconductors and electronics), for which e.g. ICT skills were needed and which did not concern ICT professionals alone (OECD, 2009; Dedrick and Kraemer, 2008). These observations reveal another challenge to high-tech regions: investment in human capital and continuous upgrading of skills.

The vulnerability of EU high-tech manufacturing employment to the business cycle may have several causes; firstly, the participation of many smaller EU-10 economies in offshore outsourcing[9] activities as part of a bigger value chain. Many companies, especially

---

[9] Subcontracting abroad or offshore outsourcing occur when one firm (the manufacturer or contractor) contracts another firm (the subcontractor) for a given production cycle. *Handbook on Globalization Indicators*, OECD, 2005.

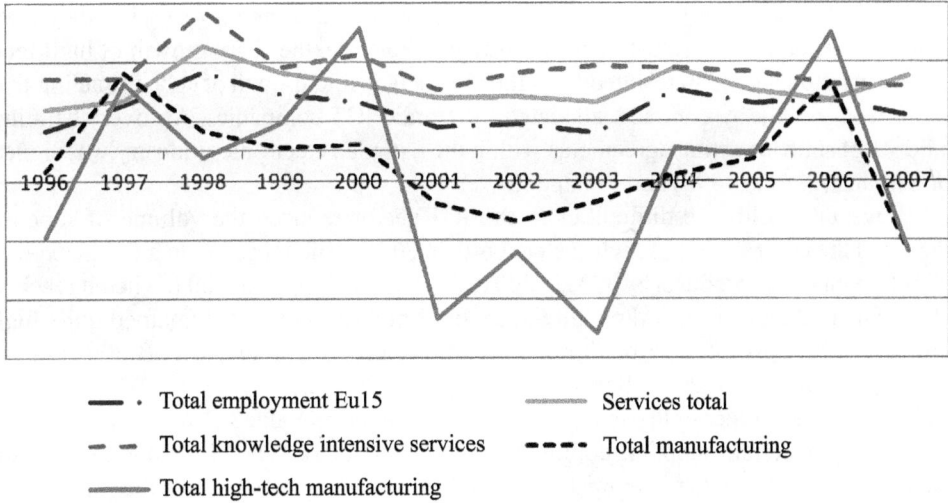

- Total employment Eu15   Services total
- Total knowledge intensive services   Total manufacturing
- Total high-tech manufacturing

Figure 3. The high-tech sector aligns with the business cycle 1996–2008 for the EU-15 regions (year-by-year dynamics of average values)
Source: own calculations, based on Eurostat data.

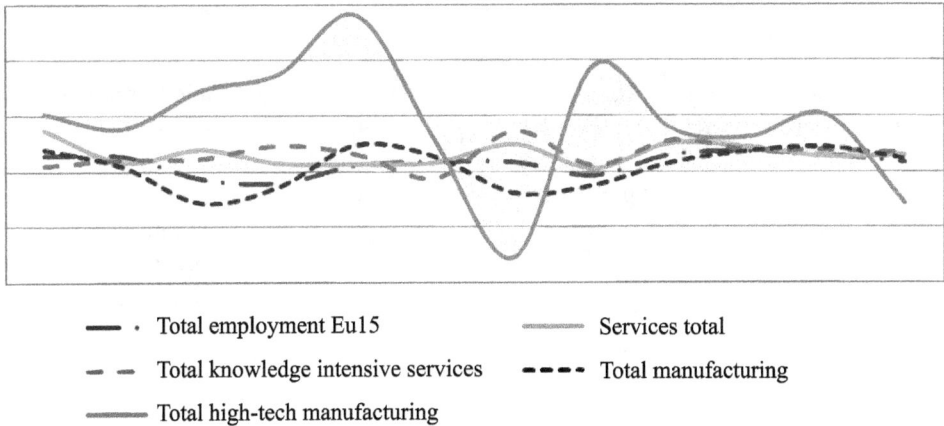

- Total employment Eu15   Services total
- Total knowledge intensive services   Total manufacturing
- Total high-tech manufacturing

Figure 4. The high-tech sector aligns with the business cycle 1996–2008 for the EU-10 regions (year-by-year dynamics of average values)
Source: own calculations, based on Eurostat data.

from new Member States, including Slovenia, Slovakia, the Czech Republic, and Estonia, have become subcontractors for Western European and global manufacturing companies, thanks to their friendly business environment and cheaper knowledge base.

The strong presence in an important suppliers' network can make the region more attractive for other global players to follow. As a result, the region will further develop its technological infrastructure and improve the cluster environment. However, subcontracting may also pose a risk, especially for the subcontractor. Large firms use subcontractors as "buffers" to stabilize their manufacturing capacity, and during a recession they may reduce the amount of work they contract out. For example, the sharp growth of high-tech exports in Estonia in 2000 resulted from the almost two-fold growth of subcontracting that was driven mainly by contracts allocated by Nordic ICT companies. An overwhelming majority of subcontracting agreements within the Estonian electronics industry was signed for Sweden (55% in 1995) and Finland (34%).

However, worldwide difficulties in the ICT sector reduced the volume of subcontracts and the contribution of high-tech exports in 2001, which resulted in a fall in exports of high-technology products by 32% in 2001; the decline stopped in 2003, when it reached a lower level than in 1999. Although the share of high-tech exports remained quite high throughout this downturn period, it indicated that Estonia's high-tech export was vulnerable (Rajasalu and Laur, 2003; Berg-Andersson, 1998, p. 24).

The regions' vulnerability to high-tech cycles can be explained also by the economic dependence on certain suppliers coming from the same region. Therefore, this can explain Estonia's vulnerability to the Finnish and Swedish economic recessions in the early 1990s (King, 1994). It is also worth mentioning the concern of regions dependent on the few international contractors of being dumped by the re-location of high-tech manufacturing to areas of cheaper labour cost, e.g. China, Russia or India (Tiits *et al.*, 2003).

5. Summary and conclusions

In sum, employment in knowledge-intensive activities and the contribution of medium and high-tech product exports to the trade balance have been the main drivers of the countries' strong growth performance. On the other hand, high-technology sectors and globally integrated firms expose production processes throughout the economy to both internal and external shocks. When considering the vulnerability of the EU high-tech manufacturing sector to business cycles, policy efforts should focus on reducing the regions' dominance to a few large firms or a few industries and promoting a diversified industrial manufacturing value chain.

References

Anbil, R., Gelman, E., Patty, B., Tanga, R. (1991), *Recent advances in crew-pairing optimization at American airlines,* "Interfaces" 21:62–74, www.columbia.edu/~dano/courses/4600/lectures/19/fleetsched.pdf.

Andersen, B. (1999), *The hunt for S-shaped growth paths in technological innovation: a patent study*, "Journal of Evolutionary Economics", 9:487–526.

Cameron, G., Proudman, J., Redding, S. (2005), *Technological convergence, R&D, trade and productivity growth*, "European Economic Review" 49(3):775–807, Elsevier.

Dedrick, J., Kraemer, K. (2008), *Impact of globalization and offshoring on engineering employment in the personal computing industry*, [in:] *The offshoring of engineering: facts, unknowns, and potential implications*, National Academy of Engineering (NAE), Committee on the Offshoring of Engineering, National Academies Press, Washington DC.

Dyson, J. F. (1999), *The Sun, The Genome, and The Internet: Tools of Scientific Revolution*, New York.

DeVol, R. (1999), *America's high-technology economy: growth, development, and risks for Metropolitan areas*, Milken Institute, Santa Monica.

Eurobarometer (2007), Eurobarometer surveys. http://ec.europa.eu/public_opinion/archives/eb_arch_en.htm.

Eurostat (2014), *Regional Yearbook 2014*, http://bookshop.europa.eu/en/eurostat-regional-yearbook-2011-pbKSHA11001/.

Fisher, J. C., Pry, R. H. (1971), *A simple substitution model of technological change*, "Journal of Technological Forecasting and Social Change" 3(1):75–88.

Fingleton, B. (2000), *Convergence: international comparisons based on a simultaneous equation model with regional effects*, "International Review of Applied Economy" 14(3):285–305, Taylor and Francis Journals.

Freeman, C. (2003), *Policies for developing new technologies*, "SPRU Electronic Working Paper Series", No. 98, Sussex University.

Gatignon, H., Tushman, M., Smith, W., Anderson, P. (2002), *A structural approach to assessing innovation: construct development of innovation locus, type and characteristics*, "Managment Science" 48(9):1103–1122.

Guellec, D., Van Pottelsberghe de la Potterie, B. (2004), *From R&D to productivity growth: do the institutional settings and the source of funds of R&D matter?*, "Oxford Bulletin of Economics and Statistics", Department of Economics, University of Oxford, 66(3):353–378.

Griffith, R., Lee, S., Van Reenen, J. (2011), *Is distance dying at last? Falling home bias in fixed-effects models of patent citations*, "Quantitative Economics" 2(2):211–249.

Graevenitz, G., Wagner, S., Harhoff, D. (2011), *How to measure patent thickets – a novel approach*, J Econ Lett 111(1):6–9, Elsevier.

Greunz, L. (2004), *Interregional knowledge spillovers in Europe*, ULB Institutional Repository 2013/9483. Universite Libre de Bruxelles.

Hart, J. A. (1986), *Politics of global competition in the semiconductor industry*, Pac Focus 1 (2):93–119.

Haupt, R., Kloyer, M., Lange, M. (2007), *Patent indicators for the technology life cycle development*, "Research Policy" 36(3), pp. 387–398.

Hopkins, M., Martin, P., Nightingale, P., Kraft, A., Mahdi, S. (2007), *The myth of the biotech revolution: an assessment of technological, clinical and organisational change*, "Research Policy" 36:566–589.

Kołodko, G. W., Piatkowski, M. (2002), *Nowa gospodarka i stare problemy. Perspektywy szybkiego wzrostu w krajach posocjalistycznych*, Wydawnictwo WSPiZ, Warszawa.

McNiven, C. (2007), *Overview and discussion of the results of the Pilot Survey on Nanotechnology in Canada*, "Science, Innovation and Electronic Information Division (SIEID)", Working Paper No.005.

Nusser, M., Hüsing, B., Wydra, S. (2007), *Potenzialanalyse der industriellen, weißen Biotechnologie*, Studie im Auftrag des Bundesministeriums fur Bildung und Forschung (BMBF), Karlsruhe.

OECD, 2009; http://www.oecd.org/innovation/inno/oecdworkonpatentstatistics.htm.

Pianta, M. (2005), *Innovation and employment*, [in:] J. Fagerberg, D. Mowery, R. Nelson (eds.) *Handbook of innovation*, chap. 22, Oxford University Press, Oxford/New York, pp. 568–598.

Porter, M. E. (1998), *The competitive advantage of nations*, Free Press, New York.

Runiewicz-Wardyn, M. (2006), *Znaczenie ICT w generowaniu zdolności konkurencyjnej regionu*, [in:] M. Runiewicz-Wardyn (ed.), *Konkurencyjność regionów. Rola technologii informatyczno-telekomunikacyjnych*, Wyd. ALK, Warszawa.

Rajasalu, T., Laur, A. (2003), *Contribution of the new economy to Estonia's economic growth and convergence with the European economy*, "TIGER working paper series" no. 41, pp. 1–17. www. tiger.edu.pl/publikacje/TWPNo41.pdf.

Runiewicz-Wardyn, M. (2006), *Znaczenie ICT w generowaniu zdolności konkurencyjnej regionu* [in:] Runiewicz-Wardyn M. (ed.), *Konkurencyjność regionów. Rola technologii informatyczno-telekomunikacyjnych*, Wyd. ALK, Warszawa.

Rasheed, A., Manarvi, I. A. (2008), *A framework of technology diffusion in Aircraft Manufacturing Industry Environment*, Lecture Notes in Engineering and Computer Science 01/2008.www. researchgate.net/publication/44261831_A_Framework_of_Technology_Diffusion_in_Aircraft_ Manufacturing_Industry_Environment.

Subramanian, R., Scheff, R. P., Quillinan, J. D., Wiper, D. S., Marsten, R. E. (1994), *Coldstart: fleet assignment at Delta air lines*, "Interfaces" 24: 104–120.

Swann, G. M. P. (2005), *High technology clusters: specialisation and interaction,* [in:] A. Quadrio Curzio, M. Fortis (eds.), *Research and technological innovation: the challenge for a New Europe*. Springer, Berlin, pp. 129–150.

Tiits, M., Kattel, R., Kalvet, T., Kaarli, R. (2003), *Competitiveness of Estonian economy and future outlooks*, Research and Development Council of Estonia, Tallinn.

Utterback, J. M., Abernathy, W. J. (1975), *A dynamic model of process and product innovation*, "International Journal of Management Science" 3(6): 639–656.

Watts, R. J., Porter, A. L. (1997), *Innovation forecasting*, "Technological Forecast Social Change" 56: 25–47.

Wunderlich, S., Khalil, T. (2002), *Introducing technology timeline interpretation to technology diffusion and maturity analysis as applied to different industrial sectors*, University of Miami, Miami.

van Ark, B., Piatkowski, M. (2004), *Productivity, innovation and ICT, in old and New Europe*, Research Memorandum GD-69, Groningen Growth and Development Centre, Groningen.

Chapter II

Entrepreneurship and Corporate R&D as Drivers of Innovations

Hermann Simon

Hidden Champions as Drivers of Innovations

1. Introduction

The globalized world holds unlimited growth opportunities. Global exports per capita were 6 US dollars in 1900; today they are at close to 3000 dollars, in spite of a much larger global population. Two thirds of this growth has occurred since 2000. Individual countries profit very differently from the opportunities globalization offers, as Figure 1 illustrates for the decade 2004–2013.

Among the larger countries, Germany's export performance is an extreme outlier. In absolute terms, Germany exports almost as much as France, Italy and the UK together. These three countries represent a population of 180 million, compared to 82 million Germans. On a per capita basis, German exports are about twice as high as those of its large European neighbours and about three times higher than Japanese or American exports.

Why is Germany so strong in exports? The explanation does not lie in large corporations, of which the country has relatively few. For instance, Germany has fewer Fortune Global 500 corporations than France. No, Germany's outstanding export performance is due to its "Hidden Champions". My total count of Hidden Champions stands at 2746 worldwide, and 1307 or 47% of them are from Germany. These little-known mid-sized global market leaders are the elite of Germany's famous "Mittelstand" and the backbone of its export strength.

2. What is a Hidden Champion?

A Hidden Champion is a company that belongs to the top three in its global market or is number one on its continent, has less than 5 billion $US in revenue and is little-known to the general public. To give some examples: 80% of all smart cards in the world and more

Country Exports, billion US-$

Country	Value
China	13 909
Germany	12 592
USA	12 234
Japan	6986
France	5238
Italy	4566
United Kingdom	4424
Korea	4155
Russia	3814
Spain	2638
Poland	1458

0   2000   4000   6000   8000   10 000 12 000 14 000 16 000

Country Per capita exports, US-$

Country	Value
Germany	153 936
Korea	84 796
France	79 605
Italy	75 347
United Kingdom	71 355
Spain	57 100
Japan	54 578
USA	39 338
Poland	37 841
Russia	26 671
China	10 372

0   20 000 40 000 60 000 80 000 100 000 120 000 140 000 160 000 180 000

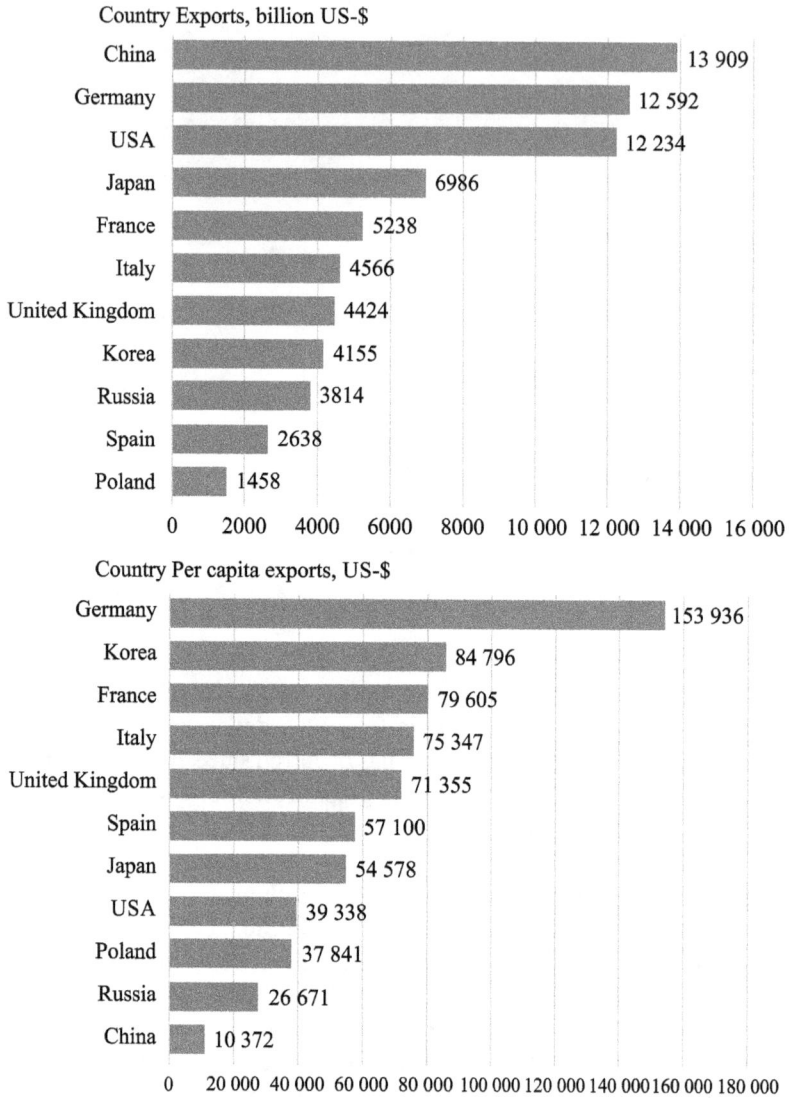

Figure 1: Exports 2004–2013, absolute and per capita

than 50% of all mobile phones, including the iPhone, are held together by the adhesives of Delo, a producer of special adhesives for electronic applications. Tetra is the world leader in feeds for ornamental fish, with a 60% global market share. Belfor, an industrial service company, is a world leader in the removal of water, fire and storm damages and the only company in the world to provide these services. Figure 2 shows the number of Hidden Champions for the same countries as in Figure 1, again in absolute terms and per capita, here expressed as the number of Hidden Champions per million inhabitants.

Country Number of Hidden Champions

Country	Number of Hidden Champions
Germany	1307
USA	366
Japan	220
Italy	76
France	75
China	68
United Kingdom	67
Poland	27
Korea	23
Russia	14
Spain	11

Total number worldwide:
2734

Country Number of Hidden Champions per million inhabitants

Country	Number of Hidden Champions per million inhabitants
Germany	16,0
Japan	1,7
Italy	1,2
USA	1,2
France	1,1
United Kingdom	1,1
Poland	0,7
Korea	0,5
Spain	0,2
Russia	0,1
China	0,1

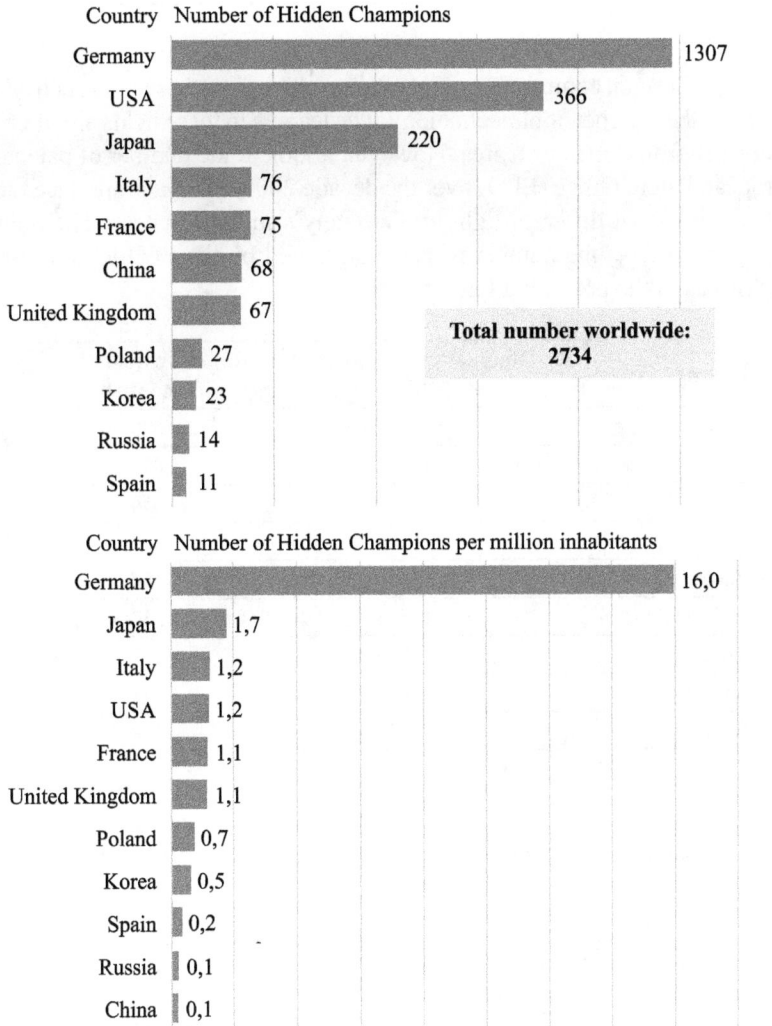

Figure 2: Hidden Champions by country: absolute number and number per million inhabitants

The Hidden Champions concept increasingly attracts attention from all over the world. In the last 15 years, the 1307 German Hidden Champions created 1.2 million new jobs. With the majority of their employees now outside Germany, they are truly global companies. Their growth is driven by two factors: innovation and globalization. The Hidden Champions have increased their global market shares in spite of a bigger world market and have initiated a massive wave of innovations.

3. Innovativeness

It's true that few German companies are innovation champions in sectors such as informa-tion technology, the Internet or biotechnology. The leaders in these fields are often from the US, occasionally from Japan or Korea. However, a look at the number of patents granted by the European Patent Office (EPO) over the decade 2003-2012, a pronounced long-term view, casts a somewhat different light on Germany's innovativeness. The numbers are striking. Figure 3 shows the number of patents granted by the EPO to applicants in the same countries as in the preceding figures.

Country	Number of European patents 2003–2012	European patents per million inhabitants
Germany	130 032	1590
Japan	108 418	847
Rance	44 363	674
USA	134 306	427
Italy	21 636	357
United Kingdom	20 893	337
Korea	9 859	197
Spain	3 649	79
Roland	313	8
Russia	462	3
China	2 807	2

Figure 3. Patents issued by the European Patent Office from 2003 to 2012 by country of origin; absolute number and number per million inhabitants

Germany is the clear leader in terms of the number of patents per million inhabitants. The differences among European countries are huge. Germany has more than twice as many patents per million inhabitants as France, more than four times as many as Italy, and almost five times as many as the UK. We also see that Spain is a weak innovator. The same is true of Poland. Russia is extremely weak. However, there is a big difference between Spain and Russia on the one hand and Poland on the other hand. In the case of Spain and Russia, the annual number of patents is essentially flat over the considered decade, whereas Poland's number has gone up from 12 in 2003 to 80 in 2012, an annual increase of 21%. Chinese patents show an even stronger growth, up from 50 in 2003 to 793 in 2012, corresponding to an annual rate of 32%. Although the topic of innovation covers much more than the number of patents, these data are nevertheless a strong indicator of the innovativeness of the countries considered. To excel in global competition innovation is indispensable.

What do the Hidden Champions contribute to Germany's innovativeness? Among the 50 biggest patent applicants in Germany are 40 German companies and 10 foreign com-panies. Of the 40 German firms 19, or almost 50%, are Hidden Champions. The list of the most patent- and innovation-intensive companies is not the same as the list of the 50 or 100 largest German companies. Instead, a very large share of the innovation in Germany comes from mid-sized companies which are global leaders in their markets, usually niche markets. The record holder in terms of patents per employee is von Ardenne, a global leader in glass and solar coating technologies. With circa 600 employees, van Ardenne registered 101 patents in 2012. It comes as a surprise that they are based in Dresden, not in West Germany.

R&D spending of the Hidden Champions is twice as high as in the average industrial company. Even more important is the output. As Figure 4 shows, Hidden Champions have five times more patents per 1000 employees than patent-intensive large corporations. Figure 4 also shows that the costs per patent with the Hidden Champions are only one fifth of the costs in large corporations.

Patents per 1,000 employees   Cost per patent

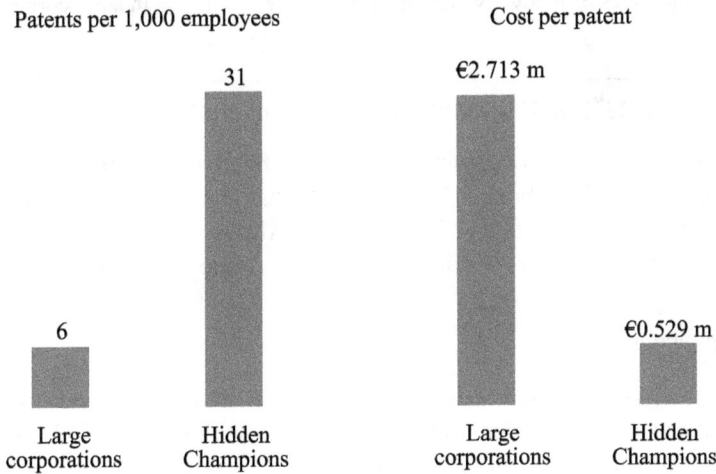

Figure 4: Patents per 1000 employees and costs per patent for Hidden Champions and for large corporations

4. Drivers of innovativeness

What are the driving forces behind the outstanding innovativeness of the Hidden Champions: customer needs, technology, or both? Figure 5 shows the answer. 65% of the Hidden Champions state that these two forces are well integrated and balanced, whereas only 19% of the large companies say so. The challenge of innovation is the integration of technology and customer needs.

There are further differences in the innovation processes. While larger companies throw huge budgets at solving problems, the Hidden Champions devote very few dedicated people to finding new solutions. This is one reason why their costs per patent are much lower. They also co-develop intensely with their top customers. The internal cooperation between functions (e.g. between R&D and marketing) is smoother and less friction-loaded. All this leads to higher speed in product development and, thus, shorter time to market.

Large corporations   Hidden Champions

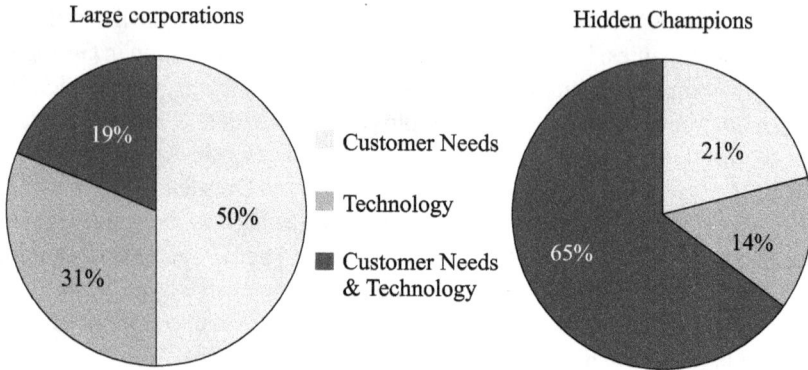

Customer Needs

Technology

Customer Needs
& Technology

Figure 5: Driving forces of innovativeness in Hidden Champions and in large corporations

5. Strategic and cultural foundations of innovativeness

The roots of a company's innovativeness are not confined to the process and the manage-ment of R&D, but are both broader and deeper. What are the Hidden Champions doing differently from large corporations? The answer is: Almost everything! Here are the main differences. All of them foster the Hidden Champions' innovativeness.

Extremely ambitious targets

Hidden Champions set themselves extremely ambitious goals regarding market leadership and growth. An example: The goal of Chemetall is the worldwide technology and market-ing leadership. Chemetall is a global leader in special metals like cesium and lithium. 3B Scientific, world leader in anatomical teaching aids, states: "We want to become and stay number 1 in the world." The Hidden Champions achieved annual growth rates of 10% in the last 15 years, which means that they are four times larger than they were then. Almost 200 €-billionaires emerged from that group in terms of revenues. Furthermore, their market shares have increased. Ten years ago, their global market share was 30%, today it stands at 33%. The cause for this has one name: Innovation.

Focus and depth

 "We always had one customer and will only have one customer in the future: the pharma-ceutical industry. We only do one thing, but we do it right." This quote comes from Uhl-mann, the world leader in packaging systems for the pharmaceutical industry. Flexi states: "We will do only one thing, but we do it better than anyone else." Flexi makes retractable leashes for dogs and has 70% of the global market. This is focus! And only focus leads to world class. Closely connected to focus is a deep value chain. One of the modern buzz-words of the last 20 years has been "outsourcing". While many companies are proud of having delegated large parts of their production to others, the Hidden Champions have a very strong anti-outsourcing attitude when it comes to their core competencies. An example is Wanzl, the world leader in shopping carts and airport baggage carts: "We produce all parts ourselves, based on the quality standards we define." Carts at airports all over the world are made by Wanzl. The airport authorities are obviously willing to pay Wanzl's high prices. Even Narita, the Tokyo airport, uses carts made by Wanzl. They look like a simple product but their quality is extraordinary. The roots of this superior performance lie in the fact that Wanzl retains total quality control by making everything on its own.

Globalization

Focus makes a market small. How can you make a market big? By globalizing! The Hidden Champions combine their focus in product and know-how with global selling and marketing, thereby expanding each market by a huge factor. If one does that, there are hardly any growth limits. The Hidden Champions have their own subsidiaries in all important markets around the globe and sell directly to their customers instead of delegating their customer relations to intermediaries, agents, importers etc. Kaercher, a world leader in high-pressure water cleaners, started in earnest its internationalization in the 1970s and since then has added one, two and sometimes three countries to their market presence every year. It has now 100 own subsidiaries all over the world.

Closeness to customer and competitive advantages

The biggest overall strength of the Hidden Champions is not technology but their closeness to the customers. This is a natural advantage of smaller and mid-sized companies. 38% of their employees have regular customer contacts, compared to larger companies where only 8% have regular customer contacts. This closeness leads to the more effective integration of customer needs and technology we outlined earlier. The strategies of the Hidden Champions are value-driven, not price-driven. They usually charge a price premium of 10 to 15% over the market average. The most important competitive advantage of the Hidden Champions is product quality. In recent years, three new advantages have emerged: advice, systems integration and ease of use. They are the attributes with the biggest increases in importance.

Loyalty and highly qualified employees

Innovativeness is ultimately based on inner competencies, especially on qualification and loyalty. The Hidden Champions invest 50% more than the average company into training their workers. They have highly qualified employees; the percentage of university graduates among the workforce has more than doubled, from 8.5% ten years ago to 19.1% today. Since global competitiveness today is more and more about qualification, it becomes increasingly important not only to hire, educate and train top talent, but to retain it. The Hidden Champions have extremely low turnover rates: only 2.7% annually as compared to the average of 7.3% for Germany, which is still low in an international comparison.

Strong leadership

The leaders of the Hidden Champions are the ultimate root of these companies' continuing success. What characterizes the leaders? First and foremost, it is the identity of person and purpose. The leadership is ambivalent: authoritarian with regard to principles and values, but flexible in the details of carrying out a job. The Hidden Champions have more women in top positions and a very high continuity with regard to the CEOs. Their average tenure is 20 years, compared to 6.1 years in large companies. The leaders are also the strongest promoters of innovation in the Hidden Champions. Most of them see permanent innovation as their personal responsibility. And since they are deeply familiar with their products, they really contribute new ideas and make sure those are implemented. At the age of 66, Dr Peter Zinkann retired as CEO of Miele, the manufacturer of high quality washing machines. Dr Zinkann is now 84 years old. Since his retirement as CEO he has registered 108 patents.

6. Summary

The main findings and insights on the role of Hidden Champions as drivers of innovation can be summarized in five points:

- Globalization offers unlimited growth opportunities, but countries differ strongly in how they exploit these opportunities.
- Innovativeness and strong mid-sized companies determine the success in global competition to a large degree.
- The Hidden Champions contribute over-proportionately to the innovativeness of a country due to radically different innovation processes.
- They are highly focussed, have a deep value chain, and effectively integrate technology and customer needs.
- Their innovation capabilities are rooted in inner strengths based on qualification, loyalty and continuity.

The ultimate lesson: The Hidden Champions go their own ways, more decisively and successfully than ever. They do most things differently from the teachings of management gurus, from modern management fads, from large corporations. They are outstanding role models for innovation and leadership in the age of Globalia.

References

Simon, M. K., Goes, J. (2013), *Scope, Limitations and Delimitations,* www.dissertationrecipes.com.

Simon, H. (2012), *Hidden Champions – AufbruchnachGlobalia: die Erfolgsstrategienunbekannter-Weltmarktführer*, Frankfurt am Main, Campus-Verlag.

Simon, H., Guinchard, S. (2012), *Les Champions Cachés du XXIe Siècle: Stratégies à Succès.* Economica.

Simon, H. (2012), through Simon Kucher on youtube.com: Hidden Champions Gipfel 2012:Der Mittelstand in der deutschenPolitik. http://www.youtube.com/watch?v=5sXRAUKlqQ.

Simon, H. (2009), *Hidden Champions of the Twenty-First Century: The Success Strategies of Unknown World Market Leaders*, Heidelberg, Springer.

Simon, H. (1996), *Hidden Champions – Lessons from 500 of the World's Best Unknown Companies*, Harvard Business School Press, Boston, Massachusetts.

Simon, H. (1996), through Business Strategy Review: You don't have to be German to be a "hidden champion" (successful medium-sized companies exist outside Germany). http://www.access-mylibrary.com/article-1G1-18463674/you-dont-have-german.html. Accessed on 13.12.2012.

Pietro Moncada-Paterno-Castello, Nicola Grassano

Innovation Without Corporate R&D? An Analysis of the Italian Case and Implications for Policy

1. Introduction

This paper analyzes the status of private R&D investment in Italy based on a collection of recent evidence and indicates possible policy actions to boost private R&D investment.

Why is business R&D investment relevant? The literature (e.g. Griliches, 2000; Mohnen and Hall, 2013) broadly reports that engaging in R&D can help firms to innovate and increase productivity, and to improve or create new products[1] and markets, thus ensuring competitiveness and growth[2], and leading to both private and social benefits[3].

However, despite the known benefits, the innovation system in Italy has long suffered from underinvestment in R&D compared to the EU average, in particular from private investment (Action Institute, 2013). Regardless of several studies in the literature supporting this diagnosis (e.g. Cerulli and Potí, 2012; Antonelli and Crespi, 2013), policy actions implemented to address this issue during the past decade have not significantly improved the situation.

Our analysis relies on microdata from an unbalanced 10 years' panel data-set (2004–2013), built using several waves of the European Industrial R&D Investment Scoreboard

---

[1] Harrison *et al.* (2014) found strong empirical evidence that innovation creates employment at firm level, especially thanks to the introduction of new products.

[2] For example, Hall *et al.* (2010) showed that R&D could explain on average 20–30% of the innovation process. However, considerable differences exist in firm's innovation and competitiveness returns on R&D investment, depending on the technology intensity of the industrial sector, the product portfolio and/or the life cycle (Kumbhakar *et al.*, 2012; Mairesse and Mohnen, 2005; Bosworth, 2005).

[3] Already Shumpeter in 1934 argued that it is the achievement of profits, through entrepreneurship and innovation, that makes possible economic growth.

and on other sources of quantitative and qualitative information (e.g. OECD, ISTAT, EUROSTAT, ERAWATCH Country Report – Italy, 2013, State of the Innovation Union, 2014). We also took into account recent academic literature on the topic.

Based on all this, we argue that: i) innovation in firms without their engagement in R&D activities is not sustainable in the medium and long term; ii) the Italian R&D and innovation (and competitiveness) gap is due to "systemic"/structural reasons, and thus targeted high quality policies are needed to address these issues; iii) such policy interventions will have little positive impact without comprehensive reform aimed at improving the innovation environment as a whole. Careful design of an "innovation strategy" that includes support for R&D is needed. This strategy should be fine-tuned to tackle the actual specificities of the Italian economic context and its R&D-led innovation difficulties.

2. Overview of business demographics and research and innovation (R&I) in Italy

The preponderance of small firms is a well-known characteristic of the Italian economy. Italy leads the EU in the number of enterprises and has the second largest number of SMEs among European countries. According to ISTAT data[4], there are just over 4.4 million enterprises in Italy, but only 3,470 of those have 250 employees or more (and hence are not SMEs). Micro firms with one to nine employees account for more than 4 million enterprises, and for half of all employment in the business sector. This makes the overall average size of Italian firms very small: 3.9 employees, compared to 6.6 as the EU average (ISTAT, 2014).

The prevalence of micro-size firms has a number of major consequences for the Italian R&I system. Such very small firms – mostly sole traders– are unable to invest significantly in R&D activities, as they are typically financially constrained and are unlikely to hire specialized employees, and thus they have low R&I development and absorptive capacity (Bugamelli et al., 2012). The fact that the innovation capacity is seriously limited by firm size is also confirmed by the evidence provided by the Community Innovation Survey (CIS) data: in the period 2008–2010, 64.1% of Italian firms with 250 employees or more were involved in innovation, whilst this figure was 47.1% for the 50–249 employee class and only 29.1% for the 10–49 employee class (ISTAT, 2012b).

One of the consequences of this reduced investment in R&D and of the low innovation activity of Italian firms is the lack of a positive and sustained growth dynamic and the low levels of international competitiveness. In fact, if we consider the period 2008–2012, the size structure of Italian firms remained unchanged, with firms of four employees or less representing between 90.2% and 90.8% of the total number of active firms in the country (Eurostat, 2014). If we look instead at competitiveness vis-à-vis other EU countries, Italy is ranked among the countries "with strong but declining competitiveness", with the classification based on the last five years' values of three indicators, namely, labour productivity, exports, and innovation (European Commission, 2014c).

---

[4] ISTAT – extract from online database on 30 September 2014; data from national survey 2011.

Italy does not have a high capacity of start-up innovative firms, nor an ability to help them survive (Audretsch *et al.*, 1999) or grow (Colombo and Grilli, 2010). In the ranking elaborated by the World Bank "Doing Business project", Italy is classified 90th for the ease of starting a new business, below countries like the UK (28) and France (41)[5]. The Italian Chambers of Commerce counted (September 2014) about 2,600 innovative start-ups in Italy, compared to, e.g. 2000 in London alone and 1000 each in Paris and Berlin in the same year. Furthermore, even though five out of six high-tech firms in Northern Italy are technology-based SMEs, only one in six of them has a realistic prospect of growth, the rest are likely to remain SMEs (European Commission, 2003).

Moreover, Italian economic specialization is mainly in low tech sectors: 14% of Italian total Value Added (VA) is represented by textile and clothing, leather and shoes, and wood and wooden products (Pagano and Schivardi, 2003). Sectors with a high R&D intensity are under-represented in terms of their relative contribution to the total Italian VA. As a consequence, Italian R&D intensity (as a ratio of R&D expenditure to GDP) in 2012 was only 1.27, while the EU-27 average was 2.06. Business expenditure on R&D (BERD) as a share of GDP was also well below the EU-27 average in 2012: 0.69% in Italy compared to an EU-27 average of 1.3% (Figure 1).

Finally, the R&I system in Italy is characterized by a high concentration of R&D expenditure and employment in just four major Northern regions – Lombardy, Piedmont, Emilia Romagna and Veneto – and one Central region – Lazio[6].

3. Closer analysis of corporate R&D investment by Italian firms

We used several waves of *The European Industrial R&D Investment Scoreboard*[7] (European Commission 2004–2013) to carry out the analysis of Italian corporate R&D investment at a firm level[8]. Italian firms represent a small part of the world's top R&D investors, not only in numerical terms (only 30 firms in the top 2000, and 46 firms in the EU top 1000), but also as a percentage of the total company R&D expenditure registered on the R&D Scoreboard in 2012 (1.6%). Two firms alone – Fiat[9] in the Automotive & Parts sector, and Finmeccanica in the Aerospace & Defence sector – represent 60% of all R&D investment of the Italian firms included in the EU top 1000 Scoreboard ranking (edition 2013).

---

[5] http://www.doingbusiness.org/.

[6] This reflects the historical pattern of industrialization and the polarized economic structure of the country, with four regions in the south – Sicily, Calabria, Puglia and Campania – eligible for EU Convergence/Objective 1 policies (ERAWATCH Country Report – Italy, 2013).

[7] This Scoreboard collects data on the top private R&D investors worldwide. Focusing on the biggest world investors in R&D, our data suffers from some limitations (e.g. big firms are more represented than SMEs). For a detailed description of the methodology and limitations of the data, see European Commission (2013a, pp. 77–79).

[8] The R&D Scoreboard data are drawn from the companies' annual audited accounts. The database contains economic and financial data of the world's top companies, ranked by their investments in research and development (R&D).

[9] Fiat has controlled Chrysler since July 2011. In the 2012 edition of the Scoreboard (it refers to the 2011 data), Fiat's data also included Chrysler's financial data.

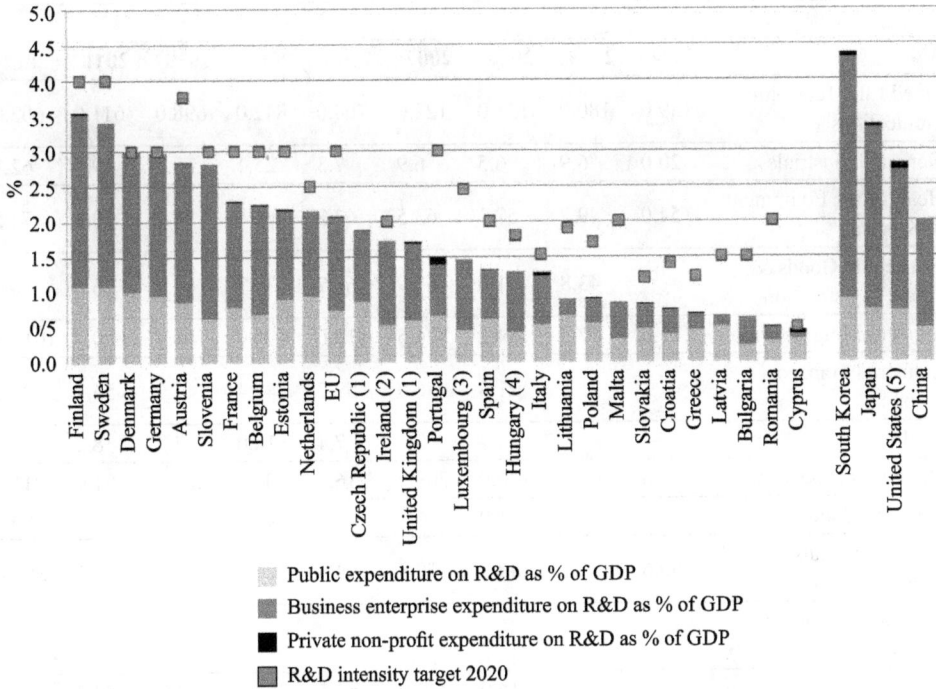

Public expenditure on R&D as % of GDP

Business enterprise expenditure on R&D as % of GDP

Private non-profit expenditure on R&D as % of GDP

R&D intensity target 2020

Figure 1. R&D intensity broken by sector, 2012 and R&D intensity targets 2020
Source: DG Research and Innovation – Unit for the Analysis and Monitoring of National Research Policies.
Data: Eurostat, OECD Member States. Notes: (1) CZ, UK: No R&D intensity targets have been set. For CZ a target of 1% is available only for the public sector. (2) IE: The R&D intensity target is 2.5% of GNP which is estimated to be equivalent to 2.0% of GDP. (3) LU: The R&D intensity target is between 2.30% and 2.60% of GDP
(2.45% was assumed). (4) HU: The R&D intensity sectoral breakdown does not add up to total R&D intensity. (5)
US: (i) Most or all capital expenditure is not included; (ii) Government expenditure on R&D refers to federal or
central government only.

Table 1. Sectoral R&D investment of Italian firms from the EU R&D Scoreboard – Absolute
values (€ million)

Sector	Year								
	2004	2005	2006	2007	2008	2009	2010	2011	2012
Aerospace & Defence	1453.7	1746.0	1891.0	2013.0	1819.7	1964.0	2007.6	1995.6	1853.2
Automobiles & Parts	1322.5	1605.6	1538.4	2033.8	2271.0	1951.8	2206.5	2481.1	3626.0
Banks		141.0	150.0	173.2	278.7	275.9	465.8	503.4	614.0
Construction & Mate-rials			51.3	66.3	73.1	78.2	75.8	70.7	67.3
Electricity	20.0	23.4	22.0	29.0	79.2	101.2	111.5	117.3	154.6
Electronic & Electrical Equipment	23.9	55.3	91.8	100.4	109.9	103.1	107.2	131.8	130.0

Sector	Year								
	2004	2005	2006	2007	2008	2009	2010	2011	2012
Fixed Line Telecommunications	139.0	180.0	133.0	122.0	704.0	842.0	698.0	611.0	602.0
General Industrials	20.0	6.9	6.5	6.9	7.3	25.1	30.2	39.3	62.1
Health Care Equipment & Services	54.0	49.7	57.1	63.5	62.2	65.6	75.0	70.1	75.5
Household Goods & Home Construction		43.8	41.0	67.9	64.7	71.7	65.9	76.0	66.4
Industrial Engineering	43.0	62.9	94.2	826.5	810.0	694.0	786.4	870.7	1015.4
Industrial Transportation		21.2	21.4	36.0	59.7	47.4	49.0	55.7	72.7
Media						7.4	10.0	7.3	8.2	8.6
Oil & Gas Producers	257.0	202.0	222.0	208.0	216.0	207.0	221.0	191.0	211.0
Personal Goods			21.0	36.2	45.3	146.9	144.9	152.0	160.4
Pharmaceuticals & Biotechnology	99.6	125.1	147.2	170.3	194.4	229.2	247.5	259.1	306.6
Software & Computer Services	12.5		0.4	0.8			9.4	5.8	7.3
Travel & Leisure			15.9	33.9	62.5	62.4	54.8	58.8	72.2
Grand Total	3445.2	4262.7	4504.1	5987.5	6865.1	6875.4	7363.7	7697.5	9105.2

Source: European Commission, JRC-IPTS – R&D Scoreboard 2004–2013.

In Table 1 it is worth noting that these 46 firms invested in R&D in 2012 a total of EUR 9.1 billion, which accounted for 84.3% of the total Italian BERD for the same year (EUR 10.8 billion).

There is a very low dynamicity of new entries of Italian firms on the R&D Scoreboard, especially in the high-tech sectors. Additionally, it is worth noting that there are no Italian

Table 2. Sectoral R&D investment of Italian firms from the EU R&D Scoreboard – % of the global annual total

Sector	Year								
	2004	2005	2006	2007	2008	2009	2010	2011	2012
Aerospace & Defence	12.9%	13.2%	13.7%	12.9%	11.6%	12.9%	12.5%	11.8%	10.2%
Automobiles & Parts	2.1%	2.4%	2.2%	2.8%	3.0%	3.0%	3.1%	3.2%	4.3%
Banks	0.0%	9.5%	7.7%	5.0%	5.7%	5.3%	7.0%	6.1%	7.7%
Construction & Materials	0.0%	0.0%	1.5%	1.8%	1.8%	1.6%	1.3%	1.1%	1.0%
Electricity	0.8%	1.0%	0.9%	1.0%	2.5%	3.4%	3.3%	3.9%	5.3%

Sector	Year								
	2004	2005	2006	2007	2008	2009	2010	2011	2012
Electronic & Electrical Equipment	0.1%	0.2%	0.3%	0.3%	0.3%	0.3%	0.3%	0.3%	0.3%
Fixed Line Telecommunications	2.1%	2.6%	1.8%	1.5%	8.2%	9.6%	8.0%	7.3%	7.2%
General Industrials	0.1%	0.0%	0.0%	0.0%	0.0%	0.2%	0.2%	0.2%	0.4%
Health Care Equipment & Services	1.0%	0.8%	0.7%	0.7%	0.6%	0.7%	0.7%	0.6%	0.6%
Household Goods & Home Construction	0.0%	1.2%	1.1%	1.7%	1.5%	1.7%	1.5%	1.7%	1.4%
Industrial Engineering	0.4%	0.5%	0.7%	4.9%	4.2%	3.8%	3.8%	3.7%	4.0%
Industrial Transportation	0.0%	5.9%	6.4%	8.0%	12.4%	10.4%	9.0%	9.3%	9.3%
Media	0.0%	0.0%	0.0%	0.0%	0.4%	0.5%	0.3%	0.3%	0.4%
Oil & Gas Producers	6.5%	4.3%	4.0%	3.1%	2.6%	2.6%	2.5%	2.0%	2.2%
Personal Goods	0.0%	0.0%	0.7%	1.2%	1.4%	4.4%	4.1%	4.0%	4.0%
Pharmaceuticals & Biotechnology	0.2%	0.2%	0.2%	0.2%	0.2%	0.3%	0.3%	0.3%	0.3%
Software & Computer Services	0.1%	0.0%	0.0%	0.0%	0.0%	0.0%	0.0%	0.0%	0.0%
Travel & Leisure	0.0%	0.0%	1.3%	2.1%	3.6%	3.8%	3.3%	3.3%	3.5%
Grand Total	1.4%	1.6%	1.6%	1.9%	2.0%	2.1%	2.1%	2.1%	2.3%

Source: European Commission, JRC-IPTS – R&D Scoreboard 2004–2013.

Table 3. Italy: Inward and outward corporate investments (July 2012 to July 2014)

	Capex (€ million)	Jobs (number)
Inward RDDT	332.1	1,190
Outward RDDT	88.7	474
Inward Manufacturing*	959.5	2,077
Outward Manufacturing	10,715.9	52,613

Source: European Commission, JRC-IPTS elaborated from © fDi Intelligence dataset (Financial Times Ltd 2014).
Includes a new investment of Philip Morris Int. in January 2014 to Italy (Bologna) in the tobacco industry with a CAPEX of EUR 481,353 million and 600 jobs created.
Note: Figures based on download from FDi markets database, 29 September 2014. All types of projects (i.e. new, expansion and co-location) are included.
Legend:
– **Inward RDDT**: Data for companies investing in Italy in design, development and testing, and in research and development activities
– **Outward RDDT:** Data for companies from Italy investing in design, development and testing, and in research and development activities
– **Inward Manufacturing:** Data for companies investing in Italy in manufacturing
– **Outward Manufacturing:** Data for companies from Italy investing in manufacturing

firms in sectors like biotech and chemistry – sectors in which the EU performance is particularly strong compared to the US and Japan. More detailed information on the share of the sectoral R&D investment of Italian firms is provided in Table 2.

In regard to the internationalization of R&D, Italian firms' investment in R&D abroad is marginal, and represents only around 5% of the total private investment in R&D (Evangelista *et al.*, 2002; Cozza, 2010). Also, high R&D intensity exports decreased from 9% of total exports in 2000 to 6.8% of the total in 2010 (Ambrosetti Club, 2013). More recent data (July 2012-July 2014) show an enormous imbalance between inward and outward investment in R&D and related activities, respectively, by foreign and Italian companies (see data on inward and outward investments in Table 3).

Comparing Italian firms in the ranking of top R&D private investors with other top R&D spenders located in selected OECD economies, and by looking at their R&D investment growth rates during the last eight years (2004–2012 – see Figure 2), we can see a growth trend for Italy (both in average and absolute terms), illustrating a similar growth path to other large countries (like the US and Germany). Focusing only on the absolute R&D expenditure in 2012, Italian firms are positioned below firms located in the US, Germany, France and Japan, but above firms located in Spain and the UK. A possible reason for this is the difference in the industrial structure of the countries where the R&D Scoreboard companies are located. Some countries are characterized by the presence of high-R&D intensity sectors, while others have an industrial structure centred on more low-R&D intensity sectors.

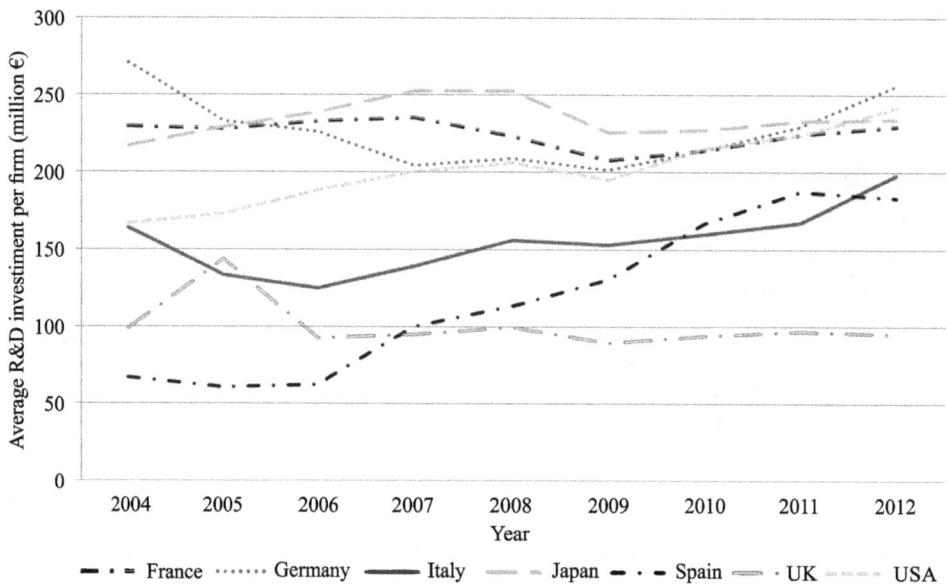

Figure 2: Average R&D investment per firm (absolute values) 2004–2012 – selected countries
Source: European Commission, JRC-IPTS – R&D Scoreboard 2004–2013.

Looking at firm size[10] in 2012, in all the countries analyzed the majority of top R&D-investing firms were medium large or large firms. It is interesting to note that in countries like the UK and the US there is a consistent percentage of small and medium small firms investing significantly in R&D. While the Italian small companies investing in R&D are the smallest ones compared to the seven countries analyzed (see Figure 3).

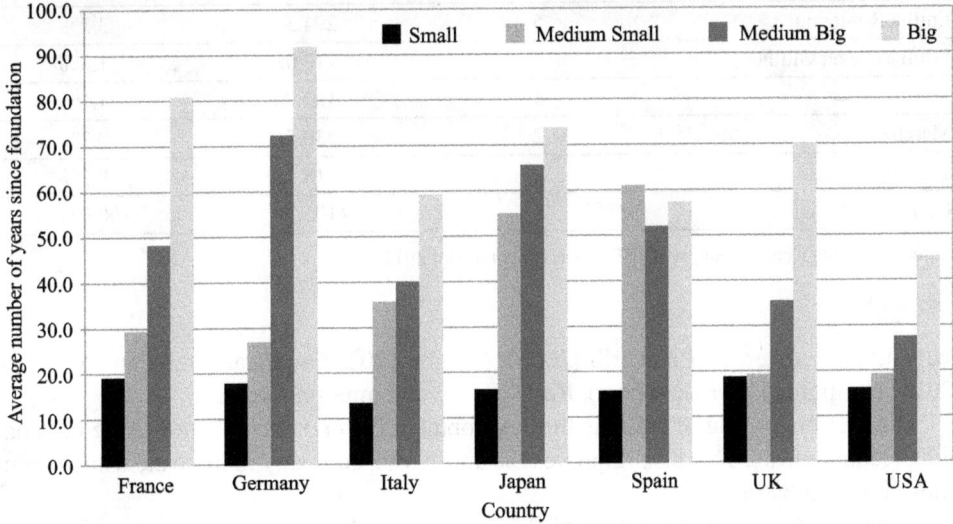

Figure 3. Average year since foundation by firm size top R&D investors 2012 – selected countries
Source: European Commission, JRC-IPTS – R&D Scoreboard 2013.

Comparing firms also from an age point of view, European countries have a higher percentage of "old and big firms" among the top R&D investors compared to the US. Italian firms are positioned in the middle; they are on average (across all size categories) younger than German firms and older than US firms (see Figure 2). There seems to be two different models: Germany and Japan on the one side with many older firms (still spending considerably on R&D), and the UK and the US on the other side, with many young firms operating alongside old firms (thus lowering the average age). The analysis of corporate R&D investment by Italian firms confirms their very high concentration in a few Northern and central regions (see Table 3 for details).

4. Further inputs from literature and analytical considerations

Current literature on the relevance of R&D to a firm's performance is controversial if the firms and their sector/industry heterogeneities (Som, 2011) are not taken fully into

---

[10] In our own definition of groups according to different sizes: <250 = 'Small' (SMEs), <1 000 = 'Medium Small (Quite Large)', <10 000 ='Medium Big' (Large), >10 000 = 'Big' (Largest).

Table 4. Regional distribution of top Italian R&D INVESTORS from the R&D Scoreboard (2012)

Region	Number of firms	R&D 2012 (€ million)	R&D 2012 (as %)
Piedmont	5	4173.5	45.8%
Lazio	9	2931.8	32.2%
Lombardia	17	1436.1	15.8%
Emilia Romagna	5	294.3	3.2%
Friuli Venezia Giulia	2	117.6	1.3%
Veneto	4	102.7	1.1%
Marche	2	30.5	0.3%
Tuscany	2	18.7	0.2%
Grand Total	46	9105.2	100.0%

Source: European Commission, JRC-IPTS – R&D Scoreboard 2013.

account[11]. However, as Bosworth (2005), Vaughn (2014) and Catozzella and Vivarelli (2014) highlighted (among others), R&D has several important roles.

The first major role of R&D is the development of fundamental knowledge or "enabling technologies". This also improves the ability of a company to innovate using inventions produced by others.

The second important function of R&D is to provide support to manufacturing, customers, and business management. R&D organizations are often the repositories of technical know-how.

The third major function of R&D is to develop and implement new technologies.

In reality, all of these R&D roles are interrelated. R&D pooled (e.g. from abroad) could be at least as important for innovation and productivity as a company's own R&D. Achieving the right balance of the different R&D roles is critical to the success of companies.

But, why should policy-makers aim at more R&D in general, and in Italy in particular? Given the role played by competitive innovation-led enterprises in the economy (i.e. the return in terms of economic and social benefits), policy initiatives typically do not aim at raising the level of private R&D per se, but aim at making R&D investment more effective and at overcoming possible barriers to innovation, and hence aim to promote economic and social prosperity by achieving a knowledge-intensive economy and society (Pessoa, 2007; Jones and Williams, 1998).

Investigating Italy, both Bugamelli *et al.* (2012) and Istat (2012a) argued that, when comparing BERD within the EU by taking into account the industrial structure – in terms of both sectoral breakdown and average size – of each Member State, Italian firms do not actually underperform in undertaking R&D activities vis-à-vis other EU businesses. This would suggest that the low level of R&D investment by Italian businesses is consistent

---

[11] See footnote 2.

with the low needs for innovation projects usually undertaken by a limited number of the Italian enterprise[12].

However, such arguments do not contradict, but on the contrary reinforce, the need for policy intervention to promote change of the Italian structure, by among other things, increasing the number and size of R&D performers. As shown by other benchmarking countries performing much better in terms of business R&D investments and competitiveness (such as Germany), there is a crucial contribution of R&D performing SMEs (which hold the capacity to growth) and of large companies operating in medium-high and high R&D intensive sectors (able to shift market/sector segmentation).

In sum, this is why Italian policy makers should aim at having more "R&D-related innovation" and not mainly (only) base companies' competitiveness and economic growth on "non-R&D-based innovation". In fact, evidence shows that that the proportion of corporate sales revenues allocated to commercially oriented R&D is one of the principal indicators (if not the main one) of subsequent sales growth performance relative to competition over 5–10 year periods (Franko, 1989)[13].

The specific characteristics of the Italian firms' demographics described earlier and of the industrial structure (i.e. the specialization in traditional and lower R&D intensity sectors), is accompanied by (and in great part due to) exogenous business environment conditions, which hardly favour the emergence and growth of R&D-intensive firms. Such an environment is characterized by difficulties in accessing financial sources for R&D (e.g. public subsidies, venture capital and private equity), together with difficult market conditions (finance[14], employment, reduced demand), and an unfavourable institutional and regulatory framework[15] for business innovation (Bugamelli *et al.* 2012; ERAWATCH Report 2013; Moncada-Paternò-Castello *et al.*, 2014). As some authors point out, part of the reason why there is a traditional low level of R&D investment in R&D by enterprise could be due to the low offer of scientific and technical skills by the Italian labour market (Rossi, 2014).

In such circumstances, unless change is implemented, the Italian productive system will continue to face ever greater difficulties, both to compete globally with producers based in countries with low labour costs and to find and defend new market niches (Moncada-Paternò-Castello *et al.*, 2006).

In fact, reversing its current private R&D investment path can help Italy to succeed further in competing globally[16]. The overall system of innovating without

---

[12] According to ISTAT, only 31.5% of the Italian firms with 10 or more employees have introduced at least one product or process innovation between 2008 and 2010 (ISTAT, 2012a).
[13] His study summarized the major changes over the period 1960–86 in the shares of world markets of the world's leading American, European and Asian corporations based in 15 major industries.
[14] Between 2012 and 2013, loans for business decreased in Italy by 4.6%. Since 2007, the percentage of accounts uncollectible tripled, reaching 22%. About a third of company failures are due to the lack of loans for business rather than the lack of competitiveness (European Commission, October 2013). This is a symptom of the long overdue problems of access to finance, rather than more recent problems derived from the 2008–9 crisis.http://europa.eu/rapid/press-release_MEMO-13–909_en.htm.
[15] Firms in Italy face the highest fiscal burden in Europe, 65.8% of revenues (PWC/World Bank, 2014).
[16] Italy in the Global Competitiveness Index 2014–2015 is ranked 49th overall (out of 144 countries) – 106th for firm-level technology absorption, 39th for innovation capacity and 35th for firms' spending on the R&D sub-indexes (World Economic Forum, 2014).

R&D[17] is not sustainable in the long run, especially if Italian firms only favour innovation buy-ins (i.e. firms' absorption of R&D and innovations done by others, e.g. in the textile industry). The strategy for moving forward is thus either to rely on a continuous race of comparative price advantages via cost reductions and productivity increases in order to increase the export of low-/medium-tech goods and services, or to increase the capacity of competing in knowledge intensive sectors. While the first strategy has serious limits in a globalized economy and presents serious risks of internal demand depression and rising inequalities in income, the second one offers the possibility to harvest higher margins for business and broader societal benefits.

Appropriate framework conditions and adequate support should therefore be established to favour business R&D investments in knowledge intensive sectors, both from existing companies (of all sizes) and from emerging new ones. Companies in medium- and low-R&D intensity sectors would also benefit from the establishment of an adequate business environment that favours the absorption of the R&D results produced in other sectors.

In this aspect, Italy could learn from both the German and the US models: in Germany, many large and old firms have been able to develop and absorb R&D and technology, and to diversify and/or shift dramatically their core business towards more knowledge intensive activities. This has allowed many firms to survive and grow, even during the latest financial and economic downturn, e.g. Siemens. In the US, there is an outstanding dynamics of the creation and destruction of firms, many of them in high-tech sectors (the US has a very large base of high-R&D performing SMEs). This has resulted in the emergence in just a few years of many global leaders in new knowledge-intensive sectors (e.g. Google and Facebook). This phenomenon is accompanied in the US by a number of large traditional companies behaving similarly to their German counterparts.

According to a recent study by Bonaccorsi and Perani (2014), in Italy, there are a disproportionally higher number of *occasional* corporate R&D investors versus the number of continuous/*systematic* ones (i.e. firms performing R&D for at least three consecutive years). The less frequent (*occasional*) corporate R&D performers are small firms and are usually attempting to play catch up in a process which is most likely influenced by exogenous factors (external sources of funding, options for tax reliefs, low cost of R&D inputs, etc.) and features a remarkable cyclicality. Furthermore, the same authors argue that most R&D support policies in Italy have actually reinforced the R&D infrastructures of large and persistent performers (those which would have invested in R&D anyway), largely neglecting the need to reduce the fixed costs which make it difficult for *occasional* performers (mostly small firms) to develop their projects on a continuous basis.

---

[17] As noted in the past by Colombo and Lanzavecchia (1996), some Italian economic actors are reluctant to invest in fields with a low likelihood of the creation and growth of a considerable number of new Italian firms. However, doing so could lead to them investing money in research more useful for foreign firms than for Italian ones.

5. Implications for policy

Malerba (1993) already pointed out the "dual" nature of the Italian industrial system, with a small set of big firms capable of performing R&D and a large group of small firms not investing in R&D. The key question then was: what could policy-makers do to favour an upturn of this structural situation?

The political target should be to improve the competitiveness of Italian enterprises by fostering more business R&D-related innovation, together with continuing to develop firms' capacity to innovate by absorbing R&D/innovation done externally (e.g. by performers adopting R&D *à la carte*), and further strengthening firms' already good performance in non-R&D-based innovation[18]. This would result in an "innovation policy strategy" which would include specific measures to support the R&D efforts of enterprises that really need it, in the presence of market failures.

If we look at national policies, Italian government funding of business R&D has been characterized by very low figures compared to its EU competitors. This has been aggravated by very strong cuts in the years 2006–11: a decrease of almost 50% in government support through direct funding and from tax incentives (Figure 4)[19].

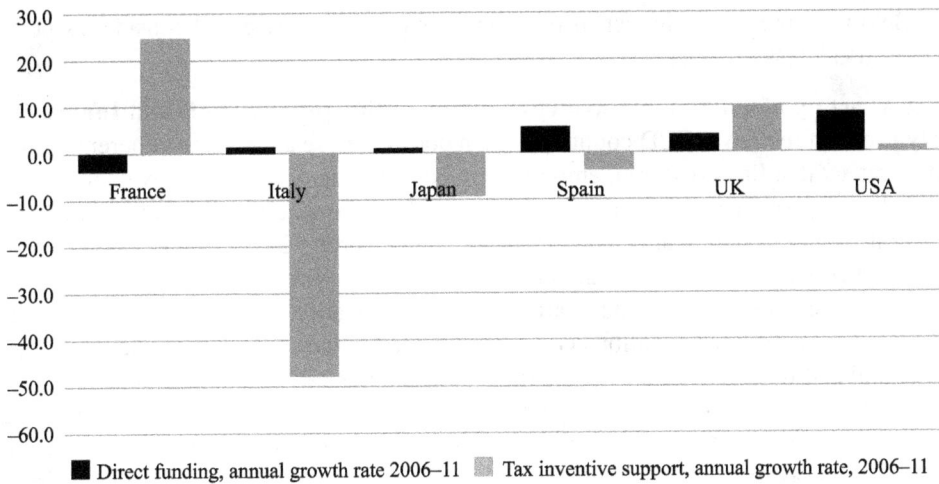

■ Direct funding, annual growth rate 2006–11 ▨ Tax inventive support, annual growth rate, 2006–11

Figure 4: Change in government support for business R&D through direct funding and tax incentives, 2006–11 (annualized growth rates)
Source: OECD 2013.

This calls for a stronger commitment from the central government to provide more support to the funding of research and innovation, as a well-recognized growth-enhancing

---

[18] Italy tends to perform better on *indicators* of non-R&D-based innovation. For example, it leads in design (OECD, 2012).
[19] According to OECD (2013), there is a lack of a long-term strategy on tax credits for business R&D incentives in Italy. In fact tax credits for 2007–2009 had come to an end in 2011, but the new exercise has not yet been launched.

public investment (Annual growth survey 2014, European Commission, 2013d). In this advocated governmental undertaking, full care should be given to the efficiency and effectiveness (quality) of the investment in R&I (European Commission, 2014e).

However, much more than just funding is needed to address the weaknesses of the national research and innovation system in Italy, including urgently addressing some of the areas where priority actions are needed most, as largely highlighted by the most relevant and recent work of the European Commission[20], namely, human capital; R&D intensity and specialization of firms; size distribution of firms; territorial inequalities; and institutional and framework conditions. These areas cover a broad spectrum of structural aspects and require a comprehensive policy mix.

In this context, and based on the previous analysis, we point to a series of specific priority policy actions aimed at stimulating the level of business R&D investment, both through the broadening of the population of R&D investing firms and a deepening of the efforts of the existing ones. These suggestions should be modulated according to more specific innovation and socio-economic targets (e.g. finding a balance between R&D-related and non-R&D-related innovation; promoting the green economy) and should be fine-tuned to tackle the actual specificities of the Italian economic context and its R&D-led innovation difficulties.

Below we present a number of recommendations that Italy could consider as policy actions to address the R&I issues.

5A. Set up of a long-term strategy for stimulating private R&D and Innovation. Italy is one of the few OECD countries which does not have a clear and coherent innovation strategy that links research, employment, education and industrial development policies. The implementation of such a strategy should be done: under the framework of the relevant European policy agenda, namely the broad Europe 2020 strategy[21] for employment and growth, by the establishment of a European Research Area, with a commitment to the European research and innovation agenda (Innovation Union), and by implementation of the Smart Specialization concept established in the context of the new European Structural and Investment Funds[22]. Some good examples can be found in other countries (e.g. in Germany, the "High-tech strategy"; or in The Netherlands, the so-called Dutch top-sectors policy). Possible strategic directions to consider are to focus on key sectors, on job skills (availability and needs)[23] and on geographical areas to leverage territorial inequalities (e.g. to look at lessons from the success of *Silicon Valley* or the failure of *Etna*

---

[20] ERAWATCH Country Report 2013 (European Commission 2014a), 2013 Small Business Act Fact Sheet – Italy (European Commission, 2013b); Research and Innovation Performance in EU Member States and Associated Countries (European Commission, 2013c); Report on "Market Reforms at Work" – Italy (European Commission 2014d).

[21] "Horizon 2020 Italia" already connects the Italian strategy to the thematic priorities (Societal Challenges) of H2020. The weak side is its implementation. https://www.researchitaly.it/uploads/50/HIT2020.pdf.

[22] http://ec.europa.eu/research/regions/index_smart.

[23] Avoiding shortage of skills and improving research quality of research for increasing graduates' employability (Royal Netherlands Academy of Arts and Sciences, 2013; Ciriaci and Muscio, 2014), thus satisfying the needs of firms.

Valley). Overall, it is suggested to set up a stronger quality assessment (*ex ante* and *ex post*) framework for R&I policy (e.g. in Finland, "Tekes' practice").

5B. Provide support for the R&D-led growth of SMEs. Direct and indirect incentives for doing R&D in high-tech and medium high-tech sectors should be put in place, *especially for small medium and young firms* (e.g. a mix of tax exemptions for R&D and a *SBIR*[24](US)-like programme for Italian innovative SMEs). Coordination and better synergy between regional, national and transnational programmes, including EU programmes, and funding should be ensured. There is also a need to go beyond the actual measures (e.g. "Decreto Crescita 2.0"[25]) to support innovative SMEs, e.g. by focusing on "industrial" firms, and favouring cooperation between SMEs in R&D investment. Under this framework, it would be prudent to launch a pilot test[26], e.g. to provide 5–10% tax credits for investment in R&D (with a generous ceiling for the maximum amount of investment) implemented in house by SMEs or in cooperation with other innovative SMEs in one or two sectors of economic activities. Help could also be provided to Italian SMEs to develop their own R&D/technological capacity by involving large national and foreign direct investments from multinational companies, e.g. by using an instrument similar to *The Irish National Linkage Programme*[27]. Finally, SMEs could be provided with automatic access to funding: with *ex post* evaluation implemented to check for the proper use of the incentive received[28].

5C. Improve bilateral R&D and innovation activities and the capacity for technology and knowledge transfer between Public Research Organizations (PROs)/universities and firms,[29]and also improve firms' R&D absorption capacity. This would imply putting in place company tax credits for investment in R&D projects performed by universities and PROs, with a requirement that firms' involvement must include a set minimum percentage of research activities performed by PRO or universities[30] – or, as an alternative, to transfer a percentage of the PRO/universities budget to firms, as "R&D Vouchers" (like the European Commission's ICT Vouchers scheme for SMEs, or the R&D Vouchers scheme in The Netherlands). Also, there should be better access to improved public R&D infrastructure and the creation of shared platforms for technology transfer, including accompanying support measures, such as extending the number of internships in firms by graduates and post-doctorates.

5D. Improve job market flexibility for scientists. Some initiatives have already been put in place by the Italian government; however, these are hampered by limitations in the resources available and in the temporary nature of the jobs offered (European Commission, 2014a).

---

[24] Small Business Innovation Research (SBIR) programhttp://www.sbir.gov/about/about-sbir.
[25] Full text available (in Italian) athttp://www.gazzettaufficiale.it.
[26] See Moncada-Paternò-Castello (2011).
[27] For a short description, see OECD and The Word Bank (2014), Box 2.1, page 39.
[28] Often in large R&D support programmes, where project proposals need months to be evaluated (*ex ante*) and payments need years to be finalized, we hardly find any SMEs applicants.
[29] See also *XI Netval Report* (2014);Ambrosetti Club (2013); and Runiewicz-Wardyn (2013).
[30] Or vice versa: as in the "Plan Estatal de Investigación Científica y Técnica y de Innovación 2013–2016" in Spain.

5E. Stimulate demand-driven innovation. This concerns policy initiatives such as public Pre-Commercial Procurement (PCP) and Public Procurement of Innovation (PPI)[31], and e-governance.

5F. Improve the legal framework, strengthen the rule of law, reduce the bureaucratic burden and improve government effectiveness. There is a considerable reform work needed to be implemented in Italy, i.e. administrative simplification (including procedures to set up start-ups), towards achieving continuous improvement in various areas to create the right environment for R&I businesses to succeed, such as the reduction of administrative costs, lowering the minimum capital requirements for limited liability companies, tempering the insolvency procedures, further simplification of the IPR system, and strengthening the evaluation system for research and innovation projects and policy measures[32]. A recent study shows that higher bureaucratic barriers are not only associated with lower business entry dynamics (i.e. business birth rate) in Italy, but also estimates that the implementation of the reforms in Italy can have a significant positive impact on business entry dynamics (European Commission, 2014e).

5G. Address territorial inequalities of public support towards private R&D investment. A positive shift towards rebalancing present territorial inequalities in the Italian polarized economic structure – also taking into account the asymmetries with regards to the different capabilities of the local stakeholders – could also be realized by the efficient investment in private R&D and innovation in those Italian regions which do not feature on the high-intensity knowledge map and in which currently businesses hardly benefit from public support.

The aforementioned policy actions[33] in points A to F could, in part, endorse such a territorial scope and convergence into regional/local R&D and innovation policies. One of the ways to achieve this that can certainly be promoted here is the full exploitation of opportunities available under the European regional development funds (ERDF)[34], through e.g. the *Smart Specialization* approach (European Commission, 2014f)[35].

6. Conclusions

In conclusion, from the available evidence on business R&D investments in Italy, both from official statistics and from the company data of the top R&D investors, as well as from

---

[31] In 2012, Italy assigned more than €150 million to pre-commercial procurement. It will be deployed in Southern Italy with the support of structural funds (European Commission, *ERAWATCH* Report, 2014a). Moreover, the higher risks related to these purchases are covered by a special risk-sharing facility established in cooperation with the European Investment Bank (European Commission, 2014a).

[32] See also Gros, 2011, Veugelers 2014, European Commission 2013c, and 2014e.

[33] Also, here the key objectives of policies to support R&D and innovation at the regional level have to be made explicit and, more importantly, have to be consistent with the specific context in which the resources are going to be spent. The quality (efficiency and effectiveness) of policy intervention has to be assured.

[34] For example, it encompasses "Strengthening research, technological development and innovation" or "Enhancing the competitiveness of small and medium-sized enterprises" as objectives to deliver EU 2020.

[35] See also Smart Specialization Platform: http://s3platform.jrc.ec.europa.eu/home.

recent literature, we can see that there has been little change over the last decade in the structural features and trends, which have led to low levels of R&D investment and business dynamics of Italian enterprises. There is therefore a critical need to step up public intervention to help promote a shift towards an industrial structure more amenable for a high level of activity in high-tech sectors, better capacity for innovation absorption from other sectors, and better framework conditions to allow the business sector and society at large to fully benefit from a more knowledge-based economy.

Acknowledgements

We are grateful to M. Dosso, F. Hervas, H. Hernandez, G. La Placa and A. Tübke (all from the European Commission, Joint Research Centre); D. Ciriaci (European Commission, Directorate-General for Economics and Financial Affairs) and G. Perani (The Italian National Institute for Statistics – Istat) for their highly valuable inputs, comments and suggestions to the previous versions of the present document. We would also like to thank the members of the Action Institute's Innovation task force who inspired the idea of this paper.

References

Action Institute (2013), "L'ecosistemadell'Innovazione in Italia" – Bozza; dicembre 2013.

Ambrosetti Club (2013), L'Ecosistema per l'innovazione: quali strade per la crescita delle imprese e del Paese – The European House, Technology Forum 2013.

Antonelli, C., Crespi, F. (2013), The "Matthew effect" in R&D public subsidies: The Italian evidence. "Technological Forecasting and Social Change" Vol. 80 (2013) 1523–1534.

Audretsch, D. B., Santarelli, E., Vivarelli, M. (1999), Start-up size and industrial dynamics: some evidence from Italian manufacturing. "International Journal of Industrial Organization", 17(7), 965–983.

Bonaccorsi, A., Perani, G. (2014), Investing in R&D in Italy: trends and firms' strategies, 2001–2010. "Journal of Economics and Industrial Policy" 3/2014, pp. 65–107. DOI: 10.3280/POLI2014–003004.

Bosworth, D. L. (2005), Determinants of firms performance, Manchester: Manchester University.

Bugamelli, M., Cannari, L., Lotti, F., Magri, S. (2012), The Innovation Gap of Italy's Production System: Roots and Possible Solutions. "Bank of Italy Occasional Paper" 121 (2012).

Catozzella, A., Vivarelli, M. (2014), The Catalysing Role of In-House R&D in Fostering Complementarity Among Innovative Inputs. "Industry and Innovation"(ahead-of-print), 1–18.

Cerulli, G., Potí, B. (2012), Evaluating the robustness of the effect of public subsidies on firms R&D: An application to Italy. "Journal of Applied Economics". Vol XV, No. 2 (November 2012), 287–320.

Ciriaci, D., Muscio, A. (2014), University Choice, Research Quality and Graduates' Employability: evidence from Italian national survey data – European Educational Research Journal Vol. 13, No. 2, 2014.

Colombo, U., Lanzavecchia, G. (1996), L'industria in Italia: innovazione senza ricerca, in «Nuova CiviltàdelleMacchine», vol. XIV, n. 3–4, pp. 96–121.

Colombo, M. G., Grilli, L. (2010), On growth drivers of high-tech start-ups: Exploring the role of founders' human capital and venture capital. "Journal of Business Venturing", 25(6), 610–626.

Cozza, C. (2010), *Measuring the internationalisation of EU corporate R&D: a novel complementary use of statistical sources*. European Commission, *JRC Scientific and Technical Reports, Luxembourg*. EUR 24564 EN.

European Commission (2003), *Growth paths of technology-based companies in life sciences and information technology* – Innovation papers No. 32, EUR 17054.

European Commission (2004–2013), *The European Industrial R&D Investment Scoreboard* – European Commission.

European Commission (2013a), *The 2013 EU Industrial R&D Investment Scoreboard* – European Commission.

European Commission (2013b), *2013 SBA Fact Sheet Report* – Italy. Directorate-General for Enterprise and Industry, Brussels, 21 Nov. 2013 ec.europa.eu/enterprise/policies/sme/.../italy_en.pdf.

European Commission (2013c), *Research and Innovation Performance in EU Member States and Associated Countries – Innovation Union Progress at country level*.

European Commission (2013d), *Annual Growth Survey 2014* – Communication from the Commission – COM(2013) 800 final, Brussels, 13.11.2013.

European Commission (2014a), *ERAWATCH Country Report 2013: Italy*, 2014 by L. Nascia and M. Pianta.

European Commission (2014b), *State of the Innovation Union: Taking stock 2010–2014* – Report (2014).

European Commission (2014c), *Reindustrialising Europe Member States' Competitiveness Report 2014*, 2014.

European Commission (2014d), *Report on "Market Reforms at Work" – Italy, Spain, Portugal and Greece* – European Economy series, No. 5/2014.

European Commission (2014e), *Research and innovation as sources of renewed growth* – Communication from the Commission COM(2014) 339 final. Brussels, 10.6.2014.

European Commission (2014f), *Enabling synergies between European Structural and Investment Funds, Horizon 2020 and other research, innovation and competitiveness-related Union programmes, Guidance for policy-makers and implementing bodies* – European Commission, Directorate-General for Regional and Urban policy.

Evangelista, R., Iammarino, S., Mastrostefano, V., Silvani, A. (2002), Looking for Regional Systems of Innovation: Evidence from the Italian Innovation Survey, *Regional Studies* 36(2), 173–86.

Franko, L. G. (1989). Global corporate competition: Who's winning, who's losing, and the R&D factor as one reason why. *Strategic Management Journal, 10*(5), 449–474.

Gros, D. (2011), *What is Holding Italy back?* – Centre for European Policy Studies. Brussels, Nov. 2011.

Hall, B., Mairesse, J., Mohnen, P. (2010), *Measuring the returns of R&D*. In: B. Hall, & N. Rosenberg, "Handbook on Economics of Innovation" (Vol. 2). Elsevier.

Harrison, R., Jaumandreu, J., Mairesse, J., Peters, B. (2014), *Does innovation stimulate employment? A firm-level analysis using comparable micro-data from four European countries.* "International Journal of Industrial Organization", *35*, 29–43.

Kumbhakar, S. C., Ortega-Argilés, R., Potters, L., Vivarelli, M., Voigt, P. (2012), *Corporate R&D and firm efficiency: evidence from Europe's top R&D investors.* "Journal of Productivity Analysis", 37(2), 125–140.

ISTAT (2012a) Statistica report Anni 2008–2010 L'innovazione nelle imprese 07/11/2012.

ISTAT (2012b) Statistica report Anno 2010 La struttura e competitività del sistema delle imprese industriali e dei servizi 29/10/2012.

ISTAT (2014) Annual Report – The state of the Nation. Rome, 28 May 2014.

Jones C. I., Williams J. C., (1998), *Measuring The Social Return To R&D,* "The Quarterly Journal of Economics", 113, 1119–1135.

Mairesse, J., Mohnen, P. (2005), The Importance of R&D for Innovation: A Reassessment Using French Survey Data, *The Journal of Technology Transfer*, Springer, vol. 30(2_2), pages 183–197, 01.

Malerba F. (1993), *The National System of Innovation: Italy*, [in:] R. Nelson, *National Innovation Systems: A Comparative Analysis*, New York, Oxford University Press.

Moncada-Paternò-Castello, P., Ciupagea, C., Piccaluga, A. (2006), Industrial innovation in Italy: the persistence of a model 'without R&D'?, *L'Industria – Journal of Industrial Economics* – Vol. 03; 2006.

Moncada-Paternò-Castello, P. (2011), "Companies' growth in the EU: What is research and innovation policy's role?", [in:] *IPTS Working Papers on Corporate R&D and Innovation* series, European Commission – Scientific and Technical Research series; July 2011.

Moncada-Paternò-Castello, P., Vezzani, A., Hervás, F., Montresor, S. (2014), *Financing R&D and innovation for Corporate Growth: What new evidence should policy-makers know? Policy Brief*, European Commission EUR 26272 EN – Joint Research Centre – Institute for Prospective Technological Studies – Scientific and Technical Research series – Luxembourg: Publications Office of the European Union, January 2014.

Netval (2014) – XI Report by A. Bax, S. Corrieri, C. Daniele, L. Guarnieri, R. Parente, A. Piccaluga, A. Ramacciotti, R. Tiezzi (2014), *Unire i puntini per completare il disegno dell'Innovazione*, 2014.

OECD (2012), Science, Technology and Industry Outlook 2012; IV.10, pp 328–331, Paris 2012.

OECD and The Word Bank (2014), *Making Innovation Policy Work – Learning from Experimentation*.

Pagano, P. Schivardi, F. (2003), Firm size distribution and growth; *Scandinavian Journal of Economics*, Wiley Blackwell, vol. 105(2), pages 255–274, 06.

Pessoa, A. (2007), "Innovation and Economic Growth: What is the actual importance of R&D?", FEP Working Papers 254, Universidade do Porto, Faculdade de Economia do Porto.

PwC and The World Bank (2014), *Paying Taxes 2014: The global picture – A comparison of tax systems in 189 economies worldwide* – Report; http://www.pwc.com/gx/en/paying-taxes/assets/pwc-paying-taxes-2014.pdf.

Royal Netherlands Academy of Arts and Sciences (2013), Public knowledge investments and the value of science. Report by 'Value of Research Committee'; Oct. 2013 https://www.knaw.nl/shared/resources/actueel/publicaties/pdf/summary).

Rossi, S. (2014), *L'innovazione nelle imprese italiane*, Intervento del Direttore Generale della Banca d'Italia alla Fondazione Luigi Einaudi onlus – Torino, 15 October 2014.

Runiewicz-Wardyn, M. (2013), *Knowledge Flows, Technological Change and Regional Growth in the European Union*. Contribution to economics (Book); Springer, September 2013.

Som, O. (2011), *Innovation without R&D*. Springer Gabler Publisher, Düsseldorf, 2011.

Vaughn, C. (2014), *Innovation and R&D: A balanced package of research and development is a key component in the success of companies*, "Chemical & Engineering News," 92(24), June 2014 http://pubs.acc.org/cen/125th/pdf/7913vaughn.txt.pdf.

Veugelers, R. (2014), *Public R&D budgets for smart fiscal consolidation* – Draft paper prepared for the second annual SMPATIC Conference – The Hague, 2–4 April, 2014.

World Economic Forum (2014), *The Global Competitiveness Report 2014–2015* -http://reports.weforum.org/global-competitiveness-report-2014–2015.

Chapter III

Sustainable Development: Facing Major Environmental Challenges of Poland and the EU

Tomasz Winnicki

Separation Processes in Solving Strategic Environmental Problems

1. Introduction

Two – air and water – out of three components of biosphere were for a long time treated as *free environmental values*. Only the third – land – including forests, arable land and other areas of pedosphere were either privately or state owned. The situation changed with growing anthropogenic impact on atmosphere and hydrosphere – the increasing pollution of both spheres.

Air and water became important media not only in everyday life, but also in all kinds of human activities from agriculture through municipal to industrial activities and other areas such as communication. For animals and plants to survive, as well as to conduct the above mentioned activities, it appeared necessary to establish air and water environmental standards and to charge adequate fees and penalties for both: using these natural components and discharging pollutants to the ambient environment. The same rules apply to the third natural component – the earth.

The more intruding became the man in his activities oriented at exploiting the natural components the more sophisticated tools were required to prevent damage in the natural environment and to repair that which already occurred. That is the origin of the environmental engineering.

The physical state of natural components of biosphere determines their mobility, as well as the mobility of natural and artificial particles in each of them. It is obvious that this mobility increases from gas through liquid to the solid state. Technical problems dealing with controlling man-made contaminants go in the same sequence and direction.

Another general and fully understandable rule is that the more complex any composition is, the more technology and energy is required to isolate a certain particle of physical or chemical nature, both to prevent its accumulation in the natural component and to enable its recycling or recovery.

To fulfil the above mentioned and some other goals environmental engineering uses a variety of techniques of physical, chemical and biological nature, which can be classified in four groups relating to the following stages of action: (1) preventing – prophylactic – undertaking any predictable action to avoid generation of pollutants; (2) employing a technology with separation tools in order to isolate and recycle or recover valuable or harmful species as early as possible; (3) implementing *end-of-the-pipe* technologies – installing adequate controlling devices before exhausting gases to the ambient air or discharging sewage to the surface water or separating and reworking separate fractions in solid wastes; (4) repairing unavoidable damage which already occurred using various remediation and re-cultivation techniques, especially in land exploitation.

The same ideology and technical approaches refer to all three natural components. While the air is volatile and its contaminants – such as dust particulates – are easy to capture by a variety of invented filters and the components of solid wastes on the contrary are so immobile that quite simple physical segregation methods can be applied; the liquid state requires a number of very complicated and sophisticated separation processes and operations. The most important and widely implemented are active bed filtrations: catalytic filtration, sorption and ion exchange, as well as membrane processes: micro-, ultra- & nano-filtration and reverse osmosis. The latter successfully compete with formerly widely used thermal methods of separation solvent (water) from mostly inorganic and some organic solids.

Separation technology allows to carry out such important technical tasks as: (1) treatment of water to make it potable or process-applicable; (2) water recovery & recycling at the exit from technological process; (3) wastewater treatment for recycling of valuable or abatement of harmful substances; (4) within-technology separation & recycling of substances; (5) abatement of harmful substances from wastewater; (6) desalination of sea water & brackish water.

Two most important separation groups of processes – active bed filtration and membrane operations as well as some major strategic applications will be presented.

2. Active Bed Filtration

Filtration has been used for centuries to isolate suspended matter from liquids. Nowadays, the filtration on sand-bed or other inert filling remains the most common operation in water and wastewater treatment.

The scheme of loading of a filtration bed is shown (in four stages) in Figure 1. Dots in the column present a volume of the bed already exhausted – completely loaded – the bottom line shows the border between upper (partly loaded) and lower (completely free of charge) parts of the bed. A *breaking point* (column three) indicates that the first drop of isolated matter appears on the exit. From now on it is the operator's decision when to stop charging the bed, which depends on outlet purity requirements. The last column shows the state of complete exhaustion of the bed capacity. Such a state could be accepted

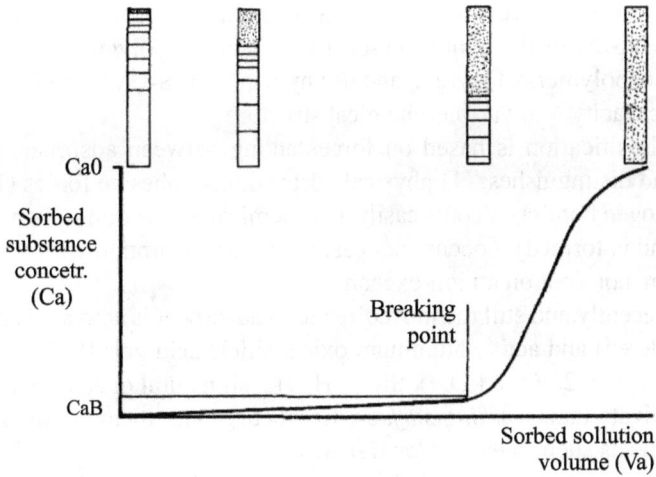

Figure 1. Four stages of loading the column filtration bed

when the operation is run in a multi-column system and another (regenerated) column is connected-in-series with the first (the 4th in the figure) to continue the abatement process.

Connection of single units (columns) into a system of the above mentioned *in-series* compositions is applied when the improvement of quality (purity) is expected, while a parallel connection provides increase of yield. The same rule is in force for membrane systems. See also two options of running the softening operation on stationary beds in Figure 6.

Sorption is a term covering two processes – adsorption – phenomenon of capturing particles penetrating from inside of one of the neighbouring (liquid) phases to the surface of the other (solid), and absorption – penetration of the components of the liquid phase into the entire mass (profile) of the second phase. Other important terms connected with the process are: adsorbent – a solid phase on which the adsorption occurs, and adsorbate – the substance which is left after the completed adsorption. The mechanism of the process is presented in Figure 2 on the example of sorption on/in the soil particle.

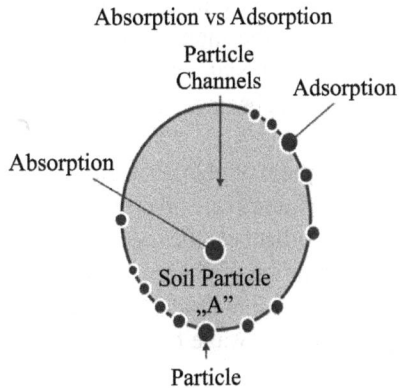

Figure 2. Model of adsorption/absorption processes

According to Kisielev's classification of sorbents, an interaction between a sorbate and a sorbent allows to divide them into: (1) specific – mainly copolymers with ester-binds, (2) non-specific – copolymers of styrene and divinylbenzene (S-DVB) and (3) sorbents with ion-exchange capacity – of various chemical structure.

Another classification is based on forces acting between adsorbate and adsorbent on interface and distinguishes: (1) physical adsorption – cohesive forces (*Van der Waals*, as well as hydrogen bonds) – occurs easily, (2) chemical adsorption – chemical compound (an atomic bond is formed) – occurs not easily and (3) adsorption with a parallel ion-exchange phenomenon (not on an ion-exchange resin).

The most recently and still the most often used adsorbent is activated carbon (grained, granular, powdered) and active aluminum oxide, silicic acid gels ($SiO_2 \cdot nH_2O$), aluminosilicate (zeolites – $Me2/nO \cdot Al_2O_3 \cdot x \, SiO_2 \cdot yH_2O$) – all natural or semi-natural – specially prepared to activate their *working surface.* Competing with them are organic, polymeric – synthetic sorbents such as *molecular sieves.*

Adsorption processes are applied in environmental engineering to carry out such important tasks as: (i) treatment of surface water, (ii) water recovery from waste following biological treatment, (iii) removal of micro-pollutants from water and wastewater, (iv) recovery of valuable components from wastewater, (v) abatement of nitrogen and sulphur oxides from spent gases, (vi) biological sewage treatment with biosorption.

All the above mentioned forms of activated carbons used to be applied in filtration beds to purify water or wastewater (sewage). Those beds can work in multi-layer filters or as separate filters. Adsorption occurs in dynamic conditions in systems with stationary (see Figure 3) or mobile beds. In each option the regeneration of a bed is necessary.

Sorption on activated carbons seems to be quite expensive because their regeneration requires steam and appropriate reactivation afterwards – therefore they are often used only one time and burned. Polymeric sorbents substituting activated carbons are easily regenerated using salt solution or organic solvents in a closed circle, which allows the recovery of a valuable solvent and using the sorbent many times.

Polymeric sorbents are usually porous, cross-linked copolymers of mono- and divinyl monomers synthesized in a form of beds of 0.1 to 2 mm diameter, insoluble and resistant up to 250°C. Polymeric sorbent resin presents micro-gels and their agglomerates with free spaces – pores among them. Their porous structure, size of pores and a specific surface depend on the manner of polymerization. Polymeric sorbents are applied for sorption from gaseous state or from solvents. In both cases the *principle of similarity* takes place – non-polar substances such as benzene are easily sorbed on non-polar, non-specific sorbents (S-DVB).

Sorption of phenols from water or sewage containing colloid suspension can by carried out on a large scale on columns filled with such a non-specific sorbent as Amberlite XAD-4. The sorbent can be regenerated using acetone or alcohol in a closed cycle. The multifold concentration of phenol can be obtained. In treating petrochemical wastes containing phenols an alkaline (NaOH) regeneration was used and residues were burned, buried or sent to the local sewage treatment plant.

3. Ion Exchange Processes and Operations

Ion exchange is an equilibrium reaction to substitute ions of functional groups in natural minerals or organic synthetic compounds usually of polymeric structure by ions of the same charge from the solution. Identically to sorption also some ion exchange processes could be found in nature as well as ion-exchangers among minerals such as zeolites. But, contrary to sorbents, where semi-natural activated carbon still plays a big role, mineral ion exchangers have a very limited applicability mainly due to their low exchange capacity. They had been very largely substituted – as it has already been mentioned – by synthetic polymeric resins with ionic groups. In a classic (conventional) deionization by ion exchange two types of resins of opposite charge are in use – cation-exchangers (see Figure 3) and anion-exchangers.

A model can be constructed with a co-polymer built of two monomers – styrene (vinylbenzene) and divinylbenzene (DVB as crosslinking agent). Introduction of ionic groups – cationic or anionic – to the co-polymer converts the resin into an adequate ion-exchanger. The higher the share of DVB in the co-polymer, the more rigid is the polymeric structure which is less accessible by ionic groups. The higher number of ionic groups, the more swollen and hydrophilic the resin becomes.

Curvy lines on Figure 3 represent a co-polymer matrix; circles with minus-charge anionic groups fixed to the polymeric skeleton and circles with plus-charge mobile cations to be exchanged for other cations from the ambient solution.

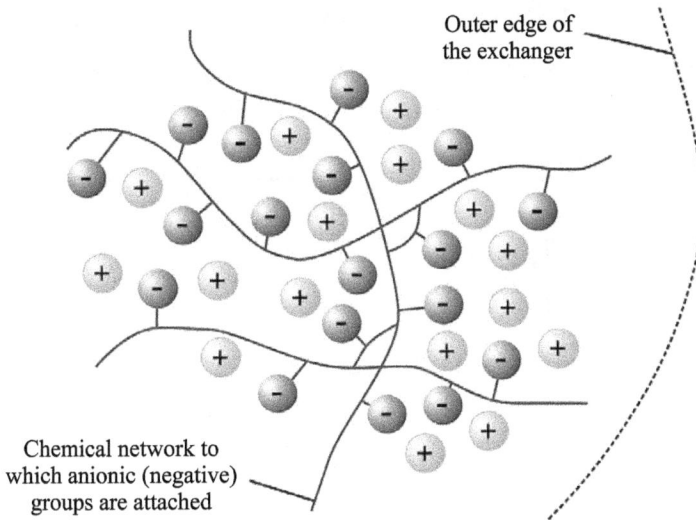

Figure 3. Model of internal cation-exchanger structure

The most often used functional ionic groups firmly fixed to the polymeric matrix are shown in Table 1. In case of cation-exchangers the mobile ion is H^+ and respectively in anion-exchangers the mobile ion is OH^-. Depending on the feature of the rest of this group mobile ions can be more or less easily dissociated. Such groups as *sulphonic* and *quaternary amines* are called respectively strong acidic or strong basic groups enabling them to exchange any ion from purely dissociated salt solution. The second in the table *carboxylic* cation-exchangers are medium acidic and other *quaternary amine* anion-exchangers medium basic, while the other ionic fixed groups act as weakly-acidic or weakly-basic ion-exchangers.

Table 1. Types of ion-exchangers with strong, medium and weak ionic groups

Cation exchangers		Anion Exchangers	
Type	Functional Group	Type	Functional Group
Sulphonic acid	$-SO_3^-H^+$	Quaternary amine	$-N(CH_3)_3^+OH^-$
Carboxylic acid	$-COO^-H^+$	Quaternary amine	$-N(CH_3)_2(EtOH)^+$
Phosphonic acid	$PO_3^-H^+$	Tertiary amine	$-NH(CH_3)_2^+OH^-$
Phosphinic acid	$HPO_2^-H^+$	Secondary amine	$-NH_2(CH_3)_2^+OH^-$
Phenolic	$-O^-H^+$	Primary amine	$-NH_3OH^-$
Arsonic	$-HAsO_3^-H^+$		
Selenonic	$-SeO_3^-H^+$		

It is time to present the most fundamental reaction of demineralization of water from sodium chloride:

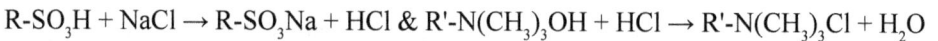

$$R\text{-}SO_3H + NaCl \rightarrow R\text{-}SO_3Na + HCl \ \& \ R'\text{-}N(CH_3)_3OH + HCl \rightarrow R'\text{-}N(CH_3)_3Cl + H_2O$$

Another basic process responsible for removal of multi-valence ions can be shown using the example of water softening – removal of cations Ca^{++} and Mg^{++}.

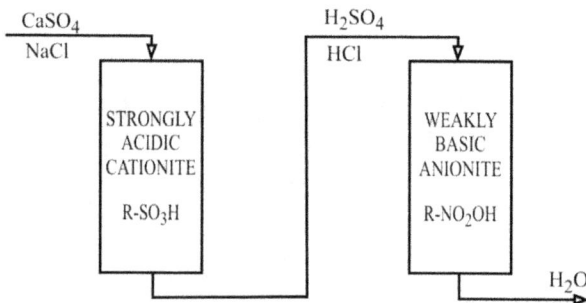

Figure 4. Two-column water demineralization by ion-exchange

The operation can be run on a single column with *sulphonic* (regenerated with HCl) or *carboxylic* (regenerated with NaCl) cation-exchanger (Figure 5) or on twin-bed systems connected *in series* or *parallel* – both options in Figure 6.

It has been already mentioned that any bed-filtration is a **periodical operation.** It means that the bed – no matter passive or active – will be sooner or later exhausted – loaded with a component to be isolated. It requires mechanical or chemical regeneration.

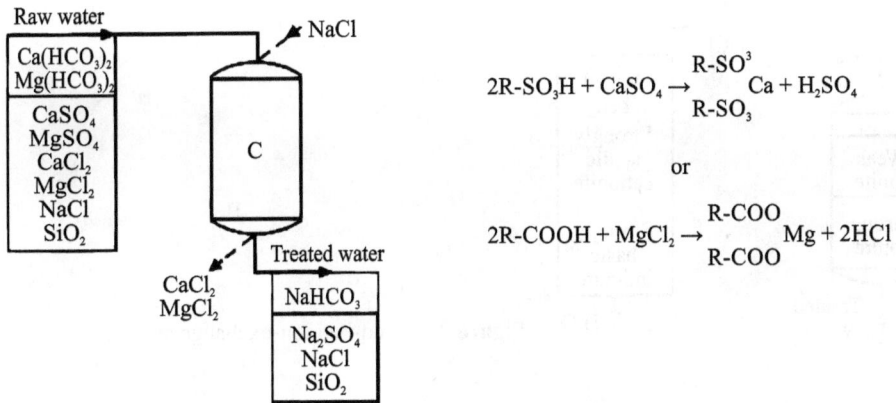

Figure 5. Softening by cation-exchanger

In a conventional two column – cation-exchanger/anion-exchanger – system the full cycle of column operation consists of: (1) moving (relaxing) of the bed, (2) regeneration with the use of a proper agent, (3) rinsing (washing) of the excess of a regenerant. Relaxing of the bed to increase the resistance against the flow is provided by counter-current flux of raw water. As regenerants for cation-exchangers solutions of mineral strong acids (5%HCl) are used or NaCl (10%) in the case of softening by a carboxylic exchanger. As regenerants for anion-exchangers alkali are applied (NaOH< 4%). The excess of the regenerant must be washed-out by raw or de-cationized water (in the case of an anion-exchanger).

Basic **ecological and economic** disadvantage of ion exchange process is linked with discharging of **post-regeneration sewage** to the surface water. The problem can be min-

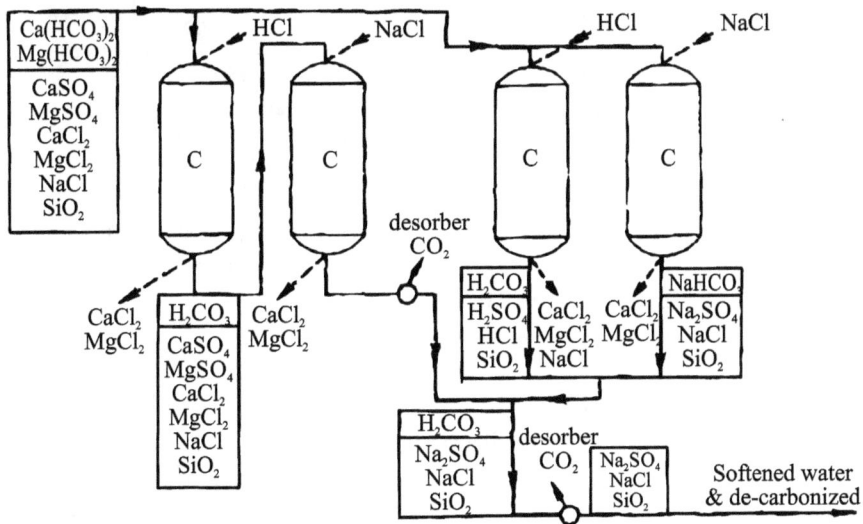

Figure 6. Water softening by ion-exchange on *in-series* and *parallelly* connected columns

125

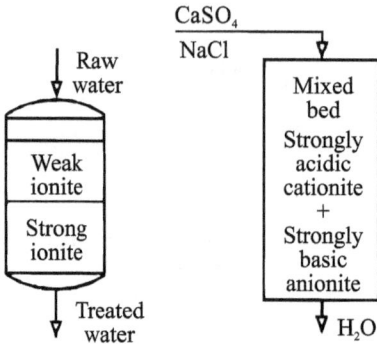

Figure 7. Mixed-bed ion-exchange system

imized by (Figure 8): (i) stabilizing of the bed in regeneration operation, (ii) multi-bed (multi-column) systems, (iii) pseudo-continuous ion exchange systems.

A number of important applications such as medicine, power generation, electronics and other, require very high purity – deeply de-ionized – water. To obtain such products by ion-exchange operation a mixed-bed system must be used in which cation- and anion-exchangers are mixed for sorption stage and separated into two layers for regeneration and wash (Figure 7).

There are several concepts to make a periodic ion-exchange process to be continuous. The most simple and quite effective is a system (Figure 8) in which an ion-exchanger is rotated by a pulsing device in a closed loop with a widened zone housing the major part of the resin while the rest is being moved through zones responsible for relaxing, regen-

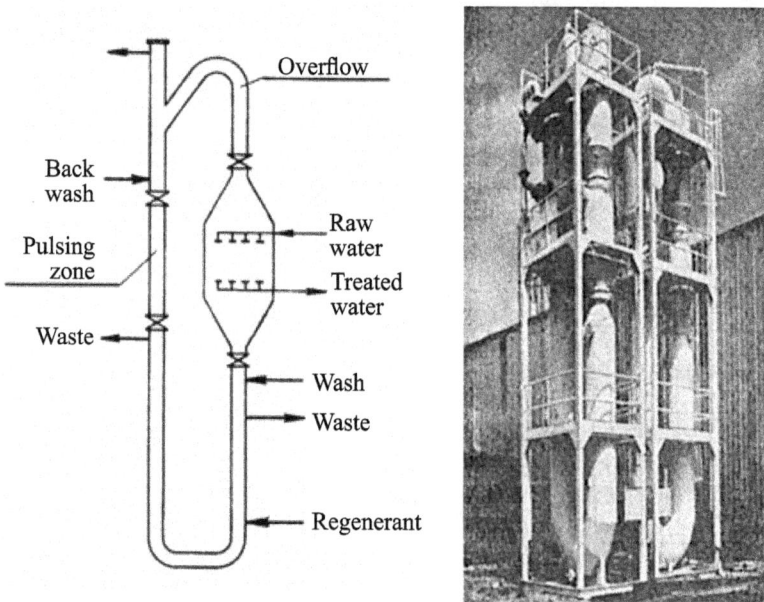

Figure 8. Continuous ion-exchange scheme of one loop and a picture of two-loops system

eration and washing-out of the excess of regenerant. One loop is filled with cation-, the other with anion-resin.

There are some other systems completing a continuous process by running an ion-exchanger through three separate vessels – sorption, regeneration and back-wash chambers.

Ion-exchange processes played an important role in water treatment substituting several conventional operations – offering higher speed and efficiency of related tasks – leading to reach better purity of the product water. But, probably even more important was the treatment of some wastewater by ion-exchangers allowing to reach the results not obtainable by any previously mentioned methods. It mostly concerns isolation of valuable and often also very harmful ionic species.

Figure 9 shows the scheme of recovering chromium compounds form chromic bath on activated carbon and cation-exchangers in a series of connected beds. Figure 10 presents less economically effective but environmentally important prevention of outflow of strong sulphuric acid.

There are dozens of similar examples of recovering or neutralizing valuable and semi-valuable metal ions by ion-exchangers of both types very often linked with other column (sorption) or membrane operations. Under consideration and implementation are the processes for metal-plating, rinsing of excess of metallic galvanic bath, recovering and neutralizing of components of pickling and de-fatting solutions. Demineralized water is usually available as a by-product.

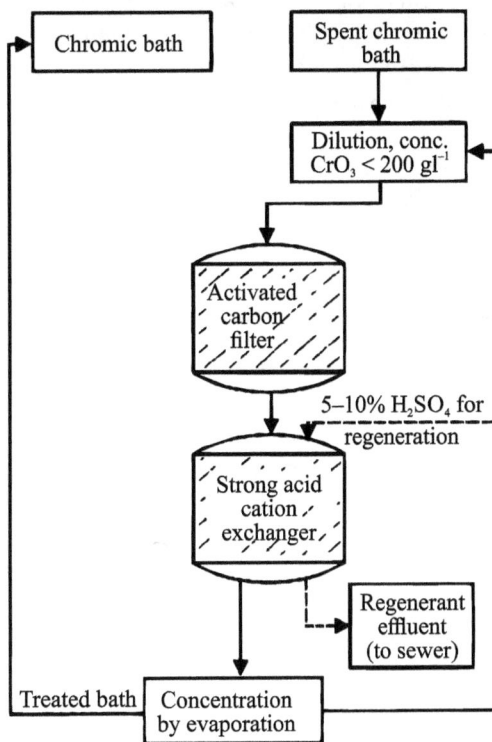

Figure 9. Recovery of chromium by ion-exchange

Exhausted pickle
liquor, conc.:
$FeSO_4 - 14\%$
$H_2SO_4 - 5.4\%$
(0.52 BV, time 1.7 min)

Water for regeneration
(0.78 BV, time 2.7 min)

Strong base
anion
exchanger

Recoverde acid
conc.:
$H_2SO_4 - 3.2\%$
$FeSO_4 - 0.5\%$
(0.8 BV)

Waste, conc.:
$FeSO_4 - 8.8\%$
$H_2SO_4 - 1.3\%$
(0.55 BV)

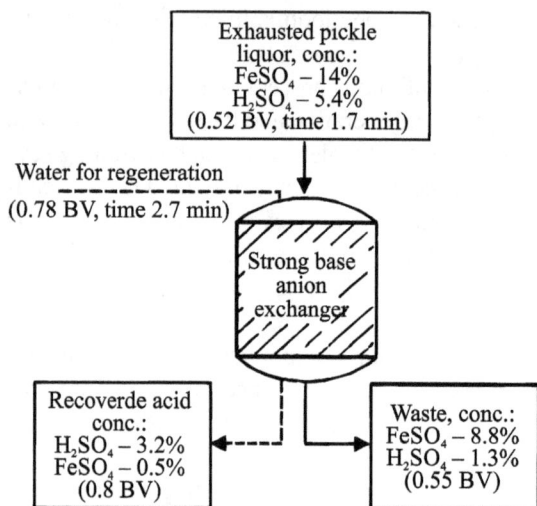

Figure 10. Recovery of sulphuric acid by IE

Environmental problems occur, of course, not only in the liquid phase – water and wastewater – but also in a very severe form in the air in two phases: solid as dust particulates and gaseous in the form acidic and other harmful, toxic and corrosive compounds.

Both already described groups of processes – sorption and ion-exchange – have been examined to abate such gaseous components. Carbon dioxide – important to be isolated because of the global warming problem – as a weakly acidic compound can be captured by an anion-exchanger, as well as by sorption. In this paper I have not so far discussed other physicochemical tools such as cryogenic and solvent separation.

Activated carbon bed for some organic gases and vapours, as well as anion-exchange resins for other acidic gases turned out to have limited applicability and a moderate efficiency.

4. Membrane Processes and Operations

Much better results were reached using membrane operations – **gas separation** and/or **pervaporation** to capture carbon dioxide – crucial for controlling the **global warming** – as well as various ways of stopping gases and vapours responsible among others for the second global air-originating conflict – ozone layer thinning – the so called ozone hole.

There is a number of gaseous compositions known to separate individual gases from the mixture. Some of them, the most common from the practical point of view, are: O_2/CO_2, O_2/CO, N_2/CO_2, SO_2/CO_2, N_2, CH_4/CO_2 (in biogas generation), hydrocarbons, NO_x, H_2S.

A general scheme of capturing and storing carbon dioxide generated by combustion of fuels is shown in Figure 11. The separation unit could be represented by sorption or a membrane system.

Membrane processes developed in the second half of the 20th century were from the very beginning seen as substitutes for ion-exchangers and other methods for water and

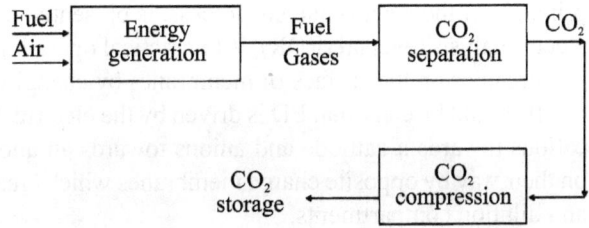

Figure 11. Capturing of carbon dioxide by one of available separation tools

wastewater treatment – in the first instant for water desalination. Ion-exchange was also tested if it could be used for that task, but the upper economic salt concentration (about single grams per litre) appeared to be far from the average salt concentration in the sea water (about 36 g/dm^3).

The first designed membrane process – electrodialysis – was primarily applied to desalt brackish water from a South African gold mine. This operation also turned out to be not economically optimal for water desalination. The comparison of a range of applicability of various processes for sea water desalination – in terms of the operation cost – is shown in Figure 12. It is clear that the ion-exchange (IE) could be used for low (<1 g/dm^3) mineralization of water while electrodialysis (ED) up to $5 - 10$ g/dm^3 could be substituted by reverse osmosis (RO) in all range of ED efficiency.

Therefore ED was almost completely eliminated from its early application for water desalination, but there are some large scale examples of using this operation for only slightly mineralized water, such as the construction of a demineralization plant in Yuma on Colorado River just to meet the standards of the US – Mexican treaty concerning cleanliness of the river at the border crossing. A scheme of the ED-desalination, as well as the

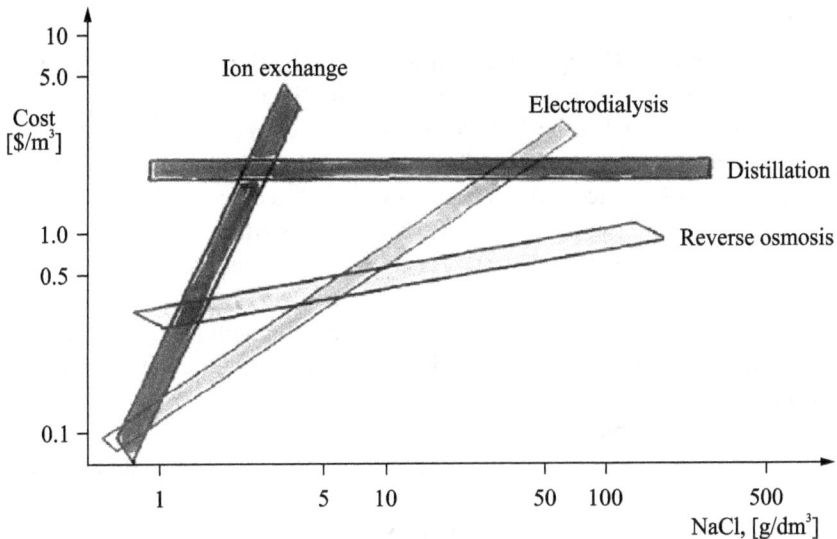

Figure 12. Cost of water desalination by available separation processes

principle of the electrodialysis process, is presented in Fig. 13. Nowadays a new process, electrodialysis reversal (EDR), is in practical operation preventing the settling of minerals and organics on the surface of membranes by changing polarity of electrodes.

It should be clear that ED is driven by the electrical potential gradient (ΔE) which runs cations towards a cathode and anions towards an anode. Both types of ions are stopped on their way by opposite charge membranes which create alternately located concentration and dilution compartments.

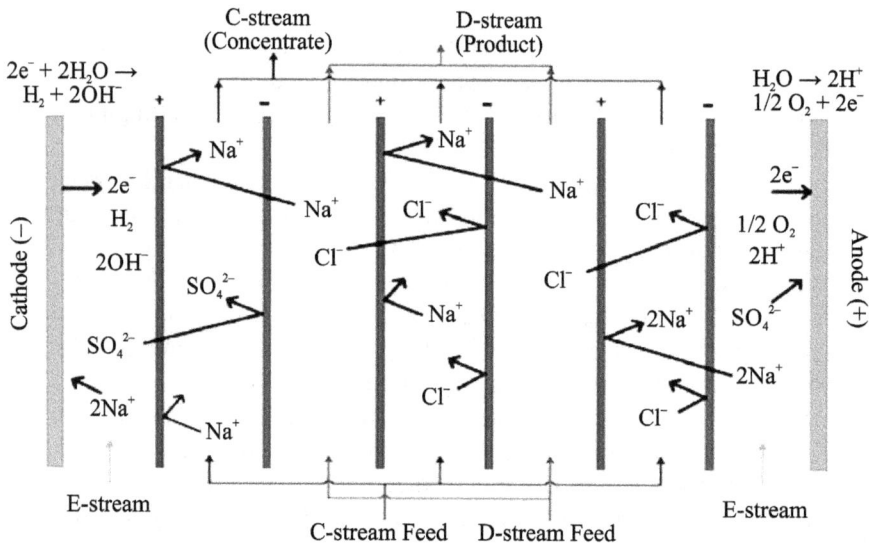

Figure 13. The scheme of electrodialysis process for water desalination

With the loss of the ED applicability in water desalination its importance grows permanently in wastewater treatment. This happens in all cases where ionic species have to be separated or isolated – the ED usually substitutes IE. The advantage of the use of membrane instead of bed operation allows to avoid the use of regenerants which cause secondary pollution of surface waters when they are in excess and back-washed.

Again, like with IE, the most effective applications of ED occur when the valuable and toxic metal can be separated and recycled for the same technology or recovered as a by-product.

Electronic industry for noble metals and metal-plating technology for semi-precious metals can supply dozens of good examples of the ED implementation. One is shown in Figure 14.

The ΔE was the first, but not the most important driving force for transport of solutes or solvents (water) through a membrane. The next developed process, already mentioned, reverse osmosis is driven by pressure gradient (ΔP), as well as other membrane operations elaborated parallelly or later – microfiltration (MF), ultrafiltration (UF) and nanofiltration (NF). Figure 15 shows a principle of pressure driven separation and Figure 16 the sequence

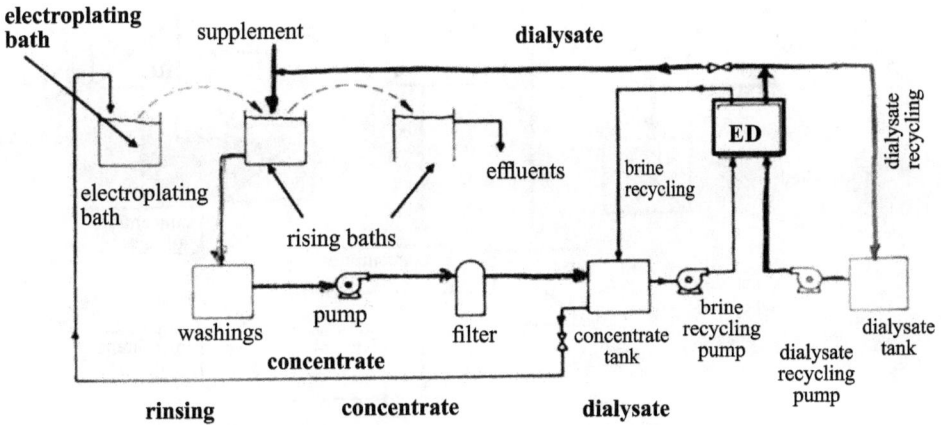

Figure 14. Recovery and recycling of nickel from plating liquors by electrodialysis

of isolating suspended particular solids on MF and UF (including colloids on the UF), macromolecules and polyvalent ions (including hardness causing Ca^{+2} and Mg^{+2}) on NF and finally all other ions on RO allowing just H_2O to pass.

There are two other driving forces used more rarely in membrane separation – gradient of chemical activity ($\Delta\mu$) in a few operations and gradient of temperature (ΔT), exploiting the excess heat, mostly in membrane distillation also for water desalination.

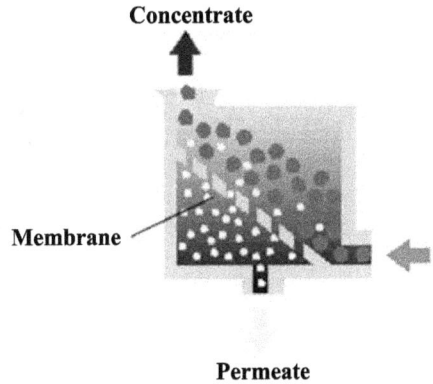

Figure 15. Separation of particulates and solutes by membrane

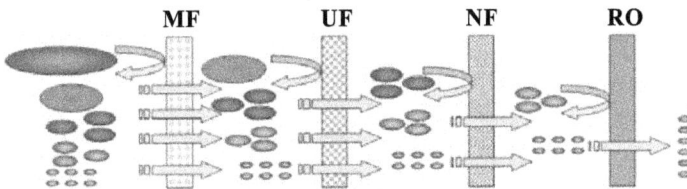

Figure 16. Separation of various species by a sequence

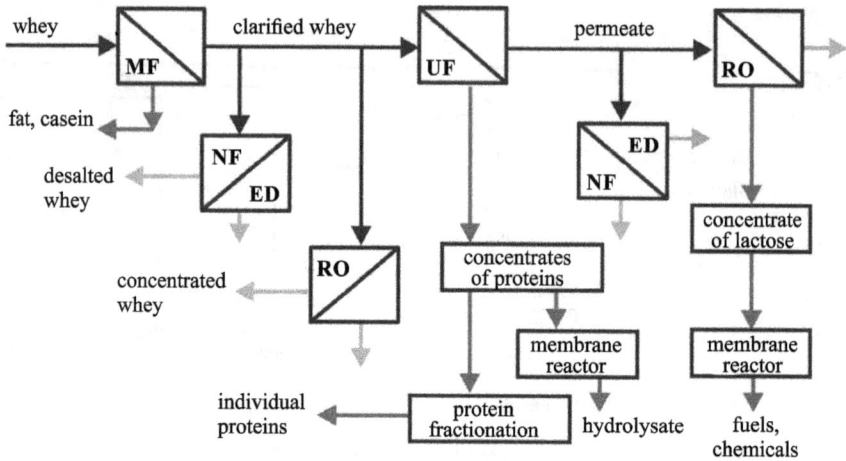

Figure 17. Pressure- and current-driven membrane operations to treat milk-whey

Another example (from the author's own laboratory) presents hybrid process com-posed of IE linked with ED to control solutions of zinc sulphate of three various con-centrations used in rayon (fibre) manufacturing. Diluted rinse water was concentrated on three-column cation-exchangers, while medium concentration excess stream treated on ED to receive concentrate ready to be recycled in the *spinning-bath* of that technology and *diluate* enriched in sulphuric acid to be used as IE beds regenerant (Figure 18).

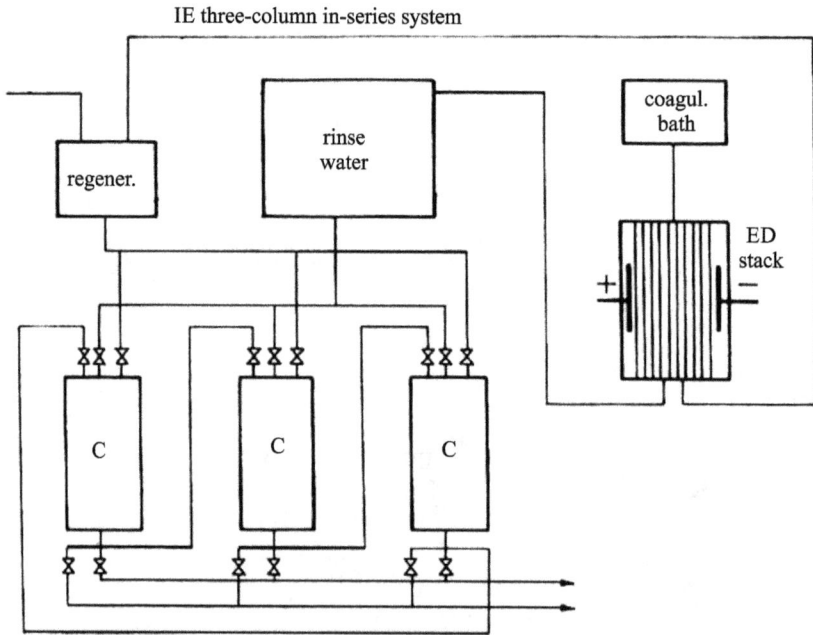

Figure 18. Hybrid IE/ED system to recycle zinc sulphate in rayon production

The second major application of membrane technology after desalination is its use in artificial organs and mainly in artificial kidney. Although it is not directly an *environmental* case, the implementation for that purpose is worth presenting (in Figure 19).

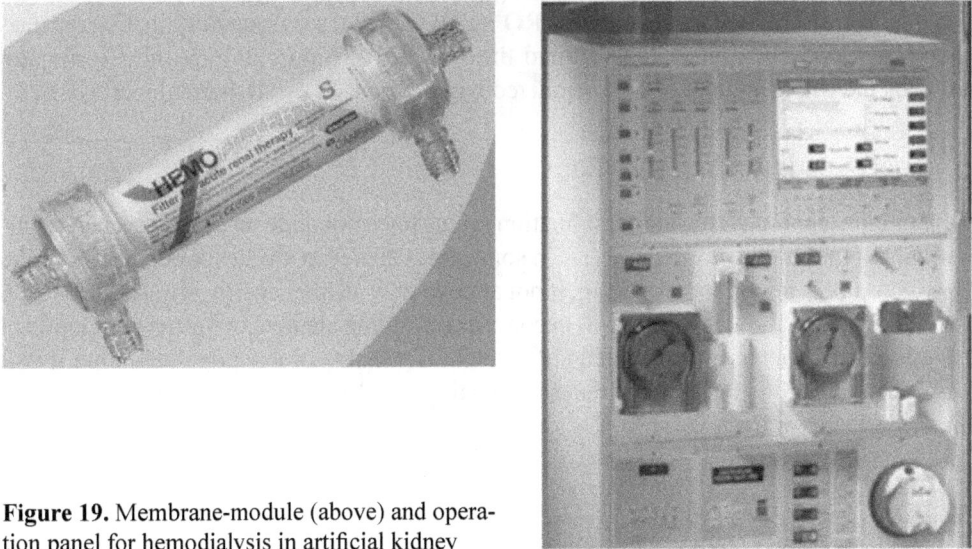

Figure 19. Membrane-module (above) and operation panel for hemodialysis in artificial kidney

The *Number One* global application of membrane separation for water desalination already exceeds previously leading thermal methods. Rich societies of the Persian Gulf and Southern Europe, North and South America, as well as Asia, are still increasing the volume of potable and industrial water gained from the sea. Japan is also a leader in isolation of salt (NaCl) from the ocean by a hybrid NF/RO process.

Figure 20. One of the world's largest sea water membrane desalination plants in Israel

The largest sea water (salinity – 40 g/dm^3) desalination plant in Ashkelon, Israel, producing 100 million m^3/a (330 000 m^3/d) of potable water (suspended solids < 300 mg/dm^3) at a cost of 0.53 \$/m^3 and maximum power consumption 4 kWh/m^3, composed of 40,000 *FilmTec*RO membrane modules in four stages, is presented in Figure 20.

The share of membrane operations (RO + ED) in global sea water desalination reached the value of 45 per cent already around the year 2010 (Figure 21) and now it already exceeds the whole amount of demineralized water produced by all thermal methods.

5. Final remarks and conclusions

Separation technology in water desalination seems to be not quite an environmental application, but the shortage of fresh water in some areas and even a water supply crisis, make this issue a very important one. Soon, if not already now, neither energy resources nor such factors as gross national product will become a controlling element in further development of individual societies and so called civilization of growing global population, but it will be water availability. It should be remembered that only less than one per cent of all global water resources is fresh water.

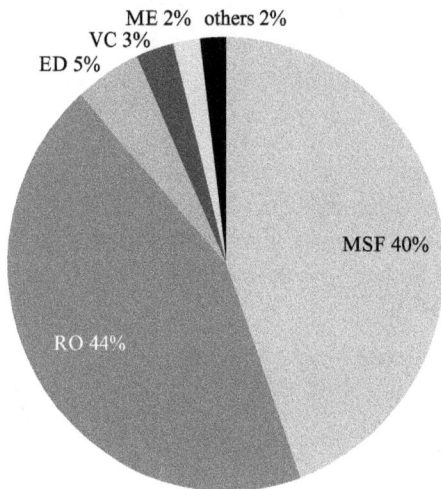

Figure 21. The share of available sea water desalination methods in the global market

The following references include a few quite recent books covering the discussed subject. They deal with presented separation processes and operations and are not linked to any specific place in this paper.

Acknowledgements

I am grateful to my former associates – professors Małgorzata Kabsch-Korbutowicz and Katarzyna Majewska-Nowak – for allowing me to use some graphics of their authorship.

References

Absorption and Ion Exchange. Perry's Chemical Engineers' Handbook, 8th Edition. McGraw-Hill, 2008.

Bolto, B.A., Pawlowski, L., *Wastewater Treatment by Ion Exchange,* E & F.N. SPON, London, New York, 1987.

Howell, J.A., Noworyta, A. (eds.), *Towards Hybryd membrane and Biotechnology Solutions for Polish Environmental Problems,* Wroclaw Technical University Press, Wrocław, 1995.

Kabsch-Korbutowicz, M., Majewska-Nowak, K., *Membrane Separation Processes in Environmental Protection,* Wrocław University of Technology Press, Wrocław, 2011.

Koltuniewicz, A. (ed.), *Membranes in clean technologies: theory and practice,* Wiley-VCH, 2008

.Konieczny K., Korus I., [eds], *Membrane and Membrane Processes in Environmental Protection,* Monographs of Polish Academy of Sciences. Vol. 118, Warszawa – Gliwice, 2014.

Li, N.N., Fane, A.G., *et al.* (eds.), *Advanced membrane technology and applications,* Wiley AIChE 2008.

Luqman, M. I., *Ion Exchange Technology I. Theory and Materials,* Springer 2012.

Noworyta, A., Trusek-Holownia, A., *Membrane Separation,* ARGI Press Agency, Wrocław, 2001.

Pawlowski, A., Dudzinska, M.R., Pawlowski, L. (eds.), *Environmental Engineering.* Taylor & Francis Group – CRC Press, Boca Raton, London, New York, Leiden, 2013.

Wilf, M., *The guidebook to membrane technology for wastewater reclamation: wastewater treatment, pollutants.* Balaban Publishers 2010.

Winnicki, T., Gostomczyk, M.A., Manczak, M., Poranek, A., *Zinc recovery from the rayon industry wastes by combining the column ion-exchange method with electrodialysis processes.* Environment Protection Engineering. 1, No 1, p.1, 1975.

Winnicki, T.: *Separation processes – a strategic technology for sustainable development. ibid.* 26, No 3, p.5, 2000.

Christopher George Gruszczynski

EU Emissions Trading System (ETS). Legislation Impact on Carbon Capture and Storage (CCS)

1. Introduction

The relationship between European Union (EU) undertakings and innovation in environmental control technology is important for the design of cost-effective policies to achieve environmental goals in Europe, where optional solution is carbon dioxide (CO_2) capture and storage technologies (CCS).[1] In the EU, the main source of CO_2 emissions is the combustion of coal at electric power plants. Measures to reduce these emissions fall into two general categories: switching to lower-sulphur or sulphur-free fuels (such as low-sulphur coal or natural gas), or installing control technology to capture CO_2 before it is emitted to the atmosphere.

Because much of Central Europe's electricity is still generated from the combustion of coal, emissions from coal-fired power plants have been the subject of substantial scrutiny and attention from the EU institutions. The main focus has been on pollutants directly linked to adverse human health effects, namely sulphur dioxide, nitrogen oxides, and air toxics, especially mercury. In addition, power plant emissions of CO_2, causing a greenhouse gas, are widely linked to global warming and climate change impacts and therefore are the subject of intense study in the context of new environmental problems – global climate change.

---

[1] Such policies cover e. g. actions on innovation in CO_2 control technology, particularly flue gas desulphurization (FGD) systems that achieve high levels of CO_2 control at coal-fired power plants and industrial boilers; see M. Taylor, *Effect of government action on technological innovation for SO_2 control*, "Environmental Science and Technology", Vol. 37, No. 20, 2003 p1 and following. http://www.energy.lbl.gov/staff/taylor/.../taylor-etal-est-2003.pdf.

2. The European Union emissions trading system

The EU Emissions Trading System (EU ETS) was the first large greenhouse gas emissions trading scheme in the world, and remains the biggest.[2] It was launched in 2005 to combat climate change and is a major pillar of EU climate policy The success of the EU ETS has inspired other countries and regions to launch cap and trade schemes of their own. The EU aims to link up the ETS with compatible systems around the world to form the backbone of an expanded international CO_2 market. For example the EC has agreed in principle to link the ETS with Australia's system in stages from mid-2015. The EU has around 2,000 million emission allowances for 12,000 industrial facilities in the whole of its territory, and its CO_2 market is valued at around 90,000 million Euro per year. Due to the oversupply, the ETS is not achieving its energy efficiency and environmental technologies goals. This is impairing the innovation and competitiveness of the EU member states The suspension of the auction will reduce the surplus of allowances by 40% and make it possible to set the price for a tonne of CO_2 somewhere between 6 and 8 Euro (today the price is 4,80).

As of 2014, the EU ETS covers more than 11,000 factories, power stations, and other installations with a net heat excess of 20 MW The installations regulated by the EU ETS are collectively responsible for close to half of the EU's emissions of CO_2 and 40% of its total greenhouse gas emissions.

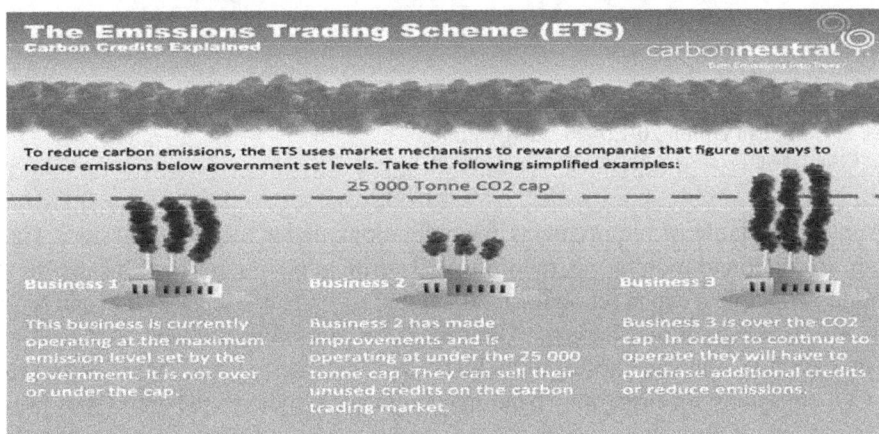

Figure 1. ETS scheme
Source: Carbon Neutral.

[2] The most important climate protection initiatives affecting energy generation are in particular: Directive of 27 September 2001 on the promotion of electricity from renewable energy sources in the internal electricity market; Directive of 27 October 2003 restructuring the Community framework for the taxation of energy products and electricity; Directive of 13 October 2003 establishing a scheme for greenhouse gas emission allowance trading within the Community; Directive of 27 October 2004 amending Directive 2003/87/EC establishing a scheme for greenhouse gas emission allowance trading within the Community, in respect of the Kyoto Protocol's project mechanisms. See IEA, *Reducing greenhouse gas emissions*, Paris 2005, p. 26 and following.

The 2020 climate and energy package. These targets, known as the "20–20–20" targets, set three key objectives for 2020:

I. A 20% reduction in EU greenhouse gas emissions from 1990 levels.

II. Raising the share of EU energy consumption produced from renewable resources to 20%.

III. A 20% improvement in the EU's energy efficiency – 20% cut in energy consumption through improved energy efficiency by 2020.

IV. The climate and energy package comprises four element of complementary legislation which are intended to deliver on the 20–20–20 targets.

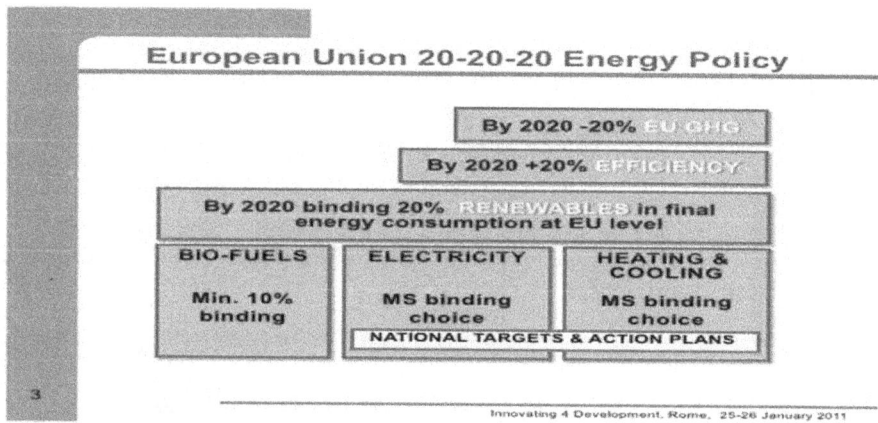

Figure 2. European Union 20–20–20 Energy Policy
Source: ENoLL FAO Workshop Alvaro Oliveira, Rome 2011.

Annual timetable of requirements for obligations under the EU Emissions Trading System, in relation to monitoring, reporting and verification of emissions. Under the "cap and trade" principle a cap is set on the total amount of greenhouse gases that can be emitted by all participating installations. Allowances for emissions are then auctioned off or allocated for free, and can subsequently be traded. Installations must monitor and report their CO_2 emissions, ensuring they hand in enough allowances to the authorities to cover their emissions. If emission exceeds what is permitted by its allowances, an installation must purchase allowances from others. Conversely, if an installation has performed well at reducing its emissions, it can sell its leftover credits. This allows the system to find the most cost-effective ways of reducing emissions without significant government intervention.

Recognizing the insufficient incentive for CCS by the EU-ETS, the European Commission (EC) introduced a specific mechanism to provide further incentives to CCS. This instrument, referred to as the "NER 300" programme, allocates 300 million EU emission allowances (EUAs) from a New Entrants Reserve to be used to support development of CCS and innovative renewable energy technologies. The reserve is made available until 31 December 2015. However, the first round of NER 300, that included the sale of the first 200 million EUAs, did not support any CCS projects in the EU. On 22 January 2014, the EC put forward 2030 energy and clime targets of a 40% reduction in greenhouse gas emissions (compared to 1990) and a share of 27% renewables in final energy consumption.[3]

According to the EC's own estimates, by 2020 a surplus of 2.6 billion emission allowances is expected to be available within the EU Emissions Trading System. In principle, the existence of this surplus has the danger of diluting the 40% target for greenhouse gas emissions reduction, because emissions reduction could be partly implemented by submitting allowances (and not by real reduction measures). Ecofys performed some analysis on the possible effects and included the proposal from the Commission for a Market Stability Reserve. Concluding, the Market Stability Reserve limits the possibility to use these surplus allowances. Surplus allowances can still dilute the target in early years of the commitment period and after 2030. Without the Market Stability Reserve, the surplus allowances could more than satisfy the additional demand for allowances resulting from the proposed stricter ET.[4]

In addition, the EC supports CCS demonstration in Europe through the European Energy Programme for Recovery. Six demonstration projects had a fast start aided by a total of EUR 1 billion. In 2009 the EC introduced Directive 2009/31/EC on the Geological Storage of CO_2 which includes provisions for the management of environmental and health risks related to CO_2 storage, requirements on permitting, composition of the CO_2 stream, monitoring, reporting, inspections, corrective measures, closure and post-closure obligations, transfer of responsibility to the state, and financial security. The programme award criteria under the specific sub-programme of the EEPR Regulation had to comply with the following conditions:

1. Projects had to demonstrate that they had the ability to capture at least 80% of CO_2 produced in the industrial operation and the ability to transport and geologically store this CO_2 safely underground.
2. In power installations, CO_2 capture had to be demonstrated on an installation of at least 250 MW electrical output or equivalent (the full amount of flue gas emitted by this installation had to be treated by the capture installation).
3. Project promoters had to make a binding declaration that the generic knowledge generated by the demonstration plant would be made available to the wider industry and to the Commission to contribute to the implementation of the Strategic Energy Technology Plan for Europe.

The Directive was transposed by most EU member states, but in many cases it was not done in full compliance with the EU requirements. The process of a complete transposition of this Directive is continuing.

---

[3] The 2030 targets are not in line with the EU's own climate goals for 2050: 80 to 95% less greenhouse gas emissions. Under the Commission's proposals, achieving the less ambitious limit of –80% would require a considerable acceleration of growth in renewables and reduction of energy use after 2030. See R. de Vos, P. van Breevoort, N. Höhne, Th. Winkel, C. Sachweh, *Assessing the EU 2030 climate and energy targets*, ECOFYS 2014. p. 4.

[4] The Market Stability Reserve limits the possibility to use these surplus allowances. Surplus allowances can still dilute the target in early years of the commitment period and after 2030. Without the Market Stability Reserve, the surplus allowances could more than satisfy the additional demand for allowances resulting from the proposed stricter ETS cap, see de Vos *et al.* (2014).

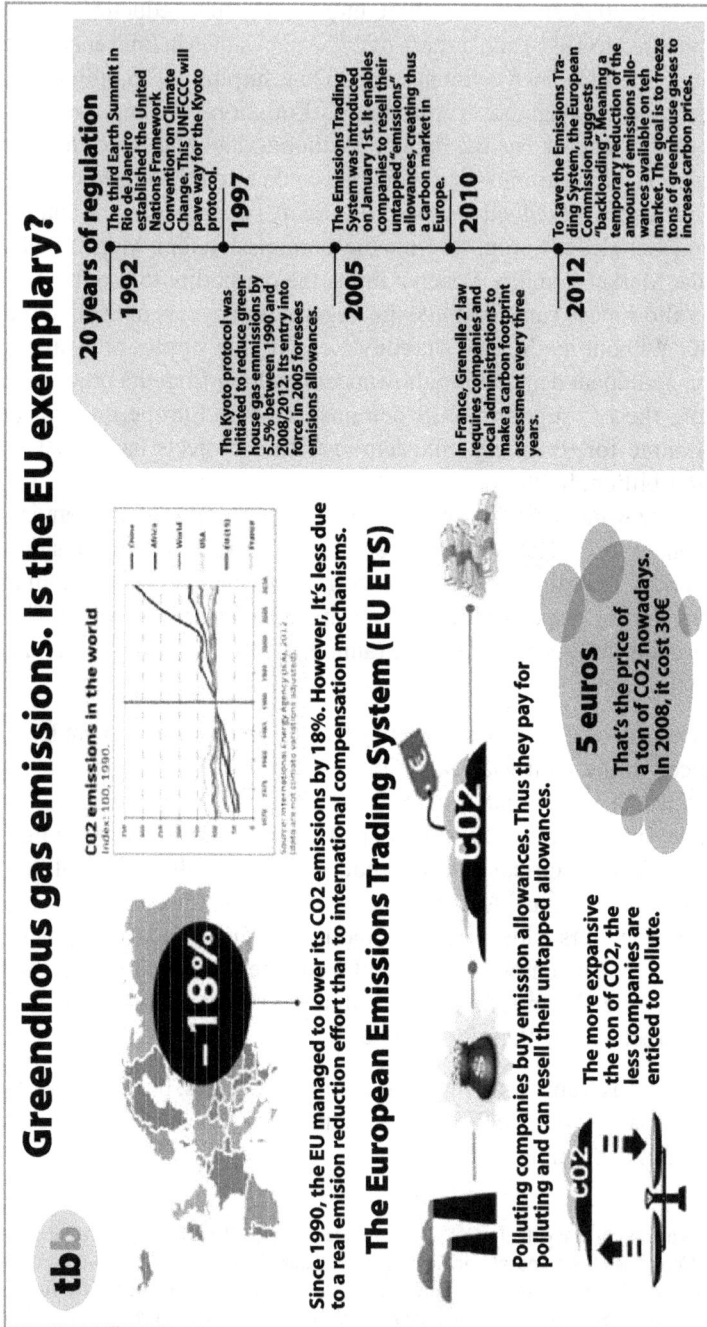

Greendhous gas emissions. Is the EU exemplary?

tbb

20 years of regulation

1992 — The third Earth Summit in Rio de Janeiro established the United Nations Framework Convention on Climate Change. This UNFCCC will pave way for the Kyoto protocol.

1997 — The Kyoto protocol was initiated to reduce greenhouse gas emmissions by 5,5% between 1990 and 2008/2012. Its entry into force in 2005 foresees emissions allowances.

2005 — The Emissions Trading System was introduced on January 1st. It enables companies to resell their untapped "emissions" allowances, creating thus a carbon market in Europe.

2010 — In France, Grenelle 2 law requires companies and local administrations to make a carbon footprint assessment every three years.

2012 — To save the Emissions Trading System, the European Commission suggests "backloading". Meaning a temporary reduction of the amount of emissions allowances available on teh market. The goal is to freeze tons of greenhouse gases to increase carbon prices.

CO2 emissions in the world
Index: 100, 1990.

China
Africa
World
USA
EU(15)
France

Source: International Energy Agency (IEA), 2012.
Data are not climate variations adjusted).

−18%

Since 1990, the EU managed to lower its CO2 emissions by 18%. However, it's less due to a real emision reduction effort than to international compensation mechanisms.

The European Emissions Trading System (EU ETS)

CO2

Polluting companies buy emission allowances. Thus they pay for polluting and can resell their untapped allowances.

The more expansive the ton of CO2, the less companies are enticed to pollute.

CO2

5 euros
That's the price of a ton of CO2 nowadays. In 2008, it cost 30€.

Figure 3. Greenhouse gas emissions
Source: Brusselsbusiness.arte.tv.

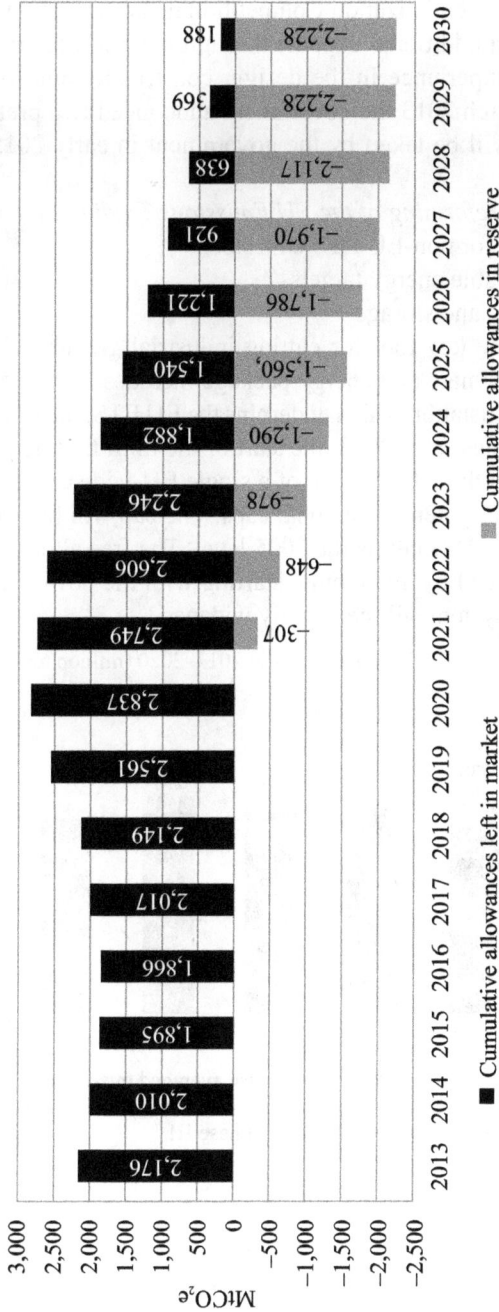

Figure 4. Supply of allowance under the European Commission
Source: www.sandbag.org.uk.

The UK CCS Commercialization Competition makes available GBP 1 billion capital funding, together with additional support through the UK Electricity Market Reforms, to support practical experience in the design, construction and operation of commercial-scale CCS. In March 2013 the government announced two preferred bidders. A final investment decision will be taken by the government in early 2015 on the construction of up to two projects.

Four measures of reforming of the EU Emissions Trading System (EU ETS):
I. National targets for non-EU ETS emissions
II. National renewable energy targets
III. Carbon capture and storage

The EU ETS is the key tool for cutting industrial greenhouse gas emissions most cost-effectively. The climate and energy package includes a comprehensive revision and strengthening of the legislation which underpins the EU ETS, the Emissions Trading Directive. The revision applies from 2013, the start of the third trading period of the EU ETS. Major changes include the introduction of a single EU-wide cap on emission allowances in place of the existing system of national caps. The cap will be cut each year so that by 2020 emissions will be 21% below the 2005 level. The free allocation of allowances will be progressively replaced by auctioning, starting with the power sector. The sectors and gases covered by the system will be slightly widened.

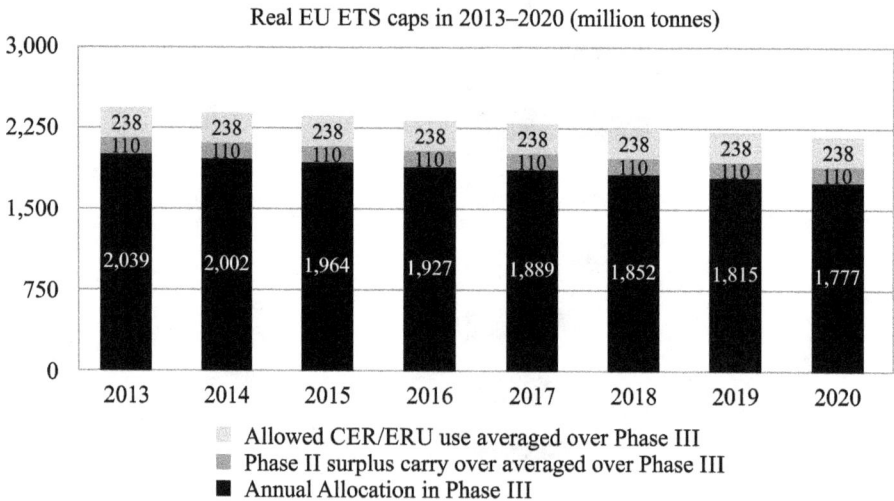

Real EU ETS caps in 2013–2020 (million tonnes)

Year	Annual Allocation in Phase III	Phase II surplus carry over	Allowed CER/ERU use
2013	2,039	110	238
2014	2,002	110	238
2015	1,964	110	238
2016	1,927	110	238
2017	1,889	110	238
2018	1,852	110	238
2019	1,815	110	238
2020	1,777	110	238

Allowed CER/ERU use averaged over Phase III
Phase II surplus carry over averaged over Phase III
Annual Allocation in Phase III

Figure 5. EU ETS caps in 2013–2020
Source: tomaswyns.wordpress.com.

Carbon capture and storage as the fourth element of the climate and energy package is a directive creating a legal framework for the environmentally safe use of CCS. Carbon capture and storage involves capturing CO_2 emitted by industrial processes and storing it in underground geological formations where it does not contribute to global warming. The directive covers all CO_2 storage in geological formations in the EU and lays down requirements which apply to the entire lifetime of storage sites. The scheme has been divided into four "trading periods". The first ETS trading period lasted three years, from January 2005 to December 2007. In the first phase (2005–2007) the EU ETS included more than 11,000 installations, representing approximately 40% of EU CO_2 emissions, covering energy activities: combustion installations with a rated thermal input exceeding 20 MW as well as production and processing of ferrous metals, mineral industry. From 2005 through 2007, the ETS reduced CO_2 emissions by 120 million to 300 million tonnes, or roughly 2–5% below the "business-as-usual" scenario.[5]

The second trading period ran from January 2008 until December 2012, coinciding with the first commitment period of the Kyoto Protocol. The second phase was expanded by the introduction of the EU's "Linking Directive" Clean Development Mechanism defined in the Kyoto Protocol (IPCC, 2007). It provides that the emissions reduction projects (Certified Emission Reduction units) may be traded in emissions trading schemes. Joint implementation credits – one of three flexibility mechanisms set out in the Kyoto Protocol to help countries with binding greenhouse gas emissions to meet their obligations. Phase 2 coincided with the global economic recession but introduced tighter emissions targets and achieved additional reductions of approximately 340 million tonnes in its first two years (2008–2009), or roughly 8% below projected business-as-usual emissions.

The third trading period began in January 2013 and will last until December 2020. For Phase 3 (2013–20)the European Commission has proposed a number of changes, including the setting of an overall EU cap, with allowances then allocated to EU members; tighter limits on the use of offsets, limiting banking of allowances between Phases 2 and 3; and a move from allowances to auctioning. At the start of Phase 3 running from 2013 to 2020the surplus stood at almost two billion allowances, doubled their level in early 2012, and by the end of 2013 had grown further to over 2.1 billion. The surplus was caused by several factors, principally the economic crisis and high imports of international credits. To achieve the target of a 40% reduction in EU greenhouse gas emissions below 1990 levels by 2030, set out in the 2030 framework for climate and energy policy, the cap will need to be lowered by 2.2% per year from 2021, compared with 1.74% currently.[6]

Phase 4 will commence on 1 January 2021 and finish on 31 December 2028. On 22 January 2014, The European Commission proposed two structural reform amendments to the ETS directive of the 2008 Climate Package: a) the linear reduction factor, at which the overall emissions cap is reduced, from 1.74% (2013–2020) to 2,2% each year from 2021 to 2030, thus reducing 43% of EU CO_2 emissions in the ETS sector as compared to 2005; and b) the creation of a 12% "automatic set-aside" reserve mechanism of verified annual emissions (at least a 100 million CO_2 permit reserve) in the fourth ETS period from 2021 to 2030, thus creating a *quasi* carbon tax or *carbon price floor* with a price range set each year by the EC Directorate General for Climate Change as of 2013.[7] The EU Emissions Trading Scheme, which is supposed to limit the greenhouse gas emission of all

---

[5] EDF, The EU Emissions Trading system, 2012 p. 8 and following, http://www.edf.org/.../EU_**ETS**_Lessons_ Learned_Report_...

[6] http://ec.europa.eu/clima/policies/2030/index_en.htm.

[7] A policy framework for climate and energy in the period from 2020 to 2030, page 5, http://ec.europa.eu/clima/ policies/2030/docs/com_2014_15_en.pdf.

of Europe's power stations and factories, is oversupplied by 2.1 billion CO_2 allowances. With total 2013 emissions under the ETS at 1.9 billion tonnes, this leaves over a year's worth of spare allowances flooding the market. The surfeit of allowances has lowered the price of CO_2 to the region of €5 per tonne of CO_2 emitted, too low to drive even the cheapest known forms of emission reduction. This has left many of Europe's gas-fired power stations idling, because the price of CO_2 can no longer bridge the price differential between coal and gas.

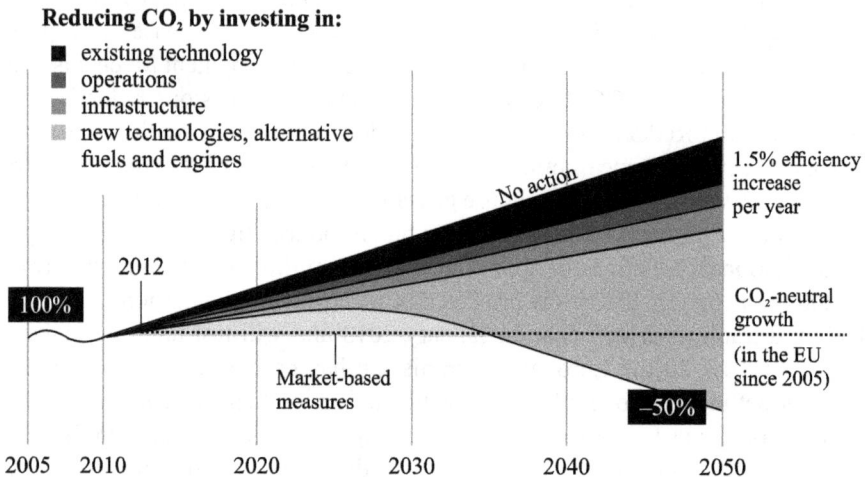

Figure 6. Measures to achieve CO_2-reduction targets
Source: Bundesverband der Deutschen Luftverkehrswirtschafte.V.

In November 2014, the European Council endorsed a binding EU target of an at least 40% domestic reduction in greenhouse gas emissions by 2030 compared to 1990. This is the toughest climate change target in the world, and would project the production of 27% of its energy from renewable sources by the same date. The two neighbours, Germany and Poland, might appear at opposite ends of the spectrum on the European climate debate, but both rely heavily on coal and therefore face similar challenges. CO_2 allowances would need a market value of 40 Euro to impact the price of coal-fire power, but the average price is currently around 5 Euro. The Climate and Energy Framework 2030 was first presented by the EC in January 2014, with the aim of creating a roadmap for energy policy beyond targets already in place for 2020. The package was debated by EU heads of state in March and June 2014, but they failed to reach an agreement, and instead gave themselves until the end of November 2014. The EC position is that a 40% reduction in greenhouse gas emissions compared to 1990 is the "centre piece" of the 2030 framework. The 2030 framework includes proposals to delay the next batch of allowances due to be auctioned in the current period, and to create a market stability reserve (MSR) to regulate the supply of allowances, which would be brought in at the beginning of the next trading period in 2021. But there are questions over whether these measures will have a sufficient impact. The Market Stability Reserve proposed by the EU commission will not increase prices in the European Trading Scheme because the allowances are only reduced partly and temporarily. With the EU potentially setting the pace for climate targets worldwide, at the UN Climate Change Conference in Paris in 2015 Sweden called for the CO_2 reduction target to be raised to 50%, while Germany spoke of 40% as a "minimum".[8] In the beginning of the November 2014 Polish Prime Minister Ewa Kopacz threatened to veto the CO_2 reduction target, saying she was not prepared to accept the economic impact of rising energy prices. Low-income and coal-dependent economies like Poland might be talked round with funds to help them reach the targets.

The main problem for the current prices on junk status seems to be the insufficient credibility of European climate policy. We have to reform emissions trading and put a minimum price on CO_2. The EU ETS has been criticized for several failings, e. g. less than 50% of fossil carbon is covered, over-allocation – because EU governments based the system's initial caps and emissions allowance allocation on *estimates of regulated* entities' emissions rather than on actual historical emissions data. Furthermore, too many emissions allowances issued by the EU governments windfall profits (by passing through to consumers the price of allowances that they received for free), as well as cause the EU emissions allowance prices volatility. Economy slump in Europe has caused the price of the emission certificates to drop dramatically, currently hovering around €5 ($6.50) per tonne of CO_2.

Carbon capture and storage CCS

CCS (or carbon capture and sequestration) is generally recognized as one of the key climate change mitigation options in several scenarios and the technology can be utilized also in the case of coal industry. Coal is still the largest incremental source of global primary energy consumption. Over the last decade, coal has been the fastest growing source of primary energy, with incremental consumption over 50% higher than the incremental demand for oil and gas combined. In 2011, coal demand grew by 4.3% (from 7,080 megatonnes (Mt) in 2010 to 7,384 Mt in 2011), with most of this growth arising in non-OECD countries as well as in the EU region.[9] This continued expansion of coal and other fossil fuels, despite strong advances in clean energy technologies worldwide, has meant that the CO_2 emissions intensity of the global energy supply has been stable, but overall energy-related emissions have grown (IEA, 2013). Thus, it is clear that in spite of rapidly increasing shares of non-fossil energy sources, coal and other fossil fuels will inevitably play a role for many decades to come. CCS offers a solution.

CCS is the process of capturing waste CO_2 from large point sources, such as fossil fuel power plants, transporting it to a storage site, and depositing it where it will not enter

---

[8] Germany's energy transition plan to simultaneously phase out nuclear power and cut carbon emissions through a push into renewable energy has the support of the grand coalition government of the Social-Democrats and the Christian Democrats and envisages that renewable power will cover more than a quarter of the country's energy needs in the first nine months of 2014. Germany already has climate reduction targets in place: of 40% by 2020 and 55% by 2030, although the country's CO_2 emissions have been on the rise again since hitting a low point in 2009; http://www.cleanenergywire.org/news/germany-faces-challenges-its-triad-targets-european-climate-negotiations.
[9] IEA, *Technology Roadmap – Carbon capture and storage*, 2013 Edition, p. 1.

the atmosphere, normally an underground geological formation. The aim is to prevent the release of large quantities of CO_2 into the atmosphere (from fossil fuel use in power generation and other industries). It is a potential means of mitigating the contribution of fossil fuel emissions to global warming[10] and ocean acidification[11].

CO_2 capture and storage (CCS) involves three distinct processes, shown in the figure below: first, *capturing* CO_2 from the gas streams emitted during electricity production, industrial processes or fuel processing; second, *transporting* the captured CO_2 by pipeline or in tankers; and third, *storing* CO_2 underground in deep saline aquifers, depleted oil and gas reservoirs or unmineable coal seams. All three processes have been in use for decades, albeit not with the purpose of storing CO_2.

Further development is needed, especially in the capture and storage of CO_2. While pipeline transport is an established technology, the siting of CCS projects can reduce the need for an extensive transportation system. The challenge, cost and environmental impact of such a CO_2 pipeline system should not be underestimated.

Once captured, the CO_2 gas is compressed and transported to a suitable location for injection and storage in deep geologic formations, such as saline reservoirs, mature oil and gas fields, and potentially unmineable coal seams, basalts or other formations. Once stored, the CO_2 is isolated from drinking water supplies and prevented from release into the atmosphere by a confining zone that includes a dense layer of rock, which acts as a seal, and through additional trapping mechanisms. Monitoring devices are also installed to ensure process integrity. CCS applied to a modern conventional coal[12]-based power plant could reduce CO_2 emissions to the atmosphere by approximately 80–90% compared to a plant without CCS.

Installing CCS on a PC coal plant could double the emissions of methane associated with coal extraction, due to the increased coal consumption, but will decrease the CO_2 emissions associated with combustion.[13] Both methane and CO_2 are GHGs that contrib-

---

[10] "IPCC Special Report on Carbon Dioxide Capture and Storage. Summary for Policymakers". Intergovernmental Panel on Climate Change. Retrieved 2011-10-05.

[11] Commonwealth Scientific and Industrial Research Organization (CSIRO) and the Global CCS Institute, *Introduction to Carbon Capture and Storage – Carbon storage and ocean acidification activity*. Retrieved 2013-07-03.

[12] Coal is an extremely important fuel and will remain so. Some 23% of primary energy needs are met by coal and 39% of electricity is generated from coal. About 70% of world steel production depends on coal feedstock. Coal is the world's most abundant and widely distributed fossil fuel source. The International Energy Agency (IEA) expects a 43% increase in its use from 2000 to 2020. http://www.world-nuclear.org/info/energy-and-environment/-clean-coal--technologies/.

[13] CCS will need to contribute nearly one-fifth of the necessary emissions reductions to reduce global GHG emissions by 50% by 2050 at a reasonable cost. CCS is therefore essential to the achievement of deep emission cuts. See more: IEA (2012g), *A Policy Strategy for Carbon Capture and Storage,* Information Paper, OECD/IEA, Paris; IEA (2012h), *Facing China's Coal Future: Prospects and Challenges for Carbon Capture and Storage,* IEA working paper, OECD/IEA, Paris; IEA (2013a), *Tracking Clean Energy Progress 2013: IEA Input to the Clean Energy Ministerial,* OECD/IEA, Paris; IEA (2013b), "Global Action to Advance Carbon Capture and Storage: A Focus on Industrial Applications", Annex to *Tracking Clean Energy Progress 2013,* OECD/IEA, Paris; IEA (2013c), *Methods to Assess Storage Capacity for CCS: Status and Recommendations,* OECD/IEA, Paris, forthcoming; IEA GHG (IEA Greenhouse Gas R&D Programme) (2007), CO_2 *Capture Ready Plants,* Report 2007/4, IEA GHG, Cheltenham, UK; IEA GHG (2011a), *Global Storage Resources Gap Analysis for Policymakers,* Report 2011/10, IEA GHG, Cheltenham, UK.

---

ute to climate change. However, methane has more ability to warm the atmosphere per gram than CO_2. Thus, to compare relative flows, these two streams must be converted into equivalent units. In this case, methane emissions are converted into $-CO_2$ equivalent units to describe the "global warming potential" of each flow. Doing this allows the two streams' impact on global warming to be compared to determine if, overall, the process has a negative or positive impact on global warming potential and the relative size of that change. In the case of a PC coal plant with CCS, the reduction in combustion emissions far outweighs the increase in methane emissions, and the result is a significant net decrease in global warming potential over the PC coal plant baseline. This same methodology can be applied to many material flows and other impact categories.

CCS technology has the potential to reduce CO_2 emissions from a coal or natural gas-fuelled power plant by as much as 90%. CCS could provide significant economy-wide CO_2 emission reductions. Due to rising global demand for energy, the consumption of fossil fuels is expected to rise through 2035, leading to greater CO_2 emissions.[14] CCS technology offers the opportunity to reduce emissions while maintaining a role for fossil fuels in national energy portfolios.

Under its 2°C Scenario (2DS), the International Energy Agency (IEA) estimates that CCS will provide 14% of cumulative emissions reductions between 2015 and 2050 compared to a business-as-usual scenario. Under the same scenario, CCS will provide one-sixth of required emissions reductions in 2050.[15]

Oil produced by CO_2-EOR projects can be considered relatively lower-CO_2 than oil produced by other techniques. For example, the CO_2 stored by the Weyburn EOR project can offset approximately 40% of the combustion emissions resulting from the oil it produces, not including emissions from electricity use due to compression, lifting, and refining. Although CO_2 has been injected into geological formations for several decades for various purposes, including enhanced oil recovery, the long-term storage of CO_2 is a relatively new concept.[16] The first commercial example was Weyburn, Canada in 2000 (Weyburn CO_2

---

[14] See more: D. Finon, (2010), *Efficiency of Policy Choices for the Deployment of Large Scale Low-Carbon Technologies: the Case of CCS*, Laboratoire d'Analyse Économique des Réseaux et des Systèmes Energétiques, Working Paper No. 27, Paris, France; C. Fischer and R. Newell (2008), *Environmental and Technology Policies for Climate Mitigation*, "Journal of Environmental Economics and Management", 55 (2), pp. 142–62; Global Carbon Capture and Storage Institute (2009), *Country Studies – The United States of America*, Canberra, Australia; Global Carbon Capture and Storage Institute (2011), *The Global Status of CCS,* Canberra, Australia; H. Groenenberg and T. Dixon (2012), *Using carbon markets to advance negative emissions from biomass and CCS,* [in:] "Energy Procedia"; K. Hamilton (2009), *Unlocking Finance for Clean Energy: the Need for "Investment Grade Policy"*, Chatham House, London, UK; P. Havlik *et al.* (2010), *Global Land-Use Implications of First and Second Generation Biofuel Targets*, EnergyPolicy: article in press; D. Helm, C. Hepburn, R. Mash (2003), "Credible carbon policy", *Oxford Review of Economic Policy*, 19:3, pp.438-450; C. Hepburn (2006), "Regulation by prices, quantities or both: a review of instrument choice", *Oxford Review of Economic Policy,* 22 (2), pp. 226-247.

[15] International Energy Agency. 2013. *Technology Roadmap – Carbon Capture and Storage.* http://www.iea.org/publications/freepublications/publication/name,39359,en.html.

[16] CCS has not yet been applied to large-scale electricity generation due to a number of technological, infrastructure, cost and legal challenges. Public policy measures and sustained funding to support continued CCS research, development and demonstration will be necessary to accelerate large-scale commercial deployment of this critical technology. See more: W. McKibben, P. Wilcoxen (2007), "A credible foundation for long-term international

Flood Project, Canada). EnCana and the International Energy Agency (IEA) began storing CO_2 from enhanced oil recovery (EOR) in 2000. During Phase 1 (2000–2004), more than seven million tonnes of CO_2 were stored, and the geology has been found suitable for long-term storage. The site will be maintained in order to study long-term sequestration. The second phase will include site characterization, leakage risks, monitoring and verification and a performance assessment.

The fourth element of the climate and energy package is a directive creating a legal framework for the environmentally safe use of CCS. Carbon capture and storage involves capturing the CO_2 emitted by industrial processes and storing it in underground geological formations where it does not contribute to global warming. The directive covers all CO_2 storage in geological formations in the EU and lays down requirements which apply to the entire lifetime of storage sites.[17] The directive on the geological storage of CO_2 establishes a legal framework for the environmentally safe geological storage of CO_2. It also contains provisions on the capture and transport components of CCS.[18] The substances captured to be stored must consist overwhelmingly of CO_2 to prevent any adverse effects on the security of the transport network or the storage site. The operation of the site must be closely monitored and corrective measures taken in the case that leakage occurs. The directive covers in addition closure and post-closure obligations, and sets out criteria for the transfer of responsibility from the operator to the Member State. The operator must establish a financial security before the injection of CO_2 starts, to ensure that the requirements of the CCS Directive and the Emissions Trading Directive can be met.

Another example is the demonstration project in Sleipner West (Norway).[19] Statoil and IEA began injecting CO_2 from the natural gas field into a saline formation under the North Sea in 1996. Currently, they store one million tonnes of CO_2 per year with no leakage. The projected cost is more than €350 million. In Salah (Algeria), Sonatrach, BP and Statoil began capturing CO_2 from natural gas production in 2004 and storing it in depleted gas res-

---

cooperation on climate change", [in:] J. Aldy and R. Stavins (eds.) (2007), *Architectures for Agreement,* Cambridge University Press, New York, NY, USA; J. Meadowcroft and O. Langhelle (eds.) (2009), *Caching the Carbon: The Politics and Policy of Carbon Capture and Storage,* Edward Elgar Publishing, Cheltenham, UK and Northampton, MA, USA; Mineralölwirtschaftsverbande.V. (2011), *Mineralölstatistik,* Berlin, Germany; Mineral Products Association (2010), *Quarterly Cementitious,* London, England; S. Nakhooda (2010), *Getting to work: a review of the operations of the Clean Technology Fund,* World Resources Institute Working Paper, Washington, DC, USA; D. Newbery *et al.* (2009), *Carbon Capture and Storage: Analysis of Incentives and Rules in a European Repeated Game Situation,* Electricity Policy Research Group, University of Cambridge, Cambridge, UK.
[17] Directive 2009/31/EC of the European Parliament and of the Council of 23 April 2009 on the geological storage of carbon dioxide; http://ec.europa.eu/clima/policies/package/index_en.htm.
[18] Though these activities are covered mainly by existing EU environmental legislation, such as the Environmental Impact Assessment (EIA) Directive, the Industrial Emissions Directive, in conjunction with amendments introduced by the CCS Directive.
[19] The Sleipner site in Norway (sub-sea storage). About 1 Mt of CO_2 per year has been stored since 1996. This project is important as it proves that storage in aquifers can work in practice. No leakage has so far been detected. Pilot projects suggest that CO_2-enhanced coalbed methane (ECBM) and enhanced gas recovery (EGR) may be viable but the experience so far is not sufficient to consider these two as proven options. Encouraged by these promising results, many more storage demonstration projects have been started or are planned, [in:] The IEA World Energy Outlook (WEO) Reference Scenario projects, https://www.iea.org/Textbase/npsum/ccsSUM.pdf.

ervoirs. They store about one million tonnes of CO_2 per year, and the projected cost is \$1.7 billion. This is the world's first full-scale CO_2 capture and storage project at a gas field. In the Netherlands, Gaz de France is investigating the feasibility of CO_2 storage in depleted natural gas reservoirs on the Dutch continental shelf. The CO_2 is injected in the place from which it first came. Injection started in 2004. (Storage) Statoil in Norway began storing CO_2 from gas production under the seabed in April 2008. At full capacity, they plan to store 700,000 tonnes of CO_2 a year. The projected cost is \$110 million.

An integrated pilot-scale CCS power plant was to begin operating in September 2008 in the eastern German power plant Schwarze Pumpe, run by utility company Vattenfall, in the hope of answering questions about technological feasibility and economic efficiency.[20] CCS applied to a modern conventional power plant could reduce CO_2 emissions to the atmosphere by approximately 80–90% compared to a plant without CCS.[21]

Another three interesting pilot projects are:

Fenn Big Valley (Canada). The Alberta Research Council began injecting CO_2 into deep coalbeds for enhanced coal bed methane in 1999, with a project cost of C\$3.4 million. Thus far, all testing has been successful, and they are assessing the economics of the project. (Enhanced coalbed methane).

Ketzin (Germany). GFZ Potsdam, as part of the European research project, CO2SINK, began storing CO_2 in aquifers at a depth of 600 metres on 30 June 2008. They plan to store up to 60,000 tonnes of CO_2 over two years, at a cost of €15 million. (Storage)

Otway (Australia). CO2CRC has begun injecting CO_2 from natural gas wells in hydrocarbon reserves; eventually, 100,000 tonnes will be stored. The object is to provide technical information on CO_2 storage and monitoring and verification. The project's budget is A\$40 million.[22]

---

[20] Schwarze Pumpe site in Germany. Vattenfall opened their pilot 30Mw coal oxy-fuel combustion plant with CO_2 capture on 9 Sept. 2008; Norwegian Statoil Hydro's Sleipner carbon capture and storage project proceeding successfully, "Energypedia", 8 March 2009. See more: P. Ashworth, T. Jeanneret, K. Stenner & E. V. Hobman (2012). International comparison of the large group process. Results from Canada, Netherlands, Scotland and Australia. CSIRO; S. Pullenvale Bachu (2008), "CO_2 Storage in Geological Media: Role, Means, Status and Barriers to Deployment", *Progress in Energy and Combustion Science*, Vol. 34, No. 2, pp. 254–273, Elsevier, Amsterdam.

[21] (IPCC, 2005) *IPCC special report on Carbon Dioxide Capture and Storage.* Prepared by working group III of the Intergovernmental Panel on Climate Change. B. Metz, O. Davidson, H. C. de Coninck, M. Loos, and L.A. Meyer (eds.), Cambridge University Press, Cambridge, United Kingdom and New York, NY, USA, 442 pp. Available in full at www.ipcc.ch (PDF – 22.8MB).

[22] There are several important projects, mainly: 1) Tjeldbergodden (Norway). Shell and Statoil will store 2.5 million tonnes of CO_2 per year, beginning 2010–2011, captured from a 700 MW gas-fired power plant. (CCS); 2) Powerfuel (UK). An IGCC plant (900 MW) that will use CCS technology after 2012; 3) E.On (UK). An IGCC plant (450 MW) will add CCS after 2013; 3) (Coal CCS) RWE (Germany). IGCC technology (400–450 MW) at which CO_2 will be captured and stored in a saline formation or gas reservoir beginning in 2014. (Coal CCS); 4) E.On (UK). Two supercritical units (800 MW each) at a power station at which CCS will begin in 2015. (Coal CCS); 5) RWE nPower (UK). Supercritical technology and post-combustion CCS (1000 MW) will be used beginning in 2016. (Coal CCS) [in]: National Mining Association, The American resources, Carbon capture and storage, Washington 2011, p3, www.nma.org/pdf/fact_sheets/ccs.pdf.

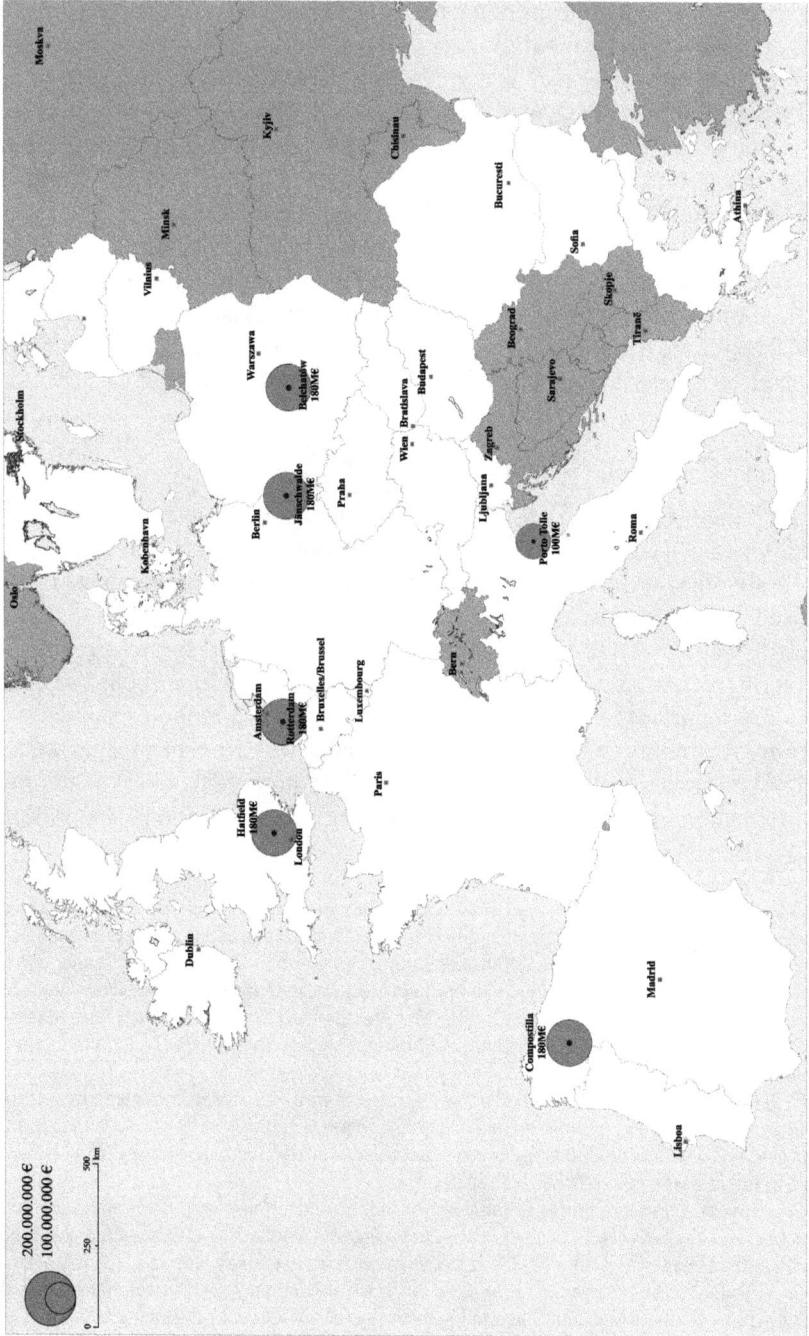

Figure 7. Carbon and storage projects
Source: European Commission Selection of offshore wind and carbon capture and storage projects for the European Energy Programme for Recovery.

The IPCC estimates that the economic potential of CCS could be between 10% and 55% of the total carbon mitigation effort until the year 2100.[23] Capturing and compressing CO_2 may increase the fuel needs of a coal-fired CCS plant by 25–40%.

These and other system costs are estimated to increase the cost of the energy produced by 21–91% for purpose built plants. Applying the technology to existing plants would be more expensive, especially if they are far from a sequestration site. Recent industry reports suggest that with successful research, development and deployment, sequestered coal-based electricity generation in 2025 may cost less than unsequestered coal-based electricity generation nowadays.

Presently, uncertainty over meeting the requirements and long-term liability issues associated with the underground storage of CO_2 have deterred project developers, financiers and insurers from moving forward with CCS. However, CCS as a tool for mitigating CO_2 emissions and ensuring a secure and affordable energy supply for EU Member States represents a vital public interest that merits a European programme to clarify and resolve these long-term liability issues and to clear the way for the rapid and widespread commercialization of the technology. Some of the key issues that must be resolved in order to foster widespread commercialization of CCS include:[24]

a) determining responsibility for post-closure monitoring;
b) avoiding characterization of CO_2 as a waste and CCS activities as waste disposal to avoid triggering expensive "cradle to grave" European regulations;
c) dealing with emissions of nitrogen oxides (NOx), sulphur oxides (SOx), and particulate matter (PM), which are also important environmental concerns for coal-fired power plants.

Another major concern with CCS is whether leakage of stored CO_2 will compromise CCS as a climate change mitigation option. Potential for human health risks is also expected to increase due to increased heavy metals in water from increased coal mining and MEA hazardous waste, although there is currently not enough information to relate this potential to actual realized health impacts. In addition to environmental and human health impacts, supply chain impacts and other social, economic, or strategic impacts will be important to consider. IPCC estimates that risks are comparable to those associated with current hydrocarbon activity. Although some question this assumption as arbitrary, citing lack of experience in such long-term storage. CO_2 could be trapped for millions of years, and although some leakage occurs upwards through the soil, well selected storage sites are likely to retain over 99% of the injected CO_2 over 1000 years.

---

[23] *Coal Utilization Research Council (CURC) Technology Roadmap*, 2005, http://www.coal.org/roadmap/index. asp; see *The CURC – EPRI Coal technology roadmap* 2012.

[24] Several studies have shown that eutrophication is expected to double and acidification would increase due to increases in NOx emissions for a coal plant with CCS provided by monoethanolamine (MEA) scrubbing. http://www.rmcmi.org/education/carbon-capture-storage#.VL0T5dLF-uE.

Costs and potential of carbon capture and storage

A substantial amount of continued research, development and demonstration of CCS technologies will be required before CCS can be applied to large-scale commercial power plants. MIT report estimates that a 10-year RD&D funding commitment of $8–8.5 billion will be required to advance the technology to a stage where it is ready for commercial deployment.[25] Similarly, the Electric Power Research Institute (EPRI) estimates that approximately $10 billion will be required through 2017. EPRI also notes that over the next 20 years, it is expected that a total RD&D investment of roughly $19 billion will be required to develop and deploy advanced coal power and CCS technologies needed to achieve major, affordable CO_2 emissions reductions. In sum, both organizations find that CCS technologies will not be available for commercial deployment until approximately 2020 to 2025. The cost for CCS can be split into cost of capture, transportation[26] and storage.[27] Current estimates for large-scale capture systems (including CO_2 pressurization, excluding transportation and storage) are US$ 25–50 per tonne of CO_2 but are expected to improve as the technology is developed and deployed. If future efficiency gains are taken into account, costs could fall to US$ 10–25 per tonne CO_2 for coal-fired plants and to US$ 25–30 per tonne for gas-fired plants over the next 25 years.

The implementation of CCS technology raises the investment costs for power and industrial projects. New power plants and industrial facilities can be designed to incorporate CCS from their inception, or the technology can be retrofitted to existing sources

---

[25] The cost of employing a full CCS system for electricity generation from a fossil-fired power plant is dominated by the cost of capture. The application of capture technology would add about 1.8 to 3.4 US$ct kWh–1 to the cost of electricity from a pulverized coal power plant, 0.9 to 2.2 US$ct kWh–1 to the cost of electricity from an integrated gasification combined cycle coal power plant, and 1.2 to 2.4 US$ct kWh–1 from a natural gas combined-cycle power plant. Transport and storage costs would add between –1 and 1 US$ct kWh–1 to this range for coal plants, and about half as much for gas plants. [in]: Chapter 8 Cost and Economic Potential, *IPCC 2010 Special Report on Carbon Dioxide Capture and Storage*, Geneva p. 341 and following. See more: Analysis from the Massachusetts Institute of Technology Future of Coal 2010.

[26] With CO_2 transportation, pipeline costs depend strongly on the volumes being transported and, to a lesser extent, on the distances involved. Large-scale pipeline transportation costs range from 1–5 USD/t CO_2 per 100 km. If CO_2 is shipped over long distances rather than transported by pipelines, the cost falls to around 15–25 USD/t CO_2 for a distance of 5,000 km. [in]: IEA, *Prospects for CO_2 capture and storage concept*, p. 11, https://www.iea.org/Textbase/npsum/ccsSUM.pdf. See also: R. A. Palmer, D. Coleman, J. Davison, C. Hendriks, O. Kaarstad and M. Ozaki (2005), "Transport of CO_2", in B. Metz, O. Davidson, H. de Coninck, M. Loos and L. Meyer (eds.), *IPCC Special Report on Carbon Dioxide Capture and Storage*, Cambridge University Press, Cambridge, UK; J. J. Dooley, R. T. Dahowski and C. L. Davidson (2010), *CO_2-driven Enhanced Oil Recovery as a Stepping Stone to What?*, US Department of Energy, Pacific Northwest National Laboratory, Richland, WA; O. B. Edenhofer, B. Knopf, T. Barker, L. Baumstark, E. Bellevrat, B. Chateau, P. Criqui, M. Isaac, A. Kitous, S. Kypreos, M. Leimbach, K. Lessmann, B. Magne, S. Scrieciu, H. Turton and D. P. van Vuuren (2010), *The Economics of Low Stabilization: Model Comparison of Mitigation Strategies and Costs*, "Energy Journal", Vol. 31, pp. 11–48.

[27] The cost of CO_2 storage depends on the site, its location and method of injection chosen. In general, at around US$ 1–2 per tonne of CO_2, storage costs are marginal compared to capture and transportation costs. Revenues from using CO_2 to enhance oil production (EOR) could be substantial (up to 55 USD/t CO_2), and enable the cost of CCS to be offset. However, such potential is highly site specific and would not apply to most CCS Project. See IEA, *Prospects for CO_2 capture and storage concept*, p. 9, https://www.iea.org/Textbase/npsum/ccsSUM.pdf.

---

of CO_2 emissions. Overall, the cost of each project can vary considerably. The incremental cost of CCS varies depending on parameters, such as the choice of capture technology, the percentage of CO_2 captured, the type of fossil fuel used, and the distance to and type of geologic storage location. Overall, as with other new technologies, the cost of CCS is expected to be higher for the first CCS projects and decline thereafter as the technology moves along its "learning curve"[28].

Retrofitting existing plants for CCS is expected to be more expensive and reduce a plant's overall efficiency when compared to building a new plant that incorporates CCS from the start. Also retrofitting CCS on existing power plants faces additional constraints: insufficient land and space for capture equipment; a shorter expected plant life than a new plant, which limits the window in which to repay the investment in CCS equipment; and the tendency of existing plants to have lower efficiency, which consequently means that CCS will have a proportionally greater impact on net output than it would have in new plants.[29] New power plants without CCS can be designed to be "CCS-ready" so that the cost of later retrofitting the plant for CCS will be lower.[30]

Although the processes involved in CCS have been demonstrated in other industrial applications, no commercial scale projects which integrate these processes exist; the costs therefore are somewhat uncertain.[31] Some recent credible estimates indicate that the cost of capturing and storing CO_2 is US\$60 per tonne, corresponding to an increase in electricity prices of about US 6c per kWh (based on typical coal-fired power plant emissions of 2.13 pounds CO_2 per kWh).[32] This would double the typical US industrial electricity price (now at around 6c per kWh) and increase the typical retail residential electricity price by about

---

[28] McKinsey & Company (2008), *Carbon Capture and Storage: Assessing the Economics*. http://www.mckinsey.com/clientservice/ccsi/pdf/CCS_Assessing_the_Economics.pdf.

[29] Finkenrath, M. (2011), *Cost and Performance of Carbon Dioxide Capture from Power Generation*. International Energy Agency, http://www.iea.org/publications/freepublications/publication/costperf_ccs_powergen-1.pdf.

[30] http://www.rmcmi.org/education/carbon-capture-storage#.VL0T5dLF-uE. See also: C. von Stechow and P. Watson (2011), "Policy incentives for carbon capture and storage technologies in Europe: A qualitative multi-criteria analysis", *Global Environmental Change*, 21, pp. 346–357; Tenaska (2009), *Tenaska's Taylorville Energy Center Selected By U.S. DOE For Loan Guarantee Program; Illinois Electric Ratepayers Could Save Up To $60 Million Per Year With $2.5 Billion Guarantee*, www.tenaska.com/newsItem.aspx?id=62; S. N. Uddin, and L. Barreto (2008), "Biomass-fired cogeneration systems with CO_2 capture and storage", *Renewable Energy*, (6) 32, pp. 1006-1019; UNEP & partners (2009), *Catalysing low-carbon growth in developing economies: public finance mechanisms to scale-up private sector investment in climate solutions*, UNEP, Nairobi, Kenya; Vereniging Nederlandse Petroleum Industrie (2010), *Productie Nederlandse Raffinaderijen*, The Hague, Netherlands; Vivid Economics (2010), *Advanced Market Commitments for low-carbon development: an economic assessment*, London, UK.

[31] One way to finance future CCS projects could be through the *Clean Development Mechanism of the Kyoto Protocol*. At COP16 in 2010, the Subsidiary Body for Scientific and Technological Advice, at its thirty-third session, issued a draft document recommending the inclusion of carbon dioxide capture and storage in geological formations in Clean Development Mechanism project activities. At COP in Durban, a final agreement was reached, enabling CCS projects to receive support through the Clean Development Mechanism. See more at http://www.globalccsinstitute.com/insights/authors/markbonner/2012/06/20/whos-who-international-al-zoo-ccs-international-forums.

[32] *Science*, 27 February 2009, Vol. 323, p. 1158, "Stimulus Gives DOE Billions for Carbon-Capture Project.

50% (assuming 100% of power is from coal, which may not necessarily be the case, as this varies from state to state). Similar (approximate) price increases would likely be expected in coal dependent countries such as Australia, because the capture technology and chemistry, as well as the transport and injection costs from such power plants would not, in an overall sense, vary significantly from country to country.

The reasons that CCS is expected to cause such power price increases are several. Firstly, the increased energy requirements of capturing and compressing CO_2 significantly raises the operating costs of CCS-equipped power plants. In addition, there are added investment and capital costs. The process would increase the fuel requirement of a plant with CCS by about 25% for a coal-fired plant, and about 15% for a gas-fired plant. The cost of this extra fuel, as well as storage and other system costs, are estimated to increase the costs of energy from a power plant with CCS by 30–60%, depending on the specific circumstances. Pre-commercial CCS demonstration projects are likely to be more expensive than mature CCS technology; the total additional costs of an early large-scale CCS demonstration project are estimated to be €0.5–1.1 billion per project over the project lifetime. Other applications are possible. In the belief that use of sequestered carbon could be harnessed to offset the cost of capture and storage.[33]

4. Poland

Poland has abundant coal resources and generates 96% of its electricity from coal, the highest rate in the EU. As a non-Annex I country under the UNFCCC, Poland does not have GHG reduction targets. But the government recognizes the need to improve the environmental profile[34] of the country's coal use in order to achieve compliance with EU Directives and realize other air pollutant reductions. CCS is expected to play a growing role in Poland's clean coal activities in the future. Poland has considerable R&D activity related to clean coal technologies, including CCS. Active organizations include companies (the Polish Oil and Gas Company PGNiG, and energy and coal companies) and three research institutes: the Kraków Technology Academy, the Central Mining Institute in Katowice and the Institute of Chemical Coal Processing in Zabrze. A Joint Technology Initiative for Clean Coal has also been established. In 2008, Poland announced a National Programme for Geological Storage of CO_2, which aims at deploying two demonstration-scale CCS projects by 2015.[35]

Poland undertook Europe's first industrial CO_2 storage in a gas reservoir in the Borzęcin field. Since 1995, acid gas by-products of an amine-gas sweetening process containing

---

[33] [IPCC, 2005] *IPCC special report on Carbon Dioxide Capture and Storage.* Prepared by working group III of the Intergovernmental Panel on Climate Change, B. Metz, O. Davidson, H. C. de Coninck, M. Loos, and L.A. Meyer (eds.). Cambridge University Press, Cambridge, United Kingdom and New York, NY, USA, 442 pp. Available in full atwww.ipcc.ch (PDF – 22.8MB).

[34] IEA, *CO_2 capture and storage – A key carbon abatement option,* 2008, p. 172.

[35] This programme will involve the National Geological Institute, the Academy of Mining and Metallurgy and the Central Mining Institute. It will develop scenarios for CO_2 capture, evaluate CO_2 storage options and identify possible policy tools that will be needed. See also: European Commission, *European CO_2 capture and storage projects,* Brussels 2014, IEA, *Energy technology roadmaps,* Paris 2009.

60% CO_2 and 15% hydrogen sulphide (H_2S) have been injected into an aquifer underlying the Borzęcin reservoir. In addition, the Polish RECOPOL project is the first ECBM project outside North America. CO_2 is obtained from an industrial gas company and injected at the Silesia coal mine. CO_2 injection began in 2004 and reached an average of 12–15 t per day in 2005. The government-owned utility BOT Elektrownia Belchatów S.A. is planning two new "zero emission" power plants of 858 MW and 959 MW capacity. These plants will burn brown coal and hard coal respectively, and are due to become operational by 2016.

The Polish utility company Południowy Koncern Energetyczny SA plans to retrofit the Blachownia power station between 2010 and 2016 to capture and liquefy CO_2. It is not clear whether this project also includes plans for CO_2 storage. A variety of possible CO_2 storage locations in Poland have a combined potential of several dozen Gt CO_2 (ZEP, 2007a), including: the Jura and Kreda aquifers; hard coal mines Krupiński and Silesia; EGR at the KamieńPomorski and Borzęcin fields and offshore Baltic reservoirs, depleted oil and gas fields in western and southeastern Poland.[36]

5. Conclusions

CO_2 capture and storage is a promising emission reduction option with potentially important environmental, economic and energy supply security benefits. But more research and investment into CO_2 capture and storage is required. This study highlights the fact that large-scale uptake of CCS is probably 10 years off and that, without a major increase in RD&D investment, the technology will not be in place to realize its full potential as an emissions mitigation tool from 2030 onwards. The implementing CCS technology could contribute to a dramatic decrease in global GHG emissions, while most other environmental and human health impact categories increase only slightly on a global scale..

CO_2 capture leads to an increase in capital and operating expenses, combined with a decrease in plant energy efficiency. In terms of cost per tonne of CO_2 captured, costs are US\$ 40–55/t for coal-fired plants, and US\$ 50–90 for gas-fired plants. In terms of cost per tonne of CO_2 abated, the figures for coal-fired plants in 2010 are around US\$ 60–75, dropping to US\$ 50–65/t CO_2 in 2030; and for gas-fired plants, US\$ 60–110 in 2010, dropping to US\$ 55–90 in 2030. The EC should ensure that new power plants either include CCS or are CCS ready, with engineering designs that provide for later carbon capture retrofit, together with identified routes to CO_2 storage sites.

The better regulatory framework necessary to support CCS projects needs to be further developed, including the recently proposed E framework.[37] Desirable is also to significantly increase efforts to improve understanding among the public and stakeholders of CCS technology and the importance of its deployment. The wishes list includes recommended reduction of the cost of electricity from power plants equipped with capture through continued technology development and use of highest possible efficiency power generation

---

[36] *Op. cit.* p. 175.
[37] Significant effort at European and national level is needed to address CO_2 transport, CO_2 storage site selection and monitoring requirements, liability for CO_2 leakage, and property rights, among other things. See also IEA, *Legal aspects of storing CO_2*, Paris 2007.

---

cycles. The latest suggestion is to encourage efficient development of CO_2 transport infrastructure by anticipating locations of future demand centres and future volumes of CO_2.

Despite important progress, no EU country has yet developed a comprehensive, detailed legal and regulatory framework that is necessary effectively to govern the use of CCS. CCS is also poorly understood by the general public. By 2020, the implementation of at least 20 full-scale CCS projects in European countries, including coal-fired power plant retrofits, will considerably reduce the uncertainties related to the cost and reliability of CCS technologies.

References

A policy framework for climate and energy in the period from 2020 to 2030, p. 5, http://ec.europa.eu/clima/policies/2030/docs/com_2014_15_en.pdf.

A Policy Strategy for Carbon Capture and Storage, Information Paper, OECD/IEA, Paris; IEA (2012).

Ashworth, P., Jeanneret, T., Stenner, K., Hobman, E. V. (2012), *International comparison of the large group process. Results from Canada, Netherlands, Scotland and Australia*. CSIRO: Pullenvale.

Bachu, S. (2008), *CO_2 Storage in Geological Media: Role, Means, Status and Barriers to Deployment*, "Progress in Energy and Combustion Science", Vol. 34, No. 2, pp. 254–273, Elsevier, Amsterdam.

CO_2 Capture Ready Plants, Report 2007/4, IEA GHG, Cheltenham, UK; IEA GHG (2011).

Coal Utilization Research Council (CURC) Technology Roadmap, 2005 http://www.coal.org/roadmap/index.asp.

de Vos, R., van Breevoort, P., Höhne, N., Winkel, T., Sachweh, C. (2014), *Assessing the EU 2030 climate and energy targets,* ECOFYS, p. 4.

Dooley, J. J., Dahowski, R. T., Davidson, C. L. (2010), *CO_2-driven Enhanced Oil Recovery as a Stepping Stone to What?,* US Department of Energy, Pacific Northwest National Laboratory, Richland, WA.

EDF, The EU Emissions Trading system, 2012. http://www.edf.org/.../EU_ETS_Lessons_Learned_Report_.

Facing China's Coal Future: Prospects and Challenges for Carbon Capture and Storage, IEA (2013).

European Commission, *European CO_2 capture and storage projects*, Brussels 2014, IEA, *Energy technology roadmaps*, Paris 2009.

Finkenrath, M. (2011), *Cost and Performance of Carbon Dioxide Capture from Power Generation*, International Energy Agency, http://www.iea.org/publications/freepublications/publication/costperf_ccs_powergen-1.pdf.

Finon, D. (2010), *Efficiency of Policy Choices for the Deployment of Large Scale Low-Carbon Technologies: the Case of CCS*, Laboratoire d'Analyse Économique des Réseaux et des Systèmes Energétiques, Working Paper No. 27, Paris.

Fischer, C., Newell, R. (2008), *Environmental and Technology Policies for Climate Mitigation*, "Journal of Environmental Economics and Management", 55 (2), pp. 142–62.

Global Action to Advance Carbon Capture and Storage: A Focus on Industrial Applications, Annex to *Tracking Clean Energy Progress 2013*.

Global Storage Resources Gap Analysis for Policymakers, Report 2011/10, IEA GHG, Cheltenham, UK.

Global Carbon Capture and Storage Institute (2009), *Country Studies – The United States of America*, Canberra.

Global Carbon Capture and Storage Institute (2011), *The Global Status of CCS*, Canberra, Australia.

Groenenberg, H., Dixon, T. (2012), *Using carbon markets to advance negative emissions from biomass and CCS*, "Energy Procedia".

Hamilton, K. (2009), *Unlocking Finance for Clean Energy: the Need for "Investment Grade" Policy*, Chatham House, London, UK.

Havlik, P. *et al.* (2010), *Global Land-Use Implications of First and Second Generation Biofuel Targets*, "Energy Policy".

Helm, D., Hepburn, C., Mash, R. (2003), *Credible carbon policy*, "Oxford Review of Economic Policy", 19:3, pp. 438-450.

Hepburn, C. (2006), *Regulation by prices, quantities or both: a review of instrument choice*, "Oxford Review of Economic Policy", 22 (2), pp. 226-247.

IPCC Special Report Carbon Dioxide Capture and Storage Summary for Policymakers.

*Intergovernmental Panel on Climate Change.*Retrieved 2011–10–05.

Introduction to Carbon Capture and Storage – Carbon storage and ocean acidification activity, Commonwealth Scientific and Industrial Research Organisation (CSIRO) and the Global CCS Institute.Retrieved 2013-07-03.

IEA working paper, OECD/IEA, Paris; IEA (2013).

IEA, *Reducing greenhouse gas emissions*, Paris 2005, p. 26.

IEA GHG (IEA Greenhouse Gas R&D Programme) (2007).

International Energy Agency (2013), *Technology Roadmap – Carbon Capture and Storage.* http://www.iea.org/publications/freepublications/publication/name,39359,en.html.

IPCC 2010 Special Report on Carbon Dioxide Capture and Storage, Geneva, p. 341.

IEA, *Prospects for CO_2 capture and storage concept*, p. 11 https://www.iea.org/Textbase/npsum/ccsSUM.pdf. See also: Palmer, R., Coleman, D.

IPCC special report on Carbon Dioxide Capture and Storage. Prepared by working group III of the Intergovernmental Panel on Climate Change.

IEA, *Prospects for CO_2 capture and storage concept*, p. 9, https://www.iea.org/Textbase/npsum/ccsSUM.pdf.

IEA, *CO_2 capture and storage – a key carbon abatement option*, 2008, p. 172.

Metz, B., Davidson, O., de Coninck, H., Loos, M., Meyer, L. A. (eds.). (2005), *JPCC Special Report on Carbon Dioxide Capture and Storage*, Cambridge University Press, Cambridge, United Kingdom and New York, NY, USA, 442 pp. Available in full at www.ipcc.ch (PDF – 22.8MB).

McKibben, W., Wilcoxen, P. (2007), *A credible foundation for long-term international cooperation on climate change*, [in:]J. Aldy and R. Stavins (eds.), *Architectures for Agreement*, Cambridge University Press, New York.

McKinsey & Company (2008). *Carbon Capture and Storage: Assessing the Economics.* http://www.mckinsey.com/clientservice/ccsi/pdf/CCS_Assessing_the_Economics.pdf.

Meadowcroft, J., Langhelle, O. (eds.) (2009), *Caching the Carbon: The Politics and Policy of Carbon Capture and Storage*, Edward Elgar Publishing, Cheltenham.

Mineralölwirtschaftsverbande.V. (2011), *Mineralölstatistik*, Berlin, Germany. Mineral Products Association (2010), *Quarterly Cementitious*, London.

Nakhooda, S. (2010), *Getting to work: a review of the operations of the Clean Technology Fund*, World Resources Institute Working Paper, Washington, DC.

Newbery, D. *et al.* (2009), *Carbon Capture and Storage: Analysis of Incentives and Rules in a European Repeated Game Situation,* Electricity Policy Research Group, University of Cambridge, Cambridge, http://ec.europa.eu/clima/policies/2030/index_en.htm.

The IEA World Energy Outlook (WEO) Reference Scenario projects, https://www.iea.org/Textbase/npsum/ccsSUM.pdf.

OECD/IEA, Paris; IEA (2013c), *Methods to Assess Storage Capacity for CCS: Status and Recommendations*, OECD/IEA, Paris.

The American resources. Carbon capture and Storage, National Mining Association, Washington 2011, p. 3, www.nma.org/pdf/fact_sheets/**ccs**.pdf. http://www.world-nuclear.org/info/energy-and-environment/-clean-coal--technologies/.

Tenaska (2009), *Tenaska's Taylorville Energy Center Selected By U.S. DOE For Loan Guarantee Program; Illinois Electric Ratepayers Could Save Up To $60 Million Per Year With $2.5 Billion Guarantee*, www.tenaska.com/newsItem.aspx?id=62.

Uddin, S. N., Barreto, L. (2008), "Biomass-fired cogeneration systems with CO_2 capture and storage", *Renewable Energy*, (6) 32, pp. 1006-1019. UNEP & partners (2009), *Catalysing low-carbon growth in developing economies: public finance mechanisms to scale-up private sector investment in climate solutions*, UNEP, Nairobi, Kenya.

Vereniging Nederlandse Petroleum Industrie (2010), *Productie Nederlandse Raffinaderijen*, The Hague, Netherlands.

Vivid Economics (2010), *Advanced Market Commitments for low-carbon development: an economic assessment*, London, UK.

Chapter IV

The Role of Culture and Social Capital in Promoting Innovations and Competitive Advantages in High-Tech Industries

Zbigniew Bochniarz[1], Katherine Faoro

The Role of Social Capital in Cluster and Regions' Performance: Comparing Aerospace Cases from Poland and USA[2]

1. Introduction

Social capital became popularly applied in the social sciences over the last 30 years. Economists, sociologists, social psychologists, political scientists, and even philosophers are writing extensively on the role of social capital in families, communities, regional and national economies, and in global affairs. There are many inspiring concepts of social capital in academic literature but not many contributions indicating how to create, apply, and utilize it in practice towards a collective good. Our view of social capital, from the point of view of economists, is that of a form of capital that contributes to cluster integration and to regional development. There are a growing number of publications indicating that national development is uneven and highly dependent on regional boundaries. To a large extent, national development is dependent on contributions from rather a limited number of prosperous regions – the real engines of national economies – while the other regions are lagging behind (Runiewicz-Wardyn 2013; Kourtit & Nijkamp 2012; Landabaso *et al.* 2007). If regions are such an important unit of analysis, then we must address how to improve their performance, competitiveness, innovative capacity, and ability to overcome negative community outcomes. One of the most important discoveries in social sciences in the last 25 years was identifying regional clusters as economic drivers (Porter

[1] In collaboration with Barbara Sieńko-Kułakowska and Grzegorz Pisarczyk, Rzeszów School of Business, Poland.

[2] Authors utilized data collected by the "*Effective Clusters—The Basis for Innovation and the Source of Sustainable Regional Development*". Project No.:WND-RPPK.010300-18-009/12 based on Agreement No. 01-05/US/2014 of 5 May 2014 between Rzeszów School of Business (Wyższa Szkoła Zarządzania), Mickiewicza 1, Rzeszów 35-064, Poland, and University of Washington, 4333 Brooklyn Avenue NE, Seattle, WA 98195, USA.

1990). The significance of industrial clusters identified by M. Porter led to the creation and adoption of cluster-based policies at the regional level (e.g. the Basque Country and Catalonia in Spain) and later at national level (e.g. Scandinavian countries).

Early implementation of cluster-based regional development policies was successful and led the European Union (EU) to offer initial support for cluster initiative pilot programmes through its Regional Development Fund (RDF) between 2000 and 2006. These cluster pilot programmes produced positive results and encouraged the European Commission to modify the rules of regional policy and to re-allocate the bulk of its resources to support existing and emerging clusters in the 2007–2013 period. This policy change significantly boosted the numbers of emerging clusters and cluster initiatives throughout the EU. In Poland, for instance, this new policy resulted in the establishment of about 250 clusters and cluster initiatives by the end of 2012. Unfortunately, according to the Polish Agency for Enterprise Development (PARP), about 75% of their support for roughly 80 cluster initiatives failed to meet the promised objectives (PARP 2012, Zachariasz 2012). France experienced a similar "success" ratio as Poland, while Finland, Germany, and the UK reached at least 75 to 80% effectiveness in cluster programmes (Czyżewska 2013).

These findings from the EU cluster support policy inspired a group of researchers from Europe and the US to design a research proposal developing a new evaluation methodology and collection of best practices of cluster management. After securing funding from the Marshal Office of the Podkarpackie Voivodship in Poland, an international research project was born: "Effective Clusters – the Basis for Innovation and the Source of Sustainable Regional Development". This research began in the Podkarpackie Region in autumn 2013 and then moved to Washington State, USA in the spring of 2014. This project will be completed in late summer 2015 with an international conference planned in Poland for October 2015. The project is hosted by the Rzeszów School of Business (Wyższa Szkoła Zarządzania w Rzeszowie) and the Evans School of Public Affairs at the University of Washington (Seattle), in collaboration with the Adam Mickiewicz University in Poznań (Poland) and the Free University of Amsterdam (The Netherlands).

The main goal of this research project is to develop a methodology to analyze and evaluate cluster performance and apply it to aerospace clusters in Poland (Dolina Lotnicza) and the United States (Washington State Aerospace Cluster). The new cluster evaluation methodology will identify effective clusters and collect their best practices and problem solving procedures for key aerospace cluster stakeholders – business, public, and non-governmental sector leaders. These two clusters are the most advanced in their respective regions and are the major contributors to their regional economies. For that reason, the application of research findings should lead not only to measurable improvements in these clusters' performance, but also significantly contribute to sustainable regional development and prosperity.

Despite the growing significance of industrial clusters in the Polish economy, their potential is still far behind the world's leading economies. Effective cluster policy is particularly critical for the poorest European regions – among them the Podkarpackie Voivodship (one of 16 administrative regions– or "voivodships" – in Poland) which had the country's lowest GDP per capita in 2012. However, at the turn of the 21st century, the region began to develop faster than most of the other poorest regions in Europe, thanks to visionary leadership and entrepreneurship in all sectors and good governance at the local and regional levels (Bochniarz & Sieńko, 2008). As a result, industrial clusters started to emerge in the region and were further supported by the European Union's structural funds. One of the most dynamic and high-tech clusters in the region is called Dolina Lotnicza (Aviation Valley), with about 120 firms and approximately $2 billion in revenue in 2013. It is worth mentioning that the initial resources for the Aviation Valley cluster support came not from the governmental but from the corporate sector – from the United Technology Corporation (UTC), which owned several large manufacturing firms in this region – with a modest initial funding of $300,000 (split equally $60,000) for five years since 2003.

Today, Dolina Lotnicza hosts representatives of the major global aviation manufacturers (e.g. Airbus, Boeing, GE, Goodrich, Sikorsky, Whitney & Pratt, etc.) and is regarded as the future regional flagship. However, it is still far from reaching the necessary level of synergy to realize its full potential. Internal communication, management, and innovation are not yet operating at levels expected by its major stakeholders.

2. The role of region in economic development and innovation

Economic development, from a regional perspective, is often very uneven. There are regions in EU which have over 300% higher GDP per capita than the EU average, and other end regions which have below 30% average EU GDP, or stated differently, over 100 times lower than in the richest regions (Eurostat 2013). The differences in GDP per capita are not that high between the states in US, but still there are several states which make about 50% as much as the richest ones. Although GDP is not the best indicator of economic development, wealth or prosperity, it shows the relative economic activity between particular regions. It also raises questions about the reasons for such significant income differences. One of the major reasons for lagging economic development is the less competitive or attractive position of a region, which can be rooted in historical, geographical, or geopolitical foundations.

In the EU regional competitiveness index (RCI), authors ranked as NUTS2 level 262 regions from the most competitive region (NL31, Utrecht region in the Netherlands) to the worst performing region (BG31, Severozapaden in Bulgaria) (Annoni & Dijkstra 2013). They took into account 73 indicators originally developed by the World Economic Forum and adapted them to the various EU regions. Among top 10 EU regions, seven were connected to capital cities and the remaining three to large cities. This fact indicates clearly that the urban areas with large cities have competitive advantage over the rural areas. The Podkarpackie Region falls into the second category with a prevailing rural population, without big cities (the largest city Rzeszów has less than 200,000 inhabitants) and for that reason was ranked as 214 (PL3), ahead, however, of two other Polish regions.

Analyzing this highly diversified index, one might ask what regional competitiveness means: how it is different from the Ricardian national *comparative advantage* and Porterian *competitive advantage* of a firm; and why it matters for regional wealth and sustainability. Annoni & Dijkstra defined regional competitiveness as ...*the ability to offer an attractive and sustainable environment for firms and residents to live and work (ibid. 18).* This definition is similar to an earlier concept of Meyer-Stamer (2008) but emphasizes sustainability. However, both concepts underlined the notion of productivity of the region to serve their residents' needs, and for that reason, regional competitiveness is rather close to Porterian *competitive advantage* as compared to the Ricardian concept, which gives each nation a niche to compete. Roberto Camagni (2013) shows that regional governments do not have policy instruments like the national government (e.g. monetary policy) to create a *comparative advantage* because they have to compete with other regions, cities, or territories based on *absolute advantage*, like companies do. For that reasons they are exposed to external competition to attract external investors and expand their territorial capital (*ibid.*). They need to continually observe the global market and look for appropriate responses to secure their attractiveness (Nijkamp & Kourtit 2012). This also shows the significance of the quality of elected regional and local governments, their institutions, and policies in shaping regional business environment.

The competitiveness implemented in RCI 2013 reports is based on three groups of indicators assessing performance: (1) basic indicators, (2) efficiency and (3) innovation indicators. The Podkarpackie region has a pretty good position in basic indicators, is in the middle of the EU regions in terms of efficiency, and is lagging significantly behind in innovation indicators. The last group of indicators is the most important to build sustainable competitive advantages in the 21st century. This is the big challenge for new EU members, particularly for the underdeveloped regions. They have to follow best practices from the most competitive countries and regions and adapt the best models to their own conditions. One of the most important features of the most competitive EU regions, similar also to the US regions, is the geographical proximity of similar and related industries offered by urban areas – usually big cities – in the form of industrial districts or clusters. Cities often house world class universities – hubs of knowledge generation and human capital building. It is no coincidence that Silicon Valley grew up in the proximity of the San Francisco Bay area with top universities like Stanford and UC Berkeley. They created a unique innovative ecosystem full of distinguished culture that is impossible to replicate in other places (Saxenian 1994).

There are, however, some structural elements that should be taken into account in policy design to speed up innovation. Unfortunately, there is no correlation between investment in research and design (R&D) at universities and successful business innovation, it is a more complex and rather circular relationship (Runiewicz-Wardyn & Lopez-Rodriguez 2013). Investment in R&D without appropriate absorption capacity – measured by the matrix of student enrolment at tertiary level education and employment in college and higher education – might be ineffective and wasteful. However, it is no coincidence that the states with the best absorption capacities are ranked highest in the innovation category, measured by the number of patent applications and R&D intensity in knowledge-based sector (*ibid.*). In fact, the 10 top innovative states absorbed about two-thirds of the total investment in R&D between 2000 and 2005 (*ibid.*). Washington State is listed among the top 10 US states in all of these categories. In the EU, these regional differences related to innovation are even more dramatic (Runiewicz-Wardyn 2013; Annoni & Dijkstra 2013).

For that reason the EU has established structural funds, with the Regional Development Fund (RDF) at the top, to assist in catching up with the most competitive and innovative regions. One of the most important mechanisms of RDF distribution was the support for cluster initiatives to encourage regional cooperation within certain industries with active participation of their related and supporting industries. There is no doubt that bottom-up initiatives supported by wise governmental policies for clustering could facilitate good business environment for innovations and should contribute to regional prosperity.

3. Defining clusters and their role in regional development

The use of the term "clusters" in the earlier part of this paper requires a rigorous definition. The authors embraced the most popular definition, credited to Michael Porter: Clusters are geographic concentrations of interconnected companies, specialized suppliers, service providers, firms in related industries, and associated institutions that can cooperate and compete in particular fields (Porter 2008: 213).

There are interesting dynamics in cluster development, based on their integration from functional clusters through clumps to working clusters described (Fig. 1 and 2) by Derik Andreoli (Bochniarz, Andreoli 2008). Functional clusters are spatial networks of like and functionally-linked industries, which enjoy basic positive externalities from geographic proximity (co-location), known in economic literature as Marshallian externalities (Runiewicz-Wardyn 2013). Higher levels of integration represent clumps, groups of functionally-linked firms in which the physical distance separating member firms does not prohibit the range of benefits that are made possible through frequent interactions. The progress of integration moves up to the level of working clusters of firms and other organizations, including academic, governmental and other institutions. These working clusters maximize

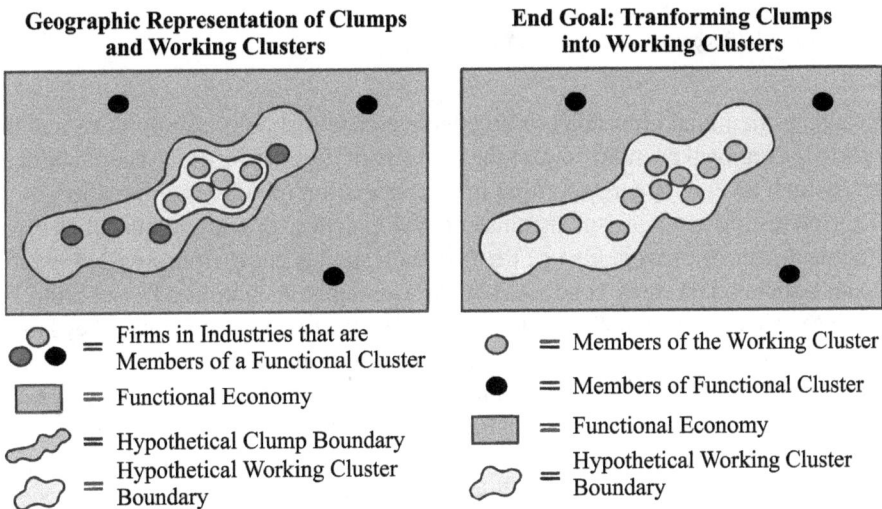

Figure 1. Cluster Development Process
Sources: D. Andreoli (Bochniarz, Andreoli, *op.cit.*).

benefits from synergetic effects coming from integration, cooperation, and competition within the clusters – Porterian externalities (*ibid.*). Finally, there are some other externalities coming from urban-related diversity commonly offered by big cities, creating benefits from cluster openness and innovation spillover between co-located clusters – Jacobsian externalities (*ibid.*).

Taking into account the dynamics of cluster development, growing synergy, and cluster integration, the authors came to formulate the following definition:

*The **effective cluster** is characterized by rich social capital that enables all participants to efficiently cooperate with one another, which leads to the increased generation of positive externalities coming from co-location and building collaborative synergy within the cluster, as well as openness for cooperation with other clusters, which leads to knowledge spillovers among them and increasing innovations.*

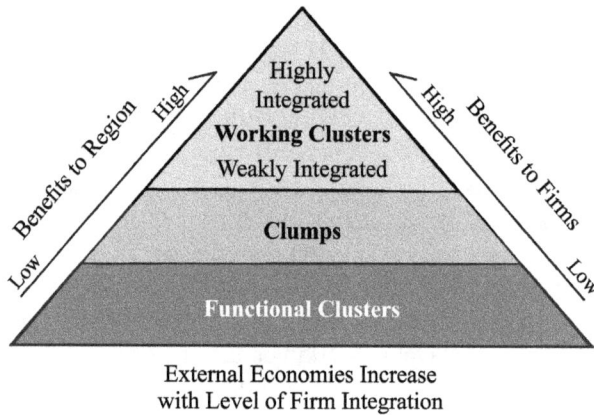

Figure 2. Benefits of Cluster Development
Sources: D. Andreoli (Bochniarz, Andreoli, *op.cit.*).

Reaching the integration level of an effective cluster should also produce maximum benefits to the regional economy due to the maturity of the cluster, which should be accompanied by high level of synergy coming from cooperation of all cluster members.

This interesting concept, linking cluster development with positive impact on regional development, can be proven. One of the first such studies came from Sweden, a pioneer of cluster policies. The study conducted by Per Lundquist & Dominic Power (2002) confirmed this positive impact of cluster development on the regional economy. They indicated that cluster supportive policy enhanced brand recognition, strengthened connection with global markets, boosted innovation and improved competitive advantages. Almost simultaneously completed research by Michael Porter confirmed a significant correlation between the active presence of industrial clusters and improved performance of the regional economy (2003). There were also several studies questioning the significance of clusters for regional economies (e.g. Martin *et al.* 2008). However, one of the recent studies by Örjan Sölvell and Matt Williams (2013) presents a convincing evidence supporting significant impacts from the 12 cluster organizations in North Mid Sweden on innovation and financial performance among the cluster firms and the whole region.

In order to verify the concept at a large scale, the team of Christian Ketels & Sergiy Protsiv pioneered research focusing particularly on how clusters influence New Growth Path for Europe in 27 members of EU with over 1,000 clusters (2013). They not only took into account existing clusters, but also analyzed the influence of about 2,000 cluster initiatives on "high road" strategy versus "low road" or "no road" strategies. They defined "high road" as a strategy based on enhancing the value of products and services by investing in innovation, technology, and skills, and improving quality standards at lower costs compared to the new value. "Low road" strategy is based on lowering the production cost of goods and services through more efficient use of capital, executing pressure on wages and prices from the suppliers and lobbying for lowering environmental and social regulations (*ibid.*3–4). The team developed a complex methodology to conduct this comprehensive research and produced impressive results. They confirmed that the presence of clusters has a positive and statistically significant impact on the average wages, and in this manner, contribute to the regional wealth. The impact of strategy selection on cluster performance produced differentiated results among prosperous and "catching up" regions, which were located mainly in Central and Eastern Europe. Among prosperous regions, three groups appeared: those performing high road strategies, those performing low road strategies, and those without any strategies. The authors noticed that the first strategy was mostly implemented in northern regions of EU and two other strategies were predominant in southern EU regions. The final conclusion of this very comprehensive study was that economic performance of a region is driven by the quality of its business environment and the strength of its cluster portfolio (*ibid.* 58).

4. Defining social capital and its relationship to other forms of capital

Although the term "social capital" appeared sporadically in social science literature in the 1970s, the real breakthrough in defining this category happened in the 1980s with contributions from Bourdieu (1986), Coleman (1988), and Lin (1986). The following decades saw an explosion of studies on social capital. There is also an ongoing process of institutionalization of the category of social capital as an important factor influencing social and economic development by international organizations, such as the United Nations, IMF, World Bank and OECD. For instance, the World Bank decided to support over 260 cluster projects worldwide at the end of 2000.

In a comprehensive study on SC, Nan Lin (2001) defines capital, as "investment of resources with expected returns in the marketplace" (Lin 2001:3). Making a clear distinction between capital and human capital, he then defines social capital as "investment in social relations with expected returns in the marketplace" (*op.cit.* 19). Lin was also critical of many authors identifying social capital with its "products", such as trusts, shared value, and norms.

Pierre Bourdieu defined social capital as a private investment in social networks that brings the owner expected benefits, such as wealth, and "symbolic capital" – representing symbols of social position and strata (1986). James Coleman regarded social capital as an individual good that could be traded through social networks for the advancement of human capital or for getting things done (1988).

Contrary to earlier researchers that treated social capital as an individual or private good, there is another group of authors defining social capital as a collective or even public good: Fukuyama (1997, 2000), Grootaert (1997), Huber (2008), Putnam (2000, 2003), Rosenfeld (2007), Roman (2007) and Woolcock & Narayan (2000).

According to Francis Fukuyama, social capital is a set of informal norms and rules as well as ethical values shared by individuals and social groups that enable them to cooperate effectively (1999, 2002). For Robert Putnam, social capital does not belong to anybody, but is a public good representing a set of social norms and civic attitudes supporting common actions and trust both interpersonal and in public institutions (1993). In a similar way, social capital is defined by experts from the Organization for Economic Cooperation and Development (OECD) as "networks together with shared norms, values and understanding that facilitate cooperation within or among groups" (OECD 2001). The World Bank expands this definition further by adding "institutions, relationships, attitudes and values that govern interactions among people and contribute to economic and social development" (Grootaert & van Bestelaer 2002).

Roberto Camagni defines social capital in a similar fashion "as the set of norms and values which govern interactions between people, the institutions where they are incorporated, the relationship networks set up among various social actors and the overall cohesion of society. In a word, social capital is the glue holding societies together" (*op.cit.* 8). Camagni brings social capital into a matrix of other forms of capital that composes the territorial capital of a region, which will be further explored.

Franz Huber proposes an interesting definition of social capital as "resources embedded in social networks which can be potentially accessed or are actually used by individuals for action" (Huber 2008:19). In addition to this, he distinguishes "internal social capital (resources mobilized through relationships between members of the collectivity)" from "external social capital (resources mobilized through relationships between members of the collectivity and actors outside of the collectivity)" (*ibid.* 20). As an example for this dual character of social capital, Huber uses economic clusters, where the distinction depends on access to knowledge within the cluster and access to other clusters and outside individuals.

Phil Cooke adds the notions of reciprocity, trust and "exchange for political or economic purposes" to his definition of social capital (Cooke 2007: 102), arguing that knowledge-based industries are more engaged than others in building and performing social capital.

Social capital is defined in a similar way by Carlos Roman – a system of social relationships based on trust and working according to well-known rules (Roman 2007). Roman's methods of measurement of social capital will be discussed later in this paper.

Finally, Stuart Rosenfeld summarizes the notion of social capital in clusters as that which gives opportunities to "know-who" leading to build "know-how" (2003). He also classifies social capital from the point of view of openness as positive or negative (Rosenfeld 2007). Positive social capital creates economic advantages that are major forces for clustering. Negative social capital can develop when there are efforts to limit membership in clusters and cultivate insularity or "lock-in".

In summary, we conclude that *social capital is defined as a special type of capital resulting from investments in building relations, institutions and networks that produce collaborative attitudes, shared norms and values, mutual understanding and trust.* These are critical factors for cooperation with other types of capital and thus contribute to sustainable development.

There are thousands of definitions of sustainable development but most of them are difficult to operationalize and assess. We believe that for human beings, sustainability means the long-term maintenance of their carrying capacity that secures their non-declining wealth and reproduction with limitation to natural endowments (natural capital), making the foundation for carrying capacity to secure intergenerational equity (Pezzey &Toman 2002). From economists' point of view sustainable development with respect to intergenerational equity will require securing non-declining resource endowment (Solow 1974; Hartwick 1977) or, what means exactly the same, non-declining total capital (Pierce 1987; Bochniarz & Bolan 2005).

Taking into account two approaches to assess sustainability: (1) maximizing wealth (usually based on GDP) and (2) maintaining non-declining capital (Non-Declining Total Capital), we prefer to focus on the second approach. For that reason we define the Non-Declining Total Capital as sustainability indicator as a sum of four types of capital:

$$TK = Km + Kn + Kh + Ks = \text{constant (non-declining)}$$

Where: Km = man-made capital (physical and financial); Kn = natural capital; Kh = human capital; Ks = social capital.

We also define Territorial Capital as the total capital related to cluster and/or region, which is unique and could be a source of their competitive advantage.

---

5. Measuring the value of social capital

There are two basic approaches to measurements of the value of social capital – according to Fukuyama (1999) – either by conducting census of groups and their members or by using surveys (1999: 6).

Due to the interest of the Effective Cluster project in measuring social capital within clusters, a combination of survey and interviews method will be applied.

Based on the accepted definition, the economic value of social capital depends on time invested in developing relationships and networks, institutions and shared values, attitudes and trust within a certain group of people. This begins at the micro level, for example a family, and continues through firms, clusters and regions to the macro level of a nation or global community (Bochniarz, Andreoli *et al.* 2008). It is worth to mention that this is a cost-based or reproductive value of social capital. It does not take into account either market or community valuation of social capital based on economic results or social impacts resulting from the existing social capital. Neither does it take into account potential depreciation of social capital that could be caused by many different reasons. This part of evaluation methodology should be further elaborated.

A very similar approach to the measurement of social capital was published by Carlos Roman (2007), with a set of complex indicators assessing its value mainly through surveys. For that reason, the research team adapted Roman's following indicators and applied them to the Podkarpackie Region to verify their usefulness.

There are four groups of indicators for measuring social capital:

- Indicators measuring associations: assessing the size of the investment in social capital
- Indicators measuring trust: assessing one of the most desired impacts of social capital
- Indicators measuring existing institutions: assessing business and political environment
- Indicators measuring results: assessing the impact of social capital.

The researchers divided the four groups of indicators into a series of specific questions, which included a variety of research methods, from simple surveys through in-depth interviews and participatory assessment workshops. The attached appendices explain methods implemented in calculating social capital in Podkarpackie region and in the Washington State.

6. Research hypotheses and verification of research hypotheses

Based on the above assumptions and definitions of the basic categories, as well as on several studies in this field, including Karima Kourtit & Peter Nijkamp (2012), Andrea Caragliu & Peter Nijkamp (2011) and Hans Westlund & Frane Adam (2010), the researchers formulated the following three hypotheses to be verified:

Hypothesis 1: The process of cluster development from its functional stage to the stage of the effective cluster is strongly influenced by increases in social capital.

Hypothesis 2: The integration process of a cluster fuelled by social capital has a positive effect on its economic performance.

Hypothesis 3: The progress in cluster development accompanied by growing social capital contributes to the sustainability of the regional economy.

At the end of February 2014, a field research project began work to test these hypotheses.

There were two methods applied: first based on the declared value of time contribution to cluster activities in either surveys or in interviews; second based on the calculation of the time invested in participating in cluster activities according to annual cluster management organizations (CMO) reports (see Appendices 1 & 2).

The first two stages of the field research – surveys and interviews – in the Podkarpackie Region were conducted in April 2014. The results indicate that there has been a significant investment in social capital by business leaders of the Aviation Valley cluster in order to move toward the goal of higher efficiency. We applied two methods of social capital assessment: (1) based on interviews and (2) based on the time invested in regular meetings, seminars, and training provided by the CMO.

The interviews provided data indicating that the top business leaders invested about 12.5% of their time for cluster activities, the equivalent of US$ 900,000 in 2013. The cluster association held regular monthly meetings, and established working groups to resolve emerging problems and to respond to future challenges and opportunities. The monetary value of social capital created in 2013 – measured by the time invested in building cluster relations, participating in joint activities, and resolving problems – was 3,180,000PLN or about 1M US$.

The second method based on the calculation from the time invested in CMO meetings and other joint activities (excluding cluster promotion and exhibitions) resulted in total value of social capital of US$ 430,000 created in 2013. It was lower than that based on interviews because it did not take into account all cluster activities. However, this very conservative value of social capital was seven times higher than in 2004. If one were to add time invested in cluster promotion, including domestic and foreign fairs, exhibitions and conferences, the value would increase easily to 1M US$, similar to the value declared in interviews. As a result of their significant investment in social capital, the trust in the association has significantly increased and is well illustrated by the number of cluster members, which has quadrupled since 2003 (18 members), reaching 120 members in April 2014. This way the Aviation Valley cluster became much more integrated and effective in 2013 and the process was continued in 2014.

In the case of the Washington Aerospace Cluster (WAC), the surveys and interviews were conducted from mid-July until the end of September 2014. Assuming the value of social capital depends on the time invested in building relations within the cluster, the authors calculated the time invested in WAC relations by four categories of stakeholders: (1) business leaders; (2) managers; (3) staff from the five CMOs: Washington Aerospace Partnership (WAP), Aerospace Futures Alliance (AFA), Pacific Northwest Aerospace Alliance (PNAA), Inland Northwest Aerospace Consortium (INWAC), and King County Aerospace Alliance (KCAA); and (4) volunteers.

Below are indicators illustrating the development of social capital in the WAC:

- Over 60% of survey participants indicated that the geographic proximity of firms and institutions had a moderate to high impact on the level of collaboration between firms.
- The interests in collaboration measured by the number of CMOs had increased five times over the last 8 years – from one CMO in 2005 to five CMOs in 2013.
- The most popular CMO was the PNAA with over 60% recognition.
- The majority of aerospace firms invested on average 1 hour per month in CMO activity.
- Total social capital created by the five CMOs was about $2,779,962 in 2013 with the following distribution: PNAA $1,669,364; AFA $439,713; INWAC $365,116; KCAA $259,882; and WAP $60,885.
- The accumulated social capital in the WAC produced a significant level of confidence (trust) in collaboration – the CMO members were ranked third (2.6) behind business partners (3.4) and employees (3.6).

Conclusion 1: Significant investment in social capital in Aviation Valley in Podkarpackie Region and by the five CMOs in WAC influenced the cluster integration process leading to higher effectiveness and confidence in collaboration between companies, but there is room for further advancement. This way we assume that Hypothesis 1 was verified.

In terms of economic performance, the Aviation Valley (AV) cluster has been growing drastically, with sales quadrupling during the period of 2003–2008 (PAIZ, 2012) and during the Global Financial Crises (2008–2012) further doubled. This unprecedented growth is closely tied to foreign direct investment (FDI), since the majority of sales came out of companies that were privatized by large multinational corporations. They had invested more than $2 billion in new machines and technologies and introduced thousands of new patents since 2003 (ResEco 2014).

In the case of the Washington Aerospace Cluster, it is hard to measure the influence of the social capital generated by CMOs on the economic performance of the WAC dominated by a single original equipment manufacturer (OEM) – the Boeing Company (TBC) – which controlled 96% of cluster revenues in 2012. However, significant increase in CMO activities, particularly related to the development of human and social capital, as well as improvements in technical and R&D infrastructure, facilitated the impressive economic performance of the WAC, which can be illustrated by the following indicators:

- In 2012, the aerospace industry reached $51.2 billion revenues, with another $8.7 billion generated by firms in related sectors – the most successful year on record.
- Total aerospace and supporting industry revenues grew by $15.9 billion, representing a 35% increase in growth between 2010 and 2012.
- Total jobs in 2012 were up by 15,000 since 2007, representing a 12.8% increase.
- Particularly dramatic was the increase in manufacturing jobs at TBC – of about 69% in 2012 compared with 2004 (CAI Report, 2014).
- TBC offered more energy efficient and environment friendly planes (e.g. 787), stabilized GHG emission at 2012 levels, moved toward renewable energy, and significantly reduced water use and wastes in their facilities.

Conclusion 2: Cluster integration was one of the contributors to the strong economic performance of both the AV & WAC and sets the stage to create shared value. This way we assume that Hypothesis 2 was initially verified but further research on exact causality is needed.

Finally, Polish aviation companies from the poorest (according to GDP per capita) Polish region offer advanced products and services and are present in all major supply chains, to the extent that almost every passenger aircraft in the world is equipped with at least one part manufactured in Poland. Aviation Valley represents a very sophisticated and technologically advanced industry with over 90% of production targeted toward the most competitive global markets. This cluster has a well-educated and skilled workforce that is earning decent salaries and thus contributing to the wealth of the region and its economic sustainability. The number of employees in the cluster has increased significantly, from 9,000 in 2003 to 23,000 in 2014. This positive picture is illustrated in economic terms by the growth of total export sales from $250 million in 2003 to $2 billion in 2013 (*ibid.*).

The WAC has significantly impacted Washington State's (WAS) economy. Indicators illustrate its contributions to the sustainable development of the region and examples of shared value creation by industry, public sector, and CMOs:

- CMOs effectively contributed to legislative efforts to bring new investments – mainly from Boeing – that generated (direct, indirect, and induced) over 253,000 jobs, nearly $76 billion in total sales and over $20 billion income to WAS economy in 2012.
- Direct aerospace wages paid more than 86% above the WAS average in 2012 – slightly down from 2006 (when aerospace wages were 110% above).
- WAS aerospace exports reached a historic peak of $37.1 billion – equal to 49% of all WAS exports – in 2012.
- The WAC total in-state direct and indirect purchases were more than $5.2 billion in 2012; however, the aerospace industry directly purchases approximately 8% of its total inputs from suppliers within WAS, with another 35% of purchases from value added – mainly labour inputs – meaning that about 44% of the input comes from WAS (CAI, 2014).
- The estimated total fiscal benefit from the WAC was over $544 million (including B&O and sales taxes).

There are selected examples of shared value created by the WAC in recent years in collaboration with CMOs: (1) the Washington Aerospace Training & Research Center in Paine; (2) the Joint Center for Aerospace Technology Innovation; (3) the Aerospace Joint Apprenticeship Committee and its programmes; (4) several aerospace training centres, internships, and new curricula at the community colleges and universities; (5) the modified state tax system, which is more favourable for small commuter air carriers and private airplane modification; and (6) in January 2015 a Boeing Advanced Research Center at the University of Washington was inaugurated. In addition, it is worth mentioning that TBC employees, retirees, and charitable trust invested $176 million in building better communities worldwide, including in WAC communities in 2013.

Conclusion 3: Progress in both AV & WAC development is accompanied by growth in social capital and the shared values contributed to the sustainable development of the whole region; however, there is still potential for improvement in sustainability and resilience of the cluster. This way we assume that Hypothesis 3 was initially verified.

7. Final conclusions

Participatory workshops conducted last autumn in Poland and still ongoing in the Washington State in US, based on the results of surveys and interviews of the Effective Cluster project, indicated that despite huge differences between both clusters, there is similar appreciation to the value of social capital and readiness to continue investments.

One of the major problems coming out of both the surveys and interviews is insufficient communication and information exchange – the key ingredient of cluster integration – within the AV and WAC. This is particularly felt by SMEs and non profits. Explanations include proprietary limitations, a culture of competition over collaboration, and insufficient understanding and/or appreciation of the value of the cluster and its social capital for building competitive advantage. At the same time in USA, 95% of survey participants supported new initiatives promoting the WAC in the region, and 80% supported economic initiatives – far ahead of support for environmental (68%) and social initiatives (55%). For that reason the authors conclude that **Aviation Valley and Washington Aerospace Cluster have the potential for creating more synergy of collaboration and to become an even more effective cluster.**

The descriptive analysis of the initial results from the field looks promising, but it should be further verified by more rigorous quantitative analysis of the three hypotheses. There is no doubt that the cluster and the region as a whole are moving towards a more sustainable path of development. Completing field research and analysis will lay the foundation for designing an appropriate cluster upgrading policy. This policy will be focused on further decreasing the weak links within the cluster and enhancing its strengths to improve its global competitiveness. It will also include the elimination of existing bottlenecks and unnecessary red tape, and investment in necessary types of capital, including human and social capital.

There is hope that this project will convince more business and political leaders that investing in social capital helps the participating actors to advance from a functional cluster to an effective one by reaching a higher level of development, better economic performance, and more effective contributions to the prosperity of the regional community.

References

Annoni, P., Dijkstra, L. (2013), *EU Regional Competitiveness Index:* RCI 2013.

Bochniarz, Z., Andreoli, D. *et al.*(2008), Clustering and Social Capital: Past and Current Research at the University of Washington and Unanswered Questions, at the Annual MOC Faculty Workshop of the Harvard Business School, 7 December.

Bochniarz, Z., Bolan, R. (2004), "Building Institutional Capacity for Biodiversity and Rural Sustainability" [in:] S. Light (ed.), *The Role of Biodiversity Conservation in Rural Sustainability*, IOS Press, Amsterdam. 79–94.

Bochniarz, Z., Sieńko, B. (2008), "Globalization, Clustering and Innovation: Some Regional Aspects", [in:] A. Herman & A. Szablewski (eds.), *Enterprise towards Global Challenges*, SGH: Warsaw. Vol. 2:152–168.

Bourdieu, P. (1986) ,*The Forms of Capital, Handbook of Theory and Research for Sociology of Education*, Richardson, JG, Greenwood Press.

Brundtland, G.H. (1987), *Our Common Future*, Oxford University Press, Oxford.

Caragliu, A., Nijkamp, P. (2011), The impact of regional absorptive capacity on spatial knowledge spillovers: the Cohen and Levinthal model revisited, "Applied Economics", 44:11, 1363–1374.

Coleman, J. (1988), Social Capital in the Creation of Human Capital, "American Journal of Sociology", 94:95–121.

Cooke, P. (2007), "Social Capital, Embeddedness, and Regional Innovation", [in:] M. Landabaso, A. Kuklinski and C. Román (eds.), *Europe: Reflections on Social capital, Innovation and Regional Development :The Ostuni Consensus,* Nowy Sącz: Wyższa Szkoła Biznesu, Oficyna Wydawnicza „Rewasz".

Czyżewska, D. (2013), Empirical evidence and first assessment of the competitiveness clusters policy in France, "International Journal of Management and Economics" 39. SGH.

Dasgupta, P., Serageldin, I. (2000), *Social Capital. A Multifaceted Perspective*, Washington, DC: The World Bank.

Flap, H.D., Völker, B. (2005), *Creation and Returns of Social Capital.* London: Routledge.

Francois, P. (2002), *Social Capital and Economic Development.* London, New York: Routledge.

Franke, S. (2005), *Measurement of Social Capital,* Reference Document for Public Policy Research, Development, and Evaluation. PRI Project Social Capital as a Public Policy Tool, Canada: Policy Research Initiative.

Fukuyama, F. (1999), *Social Capital and Civil Society.* IMF lecture.

Fukuyama, F.(2002), *Social Capital and Development: The Coming Agenda.* SAIS Review, 22(1).

Grootaert, C. (1997), *Social Capital: The Missing Link*?, World Bank, Expanding the Measure of Wealth: Indicators of Environmentally Sustainable Development. Washington, D.C.

Grootaert, C., Bastelaer, T. van (2002), "Conclusion: measuring impact and drawing policy implications", [in:] T. van Bestelaer (ed.), *The Role of Social Capital in Development.* Melbourne: Cambridge University Press.

Hartwick, JM. (1977), Intergenerational Equity and the Investing of Rents from Exhaustible Resources, "American Economic Review" 67(5): 972–974.

Huber, F. (2008), *Social Capital of Economic Clusters: Toward a Network-Based Conception of Social Resources*, Economic Geography Research Group. Working Paper Series No. 02.08, Cambridge.

Jacobs, J. (2000), *The Nature of Economies*, New York: Random House.

Ketels, Ch., Protsiv, S. (2013), *Clusters and the New Growth Path for Europe*. Working Paper No 14. www.foreurope.eu.

Kourtit, K., Nijkamp, P., Stimson, R. (eds.) (2011), *Innovation and Creativity as the Core of Regional and Local Development Policy,* "Regional Science and Practice", Vol. 3 (3).

Kourtit, K., Nijkamp, P. (2012), *Creative Firms as Change Agents in Creative Spaces. "*Quaestionaes Geographicae", December.

Landabaso, M., Kuklinski, A., Román, C. (eds.), *Europe. Reflection on social capital, innovation and regional development: The Ostuni Consensus*, Nowy Sącz: Wyższa Szkoła Biznesu – National-Louis University w Nowym Sączu, Oficyna Wydawnicza „Rewasz".162–175.

Lin, N. (1986), "Conceptualizing Social Support, Social Support, Life Events and Depression" [in:] N. Lin *et al.* (eds.), Academic Press Orlando.

Lin, N. (2001), *Social Capital. A Theory of Social Structure and Action*, Cambridge.

Lundequist, P., Power, D. (2002), Putting Porter into Practice? Practices of Regional Cluster Building: Evidence from Sweden, "European Planning Studies", Vol. 10, No. 6, 2002.

Marshall, A. (1920), *Principles of Economics*, 8th edition, London, Macmillan.

Martin, Ph., Mayer, Th., Mayneris, F. (2008), Spatial concentration and firm-level productivity in France, CEPR Discussion Paper 6858, London.

Nijkamp, P. (2003), Entrepreneurship in a Modern Network Economy, "Regional Studies", 37, 395–405.

OECD (2001), *The Well-Being of Nations: The Role of Human and Social Capital*, Paris.

Ott, K. (2003), The Case for Strong Sustainability, [in:] K. Ott & P. Thapa (eds.), *Greifswald's Environmental Ethics*. Greifswald.

PARP (2012), *Cluster Benchmarking in Poland*.

Pearce, D. (1989), *Energy and environment: Editor's introduction*. Energy Policy. Elsevier: 17(2): 82–83.

Pezzey, J.,Toman, M.A. (2002), Progress and problems in the economics of sustainability, [in:] T. Tietenberg and H. Folmer (eds.), "International Yearbook of Environmental and Resource Economics" 2002/3, 265–232.

Polish Information and Foreign Investment Agency (2012), Invest in Poland, Aviation, Online, Available HTTP: <http://www.paiz.gov.pl/sectors/aviation>.

Porter, M. (1990), *The Competitive Advantage of Nations*, The Free Press, New York, NY.

Porter, M. (2003), The Economic Performance of Regions, "Regional Studies", Vol. 37 (2003), No 6/7.

Porter, M. (2008), *On Competition: Updated and Expanded Edition*, HBS Publishing, Boston.

Porter, M., Kramer, M. (2011), Big Idea: Creating Shared Value, "Harvard Business Review", January-February.

Putnam, R. (1995), Bowling Alone: America's Declining Social Capital, "Journal of Democracy" 6, pp. 65–78.

Putnam, R. (2000), *Bowling Alone: The Collapse and Survival of American Community*, New York, Simon and Schuster.

ResEco, Firma (2014), *Raport końcowy z badań w małych i średnich przedsiębiorstwach klastra lotniczego* (Final Report from the Aviation Cluster SME) – Effective Clusters Project's study.

Román, C. (2007), Why Social Capital? What Social Capital? [in:] M. Landabaso, *op.cit.* 80–92.

Rosenfeld, S.A. (1997), Bringing business clusters into the mainstream of economic development, "European Planning Studies" 5: 3–23.

Rosenfeld, S. (2007), The Social Imperatives of Clusters, [in:] A. Landabaso, *op.cit.* 176–182.

Runiewicz-Wardyn, M. (2013), *Knowledge Flows, Technological Change and Regional Growth in the European Union*, Springer.

Runiewicz-Wardyn, M., Lopez-Rodriguez, J. (2013), *Knowledge Creation and Knowledge Linkages in the US Regions*, Fundacion de Las Cajas de Ahorros, Documento de Trabajo, No 725/2013.

Saxenian, A. (1994), *Regional Advantage: Culture and Competition in Silicon Valley and Route 128*, Harvard University Press, Cambridge, Massachusetts.

Sobel, J. (2002), Can we trust social capital?, "Journal of Economic Literature" 40: 139–154.

Solow, R. M. (1974), *Intergenerational Equity and Exhaustible Resources*, Review of Economic Studies, Symposium.

Sommers, P. (1998), Rural networks in the United States: lessons from three experiments, "Economic Development Quarterly" 12: 54–67.

Sölvell, Ö., Williams, M. (2013), *Building the Cluster Commons – An Evaluation of 12 Cluster Organizations in Sweden 2005–2012*. Stockholm: Ivory Tower Publishers.

Westlund, H., Adam, F. (2010), Social Capital and Economic Performance: A Meta-analysis of 65 Studies, "European Planning Studies", 18:6, 893–919.

Woolcock, M., Narayan, D. (2000), *Social Capital: Implications for Development Theory, Research, and Policy*, World Bank Research Observer 15 (2): 225–50.

Zachariasz, K. (2012), Pół miliarda i... zaklajstrowane Klastry, „Gazeta Wyborcza" nr 281, 01/12/2012:12.

Appendix 1

Table 1: Estimated Value of Social Capital in Aviation Valley Dynamics 2003–2013

Years	Number of AV members	Number of AV leaders involved	Annual contributions to SC by AV leaders in PLN	Number of AV staff involved	Annual contributions to SC by AV staff	Total annual contributions to SC of leaders and staff (6 + 10) in PLN	Annual growth of SC in %
1	2	5b	6	9c	10	11	12
2003	18	6	72,000	6	100,800	172,800	100
2004	22	7	115,920	8	134,400	250,320	145
2005	40	8	138,240	10	194,400	332,640	133
2006	56	8	155,520	10	194,400	349,920	105
2007	63	10	216,000	10	240,000	456,000	130
2008	71	11	277,200	12	332,640	609,840	134
2009	78	12	403,200	12	372,240	775,440	127
2010	82	13	491,400	12	396,000	887,400	114
2011	92	13	491,400	14	508,200	999,600	113
2012	98	14	588,000	14	554,400	1142,400	114
2013	110	14	588,000	15	730,800	1318,800	115

Source: Authors' calculation utilized data provided by the Aviation Valley Association based on their files with the following assumptions: a. Average time committed to AV cluster activities by CEOs based on interviews; b. This number includes average number of CEOs, their deputies and members of Board of Directors; c. This number is a total of AV employees participating in AV cluster activities during the whole year, including full-time staff of the AV management.

The value of social capital has increased over 7 times since 2003 and was approximately $430,000 in 2013.

Appendix 2

CMO Contributions to Social Capital, 2013

Assumption: CMO membership demographics mirror the weights of Leadership and Management proportions in the industry as a total of all membership.

Leadership proportion of CMO membership:	0.00693909
Management proportion of CMO membership:	0.99306091

Assumption: Average monthly salaries for Leadership and Management adopted from average proportion of salaries in all Washington industries (see "Breakdown of Aerospace Leadership vs. Management vs. Staff" Excel Workbook)

Aerospace Leadership hourly wage:	$740.85
Aerospace Management hourly wage:	$109.54

Aerospace Staff hourly wage: $42.45

Assumption: CMO Management is valued as equivalent to an Aerospace Management salary.

Assumption: CMO Paid Staff is valued as equivalent to an Aerospace Staff salary.

Assumption: CMO Volunteer hours are valued as equivalent to the 2013 WA State minimum wage.

Table 2. Social Capital created by Members of CMOs in 2013

Cluster Management Organization (CMO)	Hours Committed by Attendees to CMO Activity, 2013	Value of Annual Attendance by Aerospace Leadership at CMO Activities	Value of Annual Attendance by Aerospace Management at CMO Activities	Value of Membership Attendance at CMO Activities, 2013
Aerospace Futures Alliance (AFA)	2,800	$14,394.25	$304,595.42	$318,989.67
Inland Northwest Aerospace Consortium (INWAC)	1,176	$6,045.59	$127,930.08	$133,975.66
King County Aerospace Alliance (KCAA)	420	$2,159.14	$45,689.31	$47,848.45
Pacific Northwest Aerospace Alliance (PNAA)	6,545	$33,646.57	$711,991.80	$745,638.36
Washington Aerospace Partnership (WAP)	525	$2,698.92	$57,111.64	$59,810.56
TOTAL	11,466	$58,944.47	$1,247,318.25	$1,306,262.72

Table 3. Social Capital created by the Paid CMOs Managers

Cluster Management Organization (CMO)	CMO Paid Managers	Hours Worked by Paid Managers, 2013	Value of CMO Management, 2013
Aerospace Futures Alliance (AFA)	1	720	$78,871.84
Inland Northwest Aerospace Consortium (INWAC)	1	1920	$210,324.89
King County Aerospace Alliance (KCAA)	1	1920	$210,324.89
Pacific Northwest Aerospace Alliance (PNAA)	6	1056	$694,072.15
Washington Aerospace Partnership (WAP)	0	0	$0.00
TOTAL	9	5616	$1,193,593.78

Table 4. Social Capital created by the Paid CMOs Staff

Cluster Management Organization (CMO)	CMO Paid Staff	Hours Worked by Paid Staff, 2013	Value of CMO Staff, 2013
Aerospace Futures Alliance (AFA)	4	240	$40,748.91
Inland Northwest Aerospace Consortium (INWAC)	1	480	$20,374.45
King County Aerospace Alliance (KCAA)	0	0	$0.00
Pacific Northwest Aerospace Alliance (PNAA)	5	1080	$229,212.61
Washington Aerospace Partnership (WAP)	0	0	$0.00
TOTAL	10	1800	$290,335.98

Table 5. Social Capital created by the Volunteers

Cluster Management Organization (CMO)	CMO Volunteers	Hours Worked by Volunteers, 2013	WA. State Minimum Wage	Value of CMO Volunteers, 2013
Aerospace Futures Alliance (AFA)	6	20	$9.19	$1,102.80
Inland Northwest Aerospace Consortium (INWAC)	1	48	$9.19	$441.12
King County Aerospace Alliance (KCAA)	31	6	$9.19	$1,709.34
Pacific Northwest Aerospace Alliance (PNAA)	6	8	$9.19	$441.12
Washington Aerospace Partnership (WAP)	13	9	$9.19	$1,075.23
TOTAL	57	91		$4,769.61

Table 6. Social Capital created by All CMO Participants in their 2013 Activities

Cluster Management Organization (CMO)	Potential Contribution to Social Capital by All CMO Activities and Workforce, 2013	Net Present Value of Legislative Activities
Aerospace Futures Alliance (AFA)	$439,713.22	$3,781,588,068.43
Inland Northwest Aerospace Consortium (INWAC)	$365,116.13	
King County Aerospace Alliance (KCAA)	$259,882.69	$710,789,638.33
Pacific Northwest Aerospace Alliance (PNAA)	$1,669,364.25	
Washington Aerospace Partnership (WAP)	$60,885.79	
TOTAL	$2,794,962.08	$4,492,377,706.76

Philip Kurz, Dirk Nicolas Wagner

Innovative and Entrepreneurial Opportunity Recognition – An Analytical Approach Using the Example of Poland

1. Introduction

In the last two decades, the discipline of entrepreneurial research has grown vastly and has become one of the most dynamic research fields in business, economics, psychology and also sociology (Wiklund *et al.* 2011). Despite the fact that the opportunity recognition (OR) process can be classified as the "heart" of entrepreneurial research – as every entrepreneurial activity has its roots in the recognition of an opportunity – there is still only little understanding of how people perceive business opportunities in their environment (Venkataraman 1997). What specifically is enabling successful entrepreneurs to see what others do not see and which abilities and characteristics play an important role in this process? Models that have been developed in order to find an answer to these questions are rare. Furthermore, most of these models have been constructed only one-dimensionally – wherefore other important factors of influence are faded out (e.g. Bhave 1994; Schwartz & Teach 1999; Hills, Singh & Lumpkin 1999; De Koning 1999; Sigrist 1999 as cited in Ardichvili *et al.* 2000). So far, only Ardichvili *et al.* (2000) as well as Baron (2006) have dared to develop complex multi-dimensional models. But the question arises if their approaches can be used for a quantitative examination as these models convey the impression that they have not been developed from an analytical point of view. Anyhow, the latest evidences provided by the few scientists who have been studying the OR-ability can be isolated in order to develop a new empirical framework. Within this paper, these elements will be identified, examined, and evaluated according to their usability, with Poland serving as an example. After explaining the purpose and the relevance of this paper, an overview of the current level of entrepreneurial activity in Poland and the perceptions and attitudes towards entrepreneurship amongst Poles will be provided. Furthermore, behaviour-focused concepts, which have been developed to conceptualize the entrepreneurial process, will be examined in order to understand the ambiguous attitudes and perceptions of Poles towards entrepreneurship. Additionally, this will provide a knowledge base for the OR-theory that will be fundamental for the later development of an analytical framework. After the review of state-of-the-art literature, elements of OR will be extracted and operationalized in order to make them measurable and to use them in a quantitative research. Last but not least, the outcomes will be discussed to determine their influence on the weakly developed OR-ability amongst Poles and consequently the reason for a low level of entrepreneurship in Poland.

First of all, the findings resulting from this paper can be a further progress in the search for the question what elements primarily influence the OR process. But the resulting evidence would not only provide input for further theoretical approaches or frameworks. As entrepreneurs and therefore entrepreneurial activities are a major factor for the national economic growth, it is of course a desirable goal to gather evidence about the ability to recognize opportunities which could later on be used to conduct cultural-adapted entrepreneurship trainings in order to foster the ability to recognize opportunities of individuals (Baron 2006).

Due to the identified lack of the restricted usability of the latest models in a profound macro-analysis and the stated characteristics of entrepreneurship in Poland, this paper has the following purposes: 1. to develop a multi-dimensional framework that can be used to examine empirically the ability to recognize business opportunities; 2. to test this framework's validity using the example of Poland; 3. to examine the ability to recognize opportunities amongst Poles.

2. Entrepreneurship in Poland

Primarily, it is necessary to explain the previously mentioned characteristics of entrepreneurship in Poland. Hence, this chapter provides an overview of the level of entrepreneurial activity in Poland as well as of the attitudes and perceptions. The Global Entrepreneurship Monitor (GEM) gathered the data presented in this chapter for its Polish National Report in 2013. The following table summarizes the data in comparison with the global averages.

Current level of entrepreneurship and entrepreneurial attitudes in Poland	Poland	Total Global Average
Attitudes & Perceptions		
Entrepreneurial intentions	24.2%	30.2%
Perceived opportunities	20.4%	45.6%
Perceived capabilities	53.9%	53.7%
Fear of failure	58.7%	36.3%
Entrepreneurship as a desirable career choice	67.9%	66.9%

Current level of entrepreneurship and entrepreneurial attitudes in Poland	Poland	Total Global Average
Level of entrepreneurial activities		
High-status of successful entrepreneurship	57.1%	73.1%
Nascent	4.8%	8.0%
New entrepreneurs	4.6%	7.1%
TEA entrepreneurs (Nascent + New entrepreneurs)	9.4%	14.6%
Established enterprises	5.8%	8.6%
Discontinuation of business	3.9%	6.8%

Nascent entrepreneurs are defined by the GEM as individuals who have not launched a venture yet but plan to establish a business in the next three months and are at an early stage. With a proportion of 4.8 % in Poland this rate was far below the global average of 8.0 %. *New entrepreneurs* are classified as individuals who have just established a business within the time frame of three to 42 months before the GEM's research. This rate, amounting to 4.6%, was again far below the average of 7.1%. The level of already *established enterprises*– businesses that have been operating on the market for more than 3.5 years – was also below the average (5.8%) of 8.6%. As the rate of nascent and new entrepreneurs is currently below the level of established enterprises, and statistically 3.9 %[1] thereof will be discontinued, the level of established enterprises is expected to even decrease further during the next years. Considering the data provided by the GEM in the table, there seems to be a phenomenon which seems to be inexplicable: Poles see being an entrepreneur as a desirable career choice, think they have sufficient skills and resources to fund an enterprise but – like expounded before – the level of entrepreneurial activities is far below the global average. To get a better comprehension of the possible factors influencing these entrepreneurial activities, it is necessary to outline the entrepreneurial attitudes and perceptions of Poles.

The rate of entrepreneurial intentions – people who plan to establish a business within the next three years – does not differ drastically from the global average, as it is only roughly one sixth below. The status of entrepreneurship as a desirable career choice is even above the global level. Contrary to these quite positive indicators, there are factors that seem to influence the level of entrepreneurship negatively. The fear of a possible business failure is one of these. The *fear of failure* is, according to the GEM's data, 22.4 % higher (!) than the global average. So the factor *fear of failure* seems to strongly influence Poles. Hofstede's statistical evidence about the cultural dimension of *uncertainty avoidance*[2] underlines the circumstance that Poles do dislike uncertain, ambiguous situations as this indicator, with a value of 96[3], is one of the highest in the world (Hofstede 2000). Addition-

---

[1] Average rate of discontinued business in Poland according to the GEM National Report Poland 2013.
[2] Defined as the "degree of risk felt by members of a particular culture in the face of new, unknown or uncertain situations. This feeling is expressed, *inter alia*, by stress and the need for predictability, which may be satisfied by all kinds of laws, rules and customs" (Hofstede 2000: 180–181).
[3] Maximum is 100.

ally and most importantly, Polish society struggles with the process of noticing suitable business opportunities. The proportion of Poles noticing business opportunities has even decreased (by 13%) between 2011 and 2012. This becomes even more incomprehensible as according to the survey done by Polish experts during the GEM's National Expert Survey 2013, the Polish market holds a lot of great opportunities for nascent entrepreneurs. So the level of entrepreneurial activity seems to be negatively affected by two main factors: first, the high fear of failure, and secondly, the weakly developed ability to recognize business opportunities.

Despite the fact that a high *fear of failure* can distract a person from launching a venture, the recognition of a business opportunity is the main precondition for an entrepreneurial venture, since without a recognized business opportunity, one would not be able to establish a successful business. Based on this assumption, this paper focuses its analysis on this determinant. Like expounded previously, Poland seems to be an insightful example for testing the hereafter developed framework. Nevertheless, for the purpose of a better understanding of the ambiguity of the Polish attitudes and perceptions towards entrepreneurship, it is necessary to understand conceptualizations of the entrepreneurial process, wherefore these will be explained in the following chapter.

3. Theoretical background

Only by understanding action- and behaviour-focused entrepreneurship models, it is possible to comprehend the paradox situation of entrepreneurship in Poland. These models and theories, presented in this chapter, are also a starting point for building a knowledge base with the aim to understand the conceptions of the OR process, as there are many linkages between these two research fields. Therefore, the theoretical part of this paper is divided into two parts. Primarily, an overview of state-of-the-art theories and models of entrepreneurial research thematizing the entrepreneurial process will be given. Secondly, theories and models and the included elements of OR will be examined and "isolated" step by step according to their usability for a framework. In this part of the paper, the conceptualizations of the entrepreneurial process, developed by Ajzen & Fishbein (1975; 1980; 1985; 1987; 1991; 2005), Shapero & Sokol (1982) and Krueger and Brazeal (1984), will be presented step by step.

The most suitable predicator for evaluating the behaviour of a person is the individual intention, which is a person's readiness to perform a given behaviour – for instance towards the formation of a business (Pohja 2009). This assumption is the basis for the theory of reasoned action (TRA), which has been developed by Ajzen & Fishbein in 1975 and was modified by them in 1980 (Ajzen & Fishbein 1975, 1980). The theory suggests that an individual's *behavioural intention* depends on his or her *attitudes* towards the *behaviour* and its *subjective norms*, whereas attitudes are defined as "the sum of beliefs about a particular behaviour weighted by evaluations of these beliefs" (Pohja 2009: 9). *Subjective norms* describe the influence of one's social environment, while beliefs of people within the social environment are "weighted by the importance" (Pohja 2009: 9) and the attributes to each individual opinion. Therefore, social norms influence one's perception "of what important people in our lives would think about" (Krueger & Brazeal 1994: 97) the launch of a venture – that is, for instance, if our family or friend approve or disapprove our starting a venture. *Behavioural intention* is defined as both, the *attitude* toward the behaviour and the *subjective norm* toward the behaviour. When Ajzen & Fishbein (1985, 1987, 1991) realized that actions are highly influenced by external and internal forces, they advanced their TRA to the theory of planned behaviour (TPB), which is illustrated in Fig. 3. Internal forces can be skills, abilities, knowledge or planning, whereas external forces can be time, opportunity or dependence on other people (Ajzen & Madden 1985). These background factors directly influence a person's behavioural intention. TPB was modified again in 2005 by Ajzen & Fishbein, when they added new antecedents: *behavioural beliefs*, *normative beliefs* and *control beliefs* which are assumed to be influenced by the background factors and are in their sum affecting the *behavioural intention*.

Behavioural beliefs are defined as considerations of the likely consequences – outcome expectancies, such as costs and benefits – of a particular behaviour (Ajzen & Fishbein 2005). Added up, these beliefs are assumed to produce an overall positive or negative evaluation or attitude toward performing "the behaviour in question" (Pohja 2009: 10). If the perceived benefits outweigh perceived negative consequences, it is likely that an individual has a favourable attitude toward the particular behaviour (Ajzen & Fishbein 2005). Logically, this works also the other way around.

Normative beliefs are defined as the influence on the approval or disapproval of a given behaviour by important people (e.g. by friends, family members or co-workers). These beliefs in total are assumed to lead to perceived social pressure (resulting from *subjective norms*) to perform or not to perform the behaviour in question. If an individual perceives that his/her most respected others share the opinion that he or she should proceed with or should not proceed with the particular behaviour, the subjective norm is applying pressure to engage or not to engage in the behaviour. *Control beliefs* are defined as beliefs which concern the presence or absence of factors that make the performance of a behaviour more convenient or more difficult. In sum, these beliefs lead to the individual's perception that he or she has or does not have the skills or resources to perform the behaviour. People who believe that they have sufficient skills or resources needed to perform the particular behaviour are likely to develop a strong *behavioural control.* The derived factors – *attitude toward the behaviour*, *subjective norm* and *perceived behavioural control*– are in their sum influencing the intention to perform the behaviour. Additionally, the *perceived behavioural control* is believed to directly influence the behaviour. *Perceived behavioural control* and *behaviour* are directly interconnected. Due to this, Ajzen & Madden (1985 as cited in Pohja 2009) suggested that the *actual behavioural control* directly influences the behaviour of an individual as the *perceived behavioural control* reflects directly the available resources as well as the perceived opportunities. A wide range of social-psychological literature supports this behaviour predictability-tool (Shaver 2005, Krueger & Brazeal 1994, Krueger, Reilly & Carsrud 2000 as cited in Pohja 2009). The pioneer of the cognitive approach toward the entrepreneurial process was Israel Kirzner (1979). He developed the theory of *entrepreneurial alertness*, which deals with an individual's ability to discover and exploit opportunities. Most of today's conceptualizations of the entrepreneurial process as well as the OR process are based on his work – and also Shapero & Sokol's model of the *entrepreneurial event*. This model includes three main elements that are believed to be fundamental for an entrepreneurial event: *situation, perception of desirability* and *perception of feasibility* (Shapero & Sokol 1982 as cited in Pohja 2009). A *displacement event*, either positive or negative, can, for example, be an inheritance or sudden unemployment. Research also offers evidence how specifically significant life events can make an increase in a countries' level of entrepreneurial activity, predictable through indicators like a rising rate of unemployment or migration (Krueger & Brazeal 1994). Krueger & Brazeal assume that individuals do not really change, but their perceptions of the new circumstances do. Therefore, it is assumed that entrepreneurial potential has always been there, but it was the *displacement* that brought the potential to the surface and changed the behaviour. The result of this change is that individuals seek the best perceived opportunities out of the enacted set of opportunities (Krueger & Brazeal 1993). The *perception of desirability* of an individual depends on two main features: *attitude toward the act* and *social norms*. The *attitude toward the act* explains what an individual perceives as desirable. This perception itself "depends on the likely personal impact of outcomes from performing the target behaviour" (Krueger & Brazeal 1994: 96). The second factor that influences the *perception of desirability* is the *social norm*, which has been explained previously as an element of Ajzen & Fishbein's frameworks. *Perception of feasibility* was defined by Shapero & Sokol as one's perception of the available resources (e.g. financial resources), personal competences (e.g. a business school degree), the environment (e.g. governmental supports), social networks (family, colleagues, mentors, etc.) and last but not least, self-efficacy (Shapero & Sokol 1982; Sokol 1985 as cited in Pohja 2009). Perceived *self-efficacy* is defined as one's ability to perform a particular target behaviour. *Self-efficacy* is also an attribution of the individual control in a particular situation and has been linked to managerial as well as directly to entrepreneurial behaviour (Krueger & Brazeal 1994). Usually, potential entrepreneurs are likely to make decisions with only little information about the possible obstacles. They are also believed to see obstacles which are non-existent in reality but tend not to see obstacles which exist in reality. To develop actual entrepreneurial intentions, it is necessary that evident obstacles do not deter one. Self-efficacy helps potential entrepreneurs to overcome this deflection (Krueger & Brazeal 1994). Shapero & Sokol's concept "separates the entrepreneur from the entrepreneurial event", as the external influences are in the centre of interest (Pohja 2009: 7). The concept also highlights that it is not important what skills and resources people have in reality, but what their perceptions of their skills and resources are (Krueger & Brazeal 1994).

Krueger & Brazeal have developed a model that is built upon the previously stated scientific concepts. It includes the following elements: *perceived desirability, perceived feasibility, credibility, propensity to act, entrepreneurial potential, displacement event* (here *precipitating event*) and *entrepreneurial intention*. The *credibility* of an entrepreneurial venture requires a *perception of desirability* (do I want to be an entrepreneur?) and *feasibility* (am I able to be an entrepreneur?). High *credibility* plus the *propensity to act* – without which one would not act – are believed to be the basis for one's *entrepreneurial potential*. *Propensity to act* is defined as the propensity to "act as a stable personality" (Krueger &

Brazeal 1994: 98). This *propensity to act* is closely related to the so-called *locus of control*, which is meant to be the control of "initiating and maintaining goal directed behaviours" (Krueger & Brazeal 1994: 98).

Krueger & Brazeal's concept research work shows us that the main cognitive foundation for every entrepreneurial venture is *perceived desirability* and *feasibility*. This explains why the attitudes and intentions of Poles were previously defined as highly ambiguous and paradoxical, as Poles assessed an entrepreneurial venture desirable and feasible. Based on this, an entrepreneurial venture should be seen as highly credible – only a lack of *propensity to act* or a missing *precipitating event* could "interfere". Based on the *perceived desirability* and *feasibility*, Poles are believed to have one of the two preconditions for *perceived behavioural control*. If they would now also recognize an opportunity, their *intention* and *behaviour* would presumably be directly influenced, wherefore an entrepreneurial venture is highly probable. Based on these findings, it is assumptive that one of the main negative factors in Poland – the weakly developed ability to recognize opportunities – is the reason for the low level of entrepreneurial activity, as a high fear of failure would possibly also influence both *perceived desirability* and *perceived feasibility* negatively, and something that can be categorized as risky might not seem desirable and feasible. Consequently, the ability to recognize business opportunities is one of the most important abilities a successful entrepreneur should have as no venture could be launched without a recognized opportunity (Ardichvili *et al.* 2000). So this discipline of research can be identified as the "heart" of entrepreneurial research (Venkataraman 1997). It is important to differentiate the term of what is broadly known to us as "opportunity recognition". Ardichvili *et al.* have defined opportunities as "a range of phenomena that begin uninformed and become more developed through time" (2003: 108). Ardichvili *et al.* therefore differentiate between *opportunity recognition* (including *perception, discovery* and *creation*), *opportunity development*, and *opportunity evaluation*.

Many definitions of the term "opportunity" have been proposed by literature during the last 30 years (Bhave 1994, Herron & Sapienza 1992, Kirzner 1979 & 1985 as cited in Baron & Ensley 2006). The most frequently mentioned are opportunities with a high potential economic value. Secondly, there are opportunities with a high "newness" to the society, and thirdly, opportunities, which are perceived as highly desirable. Baron has used the firstly stated definition of opportunities for his OR framework. So he defines OR as "the cognitive process (or processes) through which individuals conclude that they have identified an opportunity" (Baron 2006: 107) with a favourable economic output for them. Opportunity recognition was defined by Ardichvili *et al.* as the process of sensing or perceiving market needs and/or underemployed resources and as well the recognition of ties between needs and resources in order to create a new fit between those in the form of a business concept (Ardichvili *et al.* 2000). According to Ardichvili *et al.*'s definition, the process of opportunity recognition involves several processes: *perception, discovery*, and *creation*. *Perception* is defined as the phenomenon that some individuals perceive market needs and underemployed resources and others do not. Ardichvili *et al.* believe "that these differences are due to the heterogeneity in individuals' sensitivity to opportunities and delivery of new value" (Ardichvili *et al.* 2000: 110). *Opportunity discovery* involves the development process of a "fit" between those, whereas opportunity *creation* is defined as the development of a business concept. *Opportunity development* is the cognitive process toward the final formation of a business opportunity. Lastly, *opportunity evaluation* is defined as the continuous process of the investigation of the current market needs and resources that can redirect the development process as the opportunity is adjusted to the current evaluations. This evaluation process is collateral to Mintzberg's concept of an "emergent strategy" (Mintzberg 1998 as cited in Ardichvili *et al.* 2000).

In order to develop a sophisticated analytical framework, it is necessary to clarify what makes an entrepreneur differ from a non-entrepreneur in the way of each of them recognizes business opportunities. The most popular stated differences between entrepreneurs and non-entrepreneurs are *personality differences, cognitive differences* and *social network differences* (Dyer, Gregersen & Christensen 2008). Baron (2006) and Ardichvili *et al.* (2000) were the first to develop comprehensive models which combine multiple factors of OR.[4] Before, as stated in the beginning, these factors had been mostly examined independently from each other. Ardichvili *et al.* and Baron developed frameworks that combined all variables of OR that are contemporarily accepted in entrepreneurial research. Still, both shared the opinion that their models are not perfect and must be developed further in the future. In this chapter it will be explained what these elements of OR are and how they are believed to influence each other. Both models will be presented and explained parallel as both are partly similar. Baron (2006) has extracted three main factors that are believed to play an essential role in the process of the recognition of a business opportunity: engagement in an *active search* for opportunities, *alertness* or *sensitivity* to opportunities and *prior knowledge* of a market, industry or customer segment. Ardichvili *et al.* (2000) have defined a three-step OR-core process, which is quite similar to Baron's approach and has been explained previously (*recognition, development, evaluation)*. After this three-step process, the opportunity "enters" the process of *opportunity development* and *opportunity evaluation*. This core process is influenced strongly by external forces that are in their sum defined as *entrepreneurial alertness*. This *entrepreneurial alertness* is also affected by the characteristics of an individual's *social network*, whereas this unit is affected by *prior knowledge* and *personality traits* in a sum. Ardichvili *et al.* have proposed that individual differences to perceive opportunities have their origin in a person's genetic makeup, background and experience as well as the amount and type of information one possesses about a particular opportunity. But "being born" with an *entrepreneurial alertness* does not automatically mean that one is keen to become an entrepreneur since "not everyone who is good at asking questions is equally adept at creating answers" (Ardichvili *et al.* 2000: 110).

On the other hand, Baron has developed the approach of the *process of pattern recognition*. According to his theory, the so called process of *pattern recognition* makes individuals "perceive complex and seemingly unrelated events as constituting identifiable patterns" (Baron 2006: 106). In other words, people who are able to recognize patterns

---

[4] Also Hansen *et al.* (2011), but they have focused their research on the role of creativity in the process of opportunity recognition.

are able to draw links between trends and changes in their environment. These links are the foundation for the recognition of possible business opportunities. An evidence for this is that a majority of business opportunities already existed for many years until one was able to recognize these links. Baron mentions a very good example for this phenomenon: wheeled luggage had been used by air flight crews for years, before one was able to recognize the links between several trends, such as the large increase in the number of luggage, much bigger airports and a greater passenger volume. Finally one was able to "connect the dots" and started the retail of such suitcases to a large majority of people (Baron 2006). Secondly, cognitive science suggests that *pattern recognition* is "a basic aspect of our efforts to understand the world around us" (Baron 2006: 106). This theory of the process of *pattern recognition* was successfully proven in a survey amongst experienced entrepreneurs, carried out by Matlin and Foley (1997). Each of the participating entrepreneurs had established at least two successful companies. As most of the entrepreneurs were engaged in an active search, restricted in an area they had already had experience in, it can be assumed that they connected their already existing *cognitive frameworks* with several perceived trends, events and changes. These outcomes challenge Ardichvili *et al.*'s non-inclusion of *active search* in their framework. As has been stated, the occurrence of changes, trends and events is perceived and interpreted through *cognitive frameworks* – more specifically through *prototypes* and *exemplar models* (Smith 1995, Hahn & Charter 1997 as cited in Baron 2006). *Prototype models* are defined as models "that individuals employ […] as a basis for recognizing patterns" (Baron 2006: 109). So new trends, changes and events are compared with existing *prototypes*, whereas these are defined as "the modal or most frequently experienced combination of attributes, associated with an object or pattern" (Baron 2006: 109). Prototypes are defined by Baron as an idealization of "the most typical members of a *category*" (Baron 2006: 109), whereas *category* is specified as a class of objects or events that are believed to belong together. A good example for this model is the prototype of a "house". Most of us associate specific *objects* with a house. Such as a roof, windows or a door. Anyhow, a house can be a small cottage, a town house or else a huge mansion (Baron 2006). The concept of *exemplars* suggests that if people perceive new events, changes or trends, they compare these with "specific examples (exemplars) of relevant concepts already stored in memory" (Baron 2006: 109). Therefore, knowledge and experiences are seen as the "raw material" (Baron 2006: 112) from which *exemplars* are developed in the cognitive framework. These *exemplars* are particularly interesting for an OR-framework, as they do not require a complex construction of a *prototype*. Straightforward, individuals compare perceived occurrences in the external world with knowledge and experience already stored in their memory and due to that, they are recognizing the opportunity "just when they see it" (Baron 2006: 110). Both of the concepts are according to Baron crucial for the understanding of OR, as each of them is believed to be processed in different parts of the brain (Gazzaniga & Mangun 1998 as cited in Baron 2006). *Prototypes* are assumed to be processed in the left cerebral hemisphere, whereas *exemplars* are believed to be processed in the right cerebral hemisphere. Furthermore, *alertness* and the *search* are crucial to the perception of patterns. Like mentioned before, *active search* is the involvement into the – logically – active search for links and connections between events, changes and trends. The second step – the drawing of lines and connections between those – is the much more challenging part since many people recognize these, but only a few are able to connect them. *Alertness* is being understood as "the capacity to recognize opportunities when they exist" (Baron 2006: 112). Based on his researches, Baron also proposed that if the alertness of a person is high enough, an active search for opportunities may not be necessary to recognize patterns, because one would be so sensitive to these, that he or she would not have to "engage in formal, systematic search processes" (Baron 2006: 113). If you think about the well-known "eureka"-moment many of us have already experienced, the impression might come up that the process of OR is a single-step process that happens like a sudden inspiration within a few seconds or minutes. But this process is much more complex. The first step of an OR-process is, like already stated, the observation of events, changes and trends and linking or connecting them with prior knowledge and other experiences, which leads to a business opportunity. Baron and other literature suggest (Baron 2006; Solso 1999) that OR and therefore *pattern recognition* is a much longer process as an individual is maybe able to observe several related to external happenings but without recognizing a "clear-cut pattern" (Baron 2006: 110) which could have been already translated into a fully-fledged business plan. First of all, individuals usually recognize that "something is there" (Baron 2006: 110) but much more information is needed to shape the pattern. Potential entrepreneurs may have already recognized business opportunities but with more information they are enabled to expand these – and the process is usually never really completed, rather it "evolves just as growing businesses do" (Baron 2006: 111).[5] Ardichvili *et al.* (2000) have defined this as the process, already earlier explained, of *opportunity development*.

After understanding how the process of opportunity recognition works, it is possible to "extract" the most important elements, which are believed to influence this process. Several traits of individuals have been linked with the ability to recognize business opportunities, such as knowledge, information, social networks, creativity, risk-acceptance, optimism and self-efficacy (Baron 2006; Hansen *et al.* 2011; Ardichvili *et al.* 2000; Chen & Yang 2009 as cited in Hansen *et al.* 2011; Shane & Venkataraman 2000). Thereof, the following elements for the analytical framework will be derived: prior knowledge (professional and non-professional), information-seeking behaviour, networking behaviour, creativity, risk-acceptance, optimism and self-efficacy. Based on the knowledge gained from the concepts of the entrepreneurial process, the focus is particularly on the behavioural aspects, as especially our perceptions – which are crucial to the OR-process – influence our behaviour. These elements will be explained in the following chapter.

All three elements are included in one chapter altogether as each of them shares one common variable: the input of information to the process of *pattern recognition*. The first factor that will be explained is *prior knowledge*, which is gained by an individual through life experiences and/or through work experience in a particular segment. Like mentioned, it is much easier to recognize business opportunities for people who have well-founded *prior knowledge* as it enables them to construct *prototypes* and *exemplars* (Baron 2006).

---

[5] Remember the reference to Mintzberg.

The interaction between one's knowledge base and one's OR-process is continuous. Thus, the interaction results in an iterative learning process and therefore in double-loop learning. This phenomenon leads to the development of a knowledge corridor that builds the basis for increased *alertness* to business opportunities (Ronstadt 1988 as cited in Ardichvili *et al.* 2000).

The broader this basis of knowledge is and the greater the quality of knowledge, the broader the range of possible business opportunities becomes. Ardichvili *et al.* (2000) identified two different types of prior knowledge: knowledge in an area which is of an individual's special interest, such as for example knowledge one has gained through his or her involvement in a particular personal field of interest (e.g. a hobby); knowledge that has been absorbed while working in a particular job. The interaction of both types of prior knowledge is believed to lead, according to Ardichvili *et al.*, to the discovery of new business opportunities.

A key role in the active search for opportunities is, according to Baron, "access to appropriate information" (Baron 2006: 104). This can happen most successfully through unique information sources, such as personal contacts. Ardichvili *et al.* (2000) defined this "access to appropriate information" as the phenomenon of information asymmetry. The assumption postulates that "people tend to notice information that is related to information they already know" (Von Hippel 1994 as cited in Ardichvili *et al.* 2000: 114). This approach builds a bridge between the idea of *appropriate information* and *prior knowledge*. The Austrian School of economics even proposes that entrepreneurship only exists because of information asymmetry between different actors (Hayek 1935 as cited in Ardichvili *et al.* 2000). Based on these findings, we formulate the following:

Also the role of social networks has been identified as highly influencing the OR-ability (Ardichvili *et al.* 2000; Hills *et al.* 1994; Pohja 2009). A study conducted by Hills and Lumpkin (1996) suggests that the more diverse an entrepreneur's social network is, the more opportunities are identified. As a consequence, social networks can be seen as the most important source of information in the process of pattern recognition; as individuals discuss possible patterns they have identified with their family, colleagues at work or other students at university, additional input is provided to this process (Baron 2006). In this paper, the question should be answered if a favourable networking behaviour – the individual "ability" to gain information from the social environment – influences the ability to recognize business opportunities.

Scientists do not fully agree whether risk-acceptance affects the ability to recognize business opportunities positively. Stewart and Roth (2001) proposed that an individual that is more prone to take risks automatically sees more events, changes or trends as an opportunity to launch a venture. A higher propensity for risk-acceptance has also been linked with a higher self-efficacy and optimism as more risk-accepting individuals may believe that they can "overcome risk through skill" (Krueger & Dickson 1994: 387). So they see risky choices more as an opportunity instead of seeing them as a threat. Consequently, it can be assumed that many people might see these opportunities, but only a few tend to develop these opportunities explicitly. This assumption is supported by Endres & Woods (2007), Dimov (2007) and Sanz-Valasco (2006) who have agreed that an opportunity only enters the "next phase" of cognitive evaluation if it is seen as viable. In other words: the more risk-averse a person is, the more opportunities remain unconscious. Also in their empirical studies, Krueger & Dickson (1994) found out that the more risks one is ready to take, the more opportunities but also threats are seen. Optimism – as the belief that a particular event will produce favourable outcomes – has been linked with the ability to identify business opportunities (Krueger & Brazeal 1994). Self-efficacy has already been explained in this paper earlier in connection with *perceived feasibility*. Krueger & Brazeal have examined how the individual perception of self-efficacy influences the ability to recognize opportunities. According to their findings, a more self-efficient person is believed to be more enabled to recognize a business opportunity than a less self-efficient person. Studies have also shown that optimism is strongly related to self-efficacy beliefs (Krueger & Dickson 1994; Krueger & Brazeal 1994). Therefore, self-efficacy and optimism can be defined as highly similar to each other but cannot be classified as one and the same thing at the same time. One could also propose that the higher a person's optimism and self-efficacy is, the more one is prone to take risks, as more optimistic individuals would expect favourable outcomes from risky situations. But this assumption was disproven as Guth, Kumaraswamy and McEarlean (1991) ascertained that an entrepreneur's optimism can be defined as an "inside view" of the potential success of a venture based on the perception of the own skills and knowledge. Neck and Manz (1992, 1996 as cited in Ardichvili *et al.* 2000) sussed out that one's perception of his or her self-efficacy leads to optimism and therefore to a higher recognition of opportunities. Creativity is maybe the most discussed factor in the literature, as creativity is believed to enable an individual to imagine services and products that are currently non-existent (Busenitz 1996 as cited in Baron 2006). Generally, creativity plays an important role in entrepreneurship. Schumpeter (1934) already identified its important role in entrepreneurship as he suggested that entrepreneurs perceive and create things that others do not see. Research conducted by Winslow and Salomon (1993 as cited in Ardichvili *et al.* 2000) has shown that a creative process and an entrepreneurial process are one and the same. Others are supporting this idea (Ardichvili *et al.* 2000; Baron 2008; Corbett 2005; DeTienne & Chandler 2007; Dimov 2007; Long & McMullan 1984 as cited in Hansen *et al.* 2011). Also psychological scholars have come to the conclusion that entrepreneurship – and therefore also OR – "is a specific case of creativity" (Hansen *et al.* 2011: 522). Kay (1986 as cited in Ardichvili *et al.* 2000) has suggested that creativity plays a crucial role in the process of entrepreneurial decision-making. Hills *et al.* (1997) has drawn the conclusion from a conducted study that 90% of the surveyed entrepreneurs find creativity to be the most important factor in the process of OR. Interesting about this survey is that solo entrepreneurs find it much more important to be creative than networked entrepreneurs, as maybe the additional information exchange within the network replaces creativity. Lumpkin, Hills & Shrader (2004), on the basis of creativity literature, have concluded that the access to prior knowledge and experience is building a basis for creativity and therefore OR. Due to this, creativity can be seen as a link between knowledge and the identification process of a business opportunity. Ardichvili *et al.* (2000) have also linked high levels of creativity with high levels of entrepreneurial alertness, optimism and self-efficacy. Sternberg proposes that creativity is one of three types of intelligence. This *creative intelligence* has been linked by him with high proportions of flexibility, self-efficacy, perseverance, and tolerance for ambiguity – meaning a high risk-taking propensity – and unconventional thinking (Sternberg 2004). Csikszentmihalyi states that opportunities remain "below the threshold of consciousness" (1996: 79) till a sudden "eureka"-moment transfers the opportunities to the level of consciousness. Hansen *et al.* (2009) suggest that it takes high levels of creativity to overcome this.

4. Discussion of the results

Despite the fact that most of the gathered data have not been sufficiently significant, the outcomes still leave room for interpretation and discussion. When revising the data, it is obviously assumptive that there is a tendency of Poles with entrepreneurial intentions or a background to score higher results than people without any intention or background. Interestingly, respondents who have already been involved in the launch of a venture often achieve lower average scores than anyone else. It could be assumed that participants who have already been involved in a venture are more experienced and therefore assess their attitudes and abilities much more conservatively. Aside from that, the mean value charts of the Likert scales indicate that there is mostly a graphical unequivocal difference between people who have recognized at least one opportunity and participants who have identified none. But paradoxically the average values in terms of risk-acceptance of the respondents who have recognized at least one opportunity tend much more to the least risky pole of the diagram.

When reviewing again the gathered data, Hofstede's as well as the GEM's assumption – despite the insufficient significance – has been confirmed that Poles are believed to be generally very risk-averse, as the pooled average score for question concerning the risk aversion is with the value of 0.46 below the "neutral" median. Surprisingly, females scored 0.53, a much higher score than males did with 0.37 and are therefore believed to accept more risks than males do. But contrary to the results of the GEM National Report of 2013, Polish women have indicated much more often (21.25%) than men did (11.76%) that they have not recognized any business opportunity in the last twelve months. But generally, much more Poles than expected indicated that they recognized a business opportunity, which contradicts the data published by the GEM (81,95% in this paper; GEM 20,4%). This could be explained by the fact that the GEM uses a future-oriented question, whereas the question used in this paper assessed opportunities, which were recognized in the past. Nevertheless, the amount of people who have indicated they have recognized at least one business opportunity in the past twelve months was higher than expected, which could lead to the assumption that maybe "fear of failure" is the main interference factor in the entrepreneurial process. Anyhow, according to the gathered data about risk-acceptance, it can be assumed that fear of failure goes hand in hand with a weak ability to recognize opportunities.

Beside the low significance of the data, it is quite surprising to what extent the scores of people who have perceived at least one opportunity were higher than of those who have recognized none. People who have perceived at least one opportunity in the past twelve months had on average 16.08% higher scores in terms of self-efficacy, 23.07% higher scores in terms of risk-acceptance, 21.10% higher scores in terms of optimism, 7.69% higher scores in terms of creativity, 14.49% higher scores in terms of information seeking behaviour, 80.30% higher scores in terms of prior knowledge, and 9.2% in terms of networking behaviour. The high difference in terms of prior knowledge is supported by the fact that prior professional knowledge was the only element of OR which has been significantly confirmed as suitable for an OR-framework. This maybe could be explained by the fact that people with a higher prior professional knowledge are mostly already studying or working, therefore they could be more oriented toward an entrepreneurial venture than, for instance, someone who is still at high school. What is also quite surprising is that there is no difference between participants who have recognized a business opportunity actively and participants who have recognized an opportunity passively. People who are currently involved in the launch of a business indicated lower average results in comparison to participants without any entrepreneurial intention or background. Participants with plans for a business launch in the next five years achieved on average the highest scores. This leads us to the assumption that people with an entrepreneurial intention achieve higher scores in terms of OR.

Like in many other elements, females had also slightly higher scores in terms of optimism than males. This would support the finding of the GEM, whereas Polish women recognize more opportunities than males. Anyhow, this assumption was probably disproven within this research as 78.75% of the females indicated that they have recognized at least one opportunity. On the other hand, the proportion of males recognizing opportunities was 88.24%. The only elements where men scored better results than females did was in the element of creativity. The proposition made by Granovetter, that people with either casual or close acquaintances gather more information which enables them to recognize more opportunities, was assumably disproven (as 90.63% of the respondents who have indicated that they strongly disagree or disagree that most of their acquaintances are casual, have identified a business opportunity, whereas 79.21% of the participants who either agreed or strongly agreed to the question recognized at least one opportunity) (Granovetter 1973). The majority of the used elements of opportunity recognition are only weakly correlated with each other which unfortunately does not allow to draw definite conclusions. Anyhow, the strongest significant correlation (mean linear correlation of 0.566) can be identified between creativity and information-seeking behaviour. Therefore it could be assumed that creativity and information-seeking behaviour are interrelated for the reason that creativity might foster an individual's ability to identify promising information sources.

5. Conclusion

Certainly the framework has weaknesses that should be improved for future analyses. Entrepreneurial OR and especially the attempt to quantify the OR-ability is a complex process and there is only a small scientific foundation to build up on. Generally, the statistical evidence used in this paper should be interpreted with caution as the reliability of these data is questionable and the support for the model is weak – maybe due to comparably only a small quantity of participants. But it cannot be ruled out that elements were not falsified by cultural tendencies of Poles. For example the very strong propensity amongst Poles to be very risk-aversive could have led to the disconfirmation of the validity of the element "risk-acceptance" – even though that disconfirmation was not statistically significant. If this analysis would have been conducted in another country, where the fear of failure is much lower (e.g. in Latvia, Sweden or Turkey), it is possible that the element "risk-acceptance" presumably would have been confirmed as suitable for the framework (GEM National Report 2013). Therefore, it is likely that a single-country analysis does not allow the researcher to draw meaningful conclusions. Additionally, two questions to assess the element "risk-acceptance" do not seem to be sufficient in order to examine this element comprehensively. Hence, more risk-choice-questions should be added for further researches, especially questions which would not be bipolar, wherefore scientists could draw stronger conclusions as tendencies could be identified much easier.

To sum it up, the used framework should be seen as a "springboard" for future quantitative OR-models. Contrary to the approach developed and utilized in this paper, future approaches should also consider all levels of the OR-process, not only *opportunity perception*. This would allow the researcher to get an overall image of the OR-process in order to identify possible variances within the process. Especially the used measures to scale the elements in terms of score should be more homogenous (e.g. all elements are measured on a score from one to ten). This should be a goal, as it would allow comparing developments of the elements among themselves as well as generating a pooled opportunity recognition score. Though it would have been very interesting, it was unfortunately not possible to answer the question whether the weakly assessed ability to recognize opportunities in Poland is the main factor for the low level of entrepreneurial activities. Based on this, the goal for further researches in entrepreneurship should be to conduct a macro-analytical examinations in various countries in order to gather data which would allow to compare the OR-ability across nations with the goal to examine differences due to cultural, economic or educational influences. A ratio could be introduced that involves the total OR-score and a national level of entrepreneurial activity wherefore it would be possible to examine links and correlations between both variables. Also the additional use of a qualitative approach could help to simplify the interpretation of gathered data.

As stated in the beginning, these entrepreneurial opportunity recognition researches not only can help to improve the understanding of the process of OR, but also can be a base for entrepreneurial trainings with the goal to promote the engagement in an entrepreneurial activity. Of course, it is questionable if it is possible to "teach" individuals the ability to recognize opportunities. But considering Baron's implications, it would be feasible to teach people how to "use" information perceived in the world around them as well as to use these recognized events, trends and changes to recognize patterns which could lead to the creation of exemplars and prototypes and as a consequence to an opportunity recognition (Baron 2006). A cultural-adapted training – based on the empirical assessment of a nation's OR-scores – could, for instance, focus on one or several weakly assessed elements. This would enable participants of a training to improve these weakly developed abilities in order to overcome e.g. imaginary obstacles in the process of OR. In the case of Poland, this could be a training that increases the acceptance of risks, creativity, and self-efficiency, for instance, through simulations that allow the participants to realize that it is possible to overcome risky situations with the help of personal skills.

To sum it up from a scientific perspective, it is obvious that the research progress in the discipline of entrepreneurial opportunity recognition is still in its infancy. Based on the discussions, it is striking that the conceptualization and also, much more, the empirical assessment of a person's ability to recognize business opportunities is a complex process – which is hard to analyzeeither one-dimensionally or multi-dimensionally. It is to be hoped that future research will not only focus further on the entrepreneurial process but also on the "heart" of entrepreneurship: opportunity recognition.

References

Ajzen, I. (1991), The Theory of Planned Behaviour, "Organizational Behaviour and Human Decision Processes", Vol. 50, Elsevier, 179–211.

Ajzen, I., Fishbein, M. (1980), *Understanding Attitudes and Predicting Social Behaviour,* New Jersey: Prentice Hall.

Ardichvili, A., Cardozo, R., Ray, S. (2000), A theory of entrepreneurial opportunity identification and development, "Journal of Business Venturing" 18 (2003), 105–123.

Baron, R. A., Ensley, M. D. (2006), Opportunity Recognition as the Detection of Meaningful Patterns: Evidence from Comparisons of Novice and Experienced Entrepreneurs, "Management Science" 52(9), 1331–1344.

Baron, R. A. (2008), The role of affect in the entrepreneurial process, "Academy of Management Review", Vol. 33 (2), 328–340.

Bhave, M. P. (1994), A process model of entrepreneurial venture creation, "Journal of Business Venturing", 9: 223– 242.

Busenitz, L.W. (1996), Research on entrepreneurial alertness, "Journal of Small Business Management", 34, 35–44.

Busenitz, L., Barney, J. B. (1997), Differences between entrepreneurs and managers in large organizations: Biases and heuristics in strategic decision-making, "Journal of Business Venturing", 12(1), 9–30.

Chen, M. H., Yang, Y. J. (2009), *Typology and performance of new ventures in Taiwan,* "International Journal of Entrepreneurial Behaviour & Research", Vol. 15 No. 5, 398–414.

Corbett, A. (2005), "Experiential learning within the process of opportunity identification and exploitation", *Entrepreneurship Theory and Practice,* Vol. 29 (4), 473–491.

Csikszentmihalyi, M. (1996), *Creativity: Flow and the psychology of discovery and invention,* New York: Harper Collins.

De Koning, A. (1999), *Conceptualizing Opportunity Recognition as a Socio-Cognitive Process,* Centre for Advanced Studies in Leadership: Stockholm.

DeTienne, D., Chandler, G. (2007), "The role of gender in opportunity identification", *Entrepreneurship Theory and Practice,* Vol. 31 (3), 365–386.

Dimov, D. (2007),"Beyond the single-insight, single-person, attribution in understanding entrepreneurial opportunities", *Entrepreneurship Theory and Practice,* Vol. 31 No. 5, 713–731.

Dyer, J. H., Gregersen, H. B., Christensen, C. (2008), Entrepreneur behaviors, opportunity recognition, and the origins of innovative ventures, "Strategic Entrepreneurship Journal", 2: 317–338.

Endres, A. M., Woods, C. R. (2007), The case for more "subjectivist" research on how entrepreneurs create opportunities, "International Journal of Entrepreneurial Behaviour & Research", Vol. 13 No. 4, 222–234.

Gazzaniga, M. S., Ivry, R. B., Mangun, G. R. (1998), *Cognitive neuroscience: The biology of the mind*, New York: Norton.

Guth, W. D., Kumaraswamy, A., McEarlean, M. (1991), *Cognition, enactment, and learning in the entrepreneurial process*, Babson College: Babson Park, MA.

Granovetter, M. (1973), The strength of weak ties, "American Journal Sociology" 78 (6): 1360–1380.

Hahn, U., Chater, N. (1997), *Concepts and similarity*, Cambridge, MA: MIT Press.

Hansen, D. J., Lumpkin, G. T., Hills, G. E. (2011), A multidimensional examination of a creativity-based opportunity recognition model, "International Journal of Entrepreneurial Behaviour & Research", Vol. 17, 515–533.

Herron, L., Sapienza, H. J. (1992), The entrepreneur and the initiation of new venture launch activities, *Entrepreneurship Theory and Practice* 16, 49–55.

Hills, G., Lumpkin, G. T., Singh, R. P. (1997), Opportunity recognition: perceptions and behaviors of entrepreneurs, "Frontiers of Entrepreneurship Research" 203–218, Wellesley: Babson College.

Kay, C. J. (1986), *The Identification of Catalysts Preceding Decision Making as Described by Innovators and Entrepreneurs*, San Francisco: University of San Francisco.

Kirzner, I. (1979), *Perception, opportunity, and profit*, Chicago: University of Chicago Press.

Kirzner, I. M. (1985), *Discovery and the capitalist process*, Chicago: University of Chicago Press.

Krueger, N. F. (1989), *Antecedents of opportunity recognition: The role of perceived self-efficacy*, Columbus: The Ohio State University.

Krueger, N. F., Brazeal, D.V. (1994), *Entrepreneurial potential and potential entrepreneurs*, Waco: Baylor University.

Krueger, N. F., Dickson, N. (1994), How believing in ourselves increases risk taking: Perceived self-efficacy and risk taking, "Decision Sciences", 25, 385–400.

Long, W., McMullan, W. (1984), "Mapping the new venture opportunity identification process", [in:] J. A. Hornaday *et al.* (eds.), *Frontiers of Entrepreneurship*, Wellesley: Babson College.

Matlin, M. W., Foley, H. J. (1997), *Sensation and perception*, Needham Heights: Allyn & Bacon.

Neck, C. P., Manz, C. C. (1992), *Thought self-leadership: the influence of self-talk and mental imagery on performance*, J. Organ. Behav. 13, 681–699.

Neck, C. P., Manz, C. C. (1996), Thought self-leadership: the impact of mental strategies training on employee cognition, behavior, and affect, "Journal of Organizational Behavior", 17, 445–467.

Lumpkin, G. T., Hills, G. E., Shrader, R. C. (2004), "Opportunity recognition", [in:] H. P. Welsch (ed.), *Entrepreneurship: The Way Ahead*, New York: Routledge.

Ronstadt, R. (1988), *The corridor principle*, J. Bus. Venturing 1 (3), 31–40.

Schwartz, R., Teach, R. (1999), *A model of opportunity recognition and exploitation: an empirical study of incubator firms*. Presented at the 13th UIC/AMA Symposium on Marketing and Entrepreneurship Interface, Nice, June.

Shapero, A. (1984), "The Entrepreneurial Event", [in:] C. A. Kent (eds.), *The Environment for Entrepreneurship*, Toronto: Lexington Books.

Shapero, A., Sokol, L. (1982), "The Social Dimensions of Entrepreneurship", [in:] *The Encyclopedia of Entrepreneurship*, Englewood Cliffs: Prentice-Hall.

Shane, S., Venkataraman, S. (2000), The promise of entrepreneurship as a field of research, "Academy of Management Review", Vol. 25 (1), 217–226.

Shaver, Kelly G. (2005), Reflections on a New Academic Path: Entrepreneurship in the Arts and Sciences, "Academic Journal Article", Vol. 7 (3).

Sigrist, B. (1999), *Entrepreneurial opportunity recognition*. A presentation at the Annual UIC/AMA symposium at Marketing/Entrepreneurship Interface, Sofia-Antipolis, France.

Smith, E. E. (1995), "Concepts and categorization", [in:] E. E. Smith & D. N. Osherson (eds.), *Thinking* (2nd ed., 3–33), Cambridge: MIT Press.

Solso, R. L. (1999), *Cognitive psychology*, 5th ed., Boston: Allyn & Bacon.

Sternberg, R. J. (2004), *Successful intelligence as a basis for entrepreneurship,* J. Bus.Venturing 19, 189–202.

Stewart, W. H., Roth, P. L. (2001), Risk propensity differences between entrepreneurs and managers: A meta-analytic review, "Journal of Applied Psychology", 86, 145–153.

Von Hippel, E. (1994), *"Sticky Information" and the Locus of Problem Solving: Implications for Innovation*, MIT Sloan School of Management Working Paper, published in "Management Science" 40 (4), April 1994, 429–439.

Wiklund, J., Davidsson, P., Audretsch, D. B., Karlsson, C. (2011),The future of entrepreneurship research, "Entrepreneurship Theory and Practice", 35(1), 1–9

Winslow, E. K., Solomon, G. T. (1993), *Entrepreneurs: architects of innovation, paradigm pioneers and change,* J. Creat. Behav. 27 (2), 75–88.

Other sources:

Global Entrepreneurship Monitor: "National Report Poland 2013".

Global Entrepreneurship Monitor: "NES – National Expert Survey Poland 2013".

Both taken from http://www.gemconsortium.org/.

Chapter V ———————————————————————————————

Improving Quality of Life through Improved Public Services and Corporate Governance: The Case of Poland

Marta Postula

The Innovative Tax Return System in Poland to Benefit Both the Taxpayers and Economy

1. Introduction

In 2014 Poland celebrated the 25th anniversary of the social and economic transformation which triggered numerous changes to public administration, and was supposed to bring the administration closer to its citizens and improve the standard of services provided by public authorities. In essence, this modernization presumed a departure from the traditional bureaucratic model of public administration and embracement of the New Public Management model being put in place in most European countries. Overall, it involves the application of models and solutions across management, based on market principles typical of private organizations. Implementation of the managerial approach may be one example[1]. Nevertheless, it should be remembered that even though these methods are widely used, public administration continually faces limitations and tasks which are absent from the private sector. This is due to the fact that markets in the public sector are not markets of free competition, but markets in competition organized by diverse public authorities[2]. After all, by ignoring these differences, the implementation of cutting-edge management tools will produce more negative than positive effects.

Therefore, the aim of this paper is to present how the use of new measures affects the quality of public services provided, with regard to broadly understood management and illustrated with an example of tax administration.

---

[1] H. Krynicka (2006), Koncepcja nowego zarządzania w sektorze publicznym (new public management), p. 193, [in:] http://www.bibliotekacyfrowa.pl/Content/34636/014.pdf, [access: 22.12.2014].
[2] *Ibid*, p. 202.

For public administration, defining the term of quality requires defining the essence and character of the tasks fulfilled by public institutions from the perspective of management, though it is crucial to determine the following concepts:

- public services as fundamental tasks accomplished by public administration organizations. Delivery of these services (in present-day definitions of management it is assumed that all tasks assigned to administration may be defined as public services) requires the introduction of management principles that substantially differ from principles guiding the private sector;
- definition depicting the type of client, their expectations and satisfaction. For public services, a client may be typified by: a citizen or groups of citizens or local communities, another organizational unit of the specific institution, another public administration body, private sector organization, politician, legislative or regulatory body. Expectations of such clients may not be clearly specified or determined, and factors driving client satisfaction are difficult to define for many public services – specifically for services – administrative decisions or services the delivery of which relies on limited public funds.[3]

The process of public services provision comprises three fundamental elements: service standard, the manner in which service is rendered and improvement of this manner. Hence, the administration, besides planning a policy and strategy, should focus on its citizens – and respond flexibly to their needs. On the whole, in the New Public Management they are identified as clients consuming public goods. Their voice should be given great importance, and thus citizens need to have an opportunity of communicating their opinions to administration bodies. The model below illustrates the process of public services in compliance with requirements of ISO 9001:2001 standard[4].

2. The history of Polish tax administration

In 2014 Poland celebrated the 95th anniversary of the setting up of the tax administration system which continually evolved in its form, though its objective was always to raise revenue for the state budget. When analyzing the performance (transforming together with other elements of the economic system) of these bodies over the period it could be claimed that the activities undertaken over these years helped to achieve the best possible functionality of the tax administration for accomplishing the goal which is, on the one hand, to ensure a continual and timely inflow of revenues from taxes and other tax liabilities to the state and commune budgets; and on the other hand, to set up the least cumbersome process for collecting taxes from citizens. It has long been known that when collecting taxes in cooperation with other state authorities, the tax administration upholds integrity in business trading and seeks to foster healthy competition among entrepreneurs.

---

[3] http://www.mf.gov.pl/administracja-podatkowa/dzialalnosc/zarzadzanie-jakoscia [access: 11.01.2015].
[4] B. Wyrzykowska (2006), Zarządzanie jakością w instytucjach publicznych, p. 77, [in:] http://www.wne.sggw.pl/czasopisma/pdf/EIOGZ_2006_nr61_s75.pdf [access: 22.12.2014].

Quality tools:
ISO9000 norms
Quality prizes
Evaluation
Services offer

Parliament
Political will   Rating/Evaluation

Orders

Socio-political process
"what is to be provided"

Socio-political process
"how the service
is provided"

- values (ethics)
- legal acts
- norms
- financial resources

- customer choices
- customer opinion
- feedback
- complaints option

Voice of the
customer/citizen

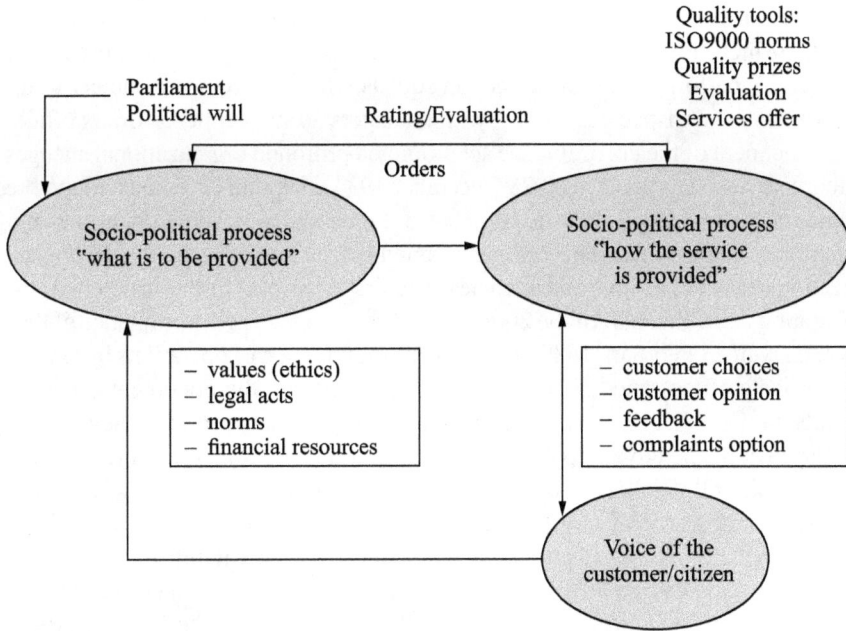

Figure 1. Model illustrating the process of public services provision
Source: M. Piotrowska (2011), Public administration model versus the quality of citizens' service in commune
offices, p. 258,[in:] http://www.ur.edu.pl/pliki/Zeszyt18/19.pdf [access: 22.12.2014].

Essentially, the original legislative act setting out the principles and assignments for this formation was the law of 31 July 1919 on temporary organization of authorities and tax agencies[5], which ushered in a three-tier organization model for tax administration, comprising the Ministry of the Treasury and tax chambers and tax agencies: dealing with direct taxes and stamp duties, excise tax and state monopolies, fiscal cash registers, as well as estimate and appeal committees.

However, the history of contemporary Polish tax administration began as early as 1918 when after regaining the independence of Poland and incorporating territories long kept under foreign rule of three other countries, the need to establish a unified tax system acquired a rare immediacy. Yet, work over setting up a new tax system was fraught with difficulties caused by uncertainty over the ultimate shape of national frontiers and, above all, by the paucity of money in circulation as a majority of people hoarded money, treating it as an extraordinary treasure rather than as means of payment.

All in all, advanced work on establishing the tax collection system in Poland only started in 1920 and continued until 1923. The levy collection system was honed step by step to attain its final form in 1925. The gradual process of evolution over several years found its reflection in the first law that comprehensively regulated the overall tax law in Poland, that

---

[5] Journal of Laws of 1919 No. 65, item 391, Internet System of Legislative Acts (ISAP), http://isap.sejm.gov.pl/VolumeServlet?type=wdu&rok=1919&numer=065 [12.01.2015].

is, the Tax Ordinance Act adopted on 15 March 1934[6]. While consolidating what at that time were ultimate measures for tax collection over 1920–1939, there also was a fiscal inspection – organized in the form of fiscal protection squads whose heads were subject to directors of tax chambers and inspected regions, with managers as subject heads of tax offices.

The enactment of the tax ordinance act prompted profound organizational changes to the tax authorities which took place on 28 December 1934 when the Ordinance of the President of Poland on normalizing authorities powers and procedures in some departments of state administration[7] was enacted. This ordinance amended the law of 31 July 1919 on temporary organization of tax authorities and agencies. The first new form of the structure of the fiscal administration in the first half of the 20th century was designed in the ordinance of the Minister of Treasury of 23 February 1939 on organization and scope of operations by tax chambers and subordinate offices and executive bodies[8]. Specifically, the document established the fiscal protection which took over tasks performed by fiscal inspection squads.

Unfortunately, the advance of public finances and taxes was interrupted for five years by the outbreak of the WW2. The work was only continued in mid-1945. The control was exercised by Konstanty Dąbrowski, the then Minister of Treasury. The Tax Ordinance act of 1934 was quickly overruled and replaced by decrees on tax liabilities of 16 May 1946[9] and penal fiscal law decree of April 1947[10]. While drawing upon experiences gained, and keeping in mind the enhanced effectiveness of operations by tax bodies, the organization of public finances and taxes was altered in January 1950, on the basis of the order of the Ministry of Treasury of 23 December 1949 on temporary organization of tax chambers and tax offices[11]. Substantial shifts sparked by the regulation entailed abandonment of organizational autonomy for fiscal inspection regions, excise offices and inspection bodies by incorporating their scope of activities into tax offices so as to enable a citizen to settle all his or her matters in one single office. Importantly, at that time a new organizational structure was implemented on tax chambers and tax offices.

The foundations of today's tax administration may be traced back to 1975–1989 when two new legislative acts regulating its operations were enacted. The first was the act of 28 May 1975 on a two-tier administrative division of the state, and amendment to the act on national committees[12], thereby establishing 23 Regional Boards for State Revenues and Fiscal Inspection. The second was the act on tax liabilities. So, approval of both legislation documents laid the foundation for adopting the act on the position of the Ministry of Finance as well as tax offices and tax chambers[13] on 29 December 1982, under which

---

[6] Journal of Laws of 1934 No. 39, item 346, ISAP, http://isap.sejm.gov.pl/VolumeServlet?type=w-du&rok=1934&numer=039 [12.01.2015].

[7] Journal of Laws of 1934 No. 110, item 975 i 976, ISAP, isap.sejm.gov.pl/Download?id=WDU19341100976&-type=2 [12.01.2015].

[8] Journal of Laws of 1939 No.18, item 118, http://dziennikustaw.gov.pl/DU/1939/s/18/118 [12.01.2015].

[9] Journal of Laws of 1946 No. 27, item 173, http://dziennikustaw.gov.pl/DU/1946/s/27/173 [12.01.2015].

[10] Journal of Laws of 1947 No. 32, item 140, http://dziennikustaw.gov.pl/du/1947/s/32/140 [12.01.2015].

[11] http://www.skarbowcy.pl/blaster/extarticle.php?show=article&article_id=643 [12.01.2015].

[12] Journal of Laws of 1975 No. 16, item 91, http://dokumenty.rcl.gov.pl/DU/rok/1975/wydanie/16 [12.01.2015].

[13] Journal of Laws of 1982 No. 45, item 289, ISAP, http://isap.sejm.gov.pl/DetailsServlet?id=WDU19820450289 [12.01.2015].

tax chambers and tax offices were revived on 1 January 1983 in a model similar to that which was in operation during the interwar period (1919–1939). All further work aimed to specify and adjust the system to advanced progress of new tools, led to the establishment of the tax administration system as it functions today.

It is worthwhile focusing on a few crucial processes occurring at that time. Principally, the essential changes were effected during the systemic transformation at the beginning of the 1990s. They engendered profound shifts in management and the internal organization of tax offices operations. Since then offices became independent bodies of the first instance having a homogenous scope of activities: tax, inspection, enforcement and fiscal penalties.

The functionality of the tax system and principle of equality in taxation in Poland grew considerably after the act of 31 January 1989 on personal income tax[14] was passed. Basically, the act put into place a uniform income tax for all business entities, thereby bringing the assumptions governing the taxation of such entities in the developed market economy into the "Polish ground".

Subsequent changes were made continually since 1 January 1992, initiated by the tax reform implemented in Poland. As a result, the law of 26 July 1991 on personal income tax[15] came into effect, and the tax on goods and services (VAT)[16] came into force on 8 January 1993. Successive laws enacted enabled the further structuring of tax issues. Among them two legislative acts should be outlined; one of them dated to 1996 required that the tax administration issue a decision under which all taxed entities operating in Poland had to receive a tax identification number (Polish acronym NIP)[17], and the other being the Tax Ordinance act of 1997 also termed as the "tax constitution".

The legal foundations of the tax obligation in Poland have their sources in Art. 217 of the Constitution of the Republic of Poland of 2 April 1997[18] which provides that "the imposition of taxes, as well as other public imposts, the specification of those subject to the tax and the rates of taxation, as well as the principles for granting tax reliefs and remissions, along with categories of taxpayers exempt from taxation, shall be by means of statute".

Moreover, it should emphasized that the reform altering the administrative division of Poland was another driver that enhanced the functionality of the tax administration. In general, it introduced a three-tier territorial structure of the state, which brought about a reduction in tax chambers from 49 to 16 and a change in the territorial scope for operations by tax offices.

Significant changes to taxes and thus to the tax administration received further impetus by the Polish accession to the European Union on 1 May 2004. Primarily, we became a part of the community, and previous import and export changed into exchange of goods

---

[14] Journal of Laws of 1989 No.3, item 12, ISAP, http://isap.sejm.gov.pl/VolumeServlet?type=wdu&rok=1989&numer=003 [12.01.2015].

[15] Journal of Laws of 1991 No. 80, item 350, ISAP, http://isap.sejm.gov.pl/DetailsServlet?id=WDU19910800350 [12.01.2015].

[16] Journal of Laws of 1993 No. 11, item 50 as amended, http://www.sejm.gov.pl/sejm7.nsf/BASLeksykon.xsp?id=BA648AC6B3E63ADDC1257A590042A4BF&litera=P [12.01.2015].

[17] Act on tax advisory services (Journal of Laws of 1996 No. 102, item 475), ISAP, http://isap.sejm.gov.pl/DetailsServlet?id=WDU19961020475 [13.01.2015].

[18] Journal of Laws of 1997 No. 78, item 483, www.sejm.gov.pl [14.01.2015].

and services which necessitated an amendment to the act on value added tax (VAT)[19], and Polish business entities started to be granted EU identification.

Since then the authorities have been launching actions intended to strengthen the operations of the tax administration so as to meet the requirements imposed by the European Union as well as to safeguard the stable economic growth for Poland.

3. Key tasks of the tax administration

The current tax administration operates under the act of 21 June 1996 on tax offices and tax chambers[20]. Its structure constantly evolves to attain excellence and to be the most functional organization maximally serving taxpayers in accomplishing their obligations towards the state, such as tax imposts and ensuring tax receipts to public finances sector.

The tax administration, harnessing advanced methods of management, has a clearly formulated mission in which the underlying assumption is "to collect budget revenues while maximizing a level of voluntary fulfilment of tax obligations by taxpayers and to provide the latter with the highest possible service through removing bureaucratic barriers, under circumstances where tax law provisions are applied in an equitable and uniform manner". Despite that, the whole staff employed in public finance and tax sector, from employees in the Ministry of Finance to employees in local tax offices, in their efforts to bolster the functionality of their work, seek to execute all their tasks in an effective manner based on extensive knowledge, high qualifications and immense experience, while not ignoring at the same time a friendly attitude to society. That's why, year after year the utility of the whole tax administration system has increased, and all entities involved into the system operate in such a manner as to be called "friendly offices".

To accomplish its mission, the tax administration has to perform numerous tasks which mainly include:

- collecting taxes and non-taxed budget liabilities;
- dividing and transferring budget revenues;
- providing taxpayers with the best possible service, including supporting them in appropriate discharge of tax duties;
- guaranteeing widely accessible and uniform tax information;
- exercising tax control;
- detecting and conducting investigations into fiscal crimes and offences;
- collaborating with both national government and local government administration bodies, as well as relevant bodies and institutions of other countries and international organizations, on tax matters, including sharing of information on the terms and to the extent specified in agreement provisions and international arrangements[21].

---

[19] Act of 11 March 2004 on VAT (Journal of Laws, No. 54, item 535 as amended).
[20] Consolidated text Journal of Laws of 2004 No. 121, item 1267as amended http://www.mf.gov.pl [14.01.2015].
[21] Draft act on Tax Administration of 17.11.2014 http://legislacja.rcl.gov.pl/lista/2/projekt/259112 [14.01.2015].

The tax administration may accomplish all these tasks due to joint actions by the Minister of Finance, directors of tax chambers, heads of tax offices and their subordinate employees. However, efficient execution of tasks by all persons employed in the tax administration would not be possible without the powers conferred on the Minister of Finance. Thus, the Minister exercises overall supervision over tax matters, organizes collection of taxes and other liabilities, creates tax law and may also grant exemption from tax for taxpaying groups.

On the whole, important tasks are also assigned to tax chamber heads. Their main duties include: oversight of tax offices, acting as the point of second instance for resolving matters falling into the remit of tax offices in the first instance, and examining appeals against decisions issued by heads of tax inspection offices.

Equally important assignments fall into the remit of tax office heads who supervise collection of taxes and untaxed budget receipts, exercise tax control, grant Tax Identification Numbers (Polish acronym NIP), divide and transfer budget revenues to the state budget and local government budgets on terms specified in separate laws, exercise administrative enforcement and collaborate with the National Centre for Criminal Information.

The scope of tasks assigned to tax offices also contributes significantly to effective operation of the whole tax administration. Office personnel in their daily works fulfil the following assignments: conduct investigation into fiscal crimes and offences, perform the function of the public prosecutor in cases of fiscal crimes and offences as well as execute proprietary penalties to the extent specified in the Executive Penal Code and Fiscal Penal Code.

The tax administration in Poland continues to undergo a process of progress and optimization aimed at addressing the problems of mutual relationships between the administration and taxpayers in an effective and advanced manner. All activities launched seek to expand the scope of services rendered to taxpayers by the tax administration and to enhance their quality.

The current tax administration is more than a body collecting revenue for the state budget. This is an advanced and professional system tasked with ensuring reliable, effective and friendly service for taxpayers while offsetting service and control functions. Additionally, this is a system that helps taxpayers in fulfilling their tax obligations, informs about applicable procedures and provides assistance in understanding complicated tax laws. Due to these activities, a positive image of the tax administration occurs and citizens' trust in tax authorities grows. The assistance in enhancing legal knowledge in respect to tax encourages taxpayers to fulfil their tax obligations voluntarily. This, in turn, supports functional collection of assumed budget revenues, thereby allowing for delivery of economic, social and administrative targets. However, execution of all these tasks would not be possible without continually boosting qualifications among tax administration employees and modernizing workplaces through implementing cutting-edge technical measures aligned to the needs and budget potentials.

4. Tax administration structure and changes to it over 2010–2014

The catalogue of tasks outlined in the previous section, that relate to the discharge of daily duties, is the responsibility of employees in the whole tax administration system. As of today its composition comprises (see Fig. 2): 16 tax chambers to which specialized units are subject, i.e. National Tax Information (Polish acronym KIP – five offices, since 1 January 20015 – six offices), one Tax Information Exchange Bureau (Polish acronym BWIP) and 400 tax offices, including 20 specialized tax offices handling the largest companies (corporations, banks) assigned[22] by the Minister of Finance on 1 January 2004. The aim behind the establishment of the latter ones was to provide better service and to more easily enforce the tax discipline among some categories of taxpayers[23]. The specified tax offices handle less taxable entities than other offices, and they employ individuals with experience in inspecting such taxpayers as well as in assisting in tax settlements, because these offices settle the taxes critical to the business entities – in particular VAT and corporate income tax.

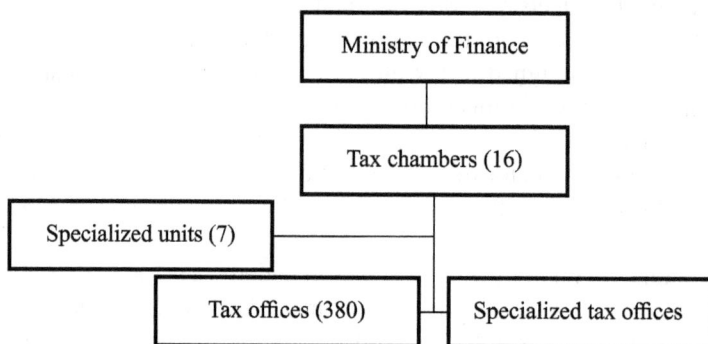

Figure 2. Organizational structure of the tax administration
Source: *Tax administration – Professional, Modern and Customer Friendly*, Document of the Polish Ministry of Finance, http://www.mf.gov.pl/documents/764034/928348/Tax+Administration+Professional,+Modern+and+Customer-friendly.pdf.

Among the institutions that have relatively recently changed their structure and scope of tasks performed is the National Tax Information (KIP). In effect, it was established in 2006, but over years its structure has been overhauled and the work over augmenting its functionality in terms of cooperation between the tax administration and the taxpayer is afoot. The institution was set up as a result of Project Phare 2003 entitled "Support for Polish tax administration – setting up of Tax Information Centres" in order to provide taxpayers with assistance in fulfilling their tax obligations through access to uniform tax information. Overall, the offices in Warsaw, Bydgoszcz, Katowice and Leszno were launched on 1 July 2006. In an attempt to facilitate access to tax information by taxpayers

---

[22] Under the act of 27 June 2003 on establishment of the Province Fiscal Councils and on amending some acts regulating tasks and competencies of agencies and organization of organizational units subject to the relevant minister responsible for public finances (Journal of Laws of 2003 No. 137, item 1302).
[23] This selected category of taxpayers was defined in Art. 5 (9b) of the above act on tax offices and tax chambers (consolidated text of 2004 Journal of Laws No. 121, item 1267 as amended).

a subsequent office with its seat in Piotrków Trybunalski (operating within the structures of the Tax Chamber in Łódź)[24] was established in 2011. Their crucial tasks include:

- provision of tax information by telephone as well as via an electronic medium;
- preparation of brochures about taxes and making them freely available;
- carrying out of training schemes devoted to taxes and preparation of educational programmes;
- developing of tax publications and placing them on websites;
- since 1 January all tax information bureaus have been recommended to introduce a convenient facility which is a preliminary analysis of applications for issuing general interpretations in individual matters at the request of those concerned and for issuing decisions on leaving these applications undecided.

Until the end of December 2014 five bureaus operated within the National Tax Information, i.e. in Leszno, Płock, Toruń, Potrków Trybunalski and Bielsko-Biała. On 1 January 2015 another KIP bureau of was opened in Będzin as a result of attempts to create an advanced and effective tax information system.

The changes also swept through tax chambers and tax offices. On 27 January 2014 a new Ordinance of the Minister of Finance on organization of tax offices and tax chambers and granting them the statutes was signed[25]. It replaced the previous Ordinance no. 39 of the Minister of Finance of 21 September 2010 on organization of tax offices and tax chambers and granting them the statutes[26].

The key reason behind effecting organizational changes in the structure of tax chambers and tax offices was modernization of the process of collecting tax liabilities and increased effectiveness of the tax administration. The ordinance of 2014 incorporates the e-Taxes Programme being currently implemented and consolidation of ancillary processes implemented put into place in tax chambers and tax offices. The methodology adopted increases the operations of the tax administration. New regulations also strengthen the supervisory and coordinating role of tax chambers over tax offices as well as the functioning of the whole tax administration with regard to inspection and execution in order to boost the tax discipline and to decrease tax arrears.

The Ordinance of the Minister of Finance of 2014 makes the following alterations in the tax apparatus:

- extends the supervision of tax chambers through devolving control powers to specific organizational units across the tax chamber, instead of assigning the inspection function to one single organizational unit;
- establishes organizational levels in tax chambers in the following domains: management, finances and accounting, inspection, collection and enforcement, judicial decisions, and organization and logistics;

---

[24] http://www.mf.gov.pl/documents/764034/11819232/20141229093658.pdf [13.01.2015].
[25] Announcement on Ordinance No. 5 of the Ministry of Finance of 27 January 2014 on organization of tax offices and tax chambers and on granting them the statutes becoming effective, http://www.mf.gov.pl/administracja-po-datkowa/wiadomosci/komunikaty/-/asset_publisher/2UWl/content/id/7449482 [14.01.2015].
[26] Journal of Laws of the Ministry of Finance, No. 10, item 45.

- extends the powers exercised by tax chambers with regard to ancillary processes through expanding the tasks performed by specific organizational units of tax chambers by supervision and organization of ancillary processes carried out by tax offices in such areas as: HR, finances, public procurement, logistics and assets, IT and legally protected information;
- enhances and standardizes oversight over the tax inspection through forming units across tax chambers that are charged with external risk management and tax inspection;
- adjusts statutes of tax chambers and tax offices to legislative changes with regard to tasks imposed on the tax administration.

Polish parliament currently works on launching further transformations in operations across tax chambers and tax offices. Principally, the aim is to reorganize tax offices so as to better use employees who proceed from internal into direct handling of taxpayers, inspection and execution. New tasks will be assigned to tax offices, which will require involvement on the part of civil servants who will be appointed to fulfil these obligations.

Few years ago the International Monetary Fund (IMF) recommended the Polish tax administration to cut down the number of tax offices. However, it is unlikely to happen over the years ahead because of new challenges facing our tax administration. Moreover, as revealed in Diagram 1, Poland, when compared to other countries across the world, ranks in the middle of the rating illustrating the number of tax offices.

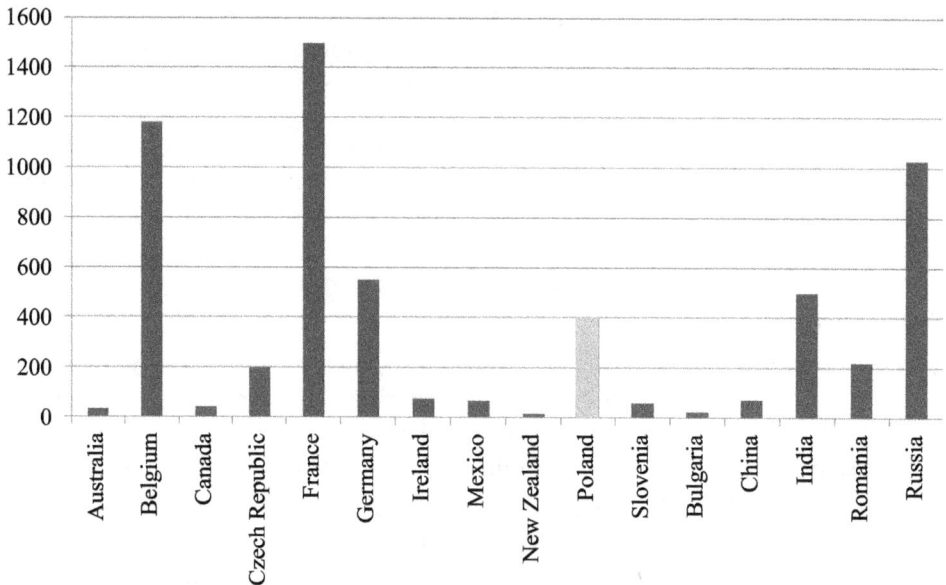

Diagram 1. Number of tax offices in selected countries globally
Source: Own study based on the data provided by OECD.

5. New projects, i.e. e-Taxes shoring up the operations of the tax administration

The Polish Ministry of Finance maintains intense focus on ongoing work on convenient facilities for taxpayers with regard to settlements with the tax offices. To accomplish this aim, an innovative information and settlement system based on cutting-edge technologies will be exploited.

Therefore, new changes were made in the Tax Ordinance, initiating the operations of the information and communication system across the tax administration, being a part of the e-Taxes Project, under the name of "Tax Portal". The system began to operate in August 2014. This is the first phase of implementing a new information and communication system designed to support taxpayers in their fulfilment of tax obligations. Until the Portal was activated the exchange of information between tax agencies and taxpayers was largely carried out using traditional means – written on paper – which was time-consuming and costly, while electronic communication between taxpayers and the tax administration was practised to a lesser extent and mostly only in one direction, that is, from the taxpayer to the tax body.

The Tax Portal reinforces the promotion of updated and current tax information. All in all, it contains both applicable laws as well as draft amendments to legislation and binding interpretation of laws, and other general information, as well as information aimed at certain taxpayers. Ultimately, the portal will comprise two blocks: one part available to general public (without registration) and the other individualized part (after logging into the Taxpayer's Account).

Currently it is possible to use the part available to general public, which allows for submission of tax returns in an electronic manner; it includes information about amendments to tax laws together with their interpretation, a calendar of important deadlines and calculators. This section of the portal offers diverse forms: traditional forms for printing out as well as interactive ones to be filed via electronic means with instructions on how to complete them. Alongside that, the new portal gives access to an e-Declaration system where taxpayers may find contact information for tax and customs administration units. The portal also includes a search engine, i.e. public benefit institutions, EU VAT numbers activation as well as general and individual interpretations by tax bodies.

Today further work over implementation of the second part of the portal is under way – the part which is individualized and will allow for direct communication with tax authorities and access to personal tax data through the taxpayer's account. By logging into the portal, a taxpayer will be able to transfer a tax remission from an account, and to electronically receive and submit documents to and from tax bodies as well as to inspect tax returns submitted and a status of matters handled.

The launch of the Tax Portal is intended to increase the functionality of the tax administration through, among others, accelerating contact among entities. Taxpayers will be able to conveniently resolve all the matters with tax bodies, to submit all applications, explanations and appeals without leaving their home.

Furthermore, the activation of the Tax Portal will fully simplify taxpayers' registration and their records. Entities entered into the National Court Register (Polish acronym KRS) will automatically receive a tax identification number (NIP) and state statistical number (REGON) due to exchange of data between the system and KRS database. Individuals commencing their business activities (CEIDG) will be granted a tax identification number (NIP) within a shortened time period, namely in one day.

The primary (strategic) goal of the e-Taxes Project is to streamline the tax collection system through honed (optimized) internal business processes across the tax administration. This goal was achieved to some extent through, among other things, enhanced effectiveness in tax information processing galvanized by formation and implementation of central information systems, widespread use of electronic documents as well as their internal circulation across the tax administration and by simplification of procedures for calculating and collecting taxes; all this being due to the use of cutting-edge ICT technologies.

The project was financed by the European Regional Development Fund at 85%, and by Beneficiary's own funds at 15% (i.e. from the state budget given the legal form of the Beneficiary). On completion of the Project, all expenses on its maintenance are covered by the Beneficiary's own funds – the total costs for accomplishing this project are outlined in Diagram 2.

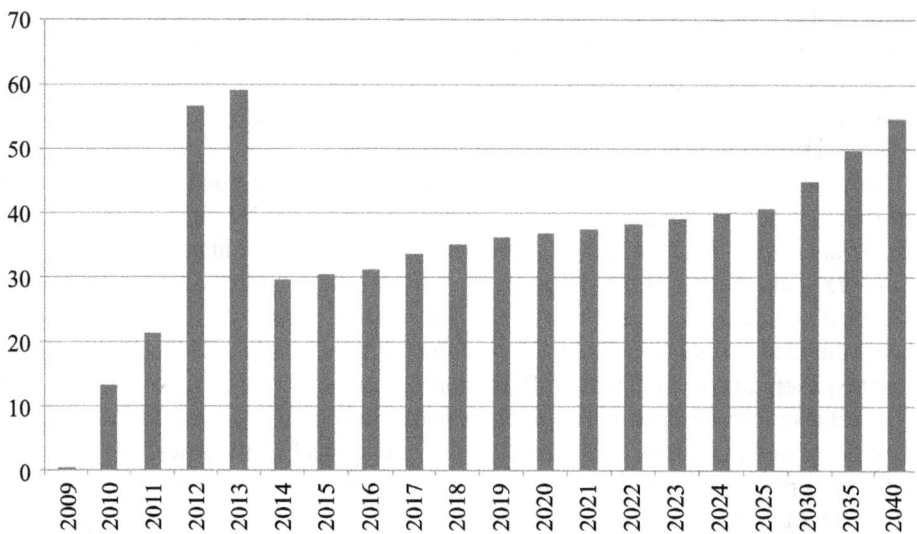

Diagram 2. Costs of the e-Taxes Project together with costs needed to maintain the infrastructure after 2014 (in million PLN)
Source: Report – Feasibility study for e-Taxes Project.

The purpose of this paper is to assess the implications of cutting-edge technologies for streamlining performance of state tasks. When answering this question in a straightforward manner, it should be noticed that notable results of the implementation of e-Taxes are a reduced tax gap through more effective detection of irregularities, streamlined procedures for assessing, collecting and distributing taxes and simplified registration obligations. The intention is to integrate the current 400 databases about taxpayers, their settlements and liabilities into one single database. The costs of implementation and establishment of this programme are small in proportion to the immense benefits produced. Tax offices, even though they do not gather information from taxpayers and despite geographical distances between the seats of offices, have all access to the same data, and taxpayers do not have to provide them repeatedly to public administration bodies (taxpayers data are automatically shared also with registers kept by other agencies, e.g. Social Insurance Institution). Every taxpayer has his or her own "account", containing all tax settlements in one place where it will be easy to verify the payment status or to approve a return initially completed by the tax administration. In addition, some types of forms, produced solely because of deficiencies in IT systems, will be eliminated.

Principal benefits yielded and services provided by the e-Taxes Project for citizens and entrepreneurs include: a radical fall in registration duties, services providing access to entrepreneur's tax information based on the Tax Portal – i.e. taxpayer's account, submission of annual tax returns by taxpayers not having a qualified electronic signature and annual tax return prepared tentatively by the tax administration. As presented in Diagram 3, the number of PIT taxpayers over 2009–2040 is diversified: at the beginning of the diagram it rises year after year, whereas beyond 2018 the number of such taxpayers is projected to drop. By contrast, another situation emerges for CIT taxpayers because over the period surveyed their number grows by about 0.5 % relative to the previous year, whereas over 2030–2040 it soars by 3%.

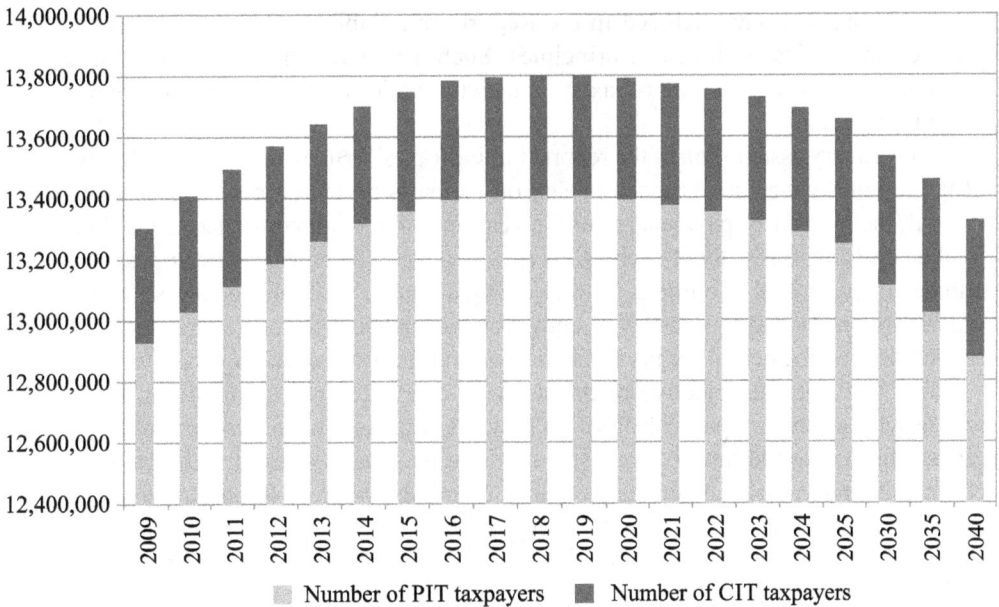

Diagram 3. Number of taxpayers – basic scenario
Source: Report – Feasibility study of the e-Taxes Project.

6. Methods for assessing operations by the tax administration

The information presented in previous sections, concerned with the scope of tasks, structure and cutting-edge technological measures in the tax administration, suggests their high dynamics. However, it fails to answer clearly the question of their effectiveness. While responding to the issue raised, it is worthwhile tapping into independent research and studies illustrating effectiveness and friendly approach to a citizen across the Polish tax administration as compared to other countries. One of the studies is the Report "Paying Taxes" compiled annually since 2007 by the consulting firm PricewaterhouseCoopers (PwC) and the World Bank Group, being a component of the Doing Business Report published by the World Bank since 2003. The ranking Paying Taxes describes the impact of complying with tax obligations on business activities. It also contains a descriptive overview of operations performed by a tax administration in a specific country, thereby responding to taxpayers' expectations which may be a driving force for the economy through removing administrative barriers. Poland is analyzed in research required for the report from the very beginning of its publication.

The report "Paying Taxes" rests on the methodology according to which investigation of the tax regime is carried out, based on the case study method, which implies measurement of tax burdens and administrative obligations with regard to business operations and is based on the activities conducted by a case study company in each country analyzed, the data being the basis for the Report obtained from the questionnaires returned by respondents.

To ensure that data included in the Report are reliable and actual, analyses of tax regimes are guided by identical principles. Such a research method makes it possible to facilitate the benchmarking of tax systems within relevant economic and geographical groupings globally.

The primary assumption of the report "Paying Taxes" is to expose the complexity level of tax regimes which are assessed mostly on the basis of: tax burdens and contributions in total, the number of payments over the year and time required to meet tax obligations by the company. Basically, it exclusively relies on rigid (technical) indicators such as the number of payments or burdens in total detailed above, while neglecting so called soft criteria which also have a substantial impact on the quality of the tax regime and are likely to include the time period for tax inspection or possibility of obtaining tax interpretation.

The fundamental objective of the research conducted when compiling the Report is to provide a comparative analysis of tax systems in selected countries worldwide (Report 2015, which provided information used in this paper, was developed with data from 189 countries; Report 2010 gave data from 183 countries, whereas Report 2009 was based on information from 181 countries), though mandatory contributions for various funds are also considered as taxes. In Poland these include the following: Social Security Fund, Labour Fund, Guaranteed Employee Benefits Fund, and State Fund for Rehabilitation of People with Disabilities.

The findings obtained from the report "Paying Taxes" over 2011–2014 helped to frame the charts below, illustrating the Polish tax system and public administration as compared to selected countries. Diagram 4 displays Poland (as compared to selected countries) relative to the total tax over 2011–2015. Undoubtedly, the rise of Poland from the 113th to 87th position stems from several factors: beneficial changes in the Polish tax regime, modified research methodology embraced by the World Bank and heightened assessment in tax terms caused by dwindling effective tax rate (from 41% to 38.5%).

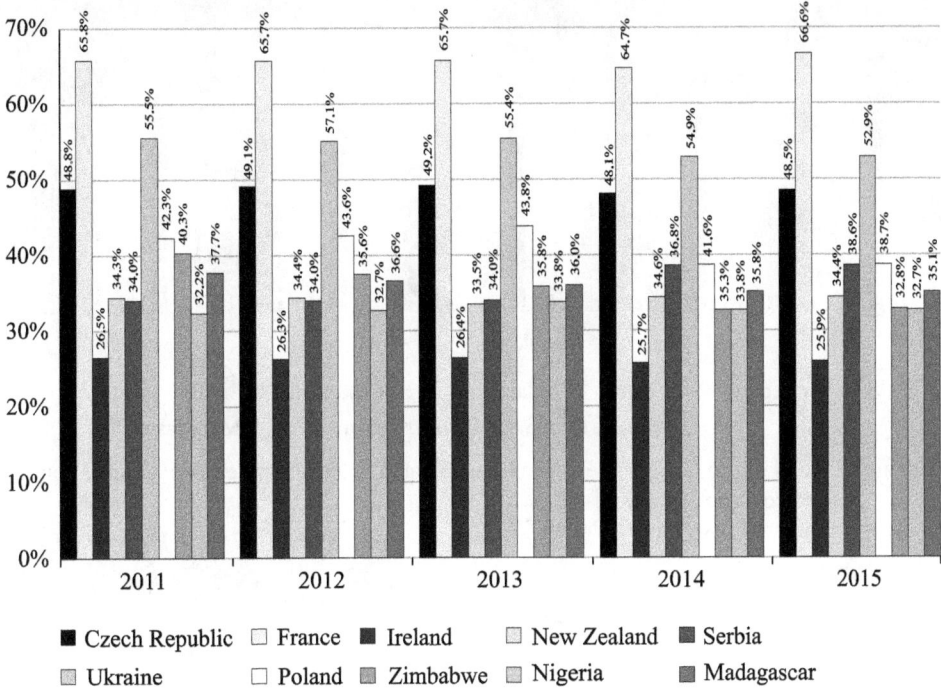

Diagram 4. Tax in total in Poland as compared to selected countries
Source: Own study based on the reports "Paying Taxes".

From the viewpoint of effective operations by the tax administration it is much more important to possess information on how much time a taxpayer requires for tasks related to the tax system in Poland as compared to selected countries – which is explicitly illustrated in Diagram 5.

According to data specified in Diagram 5 a Polish company owner has to make 18 payments per year and this takes 285 hours, whereas in Ukraine this requires as many as 350 hours. As mentioned above, in the annual report "Paying Taxes 2015" compiled by the World Bank and the consulting firm PwC, displaying tax burdens of entrepreneurs, Poland improved its position – a jump from the 113th rating last year to the 87th spot, and only in 2011 Poland was ranked 127th in this rating. Thus, a substantial improvement in this regard is evident and suggests, certainly alongside the elements previously detailed, enhanced effectiveness of the tax administration and shift of the tax system in the proper direction.

While proceeding to the analysis of performance across the tax administration system it is worth taking a close look at data concerned with the use of new technologies in han-

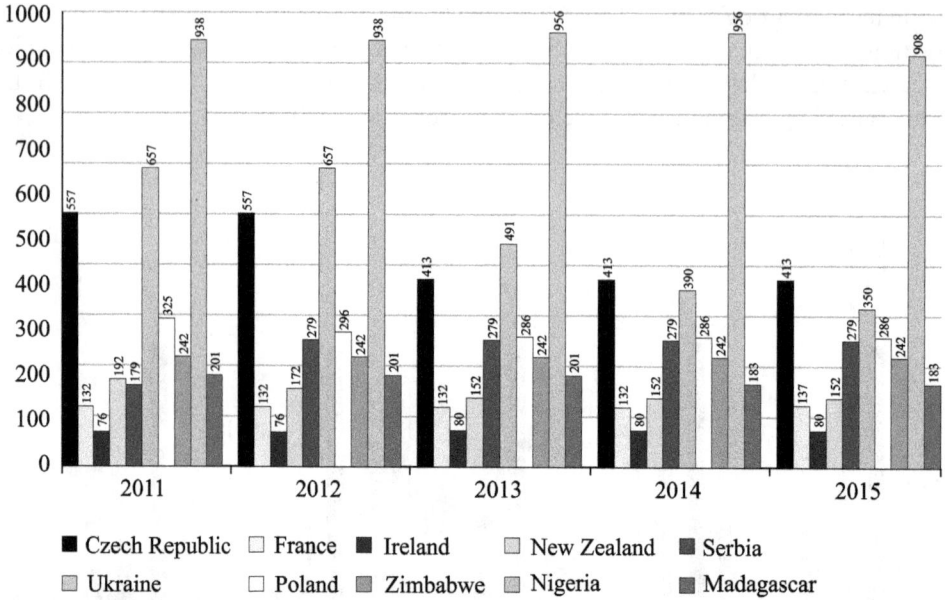

Legend: Czech Republic ■ France □ Ireland ■ New Zealand □ Serbia ■ Ukraine □ Poland □ Zimbabwe ■ Nigeria ■ Madagascar ■

Diagrams 5. Total time a taxpayer devotes to tasks related to the tax system in Poland as compared to selected countries over 2011–2015
Source: Own study based on the reports "Paying Taxes".

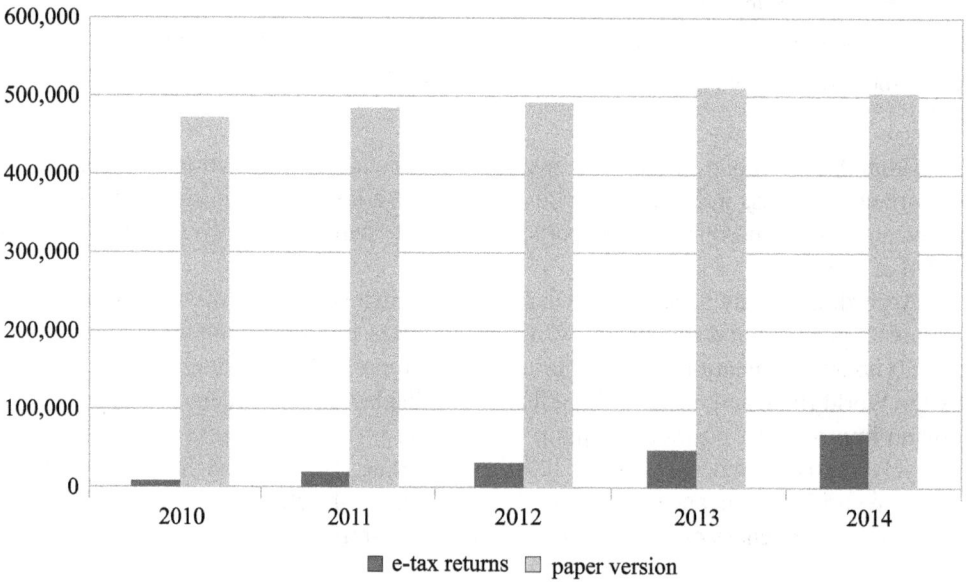

Legend: e-tax returns ■ paper version □

Diagram 6. Number of PIT-37 tax returns transferred over 2010–2014
Source: Own study based on data on www.mf.gov.pl.

dling a Polish taxpayer. In Poland, in accordance with the Tax Ordinance act, it is necessary to file various tax returns. One of them, the PIT-37 tax return, is a statement of the income generated (losses incurred) over the financial year. As presented in Diagram 5, taxpayers have two options of filing tax returns: in paper or via electronic means. It may be inferred from the findings revealed that increasingly more taxpayers select an electronic system for filing their tax returns to tax offices, which proves to be a positive trend. It should be also highlighted that data regarding 2014 cover 11 months, while it is projected that the number of tax returns filed online this year will exceed 4,000 forms. In general, emphasis should be placed on the fact that the number of tax returns sent online in 2014 increased over 15 times relative to 2010 (see Diagram 6).

7. Summary

Electronic filing of documents has been gaining momentum year after year, and thus increasingly more taxpayers choose this form for filing documents to save time on visits to tax agencies. Although statistical data shows that increasingly more tax returns are filed through electronic systems, paper documents continue to be the most popular form, and this gives a lot of potential to work with in Poland. The situation should continually improve year on year due to new reinforcing regulations, among others, the act of 26 September 2014 which became effective on 1 January 2015; specifically, this amended the act on personal income as well as some other laws, and thus introduced the electronic system for filing CIT tax returns. Technological solutions put into operation over several years by the Polish administration clearly translate into the taxpayers' attitude to new measures which allow for saving time and money. This thesis is corroborated by successive Diagrams 7–9 below which portray an increasing take-up of electronic filing of documents in the Polish tax system, which in consequence has implications for the time devoted by a taxpayer to filing tax returns.

In the first place, taking into account the government's overriding goals, stable economic growth is a significant factor entailing a boost in entrepreneurship and lessened bureaucracy. Therefore, it is worthwhile showing whether and to what extent Polish entrepreneurs make use of technological services while filing CIT-8 tax returns.

According to data provided in Diagram 7, showing CIT taxpayers' income (loss incurred) as well as the total number of CIT-8 and CIT-8A tax returns files, it may be observed that over 2010–2014 there was a dynamic increase in the number of tax returns filed electronically when compared to the overall rise in such declarations filed by taxpayers.

Similar situation occurs for CIT-10 tax returns (see Diagram 8).

Diagram 8 shows the number of CIT-10 tax returns filed; CIT-10 is a tax return on flat-rate income tax from legal persons, from income (revenue) generated by taxpayers not having a seat or management board on the territory of Poland over 2010–2014. This diagram also supports the thesis set out at the start, that increasingly more taxpayers opt for an electronic form for filing tax returns, thereby abandoning paper forms. The number of CIT-10R and CIT-10Z tax returns filed (presented together in Diagram 8) in paper form in 2014 plunged 3 times relative to 2010.

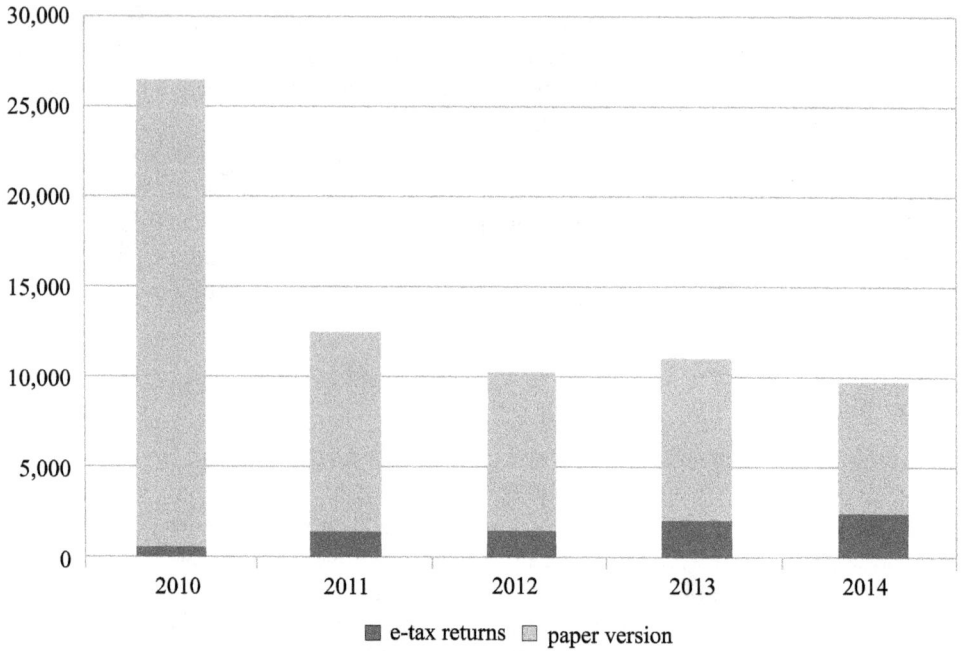

Diagram 7. Number of CIT-8 tax returns filed over 2010–2014
Source: Own study based on data presented on www.mf.gov.pl.

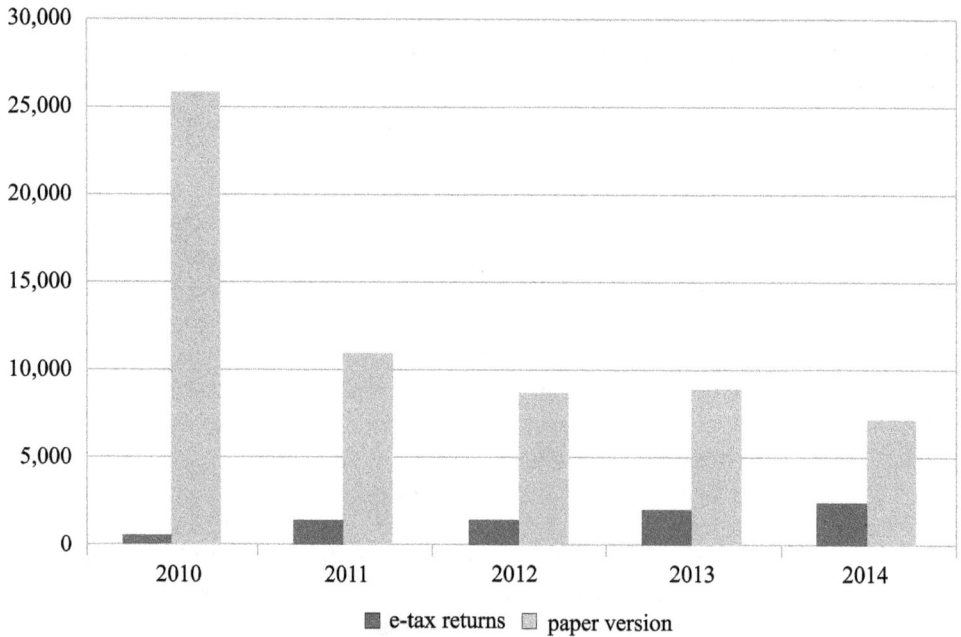

Diagram 8. Number of CIT-10 tax returns filed over 2010–2014
Source: Own study based on data presented on www.mf.gov.pl.

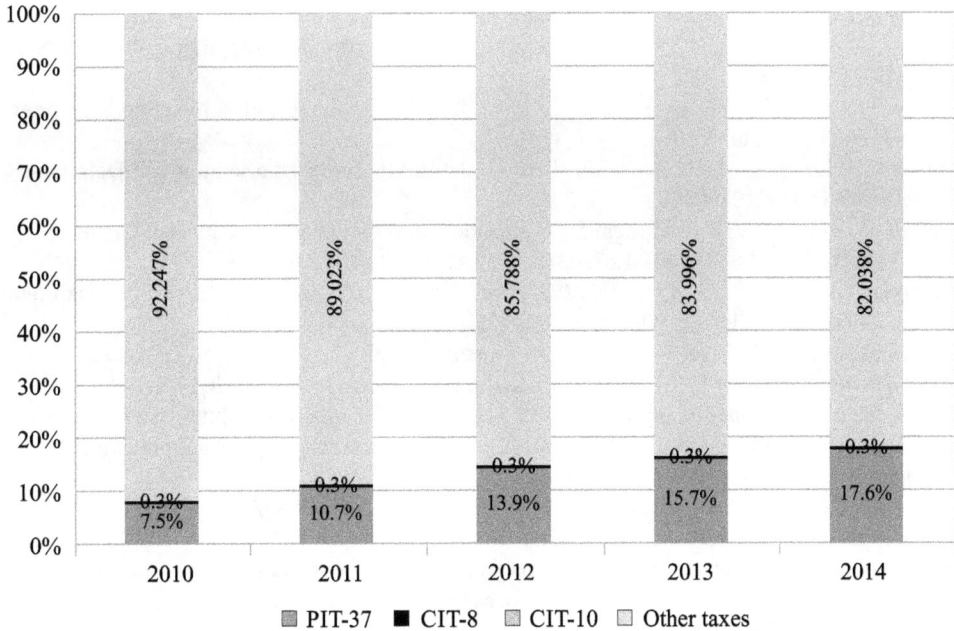

Diagram 9. Percentage share of tax returns filed online
Source: Own study based on data presented on www.mf.gov.pl.

Diagram 9, showing the percentage share of tax returns filed online, again confirms a growing interest in tax returns filed online and mounting exploitation of the electronic system. In 2014 PIT-37 tax return accounted for over 17% of tax returns electronically filed.

References

Krynicka H. (2006), *Koncepcja nowego zarządzania w sektorze publicznym* (new public management), p. 193, [in:] http://www.bibliotekacyfrowa.pl/Content/34636/014.pdf.

Wyrzykowska, B. (2006), *Zarządzanie jakością w instytucjach publicznych*, p. 77. [in:] http://www.wne.sggw.pl/czasopisma/pdf/EIOGZ_2006_nr61_s75.pdf.

http://www.mf.gov.pl/administracja-podatkowa/dzialalnosc/zarzadzanie-jakoscia.

Journal of Laws of 1919 No. 65, item 391, Internet System of Legislative Acts (ISAP), http://isap.sejm.gov.pl/VolumeServlet?type=wdu&rok=1919&numer=.

Journal of Laws of 1934 No. 39, item 346, ISAP, http://isap.sejm.gov.pl/VolumeServlet?type=wdu&rok=1934&numer=039.

Journal of Laws of 1934 No. 110, item 975 i 976, ISAP, isap.sejm.gov.pl/Download?id=W-DU19341100976&type=2.

Journal of Laws of 1939 No.18, item 118, http://dziennikustaw.gov.pl/DU/1939/s/18/118.

Journal of Laws of 1946 No. 27, item 173, http://dziennikustaw.gov.pl/DU/1946/s/27/173.

Journal of Laws of 1947 No. 32, item 140, http://dziennikustaw.gov.pl/du/1947/s/32/140.

http://www.skarbowcy.pl/blaster/extarticle.php?show=article&article_id=643.

Journal of Laws of 1975 No. 16, item 91, http://dokumenty.rcl.gov.pl/DU/rok/1975/wydanie/16.

Journal of Laws of 1982 No. 45, item 289, ISAP, http://isap.sejm.gov.pl/DetailsServ-let?id=WDU19820450289.

Journal of Laws of 1989 No. 3, item 12, ISAP, http://isap.sejm.gov.pl/VolumeServlet?type=w-du&rok=1989&numer=003.

Journal of Laws of 1991 No. 80, item 350, ISAP, http://isap.sejm.gov.pl/DetailsServ-let?id=WDU19910800350.

Journal of Laws of 1993 No. 11, item 50 as amended, http://www.sejm.gov.pl/sejm7.nsf/BASLek-sykon.xsp?id=BA648AC6B3E63ADDC1257A590042A4BF&litera=P.

Act on tax advisory services (*Journal of Laws of 1996* No. 102, item 475), ISAP, http://isap.sejm.gov.pl/DetailsServlet?id=WDU19961020475.

Journal of Laws of 1997 No. 78, item 483, www.sejm.gov.pl.

Act of 11 March 2004 on VAT (*Journal of Laws,* No. 54, item 535 as amended).

Consolidated text *Journal of Laws of 2004* No. 121, item 1267as amended http://www.mf.gov.pl.

Draft act on Tax Administration of 17.11.2014, http://legislacja.rcl.gov.pl/lista/2/projekt/259112.

Journal of Laws of 2003 No. 137, item 1302.

http://www.mf.gov.pl/documents/764034/11819232/20141229093658.pdf.

Announcement on the Ordinance No. 5 of the Ministry of Finance of 27 January 2014 on organiza-tion of tax offices and tax chambers and on granting them the statutes becoming effective, http://www.mf.gov.pl/administracja-podatkowa/wiadomosci/komunikaty/-/asset_publisher/2UWl/content/id/7449482.

Journal of Laws, Ministry of Finance, No. 10, item 45.

Barbara Kos, Joanna Kos-Łabędowicz

The Application of ICT in Urban Transport

1. Introduction

The aim of social development is to improve the quality of life of the population, which is determined through a system of indicators concerning various spheres of life (health system, access to education, the development of housing construction and municipal infrastructure etc.). The public sector plays a vital role in it, particularly local government authorities, which are responsible for the availability and level of public services – the most important services for the whole society. In recent years, more and more attention has been paid to improve the efficiency of activities for society and spending of public funds, which is achieved, among other things, through the implementation of modern management methods and the use of solutions based on innovative technologies. The use of modern communication and information technologies potentially leads to improvements in many aspects of the operation of market entities and consumers. One of these aspects is urban transport described in this study.

2. Public services

The basic feature which distinguishes services from material goods is their intangibility. Other features of services – simultaneity of delivery and consumption, heterogeneity, perishability, the inability to purchase and obtain exclusive ownership – are derived from their intangibility. Insubstantial services cannot be measured by physical measurement of size, weight, volume, and they cannot be evaluated organoleptically. Inseparability of the processes of rendering many services and their consumption means that the consumption of services takes place at the time of their delivery. Inseparability of the customer being served and the person delivering the service makes the final features of many services developed with the participation of the buyer (recipient) (Czubała, Jonas, Smoleń, Wiktor 2006).

The service sector is highly heterogeneous in terms of types of services and their functions and goals, so it is difficult to make a single division. The most commonly used services divisions are based on the following criteria (Daszkowska 1998):

- destination of the service (characteristic of consumer, manufacturing and public services),
- the type of activities (services relating to the effects on the body or an object, making available facilities for temporary use, meeting immediate physical needs of people etc.),
- result of activities (information services, renovation, distribution etc.),
- object of activities (manufacturing, personal, informational, managerial),
- the type of recipient (services for individuals and businesses) and the nature of the payment (commercial and non-commercial services).

Public services (also known as services of general interest) are a special category of services of a public nature (delivered on a non-commercial basis: free or partially paid for), aimed at meeting important social needs. Public services include, among others, health care, education, law enforcement, justice, public transport, postal services, etc. (Ziębicki 2007). These services have a common feature: they play an essential role in the functioning of the whole society by satisfying the private needs of citizens.

In most countries, ensuring an adequate level and accessibility of public services is considered to be one of the fundamental tasks of the State. Public services are supposed to satisfy the following requirements: rendering them is to be continuous, uninterrupted, safe and accessible at a proper level of quality. One of the tasks of the public authorities is to define standards and techniques to monitor public services (Wojciechowski 2012). The system of public services runs smoothly if it guarantees all citizens the same access to benefits pertaining to them legally and according to defined standards.

Both Polish law and European Union law are based on the principles of decentralization and subsidiarity of public authority.

Local governments have been assigned public issues of local and regional importance, which make up a fairly wide and diverse collection. The municipality (*gmina*), as the basic unit of local government, is responsible for several sets of tasks (Krajewski 2012):

- the delivery of public services with the use of technical infrastructure (local collective transport, telecommunications, provision of electricity, heat and gas, water supply, sewage system, rubbish collection and recycling, management of municipal cemeteries, taking care of green and wooded areas in the municipality, etc.),
- the delivery of services based on objects of social infrastructure (child care and education, health care, culture, tourism, social services etc.),
- management of other municipal public facilities (market places, marts, other public utility facilities),
- ensuring spatial and ecological order (municipal real estate management, environmental protection and water management),

- ensuring public order and safety (including fire protection and flood control),
- other tasks, the purpose of which is different from the above-mentioned (family policy, promoting the idea of self-government, support for non-governmental organizations etc.).

The above mentioned tasks have the status of public utilities and they are own tasks of municipalities, which means that they are compulsory (Wojciechowski 2012).

Urban public transport is a public service of great importance for the functioning of cities and thus for economic development in modern countries. Efficient and accessible public transport provides mobility for residents, inhibits the growth of traffic in total motorization of urban space and reduces the negative impact of transport on the surroundings, especially on the environment. All of this is particularly important in cities, which are areas of high population density. Urban public transport indirectly affects the growth of the activity of society, including professional activity, which affects the economic development of towns and investments (Michałowska ed. 2012).

3. Urban public transport services

The Public Transport Act of 16 December 2010 (OJ 2011 No. 5 pos. 13) defines the principles of organization and functioning of the regular movement of passengers on public transport in Polish territory and in border areas by road, tramway, railway, cable transport, water transport, including sea transport and inland navigation, and also determines rules of financing the regular transport of passengers on public transport, of a public utility character.

Public transport in urban areas plays an important role in meeting one of the most important needs of urban residents – mobility. This need is met through a variety of means of urban public transport (OJ 2011 No. 5 pos. 13) understood as passenger transport carried out within the administrative boundaries of:

- the metropolitan area,
- cities, towns and municipalities,
- cities or a city, towns or a town,
- towns and neighbouring municipalities (where an agreement has been reached or/ and they have created an association in order to run public transport commonly).

In Poland, under the law, urban transport services concern the activities of a public utility character. Urban transport can be carried out by a carrier. The carrier is an entrepreneur having permission to run business activity in the transport of passengers. Urban transport is a kind of subsidy for the part of society that does not have or is not able to use a personal means of transport.

The main factor determining the demand for urban transport services is the need for mobility, or desire, need or request of an individual or a particular community to move from one place to another (Pawlicka 1978). Urban transport needs to include the following features (Wyszomirski 2008):

- focus on a spatially limited urbanized area,
- prevalence,
- the changeability of occurrence,
- mass occurrence.

Urban transport needs are diverse. The most important criterion of division is a destination. It refers to the distance, the frequency and the mode of transport. The overall division of transport needs by destination includes among others: occupational, household and recreational needs. There are also multi-targeted journeys, which serve multiple needs (Wyszomirski 1998). Different means of public transport, such as buses, trams, trolley-buses, light rail or underground systems, are used to provide mass public transport services.

4. The use of ICT in urban transport services

The development of information technology and data transferring, as well as their increasing availability make the innovative solutions that improve the quality and efficiency of public transport more and more commonly implemented (Boschetti, Maurizi, Cré 2014). Multiple solutions using, among others, electronic tickets, have been developed in Poland for the past several years. Their common feature is that in most cases the cards (tickets) have been dedicated only to urban mass public transport services. There are few solutions that extend the functionality of the card (ticket) which enables payment for other municipal services, or fees for regional services (Krukowski 2008). Nowadays, consumers of transport services are becoming more and more demanding, therefore the companies providing the services of mass transport are forced to introduce ever new innovations to meet their needs and improve the quality of public transport (Lübeck, Wittmann, Battistella 2012). The essential innovation in mass public transport includes, among others, customer service, new technologies in the sale of public transport services, passenger information systems, monitoring, mobile access to timetables, etc.

4.1. Customer service system in urban transport

Keeping in contact with customers is of great importance in monitoring the reliability of customer service. An easily accessible communication channel for customers facilitates a service provider compliance with the requirements and expectations of customers in terms of offer and service quality. Without maintaining contact with the customer it is difficult to ensure the most efficient and effective service. Communication should take place in both directions, giving the service provider the opportunity to communicate to their customers relevant information on its transport services and customers to comment and evaluate these services.

Companies create different types of customer support to communicate with the customer, which takes place especially through personal communication, such as telephone, e-mail and instant messaging, giving an opportunity to exchange information between specific addressees, allowing for personalization of message content. Generally speaking, the objective of such services is to establish a dialogue with the client, to facilitate the customer getting the goods and services, and above all, to help him obtain comprehensive information about the company offer and to improve the company's image (well organized, friendly customer service is a flagship of the company and helps win new customers) (Bini 2012). Concentrating relations with the customers in one system, customer service deals with complaints, resolves problems and can simultaneously serve as a shop and an information service, customizing the content of the messages and the means of communication to customer preferences, creating comprehensive databases, updated at each contact with the customer. Customer services may function in different forms, such as (Gordon 2001):

- offices – places where direct contact between a vendor and a customer occurs. In them one can purchase goods and services, obtain the necessary information and assistance, for example technical support (help desk), take advantage of professional consulting or lodge a complaint,
- call centre (customer service centre, contact centre) used for contact with customers by telephone. The main tasks of the call centre are taking orders, providing information, receiving complaints, making reservations (e.g. in movie theatres, travel agencies). The call centre can also act as a help desk or a hotline,
- helplines, like call centres, used to contact customers by telephone; the main task of the hotline is to provide information on services and products.

Entities providing public transport services pay more and more attention to the information and feedback obtained from customers. Analyzing the tasks established by customer service departments one can distinguish the following (see web 1, web 2, web 3):

- providing comprehensive information on functioning of public transport in the area (line structure, changes in the timetables, most convenient connections, entitlement to free transport or reduced fare etc.),
- providing information about the procedures of cases handled and providing relevant forms and documents,
- retail sale of the full range of tickets offered,
- operations associated with electronic ticket (e-ticket, City Card),
- obtaining feedback from the public on the functioning of public transport, demands concerning quality, and forwarding them to the appropriate departments of the company,
- handling letters, petitions, complaints and interventions relating to the transport of persons,
- receiving payments for a variety of charges imposed, including extra charges and handling fees.

Customer service is an important element of the communication system with the passenger, therefore creating such services to give a comprehensive passenger service is a justified and right activity.

4.2 Dynamic passenger information systems

One of the elements of modern urban public transport is to inform passengers about current arrivals and departures of vehicles and transfers. Modern systems provide passengers with such information in a visual format, on specially developed electronic boards for this purpose. This allows for a constant display of updated times of arrival and departure (Rojowski, Gancarz 2009). The Dynamic Passenger Information System is an integrated information system that provides information on the implementation of transport tasks performed by public transport to passengers and to the supervising services. The main task of this system is to provide passengers with information about the estimated departure time of the vehicle from the selected stop. Information about the departure time is passed on to passengers and is presented by a system of bus boards (LED / LCD). Messages displayed on electronic boards include stop name, line number, destination, forecast and/ or scheduled departure time, waiting time, special messages (information on traffic jams, diversions, ticket prices, etc.) and advertisements (Chandurkar, Mugade, Sinha, Misal, Borekar 2013). The Dynamic Passenger Information System supplies updated electronic information depending on traffic and relating to the running of, for example, trams or buses, which have compatible onboard devices informing the control centre about the location of the vehicle.

The stop plates can be of various sizes and functions. The big ones are for passengers arriving at a stop, while the smaller ones can be installed under bus/tram shelters and they are sufficient to provide key information regarding the lines. For people with disabilities, for example for the blind, the key element is the voice function activated by pressing a button or by personal radio remote control.

From the perspective of urban transport users, information systems at stops can fulfil such functions as:

- support the choice of place to wait for journey,
- determine the required time of waiting for a means of transport,
- support the decision about alternative ways of travelling.

The Passenger Information System, through appropriate devices, should provide passengers with easy and fast access to information at all available places during the trip. Apart from boards at the stops, vehicles are also equipped with information boards. Vehicles equipped with information boards make it much easier for passengers to make sure which route they follow, and where they are at any given moment, they show the line number, the initial stop and destination, and other relevant information (Chheda, Gajra, Chhaya, Deshpande, Gharge 2012).

More and more cities in Poland are introducing dynamic passenger information boards. The towns that have introduced electronic boards include, among others, Białystok, Bydgoszcz, Gliwice, Jaworzno, Katowice, Lublin, Sosnowiec, Poznań, Puławy, Rybnik, Gdańsk-Gdynia-Sopot, Warsaw and Wrocław.

The system provides a lot of useful information for operators of public transport, facilitating transport management. The information includes (WYG 2011):

- the current position of the vehicle,
- the route of the vehicle,
- the journeys made,
- information about delays or acceleration of ongoing journeys,
- the state of selected elements of the system, for example of the boards at the stops.

Display of departures in real time may function not only at the stops, but also via the Internet. The basic operating principle and the necessary equipment are the same as in the case of information boards. Transport managers may therefore present the same type of information in two ways: at bus stops and on the Internet. Adapting information to mobile devices creates new possibilities for travellers. The use of appropriate applications enables continuous access to public transport timetables on every mobile phone that supports the proper application (Park, Kim 2015).

The dynamic passenger information system is an example of the use of ICT, which allows for improvement in transport services and lets the passengers plan their travel better.

4.3. Modern forms of sales – e-tickets, city cards

The provision of public transport services is associated with fares. A traditional and well-known paper ticket has been changing with the evolution of validating devices. Technological progress and the solutions applied in other areas of life provide opportunities to introduce into public transport other carriers informing about the payment for the journey. The paper tickets have been more and more commonly replaced by electronic information carriers that allow recording in digital form, which means replacing paper tickets with tickets with a magnetic stripe or smart cards within the city electronic travel card system. A comparison of advantages and disadvantages of various types of tickets are shown in Table 1 (Gražvydas 2006).

Table 1. Possible role, costs and benefits for regular stakeholders of integrated e-ticketing systems

Type of ticket	Validating	Advantages	Disadvantages
Paper ticket	Mechanical or electromechanical punching	Cheap to produce. Easy to use. In case of improvement of systems, costs of withdrawing are comparatively low	Weak protection, risk of falsification. Not multifunctional. Not effective for underground urban transport. Does not allow tracking of passenger flows, boarding and disembarking
Paper daily, weekly, monthly, quarterly, tourist pass	Generally no punching	Simple, easy to make	Falsification

Type of ticket		Validating	Advantages	Disadvantages
On-board single paper ticket		Ordinary punching or no punching	Advantageous mainly for passengers	If driver sells – time is wasted. Usually charged more than buying in advance
Paper/plastic card/token with magnetic strip (or two strips) – single use and passes		Card reader – contact validation	Better protected than those made of paper. More durable. Information gathering options. Very thick and light	Need for contact punching. Risk of disfunctioning or failure on readers. Magnetic strips become vulnerable to stronger crease or other contact
Smart card (electronic ticket)	Contact smart card/electronic ticket	Insertion into card reader or terminal	Very convenient validating. Gives data of passenger traffic flows, useful for optimization of routes according to the data received. Very multifunctional application of smart cards (the same card can be used for parking, library, shopping, etc.)	Expensive to introduce. Risk of fake smart card/ticket still exist. Transaction time of contact smart card is longer than that of contactless one
	Contactless smart card/electronic ticket	Remote scanning, contactless validating		
	Dual interface card and combi-card	Allow both ways of validation		

Electronic city cards with an integrated chip are modern multi-purpose cards that serve as a tool for cashless payments in public transport and other public services on the basis of appropriate information systems. They are not only more convenient, but also allow for the collection of data concerning demand for services, and thus improve the quality of services provided, particularly the coordination of public transport.

Electronic ticketing systems are implemented in large cities, metropolitan areas and agglomerations which seem more predisposed to such projects due to the scale of the market, and in small towns. In reality, small Polish towns have often been able to introduce such systems even earlier than big cities (Lubieniecka-Kocoń, Kos, Kosobucki, Urbanek, 2013). The differences between the various projects are primarily within functional range, that is, in which buildings and what cards can be used for. Many Polish cities have already implemented electronic city cards using them as a tool to standardize the collection of fees for services rendered by the municipality, to widen access and improve the attractiveness of municipal services, to optimize the costs of providing them (e.g. public transport), to optimize the costs of advertising and promotion of the city and thereby to increase the satisfaction of the public. In most of these cities, electronic city cards are used to a limited extent as a carrier of an electronic ticket authorizing the use of public transport in the area as well as an electronic wallet that enables payment for the use of municipal services, for example parking in the pay zone. The implementation of this kind of solution offers many possibilities, which include the control and optimization of the operating costs of municipal services, reducing costs of distribution fees for them, support for the collection of fines and tickets, free changes of pricing for services, electronic distribution and ticket control, monitoring the punctuality of transport, automatic billing for utility services and analysis of the quality of services, and generating different types of reports and analyses.

Tickets can be purchased with the use of the mobile phone, anywhere and anytime, regardless of the tariff system. This solution is very useful especially when one forgets or simply does not have time to buy the ticket earlier. To buy the ticket, it is enough to call or send an appropriate text message when you enter the means of transport – the price of the ticket bought this way is no different from the traditional one (Tripathi, Reddy, Madria, Mohanty, Ghosh 2009). On the market there are currently several applications allowing for the purchase of tickets via mobile phone (eg. MoBilet, SkyCash).

Such solutions as the city card or the purchase of a ticket via a mobile phone facilitate the use of services and allow the companies providing public transport services to adapt their offer to meet the needs of customers better.

5. Problems with the implementation of innovative solutions for urban transport

Implementation of the described solutions using modern technologies in urban transport is an extremely complicated process (not just for technical reasons), requiring the involvement of many parties (Vasconellos, Freire da Costa 2008). Due to the size of the paper, only examples of issues that require consideration in case of implementation of an integrated system of e-ticketing are presented.

Implementation of integrated e-ticketing in urban transport requires all parties involved to take common decisions on two aspects of the functioning of the system. The first decision should involve the technical side of the operations, e.g. selection of the devices, software and data management system. Legal and economic aspects are no less important in deciding to implement an integrated system of e-ticketing, e.g. division of tasks and responsibilities, division of earned income, ways to encourage participation in the project and others (Mezghani 2008). Described in this way, the decision-making process (concerning technical, legal and economic aspects) may seem simple. It is a wrong impression as in every city (or region) wishing to implement integrated e-ticketing, we will have to deal with a different set of actors and different conditions. Almost always, in the simplest systems, there are three types of actors: government and other administrative authorities, public transport operators and authorities, and existing and potential users. These are the three basic groups necessary for the proper functioning of the system, each of which plays a different role, bears different costs and expects different benefits (Urban ITS Expert Group 2012). Tasks and expected costs and benefits of these three stakeholders are presented in Table 2 (Kos-Łabędowicz, 2014).

In more complex e-ticket systems, additional interest groups can be observed, depending on the complexity of the system, the degree of its integration with the environment

Table 2. Possible role, costs and benefits for usual stakeholders of integrated e-ticketing systems

Role	Costs	Benefits
Governments and other administrative authorities		
Provide strategic leadership (e.g. provide incentives, encourage use of standards); support the roll-out (e.g. through additional funding); engage in the integration of existing schemes and coordination of stakeholders	Costs of financing (pilot) projects; subsidies for installation. Cost of setting up a platform for the stakeholders to push initiatives forward. In case of general project (regional or national) risk of failing to fulfil specific/local needs	Economic effects: increased expertise in ICT which can be applied to other sectors; better economic conditions for companies so that they locate or expand their businesses in that area; provide identity to the community; potential to implement nation-wide technical specifications. Environmental effects: increase in public transport usage; reductions in traffic congestion
Public transport operators and authorities		
Offer a well-established market segment (either existing users or additional passengers who will be attracted through the new medium); information about tariffs and prices	Capital costs: e.g., for buying or upgrading equipment and infrastructure. Operating costs: maintenance and replacement. Additional costs: e.g., for training staff to use and handle new technology or campaigns to inform users about new technology, cost for resolving passenger disputes (especially in the first year of operation). Costs for outsourcing clearinghouse functions for the fare and data collection system, for marketing and distribution	Reduced administrative costs through automation of manual processes: fewer cashiers needed, reduced fare-processing time, better passenger throughput in high-demand areas. Reduction of fraud resulting from cash handling and fare evasion. Better price differentiation, e.g. flexible fare structure depending on the mode and time of day. Better transport statistics for planning purposes and thus for a better exploitation of the network capacities. Multi-application potential for a better integration with other services. Safety improvements and better working conditions for operators. Reputation as a modern enterprise
Existing and potential end-users		
Purchase the products they require, based on their preferences and willingness to become involved	Burden of using new fare medium; time needed to learn handling the new medium. Costs for purchasing the card. Need to divulge personal information. Losing e-ticket poses more risks (both financial, and potential for leak of sensitive information)	Improved convenience: no (exact) tariff knowledge needed (if automatic price calculation is available), no need to take card out of the wallet (if contactless); online top-up usually possible; no need to have cash. Time savings due to faster fare processing. Cost savings due to loyalty programmes and individually targeted services (if existing). Improved availability of real-time service information (especially when mobile phones are used)

and additional services offered, e.g. the ability to recharge the card account (financial intermediary), the ability to use the card as an e-wallet (financial intermediary), using the card to obtain tourist information and discounts for tourist attractions (the tourism sector). When the role of the e-ticket is carried out by a mobile device (mobile phone, tablet), additionally telecommunications operators (European Parliamentary Research Service, 2014) are involved. Tasks and expected costs and benefits of these three stakeholders are presented in Table 3 (Kos-Łabędowicz 2014).

Table 3. Possible role, costs and benefits for additional stakeholders of integrated e-ticketing systems

Role	Costs	Benefits
Tourism sector		
Cities – as main tourist destinations and major centres of entertainment activities – offer a well-established market segment	Capital costs: e.g., for buying or upgrading equipment and infrastructure. Operating costs: maintenance and replacement. Additional costs: e.g., for training staff to use and handle new technology or campaigns to inform users about new technology. Costs for outsourcing clearinghouse functions for the fare and data collection system, for marketing and distribution	Ticketing offers a well-established market segment and thus a strong potential for additional transactions. Reduced administrative costs through automation of manual processes: fewer cashiers needed, better visitor throughput in high-demand areas. Reduction of fraud resulting from cash handling and fee evasion. Better price differentiation, e.g. flexible fee structure depending on the visitors characteristics and time of the visit. Better visitors statistics for events' planning purposes.
Intermediaries: financial service providers		
Develop interoperable application software; access to technical assistance and expertise; issuing contactless cards and promoting them to end-users	Implementation costs: issuing contactless cards; promoting services to end-users and public transport authorities	Ticketing offers a well-established market segment and thus a strong potential for additional transactions. Pushing forward the general acceptance of e-payment; replacing small-cash transactions and thus reducing cash handling costs
Intermediaries: telecommunications operators		
Provide access to customers' mobile devices; development of NFC applications for these devices	Implementation costs: building NFC chip into mobile devices, possibly promotion campaigns to motivate customers to use NFC. Costs for development and management of NFC applications for ticketing	Ticketing offers a well-established market segment and thus a strong potential for additional GSM/UMTS transactions. Additional services generated by NFC technology might attract and retain customers

It should be noted that each of the stakeholders who engage in the implementation of an integrated e-ticketing system has to play a different role. Likewise, in the case of anticipated costs of the enterprise and its anticipated benefits. Effective implementation of an integrated e-ticketing system requires the involvement of all parties and collaboration of the institutions responsible for the supply side of the project. Also, potentially high initial cost of the project (hardware, software, adapting the existing system) should be mentioned, with reimbursement spread over time – hence the leadership role of governments and other administrative authorities. Nevertheless, there have been cases of grassroots initiatives, when e-ticket systems were implemented by the transport operators, without significant support from the national administration (Vasconellos, Freire da Costa 2008). As regards potential and existing users of e-ticketing systems, it seems that the potential benefits are huge (convenience, speed, cost savings) (Lubieniecka-Kocoń, Kos, Kosobucki, Urbanek 2013). However, attention should be paid to the need for educating disadvantaged groups (due to social or digital problems – the elderly or minorities), and changing of the behaviour of the passengers. The information about the journeys of the users is obtained by other parties (which, on the one hand, allows transport operators to plan more efficiently, but on the other hand, interferes with passengers' privacy – the information can be used for profiling) (Qteishat, Alshibly, Al-ma'aitah 2014). The Silesian Public Services Card project is a good example illustrating the potential benefits associated with the implementation of modern e-ticketing systems as well as the problems associated with a high degree of complexity of it and a large number of entities involved.

6. Silesian Public Services Card project

KZK GOP - Komunikacyjny Związek Regionalny (Regional Communication Association) of GOP (The Upper Silesian Industrial Region – a conurbation in Upper Silesia and western Lesser Poland), Międzygminny Związek Komunikacji Pasażerskiej (Inter-Municipal Association of Passenger Transport) in Tarnowskie Góry, the city of Tychy and Silesian Railways up till now have organized in the central part of Silesia urban and regional public transport on the basis of paper tickets. Exceptions are solutions in purchasing tickets by mobile phones, but this form of payment for transport services has been rather marginal[1]. Daily movement by public transport takes place both within cities and between them owing to the functional and spatial structure of the central part of Silesia. This makes it necessary to organize public transport commonly (inter-municipal associations have been established, a number of agreements have been signed and consequently keep appropriate accounts). In the past, many projects concerning the integration of transport were undertaken, including the integration of tariffs; some of them turned out to be long-lasting and they have been functioning up till now, but some of them did not survive the test of time. Inaccuracy and irregularity of accounts settlements and difficulties in the distribution of income from tickets valid on the lines of different carriers turned out to be a barrier to integration, and resulted in termination of contracts and termination of sales of a common ticket for the lines of different carriers (Dydkowski 2009).

---

[1] Based on data on the sale of tickets by KZK GOP in Katowice.

The Silesian Public Services Card is a project of KZK GOP. The idea is to implement an integrated system of collecting and settling cashless payments for public services in the area of member municipalities of the union and towns of Tychy and Jaworzno, together with the information system, collecting data on the demand for particular services and relations between them (Kos 2013). The electronic Silesian Card will become a payment instrument, used in 121 public centres in 21 municipalities throughout the Silesian voivodship. Currently this project is the largest of its kind in Poland.

The introduction of the Silesian Card is to facilitate public services provided by local governments and improve the management of public administration in the region (www 4). In addition, through cashless payments, the project is to promote the so called "Information Society" (www 5).

The project has been expected to bring a lot of benefits (Dydkowski 2010):

1) to KZK GOP as there will be:
   - transportation cost savings due to efficient management of shipping offer,
   - reduction of costs associated with printing paper tickets and seals for season tickets,
   - reduction of expenses for research as system provides data for analysis,
   - an increase in income from ticket sales as a result of better price management;
2) outside the KZK GOP (i.e. external benefits), among others:
   - benefits associated with a reduction in cash payments and replacing them with cashless ones,
   - optimization of transport offer – benefits for the environment connected with maintaining the quality of the service – with less operational work,
   - obtaining data in electronic form which facilitates their processing and use for the current service management – it does not apply to public transport services.

Maximizing the card's functionality is the condition of popularizing it and consequently reducing unit costs. However, a certain limitation was the fact that the venture was partially financed by the European Regional Development Fund as a part of the Subregional Development Programme of the Central Regional Operational Programme of Silesia for the years 2007–2013. This meant on the one hand co-financing the project with funds from outside the municipality, and on the other hand, limiting the functionality of the card to payments only for public services, public taxes and fees.

As a result, the basic functions of the card are:

- identification of the inhabitants,
- payments for public transport,
- payments for parking,
- payments in municipal offices,
- payments for other communal facilities (sports and recreation facilities, libraries, museums),
- the possibility of introducing an application with an electronic signature.

An important element in the functioning of the systems involving many subjects is to ensure interoperability, to allow new users easy access to the system, or to expand the scope of services for existing ones. The Silesian Card system has been designed as an open system, meaning it can be expanded by new subjects participating in it, where charges are levied for public services. What is important here is to enable in the future payment by card for public transport services of other organizers, i.e. Jaworzno, Tychy and Tarnowskie Góry. It will also be important to integrate charges for urban public transport and regional railway transport. Interoperability is ensured by both provisions of the agreement itself, and an accepted institutional solution.

The project involves creating an appropriate infrastructure to collect and settle the fees in the cities of the Central Subregion of the Silesian Province. In particular, the following will occur:

- creation of data processing centres (primary and backup) equipped with the necessary hardware infrastructure (including telecommunications) and related software, allowing for operation of the system in the functionality presumed,
- creation of a Customer Portal – an electronic platform integrating services rendered to the public. The portal will also support the bank account associated with the card and will allow for, for example, topping-up cards through the Internet, blocking funds to pay for a specific service, previewing and printing the hard copies of transactions conducted,
- suitable equipment of public transport vehicles and depots,
- creation of a network of entities where a season ticket encoded on the card can be bought and which will be able to top up the electronic wallet,
- equipment of offices and municipal units with devices for accepting payments with these cards,
- the purchase of new machines which will be able to top up the cards, and of parking meters and the adaptation of the existing ones to payments with the cards for parking.

A lot of factors make the investment projects, particularly IT projects, risky. Risk hampers investment projects, each instance of a loss is negative, and often questions arise if these losses were really inevitable, if they could be smaller and who is responsible for them. This is particularly important during the implementation of IT projects. The innovative nature of the projects, their uniqueness, high complexity and variability of technologies mean that very often there are situations in which the planned costs of the projects are exceeded and implementation is prolonged or even unsuccessful.

Delays in the implementation of the Silesian Card project started as early as its first stage, which was commissioned on 8 October 2012 – five months after the scheduled date. The second stage commissioning was more than a year delayed and it took place on 13 November 2013, instead of 9 September 2012. Completion of the third phase of the implementation of the Silesian Card means that most of the devices of the electronic card system are already ready to operate. Currently there are 83 vending and topping-up machines. The passengers have been using these devices for a year, as the first 40 machines were introduced in 2014 and dozens were installed in March 2015. Until the whole system starts to operate, users can buy disposable paper tickets from the machines. Ultimately, the machines will handle the Silesian Card, and they will top up the cards, sell and code season tickets or sell non-personalized cards, but also disposable paper tickets. KZK GOP obtained the consent of the Marshal Office of Silesia, the Managing Authority, for the conclusion of an annex to the agreement on financing the entire project by the European Union, relating to the change of date of completion of the project. According to the existing agreement, the card was to be ready by 30 January 2015, but due to delays on the side of the contractor, which is Asseco Poland consortium and mBank (formerly BRE Bank), the deadline was not met. KZK GOP has to complete the project by 30 September 2015 (www 6).

7. Summary

Urban and regional public transport can be classified as essential public tasks. This is due to the popularity of the services offered, as well as the impact of the transport system on the living conditions and the attractiveness of urban areas. External costs of transport systems and engagement of significant public funds both for transport investments and for ongoing operations are also significant. IT tools can help to manage the services better, improve their quality and implement solutions to help passengers use them. Integration of transport, better passenger information, as well as facilities connected with the use of cards, the electronic tickets, are worth mentioning.

The Silesian Public Services Card, a project being implemented in the Silesian province currently, is an example of an innovative project in the public sector. The Silesian Card is to combine the functions of a ticket for public transportation, e-wallet, ID and a carrier of an electronic signature. The electronic system on which it is based will collect data on demand for public services and will match an offer to the needs of the people. The Silesian Card stands out among similar projects with its territorial and functional range. The complicated system of elements in a project of this scale, stages of implementation and difficulties that may occur in this process can be seen in this example. The Silesian Card, once successfully introduced, may become for the residents of and visitors to the Silesian Agglomeration a useful multifunctional tool to improve the quality and availability of public services. In the broader sense, the Silesian Card project has a positive impact on the competitiveness and image of the Upper Silesia region and the quality of life of its inhabitants.

References

Biniasz, D. (2012), Obsługa klienta i jej wpływ na efektywność funkcjonowania organizacji, „Zarządzanie i Finanse", R. 10, nr. 1, cz. 1: 471–480.

Boschetti, F., Maurizi, I., Cré, I. (2014), *Innovative Urban Transport Solutions*. CIVITAS makes the difference. How 25 cities learned to make urban transport cleaner and better, CIVITAS Initiative, http://civitas.eu/sites/default/files/civitas-plus-innovative-urban-transport-solutions-www-final.pdf.

Chheda, G., Gajra, N., Chhaya, M., Deshpande, J., Gharge, S. (2012), Real Time Bus Monitoring and Passenger Information System, "International Journal of Soft Computing and Engineering", Vol. 1, Iss. 6: 34–38.

Czubała, A., Jonas, A., Smoleń, T., Wiktor, J. (2006), *Marketing usług*, Kraków, Oficyna Ekonomiczna.

Daszkowska, M. (1998), *Usługi. Produkcja, rynek, marketing*, Warszawa, WN PWN.

Dydkowski, G. (2009), *Integracja transportu miejskiego*, Katowice, Uniwersytet Ekonomiczny w Katowicach.

Dydkowski, G. (2010), Koszty i korzyści wynikające z wprowadzania elektronicznych systemów pobierania opłat za usługi miejskie, „Zeszyty Naukowe" nr 602, Problemy Transportu i Logistyki nr 12: 29–42.

European Parliamentary Research Service (2014), Integrated urban e-ticketing for public transport and touristic sites, Science and Technology Options Assessment, http://www.europarl.europa.eu/RegData/etudes/etudes/join/2014/513551/IPOL-JOIN_ET(2014)513551_EN.pdf.

Gordon, I. (2001), *Relacje z klientem – Marketing partnerski*, Polskie Wydawnictwo Ekonomiczne, Warszawa.

Gražvydas, Jakubauskas (2006), Improvement of urban passenger transport ticketing systems by deploying intelligent transport systems, "Transport", Vol. 21:4, 252–259.

Kos, B. (2013), Rozwój e-administracji w lokalnym i regionalnym transporcie zbiorowym na przykładzie Śląskiej Karty Usług Publicznych, „Zeszyty Naukowe Uniwersytetu Szczecińskiego" nr 763, „Ekonomiczne Problemy Usług" nr 105: 117–130.

Kos-Łabędowicz, J. (2014), Integrated E-ticketing System – Possibilities of Introduction in EU, "Communication in Computer and Information Science", vol. 471, Heidelberg, Springer: 376–385.

Krajewski, K. (2012), *Gmina jako podmiot świadczący usługi publiczne*, /2012/12/gmina-jako-podmiot-swiadczacy-uslugi-publiczne/.

Krukowski, P. (2008), Warszawska Karta Miejska na tle innych systemów karty miejskiej i biletu elektronicznego w Polsce. Prezentacja, Warszawa, Biuro Drogownictwa i Komunikacji Urzędu m. st. Warszawy.

Lübeck, R., Wittmann, M., Battistella, L. (2012), Electronic Ticketing System as a Process of Innovation, "Journal of Technology Management & Innovation", Vol. 7, Iss. 1: 18–30.

Lubieniecka-Kocoń, K., Kos, B., Kosobucki, Ł., Urbanek, A. (2013), Modern Tools of Passenger Public Transport Integration, "Communication in Computer and Information Science", Vol. 395, Heidelberg, Springer: 81–88.

Mezghani, M. (2008), *Study on electronic ticketing in public transport*, Final Report, European Metropolitan Transport Authorities (EMTA), http://www.emta.com/IMG/pdf/EMTA-Ticketing.pdf.

Michałowska, M. (ed.) (2012), *Efektywność transportu w warunkach gospodarki globalnej*, Katowice, Uniwersytet Ekonomiczny w Katowicach.

Palicka, Z. (1978), *Przewozy pasażerskie*, Warszawa, Wydawnictwo Komunikacji i Łączności.

Park, D., Kim, H. (2015), SBIS$_{URBAN}$ - Secure Urban Bus Information System based on Smart Devices, "International Journal of Security and Its Applications", Vol. 9, No. 1: 205–220.

Qteishat, M., Alshibly, H., Al-ma'aitah, M. (2014), The impact of e-ticketing techniques on customer satisfaction: an empirical analysis, "Journal of Information Systems and Technology Management", Vol. 11, No. 3: 519–532.

Rojowski, R., Gancarz, T. (2009), *System dynamicznej informacji pasażerskiej. Autobusy: technika, eksploatacja, systemy transportowe*, R. 10, Nr 4: 24–31.

Tripathi, A., Reddy, T., Madria, S., Mohanty, H., Ghosh, R.K. (2009), Algorithms for validating e-tickets in mobile computing environment, "Information Sciences", Vol. 179: 1678–1693.

Urban ITS Expert Group (2012), Smart Ticketing, Guidelines for ITS deployment in urban areas, http://ec.europa.eu/transport/themes/its/road/action_plan/doc/2013-urban-its-expert_group-guidelines-on-smart-ticketing.pdf.

Ustawa z 16 grudnia 2010 roku o publicznym transporcie zbiorowym (tekst jedn.: Dz. U. z 2015 r., poz. 1440 ze zm.).

Ustawa z dnia 12 września 2002 roku o elektronicznych instrumentach płatniczych (tekst jedn.: Dz. U. z 2012 r., poz. 1232).

Vasconellos, S. C., Freire da Costa, F. (2008), Electronic Ticketing System: Implementation Process, "Research in Transportation Economics", No. 22, Sydney.

Wojciechowski, E. (2012), *Gospodarka samorządu terytorialnego*, Warszawa, Difin.

WYG International Sp. z o.o. (2011), *Pre-investment study of the passanger information system for the Airport Poznań-Ławica Sp. z o.o., Warszaw*a, http://www.champions-project.de/public_docs/4.2.6%20Pre-Investment%20study%20Poznan.pdf.

Wyszomirski, O. (1998), *Funkcjonowanie Rynku Komunikacji Miejskiej*, Gdańsk, Wydawnictwo Uniwersytetu Gdańskiego.

Wyszomirski, O. (2008), *Transport miejski, ekonomika i organizacja*, Gdańsk, Wydawnictwo Uniwersytetu Gdańskiego.

Ziębicki, B. (2007), Uwarunkowania oceny efektywności świadczenia usług użyteczności publicznej, "Zeszyty Naukowe Wyższej Szkoły Ekonomicznej" w Bochni nr 6: 149–166.

(www 1) http://www.ztm.lublin.eu/pl/dla-pasazera/biuro-obslugi-klienta-ztm-w-lublinie.

(www 2) http://www.zkmgdynia.pl/?mod=3.%20O%20ZKM%20-%20Biuro%20Obs%C5%82ugi%20Klienta&lang=pl.

(www 3) http://www.mzkzg.org/?subpage=pod&art=8&op=%2C%2C%2C.

(www 4) http://www.kartaskup.pl/strony/p-1-dwadziescia-jeden-miast-we-wspolnym-systemie.html?accept_cookie=1 (14.12.2015).

(www 5) http://rpo-promocja.slaskie.pl/strona.php?art1=1329397571.

(www 6) http://www.kartaskup.pl/news/p-1-karta-skup-coraz-blizej.html.

Jerzy T. Skrzypek

The Economic Organization Platform with Cloud Computing Architecture as a Tool of Corporate Governance

1. Introduction

The study presents the concept and implementation status of the project "The Economic Organization Platform with cloud computing architecture as a tool of corporate governance". The project combines instruments to assess the current health of the organization with tools supporting preparation of a business plan and competence level of employees management. All features are carried out in a dedicated cloud computing.

Key elements included in the Platform are shown in Figure 1.

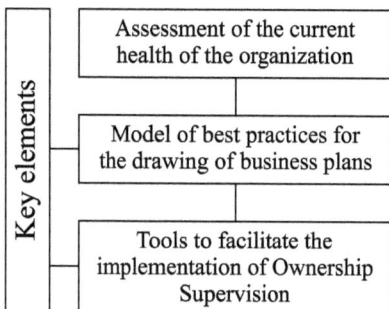

Figure 1. Key elements included in the Economic Organization Platform
Source: own elaboration.

The main tool supporting the decision-making process is a simulation model (SMOG), which allows to analyze the company's financial situation and preparation of the financial action plan to the best practices model described in Skrzypek 2012.

At the same time simulation model serves as a structural element for a set of training courses (including dynamic case studies), which aim to increase the level of competence of employees in the organization.

The implementation of these tools will bring – from the supervision ownership point of view – many advantages, among which are:

- standardization of evaluating the analyses results and action plans submitted by subsidiaries,
- the ability to monitor the achievement of strategic objectives,
- allowing comparisons of the subsidiaries results,
- the introduction of a set of warning signals regarding the worsening of the financial situation,
- the introduction of a uniform system of skills development for subsidiaries employees and supervisory board members,
- the availability of all the tools in the cloud.

As a theoretical illustration served the example of an existing company that was considering the establishment of a subsidiary. The subsidiary's task would be production of spare parts for machines produced by the parent company.

2. The idea of corporate governance

The term "corporate governance" will be used "in relation to the principles, rules and various aspects of the management of the funds that are used to control the owners of subordinate economic organizations" (Wawrzyniak 2000). Instead of this the author proposes the following functions that a corporate governance department should fulfil:

- strategic planning, including the strategic decisions level, which is used to determine targets and take strategic decisions. The level of strategic decision process management (implementation and optimization of the decision), where previously defined strategies are converted into long-term business plans, and financing plans for given entities are being created, should be transferred to subsidiaries. By contrast, coordination and control of the implementation of developed business plans falls to governance department;
- implementation of assessment standards for subsidiaries' activities (and their improvement), to assess and compare the performance of individual companies;
- developing and improving the system of monitoring the activities of subsidiaries in order to assess their current financial situation and enable the preparation of financial forecasts;
- assessing the degree of achievement of subsidiaries' strategic business objectives, together with the possibility of correcting them;
- surveillance and assessment of compliance of the subsidiaries' economic plans (including financials) with the strategy and plans set by the owner;
- cooperation through personal relationships (member of the board of the parent company should be a member of the supervisory board of the subsidiary) and substantive relationships (monitoring) of the supervisory boards of subsidiaries;
- control of the use of assets in subsidiaries to the extent recognized by the owner to be necessary.

As a result the author of this study recommends the adoption of the four steps action model:

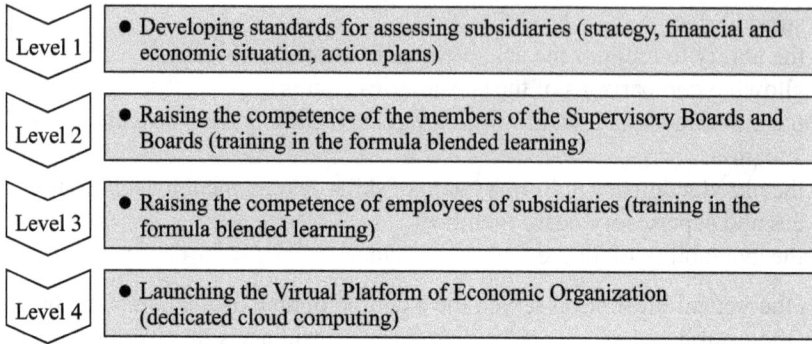

Level 1	● Developing standards for assessing subsidiaries (strategy, financial and economic situation, action plans)
Level 2	● Raising the competence of the members of the Supervisory Boards and Boards (training in the formula blended learning)
Level 3	● Raising the competence of employees of subsidiaries (training in the formula blended learning)
Level 4	● Launching the Virtual Platform of Economic Organization (dedicated cloud computing)

Figure 2. Four steps action model

3. Elements of economic organization platform with cloud computing architecture

The chart below presents the concept of the organization platform the main objective of which is effective implementation of corporate governance.

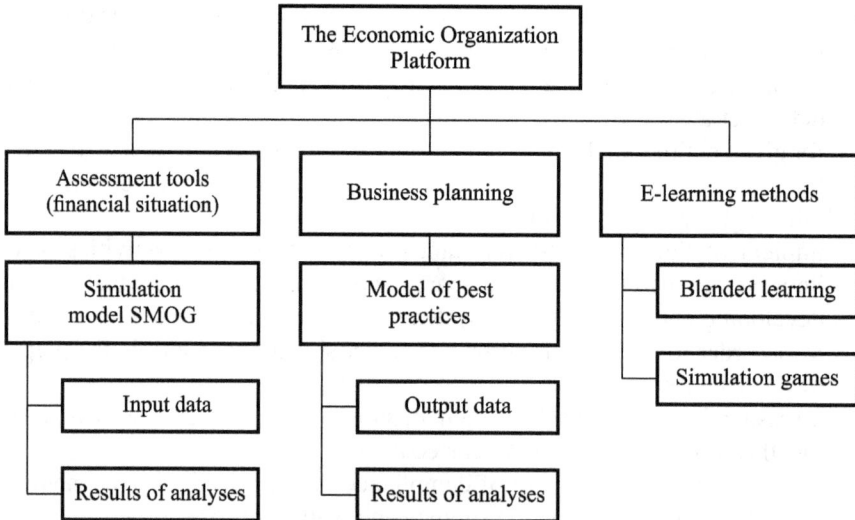

Figure 3. The Concept of the Economic Organization Platform

Tools for ongoing assessment of the financial situation are based on author's own set of analyses, and are shown in the following figure (application demo version can be found at http://jerzyskrzypek.pl in the section "Applications").

1	● Liquidity ratios
2	● Profitability ratios
3	● Debt ratios
4	● Operational efficiency
5	● Analysis of assets and sources of funding
6	● Evaluation of the effectiveness of projects
7	● Value of the firm

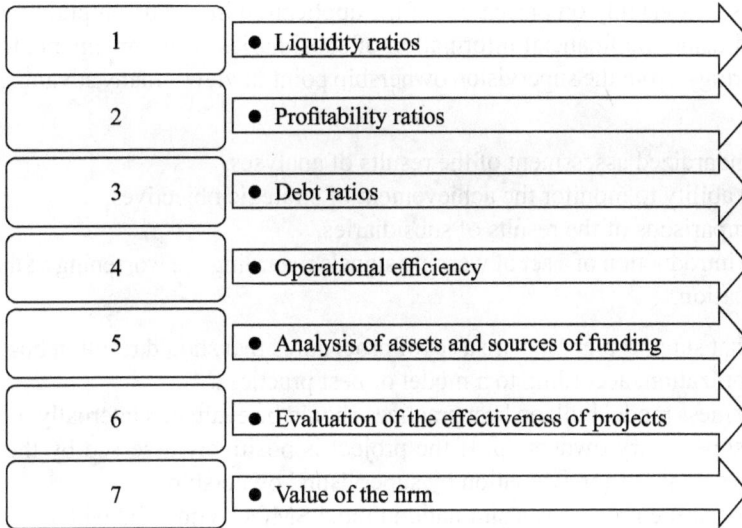

Figure 4. A set of analyses

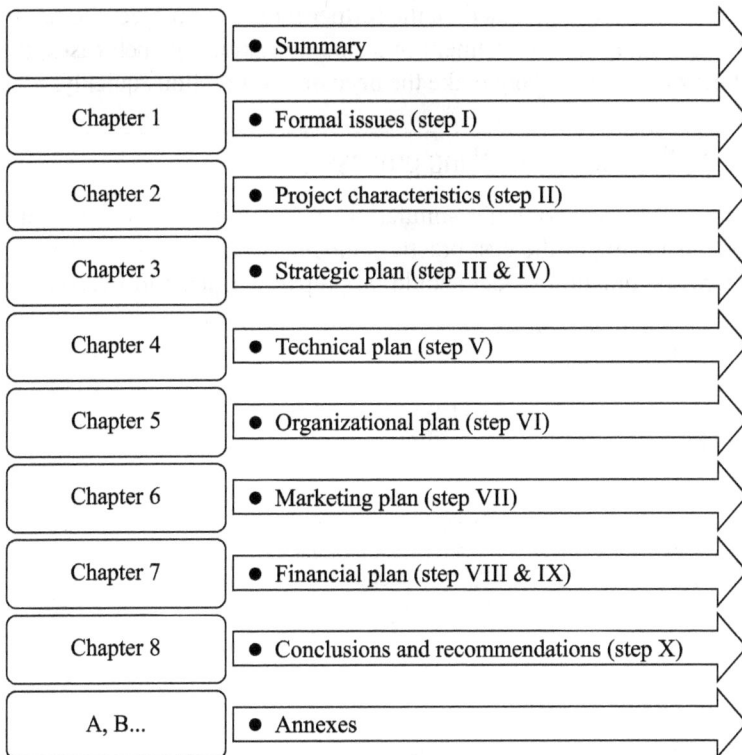

	● Summary
Chapter 1	● Formal issues (step I)
Chapter 2	● Project characteristics (step II)
Chapter 3	● Strategic plan (step III & IV)
Chapter 4	● Technical plan (step V)
Chapter 5	● Organizational plan (step VI)
Chapter 6	● Marketing plan (step VII)
Chapter 7	● Financial plan (step VIII & IX)
Chapter 8	● Conclusions and recommendations (step X)
A, B...	● Annexes

Figure 5. The structure of the business plan (Skrzypek 2012)

Target solutions rely on placement of the application in cloud computing, which will be powered using the financial information of subsidiaries. The implementation of these tools will bring – from the supervision ownership point of view – many advantages, among which are:

- standardized assessment of the results of analyses,
- the ability to monitor the achievement of strategic objectives,
- comparisons of the results of subsidiaries,
- the introduction of a set of warning signals regarding the worsening of the financial situation.

Tools that support planning are a set of procedures that should result in business plans rules harmonization, according to a model of best practices.

The business model built on best practices should be evaluated internally prior to passing to the supervisory ownership. If the project is positively assessed by the company, it should be submitted for evaluation by supervisors' ownership.

The core of the process is a simulation model SMOG, equipped with an identical set of analyses as the model assessment of the current financial situation.

Implementation of the established plan can be constantly monitored in order to be able to assess the compatibility of the results achieved against the objectives. On that basis recommendations should be formulated on the further fate of the project. Perhaps the project will require the assumptions adjustment or scope limitation. In such cases, the proposed sequence of actions can only help make the necessary corrections quickly.

4. Supporting the decision-making process

Development of an organization's simulation model requires not only project-based approach, but also using of the best practices model. As a result, it can be stated that the above-mentioned simulation model should be prepared at least in five stages (Skrzypek

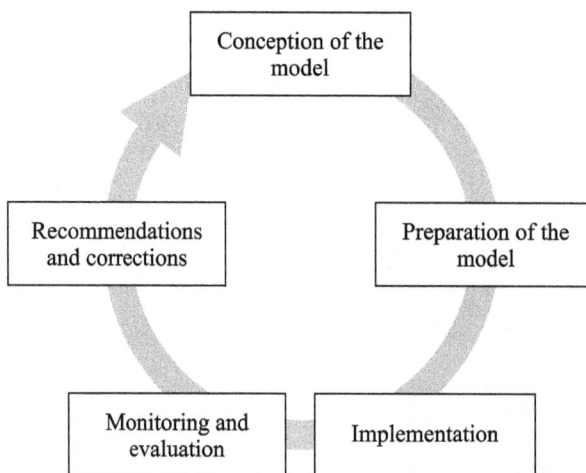

Figure 6. Steps of simulation model construction

2012): conceptualization, model development, implementation, monitoring of exploitation, using and development of possible corrections.

To prepare a concept model, assumptions should be generated. They must include an organization's model which can be implemented and then used to optimize the functioning of the organization. Then a set of assumptions must be transformed into an operational simulation model, which after the implementation, will be used to optimize functioning of the organization.

In the operation/exploitation stage, the model should be continually adapted to changes in the environment and to possible changes in strategy. Constant monitoring of the results generated by the simulation model enables the organization not only to introduce adjustments to its functioning, but also to introduce continuous improvements of the model itself.

A key element is the development of the simulation model itself (Figure 7). Simulation model's concept is created by using external and internal knowledge. Access to this knowledge can be substantially facilitated by using e-sources, knowledge and skills of all organization's parties gathered in e-resources.

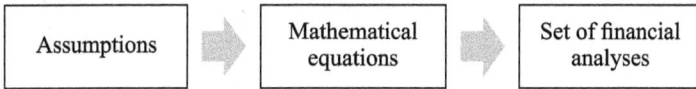

| Assumptions | ⇨ | Mathematical equations | ⇨ | Set of financial analyses |

Figure 7. Development of the simulation model SMOG. Detailed description of the model SMOG in Skrzypek 2014

At the same time, the concept of the organization can easily be disseminated through e-learning courses. Efficient and effective use of the results generated by the model depends mainly on the dissemination of results within the organization. The simulation model can still be a great base for a case study or simulation game. On the other hand, comments made by the organization's parties can play a significant role in improving the quality of the simulation model.

4.1. Application of the SMOG

Similar relations can be identified during the implementation and use of the model. It should be noted that usually the critical moment for effective implementation is disseminating knowledge about the model. For this role e-learning tools can be effectively used.

Among distance learning methods and techniques particular attention shall be paid to dynamic case studies and simulation games.

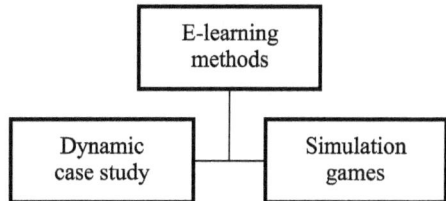

| E-learning methods |
| Dynamic case study | Simulation games |

Figure 8. Selected e-learning tools

Dynamic case study is usually an effective and efficient tool used in e-learning courses. Its value increases significantly when its construction is based on a model of a specific organization.

Decision-making simulation game is a realistic model of functioning organization which makes managerial decision gamers learn how the organization functions and what the methods of organization management are.

Author's experience gained during designing a scenario, and then during using the simulation games TEES-6 and TREND (based on the SMOG application), allows to conclude that the decision-making simulation game is an attractive tool that can be used during trainings by all interested parties of the organization. Simulation game builds and develops skills in:

- using financial analysis' outcomes to make decisions under conditions of risk,
- controlling a company's cash-flow (low or no cash-flow is the most common cause of companies' problems).

Simulation game's scenario is adapted to characteristic and specific conditions of the company.

4.2. The case study

The case study of an actual company that plans to set up a subsidiary is presented to illustrate the theoretical considerations. Subsidiary company's aim is to produce spare parts to machines manufactured by the company. To protect confidentiality of business information, the parent company was named as company "A", and the subsidiary company as company "B", and financial data were changed.

This part of the publication is a summary of the business plan "Model of start-up and operation of company B". The above-mentioned business plan was prepared at the order of company A, whose Management Board observed alarming trends in the market con-

Figure 9. The model of best practices for business plan

sisting in an attempt to take over its suppliers and customers by competitors. The business plan comprises 135 pages which present justification for the set-up of the company whose core business will be production of spare parts for machines manufactured by company A.

The study that serves as a business plan was drawn up on the basis of the model of best practices for business plan (Skrzypek 2012).

The plan's horizon covers five consecutive years. The first year is divided into quarters, the second one into half-yearly periods, and the other years are presented on an annual basis.

Therefore, the reference period can be divided into three stages:

- stage 1 – preparation of activities,
- stage 2 – launch of production process,
- stage 3 – expansion.

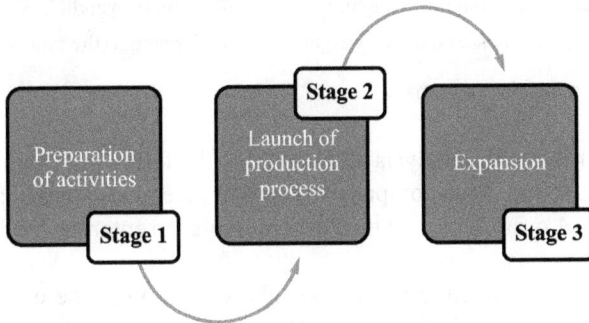

Figure 10. Stages of reference period

The whole process of preparation of the plan began with carrying out a strategic analysis, using TOWS method, which where:
- "Today" is a start-up period,
- "Tomorrow" is a period of one year after the start,
- "The day after" is a further period of 3–5 years.

The results of TOWS analysis show that as for "Today" there are unfavourable tendencies for the company, as the sum of weights of weaknesses is bigger than strengths, and the sum of weights of threats is bigger than the sum of opportunities. It means that in the first period the company must focus its efforts on minimizing the impact of weaknesses and make attempts to eliminate the impact of threats. In subsequent periods these unfavourable trends will be reversed.

Table 1. Summary of strategic analysis

Summary	Today	Tomorrow	Day after
Threats (sum of weights)	19.00	16.00	17.00
(sum of weights)	15.00	17.00	19.00
Weaknesses (sum of weights)	15.00	10.00	7.00
Strengths (the total weight)	12.00	20.00	23.00

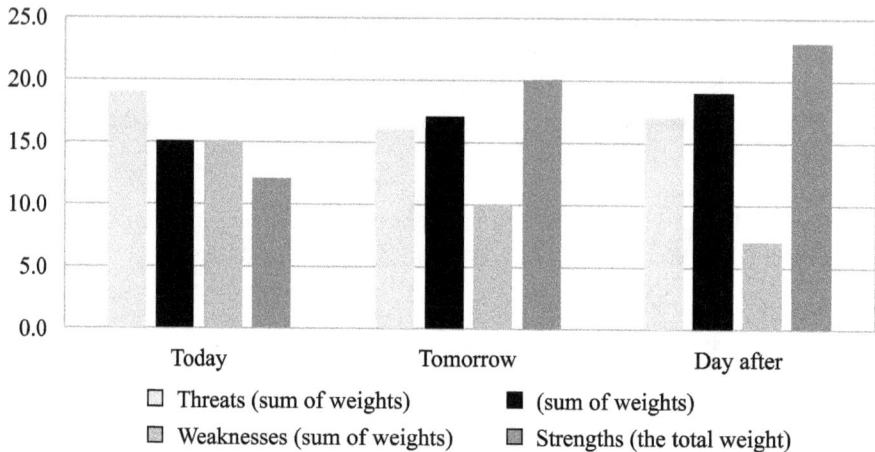

Figure 11. Strategic analysis – summary

The results of the TOWS analysis allow to draw the following conclusion: it is necessary to take actions to start up a company which will take over – in the initial period – the service of company A customers, and then take measures to enter the market of distribution of small batches of goods.

The basic strategic objective should be achieved through the entire set of detailed objectives presented in the client's financial perspective, internal and development perspective.

Basic objectives in the financial perspective are presented in the table below.

Table 2. Objectives in the financial perspective

No.	Specification of the objective	Measure	Time period
F1	Achieving and maintaining financial liquidity of the entity	Positive cash balance at the end of period; current liquidity ratios at the level of at least 1.5; positive level of net working capital	From the moment of initiation of activities
F2	Long-term increase of the value of the entity	Liquidation value measured with the use of Wilcox formula	From the moment of initiation of activities
F3	Achieving satisfactory level of net return on sales	Net return on sales at the level of at least 5%	Gradually from the moment of initiation of activities

Basic strategic objectives in the client's perspective were defined as adjustment of the offer and manner of its provision to the client's needs.

Table 3. Objectives in the client's perspective

No.	Specification of the objective	Measure	Time period
C1	Adjustment of the offer to changing expectations and needs of the client	Share in the market	Gradually from the moment of initiation of activities

Basic strategic objectives in the internal perspective are presented in Table 4.

Table 4. Objectives in the internal perspective

No.	Specification of the objective	Measure	Time period
I1	Implementation of the product quality standard system	Implementation of the system	In the first year of activities

The following table shows strategic objectives in the development perspective.

Table 5. Objectives in the development perspective

No.	Specification of the objective	Measure	Time period
D1	Permanent development of the scope of rendered services	Implementation of new types of services	Gradually from the moment of initiation of activities

Organizational chart has been adjusted to the structure of Company B. Moreover, this part of the study includes information regarding the scope of duties of employees, and proposed level of employment with nominal remuneration. It has been assumed that remuneration in the company will exceed national average pay in order to attract highly qualified employees.

Moreover, it has been assumed that the management board of the company will be composed of one member, assisted by the President's assistant. Activities of the company will be conducted in three divisions: administrative, logistic and marketing.

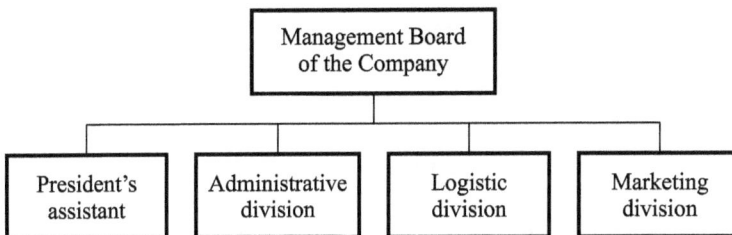

Figure 12. Proposed organizational chart of the company

The company will employ 15 production workers. The marketing plan included in this study covers a group of assumptions developed on the basis of experience of company A. Elements included in the marketing plan are presented in Figure 13.

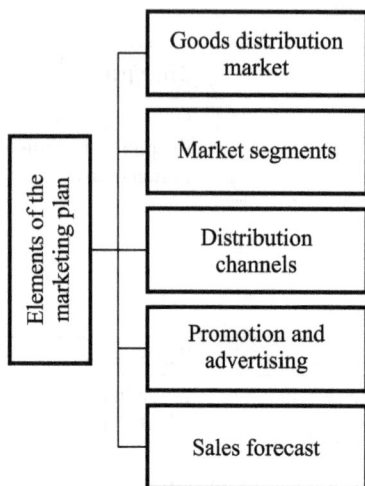

Figure 13. Elements of the marketing plan

As already mentioned, in the initial years company B will conduct its activities mainly for the needs of company A. Therefore expenditure on promotion and advertising will not be substantial, as its new customers will be won over mainly by company A.

Results of financial analyses – included in the financial plan – indicate that the project should be implemented, as:

- it generates substantial profits (except for the first year of operation),
- cash balance in all periods is positive,
- the project efficiency measures take positive values (NPV = 194.0 thousand EURO, and IRR = 20.46 %),
- value of the company is growing steadily, achieving at the end of the forecast period the following value according to:
  - net asset value method 815.8 thousand Euro,
  - adjusted net asset method (adjustment factor 0.9) 734.2 thousand EURO,
  - Wilcox method 734.9 thousand EURO,
  - DCF method 1,315.5 thousand EURO,
  - German method 1,065.7 thousand EURO,
  - Swiss method 1,049.0 thousand EURO,
- all analytical indicators show positive value.

Table 6. Liquidity analysis. Cash balance at the end of period

CASH FLOW [thousands of euros]	1Y/1q	1Y/2q	1Y/3q	1Y/4q	2Y/IH	2Y/2H	3 Y	4 Y	5 Y
I. Net profit (loss)	−102.7	−51.1	−285.8	5.4	44.6	40.7	142.9	258.5	284.8
II. Total corrections	0.0	35.6	43.0	−10.3	−34.5	3.7	6.0	−1.9	19.8
III. Net cash flow from operations (I+/-N)	−102.7	−15.5	−242.8	−4.9	10.0	44.4	148.9	256.6	304.6

Cash flow from invest-ments	1Y/1q	1Y/2q	1Y/3q	1Y/4q	2Y/IH	2Y/2H	3 Y	4 Y	5 Y
I. Income	0.0	0.0	0.0	0.0	0.0	0.0	0.0	0.0	0.0
II. Expenses	35.9	0.0	53.3	0.0	0.0	0.0	0.0	0.0	17.8
III. Net cash flow from operations (I+/-N)	−35.9	0.0	−53.3	0.0	0.0	0.0	0.0	0.0	−17.8

Cash flow from financial operations	1Y/1q	1Y/2q	1Y/3q	1Y/4q	2Y/IH	2Y/2H	3 Y	4 Y	5 Y
I. Income	478.6	0.0	0.0	0.0	0.0	0.0	0.0	0.0	0.0
II. Expenses	0.0	0.0	0.0	0.0	0.0	0.0	0.0	0.0	0.0
III. Net cash flow from financial operations (I–II)	478.6	0.0	0.0	0.0	0.0	0.0	0.0	0.0	0.0
Total net cash flow (A.III+/−B.III+/−C.III)	340.0	−15.5	−296.1	−4.9	10.0	44.4	148.9	256.6	286.8
Closing cash balance	340.0	324.5	28.4	23.5	33.5	77.9	226.8	483.4	770.2

It is worth emphasizing that cash balance at the end of each period is positive, so the project is of permanent nature. Positive values concern also the level of working capital, as demand for working capital takes negative values.

Table 7. Profitability analysis. Revenues, costs, profits

Revenues, costs, profitst (thousands of euros)	1Y/1q	1Y/2q	1Y/3q	1Y/4q	2Y/H	2Y/2H	3 Y	4 Y	5 Y
Sales revenues	0.0	0.0	280.8	581.8	639.7	1279.4	1467.5	1599.2	2163.6
Operating expenses	102.7	152	716.8	1010.7	591.5	1186.9	1317.4	1333.6	1871.6
EBITDA	−102.7	−152.0	−436.0	−428.9	48.2	92.5	150.1	265.6	292.0
Depreciation	0.0	1.8	3.6	5.4	3.6	7.2	7.2	7.2	7.2
EBIT	−102.7	−153.8	−439.6	−434.3	44.6	85.3	142.9	258.4	284.8
Interest tax	0.0	0.0	0.0	0.0	0.0	0.0	0.0	0.0	0.0
Gross profit	−102.7	−153.8	−439.6	−434.3	44.6	85.3	142.9	258.4	284.8
Income tax	0.0	0.0	0.0	0.0	0.0	0.0	0.0	0.0	0.0
Net profit	−102.7	−153.8	−439.6	−434.3	44.6	85.3	142.9	258.4	284.8

The results show that the project is characterized by a certain safety margin, from the perspective of generating positive level of profit from sales:

- revenues may drop from 6.67% in the second year to 16.97% in the last of the analyzed periods,
- costs may grow from 7.49% in the second year to 15.16% in the last of the analyzed periods.

The situation seems to be even more favourable if we eliminate depreciation which is only a cost, and it is not expense. However, it should be taken into account that in the case of company B the level of depreciation is low due to expansive use of operating leasing. The results of sensitivity analysis show that even unfavourable changes of the main variables (in assumed deviations) do not necessitate rejection of the project. Moreover, analysis was carried out regarding sensitivity of efficiency ratios to changes of the key element of the project: discount rate.

Table 8. Project efficiency assessment

Efficiency ratios	
NPV [thousands of euros]	194.0
IRR [%]	20.46%

Table 9. Project efficiency assessment – sensitivity analysis

Sensivity analysis results - discount rate	5,50%	7,50%	9,50%	13,50%	15,50%	17,50%
NPV	768.36	614.85	481.18	263.07	174.40	97.00
IRR	20.46%	20.46%	20.46%	20.46%	20.46%	20.46%
B/C	1.03	0.95	0.88	0.75	0.70	0.65

Results of the sensitivity analysis show that even increase of discount rate to the level of 17.5% will not necessitate relinquishment of the project implementation.

It should be stated that the value of company B is systematically growing and at the end of the forecast period it amounts to:

- net asset value method 815.8 thousand EURO,
- adjusted net asset method (adjustment factor 0.9) 734.2 thousand EURO,
- Wilcox method 734.9 thousand EURO,
- DCF method 1,315.5 thousand EURO,
- German method 1,065.7 thousand EURO,
- Swiss method 1,049.0 thousand EURO.

Establishment of company B is fully justified and may bring numerous benefits. The following facts support this view:

- maintaining liquidity at a safe level,
- generating net profit in all – except for the first year – periods at the level ensuring profitability of net sales appropriate for distribution business,
- relatively high safety margin resulting from possible increase of costs and decrease of revenues,
- achieving positive values of analytical indicators,
- positive values of project efficiency assessment,
- continuous growth of the value of the company.

However, the most important risk factor should be considered to be possible drop in revenues below the planned level. It is worth noting that company B will serve customers of company A on exclusivity basis, which greatly reduces the risk level.

Based on the business plans recommendations the Board of Directors of company A decided to start company B. They also decided to implement the Economic Organization Platform project in order to monitor the company's current financial situation. The Platform was also used to train company B employees. A dynamic case study was developed for this purpose, based on the SMOG model.

5. Conclusion

The results of the present study suggest that implementing "The Economic Organization Platform" project will allow businesses to effectively implement the idea of corporate governance. It is important to indicate that this Platform can be used in other business areas to:

- assess the condition of the company,
- write a business plan,
- train employees based on own case studies, compiled from companies' own data.

The proposed solutions can be addressed to the educational sector because the Platform's idea can be used to construct dynamic case studies or business games which will make the gained knowledge more memorable.

References

Hupic, V., Vebraeck, A., de Vreede, G. (2002), *Simulation and Knowledge Management: Separated but Inseparable*, SCS Europe BVBA.

Johnson, H. (2000), *Ocena projektów inwestycyjnych. Maksymalizacja wartości przedsiębiorstwa*, LIBER, Warszawa.

Skrzypek, J. (2007), *Model najlepszych praktyk oceny ekonomicznej efektywności projektów e-learningowych*, unpublished.

Skrzypek, J. (2007), *Zasady konstrukcji studium wykonalności lub biznesplanu dla projektów współfinansowanych ze środków UE*, Twigger, Warszawa.

Skrzypek, J. (2008), *e-Strategia Uniwersytetu Ekonomicznego w Krakowie na lata 2008–2012*, internal document UEK, Kraków.

Skrzypek, J. (2010), *Program odnowienia e-strategii Uniwersytetu Ekonomicznego w Krakowie*, conference on development of e-education in economic universities, Warszawa, 17 November.

Skrzypek, J. (2012), *Biznesplan – model najlepszych praktyk*, POLTEXT, Warszawa.

Skrzypek, J. (2011), *Finansowa i ekonomiczna efektywność projektów e-learningowych a wartość organizacji*, conference on development of e-education in economic universities, Kraków, 7 November.

Skrzypek, J. (2014), *Biznesplan w 10 krokach*, POLTEXT, Warszawa.

Wawrzyniak, B. (2007), *Odnawianie przedsiębiorstwa na spotkanie XXI wieku*, POLTEXT, Warszawa.

Wycena przedsiębiorstwa (2012), joint publication, POLTEXT.

Zack, M. (2003), *What is a knowledge-based organization?*, Organizational Learning and Knowledge, 5th International Conference, 30 May – 2 June.

Chapter VI

The Ageing of the Population: Technology Solutions to Demographic Challenges in Poland

Maria Zrałek

The Elderly in the World of Modern Information and Communication Technologies

1. Introduction

Poland is a country of a dynamically changing population. Much attention has recently been paid to the problem of ageing in Poland because of the growing importance of demographic changes which call for concerted action in society. Though Poland is still a demographically young country, it belongs to the group of rapidly ageing societies in Europe. The latest demographic forecast for the year 2050 made by GUS (Central Statistical Office) predicts that the process of ageing of Polish society will not only continue but will also intensify. The number of senior citizens in the country will reach 5.4 million. All variants of the forecast's scenarios (low, medium, high and very high) predict that by the year 2050 the percentage of the population at the age of 65 and over will increase about twice, i.e. from 15.8% in 2013 to 35.7% in the high scenario, and to 31.3% in the low scenario. In practice, it means that about one third of the population of Poland will be a community of senior citizens. As has been indicated in the forecast, the proportion of "younger" senior citizens (65–79 years of age) will increase by 2050, while the number of those at the age of 80 and over will decrease. However after 2050 the percentage of people at the age of 80 and over will increase sharply. In 2040 the proportion of those over 80 within the community of 65-year-olds and older will amount to 36%. In 2050 the proportions will be slightly different, and the percentage of those who are 80 and older within the community of senior citizens (65 and older) will decrease to 32%. In terms of absolute numbers it means that by the year 2050 the number of people at the age of 80 and over will exceed 3.5 million.

Such a significant increase of the proportion of elderly and oldest people in the population exerts a great influence on the type and scope of action undertaken in the sphere of social policy. The community of senior citizens is heterogeneous, differentiated by age, health condition, level of affluence, family situation, acquired education, earlier and pres-ent living conditions, knowledge and experience, and also physical and mental abilities. All these factors must be taken into consideration by those responsible for social policy in order to secure good quality of life for senior citizens. The category "quality of life" forms the basis of all action undertaken for the benefit of senior citizens today.

2. The quality of life – selected conceptual issues and definition

Anyone who takes up the issue of the quality of life faces up fundamental problems when trying to define the term, which is riddled with ambiguities both in understanding and defining. The term is complex, interdisciplinary, and unclarified, and its definition depends on the perspective from which the subject takes up the problem. Such an approach, as Doro-ta Kałuża and Piotr Szukalski point out, allows us to grasp the wide spectrum of spheres of life which conditions its evaluation and makes it possible for us to take an individual-ized approach to the question of the quality of life, but on the other hand it constitutes an obstacle to the formulation of an unambiguous definition of the term.

Walenty Ostasiewicz states that three aspects determine the quality of life:

- economic
- social
- psychological

The economic aspect means material well-being understood as satisfying the needs for food, clothing, shelter, education, culture, rest, leisure, health, and tourist travel. Things taken into consideration within the social aspect include social infrastructure and social services (health and medical care, insurance, etc.), while in the case of the psychological aspect, taken into consideration are the issues concerning the subjective perception of the quality of life. Literature on the subject contains many approaches to the question of qual-ity of life. It is important that we consider both objective (assigned) and subjective (based on self-evaluation) dimensions. Tadeusz Borys asserts that "the objective quality of life has a meaning close to the notion of conditions of living (or standard of living) which denote 'all the objective conditions of infrastructural character in which people live (social groups, households, and individuals)', while the subjective quality of life means the degree to which needs are satisfied [...] it is connected with the subjective perception of one's life within a particular ethical code and specific social, economic, and political condi-tions". An example of this approach is the definition by David Felce and Jonathan Perry, which "comprises objective descriptors and subjective evaluations of physical, material, social and emotional well-being, together with the extent of personal development and purposeful activity, all weighted by a set of values". In this approach the quality of life is analyzed on three planes: objective conditions of living, one's own satisfaction with life, and accepted values.

The situation of senior citizens depends more and more not only on previously acquired knowledge but also on the ability to learn and to adapt oneself to new challenges posed by civilization. One may argue that the only constant element of modern life are permanent changes, and that the essential requirement we all have to meet is the ability to adapt to changes. Individuals not able to keep up with change are doomed to exclusion and permanent "non-existence" in society. One of such major challenges which senior citizens have to meet is learning the skills required in using new information and communication technologies (ICT), especially the Internet. The introduction of new solutions based on information and communication technologies in the areas of security, mobility, communication, and independence of senior citizens may help elderly people significantly to maintain both their independence and a high quality of life. The rich variety of use to which this means of communication has been put makes it very popular, while "intelligent" mobile phones and other portable devices ensure an almost unrestricted access to the Internet.

Senior citizens are less likely to accept change, it is also more difficult for them to adapt to new demands. They also face the risk of a certain type of illiteracy in the form of lack of access to information technology solutions and the opportunities to use them. Those who cannot use computers are deprived of basic information and benefits accessible only in a digital form. On the one hand, revolution in information technology and the appearance of new tools of communication create unlimited opportunities of access to various kinds of information and services, but on the other hand they incur an ever greater risk of a "communication gap", which particularly affects senior citizens. Lack of skills in using modern technology isolates elderly people and makes them feel helpless and lost. In this way they become affected by the digital divide.

3. The application of new technologies in the social and health care contexts

The need to employ modern information and communication technology in order to assist senior citizens is one of the priorities of the European Union, which has recognized solutions of this type as a key factor enabling elderly people to maintain social contacts longer and to lead an active and independent life. In June 2007 Commission of the European Communities took a decision to initiate a plan whose aim is to increase the number of old age pensioners using the new media. In a communication Ageing Well in the Information Society – an i2010 Initiative – Action Plan on Information and Communication Technologies and Ageing, it was emphasized that "Information and Communication Technology may help senior citizens to improve their quality of life, maintain better health and live an independent life longer. Innovative solutions are proposed which help to overcome problems with deteriorating memory, sight, hearing and mobility, as they intensify with age. ICT also allows senior citizens to remain active in their jobs or in their communities".

In 2013 the Council for Social Monitoring conducted a research within the framework of Social Diagnosis which indicated that the percentage of senior citizens using personal computers over the last two years (compared with research results from 2011) increased only slightly by 3.3%. People belonging to the oldest section of society are considered then to be the smallest group in the space of information technology (see Table 1).

Access to the Internet at home gives not only the opportunity to deal with matters of everyday life quickly and effectively, but it is also a chance for development and active

Table 1. Use of new technologies by different groups in 2013

age	computer	Internet	mobile phone	smartphone	non-user	Using all new technologies
16–24	96.8	9.66	98.1	49.2	0.6	94.3
25–34	88.8	88.4	98.3	43.3	1.0	86.2
35–44	82.5	82.3	97.6	31.3	1.7	80.7
45–59	56.1	55.2	90.5	14.0	8.3	52.8
60–64	37.0	35.5	80.4	7.5	18.5	33.7
65 and over	14.7	14.1	55.1	3.6	44.0	12.8

Source: J. Czapiński, T. Panek, *Diagnoza społeczna 2013* (Social Diagnosis for 2013), Rada Monitoringu Społecznego, Warszawa 2013, p. 330.

participation in many spheres of life. More and more people join educational courses for senior citizens. The Internet becomes an instrument for the realization of the idea of life-long learning. Education assisted by technology contributes to helping people develop their interests in culture, medicine, entertainment, etc. In other words, it helps them remain creative and active in social life. Crucial is the ability to use Internet communicators, such as Skype and electronic mail. But using the Internet is a serious problem for senior citizens. Their access to modern technologies is limited by barriers of emotional/psychological nature (fear of new technology), by material limitations (shortage of computers and Internet connections), and by lack of skills (no competence in dealing with new media or ineptitude in using certain computer programs, or some of their functions).

Results of Social Diagnosis 2013 research indicate that senior citizens' activity on the Internet concentrates on the use of electronic mail (51%), electronic banking (35%), reading newspapers and books (28%), telephoning via the Internet (VoIP, Skype – 27%), and using communicators to stay in contact with friends (such as Gadu-Gadu, etc. – 25%). These forms of communication may be the only way for the elderly people to keep in touch with friends and family, especially in times of intensified migration of children and grandchildren. But only few senior citizens can engage in more advanced activities, such as making and publishing their own creative output (10%), buying on the Internet things and services offered abroad (10%), downloading free software (11%), and designing or modifying www sites (11%). Neither is the Internet used by elderly people to take part in coaching or training courses; it is not then used as an essential tool in lifelong learning. Similar research results are presented by CBOS (Centre for Public Opinion Research). They indicate that almost all types of activity linked to communication with other users, except for telephone conversations, are much more frequently declared by younger Internet users, especially those aged between 18 and 24. Some forms of activity, such as playing games on the Internet, are not undertaken at all by older users, i.e. those aged 55 and over (see Table 2).

Older people have also greater problems using mobile devices to connect wirelessly to the Internet. Among users connecting wirelessly to the Internet (via mobile devices such as laptops, mobile phones, net books, tablets, etc.) only 30% of people aged 65 and over can do it, and it is twice less than among the group of people aged between 55 and 64.

Table 2. Activities linked to communication with other users

Age	Internet users who during the last month:			
	talked to friends using communicators (Gadu-Gadu, Tlen)	talked on the phone (Skype, Tlenofon)	made forum posts	played games on the Net
	percentage			
18–24	89	45	68	42
25–34	64	28	38	23
35–44	41	28	18	13
45–54	36	27	15	11
55–64	35	43	14	5
65 and over	33	43	10	0

Source: *Komunikat z badań CBOS* (Communication about CBOS research), Internauci 2013 (Internet Users 2013, BS/75/2013, Warszawa 2013, p.13.

Table 3. Internet users connecting wirelessly to the Internet (via mobile devices such as laptops, mobile phones, net books, tablets, etc.) according to age

age	internet users
18–24	85
25–34	78
35–44	77
45–54	62
55–64	60
65 and over	30

Source: *Komunikat z badań CBOS* (Communication about CBOS research), *Internauci 2013* (Internet Users 2013, BS/75/2013, Warszawa 2013, p.7.

The younger the Internet users, the more frequently they choose to connect to the Internet wirelessly (see Table 3).

Nowadays using the Internet becomes indispensable because of the extending range of e-services (e-administration, e-banking, etc.) and also because of new amenities (e-health, e-library, etc.). At the time of rapid development of e-administration, people who have no access to the Internet, or have no necessary skills to use modern information and communication technologies, become cut off from more and more common channels of institutional and social communication. Michał Kaczmarczyk underlines that it concerns primarily elderly people, who are clients of various government offices, ZUS (the Social Insurance Institution), or who are patients at hospitals, clinics, and doctor's surgeries. Electronic amenities that have been introduced at these institutions are practically inaccessible to most potential older beneficiaries. This inaccessibility concerns the dimensions of information (access to website publications), interaction (the possibility of reaching institutions through electronic channels), and integration (access to portals which provide information from various institutions and databases, and which help people deal online with administrative matters at one place and in a simple and coordinated way).

Looking into the situation of senior citizens we must underline that one of the essential elements which influences the quality of life of elderly people is making it possible for them to remain in their places of living for as long as possible and assisting them in their activities. Such an approach is presented in 1991 UN Resolution No. 46 laying down Principles for Older Persons, which address, *inter alia*, issues of shelter and community support. Also the revised European Social Charter in its article no. 23 states that, among other rights, elderly people have the right to housing adapted to their needs. A noteworthy document is the 2002 Political Declaration and Madrid International Plan of Action on Ageing, which stressed the principle of "ageing in place" in the community with regard to personal preferences. Because of deteriorating health, growing number of lonely people and related difficulties with providing care, more and more attention is paid to setting new standards of living conditions and giving elderly people a sense of security.

The factor of primary importance to elderly people, one which is decisive in dignified ageing, is enjoying good health. Old age in itself is not treated as an illness, but the process of ageing increases the probability of disease, and consequently incurring the risk of no longer being fit. There is no doubt that age determines one's health condition, and that, with age, health condition worsens. It is only natural that, as life becomes longer, our physical fitness and mental agility deteriorate, though the dynamics of the process are different in each case as they depend on many factors.

It is very difficult to determine objectively the health condition of elderly people because of the natural processes which limit the body's functionality, and which are also affected by disability and multi-disease conditions. That is why when doing research on somebody's state of health we rely on the person's subjective assessment of his/her health condition. The self-assessment of one's health status is usually expressed in terms of grades ranging from very good to very bad. This kind of categorization was used by GUS in their research on the state of health of the country's population in 2009. The results show that age exerts decisive influence on how elderly people (aged 60 and over) assess their health status. Only a small percentage of them were satisfied with their health condition (judged as very good and good). The older the people, the less they are satisfied with how they feel. Subjective self-assessment of health status is given in Table 4.

Research carried out by GUS indicates that household chores are a problem because of one's health condition to every third sixty-year-old, to over 60% of septuagenarians, and almost 85% of the oldest people.

Deteriorating health condition of elderly people seriously threatens their autonomy. Such people have more and more difficulties with self-care, with participation in family, social, religious, and community life. They become more dependent on the help of others. The psychophysical condition of the elderly can be improved if they become active participants in various types of activity, which will help them to remain in good shape till very old age, and the use of modern information and communication technologies may be of great assistance to them.

Table 4. Assessment of health condition of the country's population (%)

age	assessment of health condition				
	very good	good	so-so, neither good nor bad	bad	very bad
			Percentage		
Total	23.6	42.1	23.4	8.8	2.0
15–19	48.9	42.0	7.9	1.0	0.1
20–29	41.1	49.3	7.9	1.4	0.1
30–39	26.3	57.6	13.6	2.3	0.3
40–49	11.9	52.5	28.5	6.1	0.9
50–59	5.7	39.2	39.6	12.9	2.4
60–69	3.1	25.2	47.5	19.5	4.8
70–79	1.2	13.8	45.6	31.1	8.2
80 and over	0.5	13.1	36.6	36.9	13.0

Source: *Stan zdrowia ludności Polski w 2009 r.* (State of Health of the Population of Poland in 2009), GUS, Warsaw 2011, p.108.

In the case of people who have to be closely monitored, and who need continual help and assistance, one must look for new solutions incorporating information and communication technologies that will help senior citizens to remain in their places of residence. Introduction of new ICT solutions used indoors creates great opportunities for elderly people to lead a self-reliant and independent life, and also to become active participants in various spheres of social life. The technologies are so important because they also help carers in their work with senior citizens. Actually, such technologies become indispensable as the care providing potential of society is diminishing for demographic reasons, which in practice means that there are fewer opportunities to provide care within the family. A family care providing potential can be measured with the use of three ratios: potential support ratio, which determines the ratio of people aged between 15 and 64 to the number of those aged 65 and over; parent support ratio, which is the number of persons aged 85 and

Table 5. Ratios: potential support, parent support, and potential care in the years 2010–2035

year	potential support ratio	parent support ratio	potential care ratio
2012	498.6	7.1	386.3
2015	443.7	8.5	354.4
2016	425.0	9.0	344.5
2020	359.2	10.4	323.4
2025	305.8	11.4	330.2
2030	287.5	10.3	271.2
2035	276.6	13.1	219.2

Source: Z. Szweda-Lewandowska, *Rynek usług opiekuńczych – perspektywy rozwoju w kontekście starzenia się populacji* (Care-providing Market – Perspectives for Development in the Context of Ageing of the Society), Optimum. Studia Ekonomiczne No. 2 (68) 2014, p. 151.

over to 100 persons aged between 50 and 64; potential care ratio, which relates the number of women aged between 45 and 64 to the number of persons aged 80 and over (see Table 5).

In 2008 the European Union committed itself to a project launched by 20 Member States and three Associated Countries, called Modern Technologies in the Service of Elderly People (Ambient Assisted Living, AAL). Originally the project was planned to last till 2013, but it was extended for the years 2014–2020 because of the great demand for research initiatives whose aim was to develop products and services using information-communication technologies designed for elderly people. Its objective was stated as follows: "Foster the emergence of innovative ICT-based products, services and systems for ageing well at home, in the community, and at work, thus increasing the quality of life, autonomy, participation in social life, skills and employability of elderly people, and reducing the costs of health and social care".

The programme's basic aim is to introduce new solutions based on information-communication technologies (ICT), which make it easier for elderly people to function well in society. It can be achieved through:

- extending the period of time during which senior citizens can live in their preferred environment by enhancing their self-reliance, self-confidence and mobility,
- helping elderly people maintain good health and independence,
- assisting carers, families, and care providing institutions in their care of elderly people.

The European Commission points out that the solutions adopted in the AAL programme include among other things: "smart living spaces that detect and compensate for problems that may come with age, such as memory loss, wandering, health conditions; smart products such as sensor-enabled floors and shoes with actuators to detect or prevent falls; digital information services such as security and health monitoring and telecare, or internet-connected televisions for leisure, entertainment, learning, ...".

As we can see, the adopted solutions may contribute in an important way to the improvement of living conditions at home, which will enable elderly people to remain in the environment they know very well. "Examples of such solutions may be projects: RelaxedCare, ChefMyself and VictoryaHome. RelaxedCare answers the question: 'Is my mum doing fine right now?'. It provides a new communication paradigm: being informed about the other's physical and mental state and being able to send basic messages in an easy way. The well-designed RelaxedCare cube is placed in the living environment of both the Assisted Person and the Informal Caregiver, allowing them to stay connected worry-free. RelaxedCare App is used by the Informal Caregiver when being mobile... The main goal of ChefMyself is to develop a customizable and extensible (ICT) service ecosystem built around an automatic cooking solution to support older people in preparing meals and maintaining healthy eating habits. The service provides advice on meal planning and grocery shopping, supports meal preparation through semi-automatic cooking, supports users on healthy eating, and provides a component of social interaction through activities such as recipe-sharing, developing a virtual social network... VictoryaHome is a home platform that enables caregivers to be a daily part of their loved ones' care, no matter where they live. It lets them define their own care process, gives them actionable information, and then lets them take immediate action by making a virtual visit. The open platform allows to rapidly integrate and configure any new device according to particular care needs".

In 2015 a new project was initiated – HOME 4 DEM. It is an innovative technological platform which uses new information and communication technologies and develops innovative support services in order to improve the quality of life of people with dementia (PwD) and their caregivers. The platform may enable people suffering from dementia to lead an independent life at home and take active part in social life. These are not of course the only programmes which involve the use of ICT to assist elderly people in various situations that are difficult for them. A good example here may be the initiative Silver Game, which is part of the AAL. It offers various multimedia applications which allow elderly people to use internet services and social media sites. Users may have fun playing such games as a virtual song club and a dance and fitness training. In this way they may better their physical condition and mental agility without leaving their homes. They may also use an integrated videoconferencing system if they wish to interact and communicate with one another. The project was designed in such a way that not only older people but also young may use it, which means that one's family and friends can join in, too. Apart from being helpful in assisting senior citizens, this solution exerts a beneficial influence on intergenerational relations as it gives the chance to meet new friends, to discover new hobbies, and it is intellectually stimulating. Solutions of this type may improve the quality of life of elderly people, may support their social integration, and help them contribute their experience and skills to the development of society, i.e. help them become socially active. Information and communication technologies represent a breakthrough in assisting senior citizens in a more and more mechanized environment, and they are of great help in various difficult situations.

The field in which the use of ICT becomes particularly important is designing the so-called smart homes, in which even people with serious cognitive and physical problems can remain self-reliant or will need only limited assistance. The concept of a "smart home" originated in the United States in the 1970s. The idea behind the design was to give comfort to the apartment's occupants (e.g. controlling lighting and heating), to ensure security (alarm and fire protection systems), and to save electrical and thermal energy.

An example of the concept of smart home is the project I2HOME, offering to include digital technology in the management of household appliances (e.g. washing machines, TV sets, and various connected subsystems) by elderly and disabled people. The appliances are remote-controlled by means of mobile devices (mobile phones, remote controls). They are easy to use and, which is important, are tailored to the needs of those with restrictions (e.g. voice-controlled for people with visual impairments). An even more enhanced version of smart home aimed at elderly people is Smart Home for Elderly People (HOPE) carried out as part of AAL, whose purpose is:

- "to extend the time people can live in their preferred environment by increasing their autonomy, self-confidence and mobility,

- to support maintaining health and functional capability of the elderly individuals,
- to promote a better and healthier lifestyle,
- to prevent social isolation and support social networks,
- to support carers, families and care organizations".

Still another innovative solution, one very important for senior citizens, is Mobil-Alarm, an electronic system that allows elderly people to call for help and receive assistance at any time and place. It is especially important for people living alone who remain permanently at home.

4. Summary

Introduction of technologies which assist senior citizens made it possible to improve their living conditions in such a way as to prevent their exclusion from everyday life, giving them a sense of security and improvement of their health and quality of life. Thanks to these technologies elderly people can remain in their homes and be active and independent. The Web is becoming an increasingly important means of access to knowledge, education, the job market and other kinds of information, but it is also helpful in establishing relationships with other people. Extremely important are innovative products and services based on information and communication technology which are addressed to elderly people and their carers. The ICT improves the quality of life, reduces the costs of medical care and welfare services. A crucial problem is the small number of elderly people among the users of modern information and communication technology, especially the Internet. There are various reasons behind this situation: financial and technological limitations, lack of motivation and reluctance to catch up with the quick pace of technological change, but also barriers of competence in the use of the Internet. Modern information and communication technology also gives invaluable support to caregivers in their work with elderly people. The focus of all these solutions is to let senior citizens remain and be active in their preferred environment for as long as possible.

References

AAL Joint Programme Brochure 2010, Overview of Funded and Running Projects.

Borys, T., Rogala, P. (eds.) (2008), *Jakość życia na poziomie lokalnym – ujęcie wskaźnikowe*, Warszawa.

Communication from the Commission to the European Parliament, the Council, the European Economic and Social Committee and the Committee of the Regions – Ageing well in the Information Society – an i2010 Initiative – Action Plan on Information and Communication Technologies and Ageing, COM 2007, 332.

Czapiński, J., Panek, T. (2013), *Diagnoza społeczna 2013*, Rada Monitoringu Społecznego, Warszawa, p. 330.

Decision No 554/2014/EU of the European Parliament and of the Council of 15 May 2014 on the participation of the Union in the Active and Assisted Living research and development programme jointly undertaken by several Member States, Official Journal of the European Union L169 (June 7).

Decision No 742/2008/EC of the European Parliament and of the Council of 9 July 2008 on the Community's participation in a research and development programme undertaken by several Member States aimed at enhancing the quality of life of older people through the use of new information and communication technologies, Official Journal of the European Union L201 (July30).

European Social Charter (revised), European Treaty Series nr 163.

General Assembly Resolution 46/91, 16 December 1991, United Nations.

General Assembly Resolution 57/167, 18 December 2002, United Nations.

Internauci 2013, Komunikat z badań CBOS, BS/75/2013, Warszawa 2013.

Kaczmarczyk, M. (2014), Wymiary cyberwykluczenia osób starszych, [in:] *Osoby starsze w przestrzeni życia społecznego*, Regionalny Ośrodek Polityki Społecznej, Katowice.

Kałuża, D., Szukalski, P. (2010), Jakość życia seniorów w XXI wieku z perspektywy polityki spo-łecznej – uwagi wprowadzające, [in:] *Jakość życia seniorów w XXI wieku z perspektywy polityki społecznej*, Łódź.

Komisja Europejska, *The 2012 Ageing Report*, European Economy 2012, nr 2.

McAllister, F. (2005), *Wellbeing Concepts and Challenges*. NHS Scotland, April.

Ostasiewicz, W., Przedmowa, [in:] W. Ostasiewicz [ed.] (2002), *Metodologia pomiaru jakości życia*, Wrocław.

Papińska-Kacperek, J. (ed.) (2008), *Społeczeństwo informacyjne*, WN PWN, Warszawa.

Prognoza ludności na lata 2014–2050, Central Office of Statistics, Warszawa 2014.

Report from the Commission to the European Parliament and the Council. First Interim Evaluation of the Ambient Assisted Living Joint Programme (AAL JP), COM(2010) 763 final.

Stan zdrowia ludności Polski w 2009 r., Central Office of Statistics, Warszawa 2011.

Szweda-Lewandowska, Z. (2014), Rynek usług opiekuńczych – perspektywy rozwoju w kontekście starzenia się populacji, *Optimum. Studia Ekonomiczne* Nr 2 (68).

www.i2home.org.

www.aal-europe.eu/award-2015-winners/.

www.aal-europe.eu/home-4-dem-project-starts/.

Aldona Frączkiewicz-Wronka, Sabina Ostrowska

The Development of Health Security of Elderly Citizens through the Application of Information and Communication Technologies[1]

1. The state as a healthcare policy maker: Introductory remarks

The problem of every individual is how to fulfil his or her needs, including those relating to health, and how to prevent shortage of means of subsistence in the final stage of life. Since time immemorial, two opposing ideas have been in competition: individual self-help and collective/social self-help[2]. The concept of individual self-help stems from the naturalistic conception of man, who is defined as representative of a biological species, shaped and growing according to natural laws and constantly forced to fight for his or her life. The other concept – collective/social self-help – emerged as a result of workers' protests and the attempts undertaken by Chancellor Otto von Bismarck to develop solutions that would prevent, alleviate and counteract mass-scale poverty.

Contrary to the first concept, emphasizing individual prudence and foresight, the idea of collective/social self-help underlines the necessity to develop welfare solutions created by the state as actions aiming for the systematic building of common resources allocated to protect people against the risk of poverty, which may be the result of an illness, health loss or old age. This approach to the obligations of the state towards the citizen has become the defining principle of social ideas in the European Union, built in conformity to the

[1] This publication is part of the project entitled *Human resources management in hospitals,* financed from the NCN funds allocated on the basis of decision no. DEC-2013/11/B/HS4/01062 (project manager dr Beata Buchelt). The study uses: *Raport z badania ewaluacyjnego pn. „Funkcjonowanie opieki geriatrycznej w Polsce"* (*Report on the evalaution survey "Geriatric care in Poland"*), conducted within the system project *Wsparcie systemu kształcenia ustawicznego personelu medycznego w zakresie opieki geriatrycznej (Support for the lifelong learning system for medical staff in the area of geriatric care)* – Gdańsk 2014, co-participated by the authors.
[2] T. Zieliński, *Ubezpieczenia społeczne pracowników*, PWN Warszawa-Kraków 1994, pp. 28–29.

legislation of the EU, the Council of Europe and the UN[3]. Health and life protection is the human need that should be particularly supported by the state[4]. Manifesting deep respect for the inalienable right of the individual to health and life protection, the European Union creates favourable conditions, sets strategic tasks, and coordinates and finances the initiatives aimed at the improved quality of means serving citizens' health needs, indicating the right way to develop solutions in this area to individual EU Member States[5].

The approach adopted by the EU in relation to the issues involved in serving the citizen rights to having health needs fulfilled is the consequence of the EU's understanding of the very concept of health[6]. The WHO constitution – binding for the EU Member States – defines health as *"a state of complete physical, mental and social well-being and not merely the absence of disease or infirmity"*[7]. Such an approach affords the perception of health issues in their entirety with the indication to the need for seeking multi-faceted solutions due to the diversity of factors involved. The above definition charts the directions for the developments in healthcare. If health is seen as a systemic view of life, healthcare will aim to bring back and retain dynamic balance in individuals, families, social groups, whereas a healthcare system should primarily involve the creation of a comprehensive, effective and integrated system of preventive, medical and rehabilitation care. The state in its role of a social security guarantor becomes the entity responsible for the creation of a functional healthcare system based on such rules as yield possibly largest benefits with limited public means.

The fulfilment of health needs requires an economic, political and social system that is well organized and effectively operating. A healthcare system is the reflection of a country's social policies and has a decisive influence on its population's health. Every healthcare system is designed to fulfil the health needs of a population defined in terms of a particular territory, while the actual level and degree of these needs – verified by consumer behaviours with respect to the quantity and quality of acquired services – is determined by a number of factors, especially by its resources.

Mutual dependencies within the healthcare system comprise: resources at the disposal of the system, activity measured with the quantity and quality of services provided, the population's health, and the health need fulfilment degree. The social goals of health policies embrace: eliminating health inequalities and creating equal opportunities for health development and protection, health improvement, the prevention of diseases, deaths and disabilities, as well as organizing the treatment process in such a way that it provides care and protects a patient's personal dignity[8]. In order to achieve these goals, it is necessary to build the medical services market that will:

---

[3] *Cf.* W. Anioł, *Europejska polityka społeczna. Implikacje dla Polski*, Instytut Polityki Społecznej Uniwersytetu Warszawskiego, Warszawa 2003, pp.15–44.

[4] *Cf.* P. J. Belcher, *Rola Unii Europejskiej w opiece zdrowotnej*, Wydawnictwo Ignis, Warszawa 2001.

[5] *Cf.* A. Kozierkiewicz, Zagadnienia zdrowia publicznego Unii Europejskiej [in:] J. Nosko (ed.) *Zdrowie publiczne w zmieniającej się Europie i w Polsce*, Szkoła Zdrowia Publicznego Instytutu Medycyny Pracy im. Prof. J. Nofera, Łódź 2004, pp. 31–38.

[6] P. G. Svensson, The Concept of Health. Some Comments from a Social Science Perspective [in:] "Scandinavian Journal of Social Medicine", Linkoping 1980, p. 28.

[7] Definition according to the WHO Constitution 1948.

[8] *Cf.* C. Włodarczyk, *Prakseologiczny dylemat polityki ochrony zdrowia w Polsce*, Instytut Medycyny Pracy im. Prof. J. Nofera, Łódź 1988.

- offer the fullest possible range of medical services and provide the entire population with the services that it requires, irrespective of differences in terms of their demographics, economic situation, or social, cultural, and geographical criteria (the principle of availability);
- deliver preventive, medical treatment, and rehabilitation services of the highest possible quality, adequate to the level of medical knowledge and practice and in compliance with codes of conduct (the principle on the quality of healthcare and the continuity rule);
- manage healthcare in the best possible way so that the use of the existing material, financial and human resources can be optimized (the principle of efficiency);
- implement solutions streamlining the system and contributing to patient and medical staff satisfaction (the principle of organization and management adequate to the social and economic development stage);
- employ highly qualified staff to work in a variety of healthcare areas (the principle of competence)[9].

Thanks to the healthcare system the state should monitor its population's health as well as living and working conditions, and counteract harmful phenomena. The performance of these tasks is exceedingly difficult and requires the implementation of numerous measures within a broadly defined healthcare policy as a subsystem of a social policy. Due to the current demographic trends, the fulfilment of the health needs of older citizens is of particular importance.

Ageing processes in society are recognized as one of the most important social phenomena of the 21st century and the implications are and will remain a key challenge for social policies in the coming years. The awareness of the inevitable ageing of societies is becoming an indispensible component of planning for the future in all spheres of life. Numerous scientific studies, diagnosing the situation of the elderly in Poland and globally, are published. They provide the foundation for the EU and national guidelines on necessary measures aiming to prepare people to live in a significantly changed demographic structure.

2. The identification of emerging health needs

In the last two decades in Poland, the system of social protection for older people has been seen mainly through the prism of protecting their material situation and securing livelihoods within the framework of the pension system. To a lesser degree, the social security system has developed the services that are indispensible for the protection of the social rights of senior citizens. The result is the deficit of health, activation and integration services and the condition of the social and environmental welfare system, which may lead to a conclusion that solving the problems of older people has become their own responsibility or the responsibility of the family, while the role of public institutions is insufficient in this respect.

---

[9] A. Frączkiewicz-Wronka, *Reforma systemu opieki zwrotnej w perspektywie integracji z Unią Europejską. Wybrane aspekty zachodzących zmian*, Wydawnictwo Akademii Ekonomicznej, Katowice 2001, p. 42.

Undeniably, an increase in the elderly population causes consequences for the entire society and affects the economy and social and cultural relations in a given country. In Europe, life expectancy at birth has risen by almost 10 years in the last four decades, both for men and women. The OECD statistics for European countries place this indicator for women at an average of 73.5 years of age in 1970 and 82.9 in 2011, and for men at 66.5 and 77.7 years of age respectively (OECD, 2014, *OECD Health Statistics 2014*, *Frequently Requested Data*, http://www.oecd.org/els/health-systems/oecd-health-statistics-2014-frequently-requested-data.htm (01.08.2015)).

In 2000, the proportion of senior citizens (aged 65+) in Europe's population amounted to 15% (this indicator for the entire population of the EU Member States stood slightly above 12%). 2050 forecasts point to an increase to 18.5%, while the proportion of "the oldest old" (80+) is expected to rise from 3.4% in 2000 to almost 12% in 2050.

Most European countries, including Poland, are affected by this problem to such a degree that public administration intensifies efforts to develop institutional solutions aimed at designing the system of assistance for older persons.

Demographic and epidemiological changes, in particular increased longevity, have an impact on a society's needs that can and should be fulfilled within the area defined by the social policy, especially the healthcare policy, which is one of public policies[10]. Public policies are perceived as elements of decision-making and undertaking initiatives by public authorities to achieve particular goals in the areas where market mechanisms do not apply and might not work properly on their own. They are used to regulate public tasks – from their design to implementation to the evaluation of outcomes. Public policy goals are defined in consultation with a number of actors from the public sphere, and their implementation in terms of allocating adequate sources of funding and the range of tasks is assigned to public administration bodies – often in cooperation with other entities[11].

The identification of deficit areas launched the public debate in Poland on how to create policies addressed to persons aged 60+, which led to the development of the Long-term Senior Policy in Poland for the years 2014–2020[12]. The senior policy is defined as overall activities throughout a person's life, leading to the creation of conditions conducive to prolonged activity, both work-related and social, and to independent, healthy and safe life led by older people. As one of the important areas of support for the population 60+, the guidelines included in the Long-term Senior Policy in Poland[13] highlight the creation of the environment favourable to good health and autonomy.

In Part 2.1.1., the first priority involves the development of systemic solutions allowing for the growth in medical services targeting older people and defines the main goals as:

---

[10] *Cf.* W. C. Włodarczyk, *Wprowadzenie do polityki zdrowotnej*, Oficyna a Wolters Kluwer business, Warszawa 2010.

[11] *Cf.* M. E. Kraft, S. R. Furlong, *Public policy. Politics, analysis and alternatives*. CQ Press, Washington DC, 2007, pp. 4–7.

[12] Council of Ministers Resolution No. 238 of 24 December 2013 on the adoption of the Outline of the Long-term Senior Policy in Poland for the years 2014–2020; Polish Monitor, the official journal of the Republic of Poland, Warszawa, 4 February 2014, item 118.

[13] https://www.google.pl/search?q=polityka+senioralna++dz.u&ie=utf-8&oe=utf-8&gws_rd=cr&ei=lir8Vfd-dy8vKA6qgtJAC. Accessed on 30.08.2015.

(1) the development of geriatrics as a medical specialization, (2) the professional training and development of medical staff towards holistic and comprehensive healthcare for older patients, and (3) the support for geriatric clinics and care in Poland. The scope and content of the priorities clearly indicate that issues involved with the creation of systemic solutions in the area of senior healthcare are recognized as one of the most important problems of the senior policy and, more generally, healthcare policy.

3. Contextual determinants of initiatives aiming at developing the geriatric healthcare model within primary healthcare

The attempts to find new ways of delivering medical services to older people are the result of a number of factors. The most important of them are legislative, political, social, economic, and demographic factors.

3.1. Legislative determinants

The responsibility assumed by the EU as a whole and individually by the Member States for improvement in the social and economic situation of older people is the consequence of the obligation to comply with the legislation and pragmatics enumerated in the Recommendation CM/Rec(2014)2 of the Committee of Ministers to Member States on the promotion of human rights of older people[14], in particular:

(a) the Convention for the Protection of Human Rights and Fundamental Freedoms, (b) the Convention for the Protection of Human Rights and Dignity of the Human Being with regard to the Application of Biology and Medicine, (c) the Recommendation CM/Rec(2011)5 of the Committee of Ministers on reducing the risk of vulnerability of elderly migrants and improving their welfare, (e) the Recommendation CM/Rec(2009)6 on ageing and disability in the 21st century, (f) the Recommendation No. R (94)9 concerning elderly people, (g) the Parliamentary Assembly Resolution 1793 (2011) on promoting active ageing – capitalizing on older people's working potential, (h) the Recommendation 1796 (2007) on the situation of elderly persons in Europe, (i) the Recommendation 1749 (2006) and Resolution 1502 (2006) on demographic challenges for social cohesion, (j) the Recommendation 1591 (2003) on challenges of social policy in Europe's ageing societies, (k) the Recommendation 1619 (2003) on the rights of elderly migrants, (l) Recommendation 1418 (1999) on the protection of the human rights and dignity of the terminally ill and the dying, (m) the United Nations Convention on the rights of persons with disabilities, (n) the Council of Europe Action Plan to promote the rights and full participation of people with disabilities in society: improving the quality of life of people with disabilities in Europe (2006–2015), (o) the ongoing work of the United Nations, in particular the United Nations

---

[14] Recommendation CM/Rec(2014)2 of the Committee of Ministers to Member States on the promotion of human rights of older people (adopted by the Committee of Ministers on 19 February 2014 at the 1192nd meeting of vice-ministers), https://www.msz.gov.pl/resource/161bbca4-55d0-4c79-834f-c2d4f4f4559d:JCR. Accessed on 30.08.2015.

Principles for Older Persons (1991), (p) the Madrid International Plan of Action on Ageing (MIPAA), (r) the Regional Implementation Strategy for Europe, (s) the Open-ended Working Group on Ageing for the purpose of strengthening the protection of human rights of older persons, and the decision by the Human Rights Council on the appointment of an independent expert on the enjoyment of all human rights by older persons.

The number of the regulatory documents listed above, together with the scope of issues covered in them clearly show that the problems connected with ageing of the population – equally to the problems involved with disabilities – are slowly becoming one of the dominant areas in which the European Union is seeking economically efficient and socially accepted solutions aimed at developing the systems supportive of a life in dignity for this social group.

3.2. Political determinants

The ongoing democratization of political life causes that older people are increasingly gaining in importance as a political power and their needs are reflected in the content of the key strategic documents formulated at the level of the European Union and its Member States. The regulations listed above have been strengthened by the EU's strategic documents, which point to the full participation of older people in social and economic life as a crucial success factor for the *Europe 2020* strategy, while at the same time they indicate that building a society ensuring full social inclusion is a necessary condition of sustainable economic growth and a stimulant of innovation.

In order to achieve success, the European Union proposes the use of the following instruments: awareness raising, financial backing, statistics and data collection, as well as the monitoring and implementation of coordination mechanisms in the Member States. According to the strategy initiators, the use of these instruments at different levels of governance will contribute to the creation of opportunities for living a life in dignity for the society as a whole and, in particular, for disadvantaged groups, including older people.

The achievement of the set goals requires the involvement of all organizational actors shaping the living conditions and socio-economic development in a country. In the context of the social policy goals defined in the *Europe 2020* strategy, stimulating fertility levels and ensuring generational renewal on one hand and providing proper management for a social resource of high potential, which older people are, the issue of modelling a social protection system, including healthcare services, is becoming one of the key challenges faced by the European states, including Poland.

Previous election experiences clearly show that the issues related to the provision of social services – especially to older people – often become an element of political campaigns, only to come back in vestigial form later on.

3.3. Social determinants

The social situation of older people, manifested for example by the opportunity to live a life in dignity, is the consequence of changes in the family model in Poland, in particular the breakup of the multigenerational family and the progressing atrophy of care taking functions connected with looking after a family's dependent members[15].

In the past, Poland's social life was dominated by the model based on a large, extended family, often embracing three or more generations. Over time, however, the structure of the family model has changed as a result of the atomization of society, the idea of an individual's freedom, evolving customs, increased women employment levels, lower birth rates, and rising mobility[16].

The unfavourable processes mentioned above cause the loosening of social bonds and increase the number of older people living alone, who are supported by their family to a still lesser extent, as family contacts are increasingly reduced to short visits from children and grandchildren[17]. The factors that set older people apart from the rest of society are basically gender and age: more women than men do not have life partners and with age the percentage of single people – especially women – increases.

In the 65–69 age group, 80.6% of men and 52.9% of women are married, while in the 85+ age group, the respective figures are 50.1% and only 6.6%[18]. The forms of family life that older people lead also vary depending on their place of residence – in cities more people live alone than in the country. Living alone or with a spouse only is a typically urban phenomenon[19]. These unfavourable changes are another factor that makes it necessary to develop a systemic solution – a model based on a living environment – that would allow for the fulfilment of health and care needs of older people.

3.4. Economic determinants

The assessment of the economic situation of older people is not easy. On the one hand official statistics paint a positive picture, on the other hand social surveys reveal growing exclusion (OBOP, CBOS, Diagnoza Społeczna). Social exclusion is primarily caused by low income and poor living standards, increasingly frequent cases of living in a one-man household and lack of autonomy, but also insufficient development of social services, such as lack of social support network reaching out beyond a single family, for example local care-taking establishments and welfare care services.

Senior citizens at the risk of social exclusion are mainly people who find it difficult to leave their flat or have to stay in permanently due to reduced mobility. The economic

---

[15] F. Adamski, *Rodzina. Wymiar społeczno-kulturowy.* Kraków 2002, p. 29.

[16] H. Cudak, Zaburzenie struktury rodziny jako konsekwencja makrospołecznych uwarunkowań, "Pedagogika rodziny" 2012, No. 2(4), Społeczna Akademia Nauk w Łodzi, pp. 7–18.

[17] P. Błędowski, Konsekwencje procesu demograficznego starzenia się ludności jako zadanie dla administracji publicznej, [in:] *Raport na temat sytuacji osób starszych w Polsce*, Instytut Pracy i Spraw Socjalnych, Warszawa 2012, http://senior.gov.pl/source/raport_osoby%20starsze.pdf. Accessed on 10.07.2015.

[18] B. Szatur-Jaworska, Sytuacja rodzinna i potrzeby opiekuńcze ludzi starszych w Polsce, [in:] *Raport na temat sytuacji osób starszych w Polsce*, Instytut Pracy i Spraw Socjalnych, Warszawa 2012, http://senior.gov.pl/source/raport_osoby%20starsze.pdf. Accessed on 10.07.2015

[19] B. Szatur-Jaworska, Sytuacja rodzinna i potrzeby opiekuńcze ludzi starszych w Polsce, [in:] *Raport na temat sytuacji osób starszych w Polsce*, Instytut Pracy i Spraw Socjalnych, Warszawa 2012, http://senior.gov.pl/source/raport_osoby%20starsze.pdf. Accessed on 10.07.2015.

situation of older people in Poland assessed through the prism of household budgets seems to reveal relatively high levels of average income per person in pensioner households[20]. A relatively favourable income situation in pensioner households – compared to other socio-economic groups – does not mean that it can be treated as good.

Although statistical data show that the percentage of older people at the risk of poverty is relatively lower than in the other age groups, it should be noted that the official poverty line in Poland is defined at a very low level. As a result, it is difficult to assess the actual economic situation of older people.

Indirectly, their poor financial situation can be reflected in low employment rates for people aged 50+ (a relatively small number of people in this age group are in paid employment, although income from paid employment tends to be higher than social benefits and pensions) and, in a number of surveys, high frequencies of responses on the necessity to resign from some expenses, especially prescribed medical products[21]. This applied to 18.5% of the respondents in the PolSenior project, 13.8% of men and 21.3% of women[22]. Low income is also one of the major reasons why senior citizens are reluctant to improve their living conditions by purchasing equipment and appliances that make it easier for them to run an independent household and lead an active life.

3.5. Demographic determinants

An increase in the number of older people contributes to a growing interest in economically effective and socially fair solutions aiming to deliver health and life services to this social group. A long-term population forecast for Poland for the years 2008–2035, prepared by GUS (Polish Central Statistical Office), indicates that Poland's population figures will steadily fall and the dynamics of the fall will be increasingly higher.

Importantly, these changes will significantly affect the population make-up, in particular the group of working-age population, which also means that the proportions between pre-working, working, and post-working population groups will shift. The first wave will occur as soon as in the years 2015–2020. The share of people of working age in the total population make-up will fall by almost 7 percentage points by the year 2035. Additionally, the working-age population will also decrease in size – the number of people in non-mo-

[20] *Budżety gospodarstw domowych w 2010 r.*, Central Statistical Office of Poland, Warszawa 2011.
[21] B. Szatur-Jaworska, Psychospołeczny wymiar sytuacji ludzi starych – wyniki badania „PolSenior", "Problemy Polityki Społecznej. Studia i Dyskusje" 2012, Volume 18, No. 7, pp. 155–173; B. Szatur-Jaworska, Sytuacja rodzinna i więzi rodzinne ludzi starszych i osób na przedpolu starości, [in:] M. Mossakowska, A. Więcek, P. Błędowski (eds.), *Aspekty medyczne, psychologiczne, socjologiczne i ekonomiczne starzenia się ludzi w Polsce*, Termedia Wydawnictwa Medyczne, Poznań 2012; P. Błędowski, Sytuacja materialna osób starszych, [in:] M. Mossakowska, A. Więcek, P. Błędowski (eds.), *Aspekty medyczne, psychologiczne, socjologiczne i ekonomiczne starzenia się ludzi w Polsce*, Termedia Wydawnictwa Medyczne, Poznań 2012; *Budżety gospodarstw domowych w 2010 r.*, Central Statistical Office of Poland, Warszawa 2011; J. Czapiński, T. Panek (eds.), *Diagnoza społeczna 2013. Warunki i jakość życia Polaków,* Social Monitoring Council, Warszawa 2013.
[22] P. Błędowski, Sytuacja materialna osób starszych, [in:] M. Mossakowska, A. Więcek, P. Błędowski (eds.), *Aspekty medyczne, psychologiczne, socjologiczne i ekonomiczne starzenia się ludzi w Polsce*, Termedia Wydawnictwa Medyczne, Poznań 2012.

bile age (45–60 and more) will grow, while the number of people with high job mobility (18–44) will go down. The number of non-mobile working-age people will increase by about 3% compared to the current situation. The proportion of people of post-working age will grow from 18% in 2013 to 26.7% in 2035. Finally, people of pre-working age (0–17 years) will account for only 15.6% of total population in 2035 (compared to 18% at present)[23].

The average life parameter for both men and women is growing and the average lifespan in Poland increases steadily and has changed from 81.0 years of age in 2012 to 81.1 in 2017 for women, and from 72.6 to 73.8 for men. Currently, the mortality rate for adults, especially older, is at a relatively low level, which means that the number and percentage of seniors are increasing and the number of the oldest old is growing decidedly faster. Accordingly, we are observing that the subpopulation of the oldest old, who have very specific health and life needs, has very high growth dynamics.

The age that is conventionally accepted as old age is arbitrary[24], but its delimitation is crucial for the development of systemic solutions and strongly affects their character, because advancing age is accompanied by growing needs in the area of security and health-care. This implies the necessity to design rational and effective directions for the allocation of public funds[25].

Demographic changes require the forging of new intergenerational solidarity and, as a consequence, it becomes increasingly necessary to develop networks of diagnostic, therapeutic, rehabilitation, care and assistance services aiming to create such conditions at the place of residence of older people that they can lead a life in dignity there. While formulating healthcare policies, it is of utmost importance to ensure that statutory solutions receive adequate funding and adopt clear organizational rules for primary, hospital and specialist healthcare as well as for institutional and home care, including hospice and palliative care.

A strong upward trend concerning the number of people of medium and late old age currently observed in Poland[26] is an important demographic aspect contributing to an increasingly pressing need to create the model of providing support and social and health-care services to older people at their place of living. Such a support system is both more cost-effective and more humanitarian.

---

[23] *Prognoza ludności Polski na lata 2008–2035*, GUS, http://stat.gov.pl/cps/rde/xbcr/gus/L_prognoza_ludnosci_Pl_2008–2035.pdf; *Podstawowe informacje o rozwoju demograficznym Polski do 2013 roku*, GUS, http://stat.gov.pl/cps/rde/xbcr/gus/L_podst_inf_o_rozwoju_dem_pl_do_2013.pdf. Accessed on 30.03.2015.

[24] Proposed division of the old age into stages: (1) early old age up to 74, late old age of 75–89, longevity from 90 years of age; (2) the third age, i.e. early pensioners, and the fourth age – the time of life when a person needs permanent support from others; (3) the young old of 65–74 years of age, the old old of 75–84 years of age, the oldest old of 85+ years of age.

[25] M. Mossakowska, A. Więcek, P. Błędowski (eds.), *Aspekty medyczne, psychologiczne, socjologiczne i ekonomiczne starzenia się ludzi w Polsce*, Termedia Wydawnictwa Medyczne, Poznań 2012.

[26] M. Polakowski, *Społeczne i ekonomiczne konsekwencje starzenia się społeczeństw a główne kierunki reform systemów emerytalnych w Europie*, "Studia BAS" 2012, No. 2(30), pp.169–200, http://orka.sejm.gov.pl/wydbas.nsf/0/D047CD44C3AFFD3FC1257A37002AA895/$File/BAS_30-9.pdf. Accessed on 30.03.2015.

4. The application of information and communication technologies to in-home care of older people

An increased lifespan, particularly in the developed countries, means that the state needs to assume responsibility for ensuring the adequate quality of life and care in the old age. Demographic forecasts indicate that both the world and particularly Europe are affected by the phenomenon universally known as ageing society.

Old age is characterized by an increased number of limitations in daily life. Such limitations are caused by health problems, which tend to become more acute at this stage of life, a significant decrease in physical fitness and mental condition, and growing disfunctionality in self-care. As a result of the difficulties of varying intensity and clinical condition, constant, remote monitoring of the daily activity of an older person is becoming not only a practical convenience, but also an urgent need. The fulfilment of older persons' health needs, and growing requirements and expectations as to the quality of medical and care services requires modifications in the methods of providing healthcare and social services.

E-health, telemedicine and, above all, telehomecare services are the areas of exceptional growth potential. The key element of their development is universal approval granted by their users as well as personalization and customization of care systems to varied needs and capabilities of senior citizens with their weakened sensory (e.g. sight, hearing), motor and/or mental abilities.

The studies on the attitudes and needs of older people conducted in Poland showed that 30–40% are positive about e-health services and willing to use them if given such an opportunity[27]. Among the proponents of telemedical services, most people express an interest in receiving simple recommendations from a doctor on their mobile phone or computer (84%) and reminders about scheduled visits in the clinic or prescribed medication (60%), as well as receiving medical test results by electronic mail (61%) or making appointments online (47%)[28].

The answer to growing demand may be the introduction of modern ICT solutions to the health and care services sector. This is supported by the results of research conducted as part of the evaluation of the system project *"Support for the lifelong learning system for medical staff in the area of geriatric care"* – Gdańsk 2014, co-participated by the authors. The question about the need to develop and implement the telecare system and to use innovative technologies in order to facilitate the provision of medical care to older people was answered positively by over 2/3 of the respondents.

Telecare, defined as the use of modern medical and imaging data transfer technologies and systems of remote contact with people in need of permanent in-home medical supervision, may offer a solution to the problem of improving accessibility to health and care

---

[27] M. Bujnowska-Fedak, Zastosowanie usług telemedycznych w opiece nad ludźmi starszymi ze szczególnym uwzględnieniem ich postaw, potrzeb i oczekiwań w tym zakresie, a conference speech, online source: http://www.telemedycyna.org/wp-content/ uploads/2014/10/12-M.M.Bujnowska-Fedak-Bujnowska – Telemedycy-na-w-s%C5%82u%C5%BCbie-ludzom-starszym.pdf. Accessed on 19.09.2015.

[28] M. Kielar, Teleopieka u progu starości, „Ogólnopolski Przegląd Medyczny", 2013; 12: 54–56.

The development and implementation of the telehomecare system and the application of innovative technologies according to the occupational groups of respondents

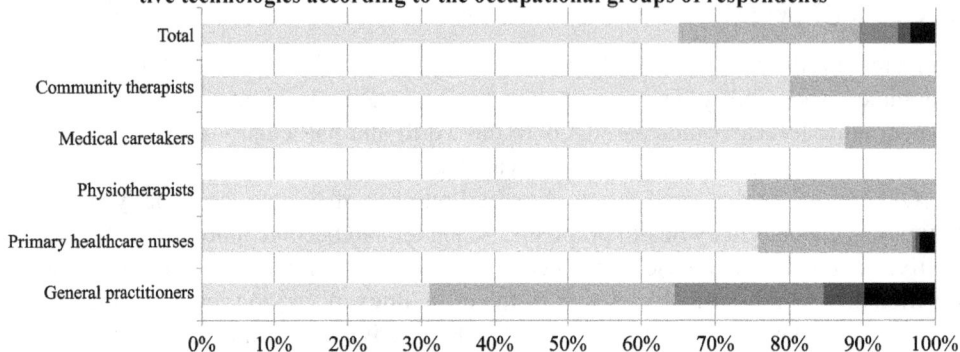

	General practitioners	Primary health-care nurses	Physiothera-pists	Medical caretakers	Community therapists	Total
Definitely yes	31.0%	75.8%	74.3%	87.5%	80.0%	65.0%
Rather yes	33.5%	21.0%	25.7%	12.5%	20.0%	24.5%
Rather no	20.0%	0.5%	0.0%	0.0%	0.0%	5.3%
Definitely no	5.5%	0.5%	0.0%	0.0%	0.0%	1.6%
Difficult to say	10.0%	2.3%	0.0%	0.0%	0.0%	3.6%

The development and implementation of the telehomecare system and the application of innovative technologies according to the occupational groups of respondents

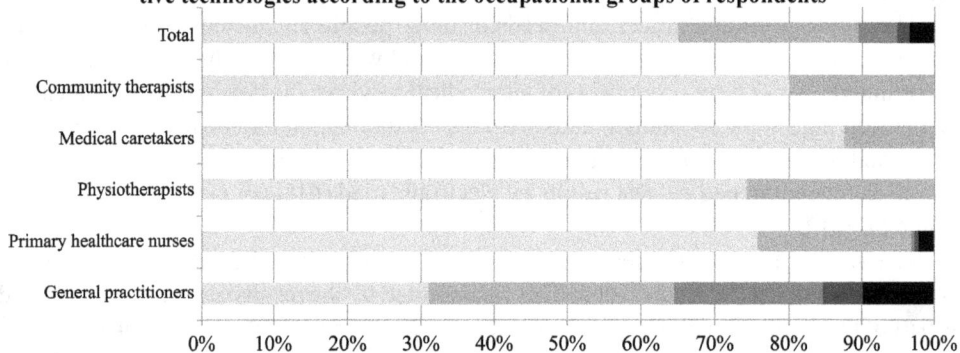

	General practitioners	Primary health-care nurses	Physiothera-pists	Medical caretakers	Community therapists	Total
Definitely yes	31.0%	75.8%	74.3%	87.5%	80.0%	65.0%
Rather yes	33.5%	21.0%	25.7%	12.5%	20.0%	24.5%
Rather no	20.0%	0.5%	0.0%	0.0%	0.0%	5.3%
Definitely no	5.5%	0.5%	0.0%	0.0%	0.0%	1.6%
Difficult to say	10.0%	2.3%	0.0%	0.0%	0.0%	3.6%

Chart 1. The assessment of the need to develop and implement the telecare system and use innovative technologies in order to facilitate the provision of medical care to older people according to occupational groups of medical staff providing health services to older people and participating in courses
Source: CATI telephone interviews with representatives of medical staff providing health services to older people and participating in the courses run within the framework of the project.

services. In recent years in Poland, we observe that the traditional health and social care model has been supplemented with innovative technological solutions, such as telemedicine and telecare. The Ministry of Health adopted adequate amendments on telemedicine to the Act of 28 April 2011, on the information system in health care[29].

In addition to increasing the effectiveness of treatment for chronic diseases, these solutions also give older people a sense of security and raise their comfort of living.

The most commonly quoted benefits stemming from the application of modern ICT solutions in the healthcare sector are interactive communication between the patient and the doctor, the general practitioner and the medical specialist (consultation), the doctor and other team members, shorter waiting time, better effectiveness of diagnostic processes and preventive measures, better chronic disease management, and rational public funds management.

The majority of respondents (80.0%) in the above evaluation study claim that there is also the need to create the system of teleconsultation for doctors working in geriatrics.

The assessment of the need to create the system of teleconsultation for doctors working in geriatrics according to the representatives of course organizers

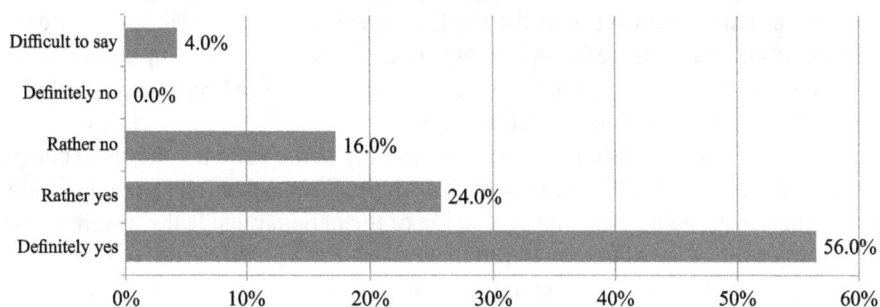

	Definitely yes	Rather yes	Rather no	Definitely no	Difficult to say
Percentage	56.0%	24.0%	16.0%	0.0%	4.0%

Chart 2. The assessment of the need to create the system of teleconsultation for doctors working in geriatrics according to the representatives of course organizers.
Source: CATI telephone interviews with representatives of organizers of the courses held within the framework of the project.

In the context of an ageing society, the benefits of telecare in the area of healthcare comprise the possibility of supporting older people in different aspects of life and offering them access to qualified medical staff according to their needs.

At the current stage, action should be taken with the aim of creating opportunities for the patient to contact and report on his health condition to the nurse or the general practitioner. Additionally, monitoring systems, modelled, for example, on the systems dedicated to people with heart condition or diabetes, should be implemented.

---

[29] Act of 28 April 2011, on the information system in health care, Journal of Laws 2011 No. 113 item 657.

Apart from monitoring selected values of clinical measures, solutions offered by tele-homecare systems also embrace remote interactive contact of the patient with the doctor, the nurse or other specialist medical staff, which gives the patient a sense of being in direct contact with the hospital worker despite the existing geographical barrier. In Poland, the implementation of telehomecare is still at test stages, while the development and improvement of the system are based mainly on research projects.

The implementation of telehomecare solutions is particularly justified in the case of older people living alone, running the risk of falling, suffering from cardiovascular diseases (e.g. cardiac arrhythmias), neurological syndromes (e.g. epilepsy) or other chronic diseases. Patient telemonitoring enables the early diagnosis of disturbing diversions from the normal health condition and the first symptoms of a disease onset, which makes it possible to undertake adequate preventive measures and/or immediate intervention.

Ageing in society, causing changes in health needs of the older population, is the challenge that seems to go beyond the current capabilities of providing integrated health and social care to Polish senior patients.

A person aged 65+ is faced with a completely new quality of relationships built between the patient and the doctor in the integrated healthcare environment. In addition to granting permanent contact with the medical specialist responsible for the treatment, telecare contributes to a more effective therapy (e.g. thanks to access to up-to-date information on one's health condition), a reduced number of visits in the healthcare establishment, and more systematic, hence more effective, treatment[30].

The merits of telecare systems are not limited only to the patient – they also benefit the service provider and the healthcare system as a whole. From a therapist's point of view, the most important ones are permanent supervision of the patient outside the hospital environment, ongoing evaluation of treatment progress involving a possibility of adjustments, and a precise and effective way of presenting the patient's medical test results as personalized individualized data that can be easily used for scientific research[31].

The beneficiary of telecare solutions is also the healthcare system, which gains access to the patient's detailed medical information and profits from increased efficiency of medical specialists. The patient's health in-home monitoring service allows for a higher care standard, while a more efficient treatment process and medical information gathering allow for the reduction in the costs of such care[32]. The potential of telecare technologies to reduce the costs involved in the care provided to senior patients is a crucial argument in the discussion on the application of remote medical care.

The provision of care to retirees generates approximately 60% of total costs in health-care[33]. Although research, which is available in literature, on economic implications of the

---

[30] Ł. Czekierda *et al.*, Aplikacje telemedyczne (slide show). http://www.malopolska.pl/Lists/DocumentManager/oferty/Aplikacje%20Telemedyczne-AGH.pdf. Accessed on 17.09.2015.

[31] Ł. Czekierda *et al.*, Aplikacje telemedyczne (slide show). http://www.malopolska.pl/Lists/DocumentManager/oferty/Aplikacje%20Telemedyczne-AGH.pdf. Accessed on 17.09.2015.

[32] Ł. Czekierda *et al.*, *Aplikacje telemedyczne (slide show)*. http://www.malopolska.pl/Lists/DocumentManager/oferty/Aplikacje%20Telemedyczne-AGH. Accessed on 17.09.2015.

[33] M. Bujnowska-Fedak, E. Puchała, A. Steciwko, Aspekty finansowe i ekonomiczne telemedycznej opieki nad chorymi przewlekle, "Family Medicine & Primary Care Review", 2011, 13, 3: 563–568.

introduction of telecare as compared to the costs of the traditional healthcare system does not point to a decisive advantage of telemedicine in terms of cost generation, most conclusions confirm financial benefits connected with remote in-home care[34].

Other factors, equally important for the implementation of such a form of care, involve mental resistance to technological innovation and the lack of acquired competences in using electronic appliances, correlated with age, weakened motor and cognitive functions, and a strong need to form a personalized bond with the doctor (face-to-face communication)[35].

Analyses, conducted in Poland, on the attitudes and needs of older people indicate that a positive approach to advanced health-related technologies and the willingness to use them – given an opportunity – are declared by 30–40% of respondents[36],[37]. The proper use of this trust capital in the largest group of potential beneficiaries of telemedicine should be a starting point for developing adequate educational strategies in the area of new electronic technologies and solutions. Despite its many benefits, however, it should be noted that telecare cannot replace medical care defined in more traditional terms, but it ought to become a useful supplementation.

Systems of remote support for older people do not offer the possibility of full specialist monitoring of particular health parameters of older patients in-home, especially when they suffer from one or more chronic diseases, and initiating clinical intervention upon the current health condition of the monitored patient. In order to deal with health problems characteristic of old age more effectively, it is necessary to provide the older patient with extensive in-home care based on the range of traditional health and care services, supplemented with remote monitoring of selected life parameters (pulse, blood pressure, temperature, blood sugar, saturation, body mass, etc.)[38].

5. Challenges faced by medical professionals involved in the provision of in-home care to older people

The expectations of older people from different community institutions are mainly addressed to medical professionals working in outpatient care, such as general practitioners, community nurses, physiotherapists, health aides. These professions are perceived as the ones of greatest importance in community care of older people due to their frequent contact with patients.

In addition to care-providing activities, increasingly greater importance is attached to educational activities aimed at improving older people's self-care and self-nursing skills.

---

[34] M. M. Bujnowska-Fedak, M. Tomczak, Innowacyjne aplikacje telemedyczne i usługi e-zdrowia w opiece nad pacjentami w starszym wieku, "Zdrowie Publiczne i Zarządzanie", 2013; 11(4): 302–317.

[35] M. M. Bujnowska-Fedak, op. cit.

[36] M. Bujnowska-Fedak, I. Pirogowicz, Support for e-health services among elderly primary care patients, "Telemedicine Journal and E-Health", 2014;1; 20(8): 696–704.

[37] M. Bujnowska-Fedak, B. J. Sapilak, Poglądy i potrzeby ludzi w podeszłym wieku w zakresie korzystania z narzędzi telemedycznych i usług zdrowotnych typu e-health, "Family Medicine & Primary Care Review", 2012; 14(2): 132–137.

[38] M. M. Bujnowska-Fedak, M. Tomczak, Innowacyjne aplikacje telemedyczne i usługi e-zdrowia w opiece nad pacjentami w starszym wieku, "Zdrowie Publiczne i Zarządzanie", 2013; 11(4): 302–317.

Another crucial thing is to facilitate the older patients' functioning at their place of residence and help them cope with difficulties related to old age.

The adoption of the patient-centred model aims to improve the older person's health and sustain their physical fitness by teaching and promoting health-oriented behaviour and life style. The analysis of medical services provided to older people within primary healthcare indicates that they should be extended with health services dedicated exclusively to patients aged 65+. A good example is the provision of screening programmes allowing for the diagnosis of particular health problems, such as risk of falling, depression, dementia, psychiatric disorders, using the tools that were proposed, for example, in the training materials developed for the participants of geriatric care workshops held within the project.

Another form of a health service dedicated to older people can be the assessment conducted in four categories: functional capability, physical health, psychological condition, and socio-economic condition. Such forms of health services could be grouped into "diagnostic packages" varying in scope, based on the patient's age and condition (identified on the VES-13 scale), offered in three age groups, for example 60–74, 75–84, 85+. The implementation of the packages would require the introduction of the "Senior Card", which would define the obligatory set of screening tests and the scope of mandatory consultations, both medical and social, in each age group. Social consultations would involve the cooperation of a general practitioner or a primary care nurse with a social worker, which should be regulated by law.

As a result, interdisciplinary teams should be formed at the level of primary healthcare in order to assess the elderly patient in terms of health, care and social problems, and to offer adequate solutions. The role and tasks of the members of the interdisciplinary team of primary healthcare practitioners in the area of Comprehensive Geriatric Care are presented in the document entitled *Pomocnicze materiały szkoleniowe dla uczestników szkoleń z zakresu opieki geriatrycznej (Auxiliary materials for participants in geriatric care training workshops)* [39]. According to the document, the tasks of general practitioners involved in the care of patients aged 65+ can be allocated to three parallel areas:

- Preventive action aiming to improve older patients' health and fitness through health counselling, regular health and fitness checkups, flu and pneumococcal vaccinations, cancer screening, cognitive disorder screening, depression screening. This allows for the reduction of a sudden health deterioration risk and increases chances of early intervention and effective treatment.
- Medical action taking into account older patients' specific needs that require improved diagnostic skills and treating complex health conditions with the changed biology of the older organism, atypical and vague symptoms, increased sensitivity to medication, and iatrogenic syndromes.
- Logistics involved in the coordination of interdisciplinary cooperation of practitioners within the healthcare system, the ability to manage a team, delegate tasks defined on the basis of comprehensive geriatric assessment to team members, and flexibility in responding to emerging health, social and care priorities.

---

[39] B. Bień, K. Broczek (eds.), Pomocnicze materiały szkoleniowe dla uczestników szkoleń z zakresu opieki geriatrycznej, Warszawa 2012, http://www.geriatria.mz.gov.pl/materialy_szkoleniowe_opieka_geriatryczna.

The obligations of the primary healthcare nurse towards people aged 65+ go beyond the scope of services provided to patients from the younger age groups, as they embrace a number of health problems typical of old age. The nurse becomes a partner/intermediary in the interdisciplinary team headed by the general practitioner and including the physiotherapist, the social worker and other professionals. She might even assume the role of the team leader, provided the patient's main health problem remains within her competences or is the result of negligence in nursing, community or educational care.

The nurse can also coordinate the work of medical caretakers and cooperate with community therapists looking after patients with psychiatric disorders. Effective cooperation is based on the ability to communicate with the patient and their family as well as within the interdisciplinary team. The nurse makes the assessment of the older patient's health condition, conducts subjective and objective examination and uses comprehensive geriatric assessment methods.

The main tasks of the primary healthcare nurse involved in the care of people aged 65+ include:

- cooperation within the interdisciplinary team providing in-home care to people aged 65+, especially with the general practitioner and the physiotherapist;
- use of scales of Comprehensive Geriatric Assessment (CGA), interpreting the results, determining the list of priority tasks, planning care activities and undertaking nursing interventions based on CGA;
- providing of nursing care to geriatric patients while taking into account the differences stemming from somatic diseases, psychiatric disorders and functional impairment;
- devising of a care plan, including the needs connected with the so-called great geriatric problems, for example falling, osteoporosis, malnutrition;
- providing of care to the older patient, embracing physiotherapeutic procedures recommended by the physiotherapist and activating the patient, also with the use of auxiliary equipment;
- recognizing of sudden somatic and mental health deterioration that requires urgent medical intervention, for example delirium caused by acute somatic disorders;
- monitoring of pharmacotherapy, instructing on how to self-administer medications (e.g. by inhalation), and choosing the method for supervising medication administration that takes into account the patient's type of disability;
- educating of patients and their families/caretakers;
- analyzing of the family/social situation of a patient, identifying the cases of negligence and domestic violence, cooperating with social workers, local community representatives and NGOs in the development of the system of support for older people;
- keeping of medical records in compliance with the statutory standards;
- help to the family to plan and organize the process of taking care of the older and disabled patient.

The main role of the physiotherapist involved in the care of people aged 65+ includes the cooperation with the general practitioner and the whole therapeutic and care taking team that participate in the treatment of older patients. They should also work closely with the patient's family or caretakers and the community in which the patient lives. Their tasks involve (the scope of competences should be based on the qualifications held by the physiotherapist):

- planning a detailed physiotherapeutic programme adequate to a given disease or dysfunction based on the medical and physiotherapeutic examination;
- prescribing physiotherapeutic procedures and methods based on the medical and physiotherapeutic examination;
- executing or supervising prescribed physiotherapeutic procedures and methods;
- issuing opinions on functional examination and the effects of physiotherapeutic procedures;
- issuing opinions on the degree of disability;
- ordering adequate orthopaedic and auxiliary equipment necessary for prescribed physiotherapeutic procedures;
- prescribing physiotherapeutic programmes aiming to sustain and strengthen the effects of the applied physiotherapeutic procedure and prevent disability;
- prescribing, conducting or supervising occupational therapy and adaptation to the new living conditions;
- scheduling the way and time of using orthopaedic and auxiliary equipment;
- developing informational materials on how to prevent hazardous occurrences, for example falling;
- heading the team of physiotherapists taking part in the physiotherapeutic programme;
- scheduling consultations with medical specialists and imaging diagnostics of locomotor organs during the diagnostic process and the physiotherapeutic programme as well as upon its completion.

The growing care needs in the ageing society on one hand and the development of technologies and medical/paramedical specializations on the other contribute to an increasingly strong demand for the profession of the older person's medical caretaker. This relatively new occupation, frequently underestimated by the traditional representatives of medical professions, has a chance of becoming popular, both among older, chronically ill and disabled patients and in interdisciplinary teams of geriatric practitioners operating within primary healthcare.

The older person's medical caretaker should cooperate with the nurse and other primary healthcare practitioners in the area of:

- planning and implementing comprehensive geriatric care in the interdisciplinary cooperation with the whole team of primary healthcare practitioners;
- devising a plan for taking care of the older and dependent patient;
- assisting during nursing procedures;
- executing the instructions given by the nurse or the doctor in relation to care taking;

- giving assistance in fulfilling the needs involved in maintaining body hygiene or providing hygienic routines and keeping the patient's surroundings clean and tidy;
- assisting the older patient with impaired mobility in fulfilling their feeding and excretion needs as well as remaining mobile and using orthopaedic and rehabilitation equipment;
- disinfecting and maintaining the instruments and tools used for nursing purposes;
- keeping records of procedures and activities;
- assisting the older person with impaired mobility in the adaptation to the living conditions in the hospital and the changes involved with the development of a chronic disease, giving emotional support, helping in communication with the care and therapeutic team as well as other people;
- providing help in life- or health-threatening conditions;
- complying with ethical standards.

An important ally of medical care providers in their work with older people should become the already mentioned telemedicine, as it allows for the constant monitoring of basic life functions (blood pressure, pulse, breathing) and signals changes in the body position (falling) or the location of a person with disturbed cognitive functions through the use of special sensors.

The community therapist, new to the Polish reality, is an occupation forming a vital link in the multidimensional care of the older patient. It is also a kind of bridge between geriatric care defined as the care for a person suffering from a somatic disease and/or impaired mobility, and the psychiatric care for the older patient experiencing mental disorders. The main task of the community therapist is the multidirectional care of the older patient remaining outside hospital care who suffers from cognitive disorders, mood swings or fluctuating consciousness. He performs his role through:

- planning and implementing the system of support for the older person with mental disorders;
- planning and implementing support for the older person with dementia, adjusting the scope of assistance to how advanced the condition of the person is, whether he suffers from other disorders and what the actual caretaker can provide;
- executing community interventions;
- giving emotional support to the patient's family/caretaker and providing them with information on the nature of his condition and guidance on how to proceed in particular situations;
- offering advice on how to adapt the rooms in a house or flat to the progressing mental and physical disability;
- defining the rules on how to act and counteract the risks related to aggressive and auto-aggressive behaviour of the older patient;
- preventing falling, giving help to an infirm patient in changing a body position, getting up and moving around; managing space around the patient and developing familiarity with the techniques of safe walking, also with the use of auxiliary equipment;

- applying elements of motivational therapy;
- cooperating with other people involved in treatment and care as part of the inter-disciplinary therapeutic team providing comprehensive care to the psychogeriatric patient.

The issues discussed in relation to the roles performed by medical professionals while providing care to people aged 65+ do not fully reflect the complexity of the problem. Apparently, the trend in shifting the focus is irreversible due to the complicated processes occurring both as global tendencies and in the immediate environment of senior citizens. The growing expectations developed in society in connection with the professionalism of medical staff working in healthcare, increased security of patients and improved quality of services, cause that medical professionals have to take a much wider view of the treat-ment process instead of dealing with its particular elements only.

6. Conclusion

Ageing in society determines the necessity of taking a still wider perspective of health problems experienced by older people, who increasingly suffer from impaired mobility as well as poorer physical and mental condition, often accompanied by disfunctionality of self-care.

Prevention, early diagnosis and immediate intervention aimed at slowing down or even stopping the development of a disease are of crucial importance. The prevention of disa-bility among older people allows them to remain independent from others and prevent the institutionalization of care that needs to be provided to them.

Ongoing demographic changes necessitate steps aimed at modifying healthcare and social policies and adjusting them to the needs of the society emerging as a result of the cur-rent demographic trends. Particular importance should be attached to the situation of peo-ple taking care of ailing seniors, as neglecting this problem may soon lead to new issues in this group, such as professional burnout, depression and other disorders.

A concerted effort should be made to build and raise people's awareness of the respon-sibility they have for their own health and help them sustain high health potential and physical fitness until old age. Social campaigns and health programmes targeting particular age groups and addressing their specific needs should play an important role in achieving this goal.

Care provided to older people should be active, versatile and professional, while its primary goal should be to keep senior citizens in good physical and mental shape as long as possible. It should also aim at preventing diseases through education of both seniors and their caretakers, at treating developed diseases, and cooperating with the older person and their caretakers, especially in difficult life situations and with the use of ICT instruments and applications.

Care of older people should be provided by the multidisciplinary team consisting of medical and non-medical staff as well as volunteers, with active support from local governments, which already today are acting in the interest of citizens aged 65+, and with the use of modern ICT tools within standard procedures for working with elderly people. Care defined and executed in this way ensures a comprehensive and holistic approach to the older person's needs, while at the same time allowing for the individualization of health and social services provided to senior citizens.

References

Adamski, F. (2002), *Rodzina. Wymiar społeczno-kulturowy*, Kraków.

Anioł, W. (2003), *Europejska polityka społeczna. Implikacje dla Polski*, Instytut Polityki Społecznej Uniwersytetu Warszawskiego, Warszawa.

Belcher, P. J. (2001), *Rola Unii Europejskiej w opiece zdrowotnej*, Wydawnictwo Ignis, Warszawa.

Błędowski, P. (2012), Konsekwencje procesu demograficznego starzenia się ludności jako zadanie dla administracji publicznej, [in:] Raport na temat sytuacji osób starszych w Polsce. Instytut Pracy i Spraw Socjalnych, Warszawa, online source http://senior.gov.pl/source/raport_osoby%20starsze.pdf.

Błędowski, P. (2012), Sytuacja materialna osób starszych, [in:] M. Mossakowska, A. Więcek, P. Błędowski (eds.), *Aspekty medyczne, psychologiczne, socjologiczne i ekonomiczne starzenia się ludzi w Polsce*, Termedia Wydawnictwa Medyczne, Poznań.

Budżety gospodarstw domowych w 2010 r., Central Statistical Office, Warszawa 2011.

Bujnowska-Fedak, M., Pirogowicz, I., Support for e-health services among elderly primary care patients, "Telemedicine Journal and E-Health", 2014;1; 20(8).

Bujnowska-Fedak, M., Puchała, E., Steciwko, A., Aspekty finansowe i ekonomiczne telemedycznej opieki nad chorymi przewlekle, "Family Medicine & Primary Care Review", 2011, 13(3).

Bujnowska-Fedak, M., Sapilak, B. J., Poglądy i potrzeby ludzi w podeszłym wieku w zakresie korzystania z narzędzi telemedycznych i usług zdrowotnych typu e-health, "Family Medicine & Primary Care Review", 2012; 14(2).

Bujnowska-Fedak, M., Zastosowanie usług telemedycznych w opiece nad ludźmi starszymi ze szczególnym uwzględnieniem ich postaw, potrzeb i oczekiwań w tym zakresie, a conference speech, online source: http://www.telemedycyna.org/wp-content/.

Bujnowska-Fedak, M., Tomczak, M., Innowacyjne aplikacje telemedyczne i usługi e-zdrowia w opiece nad pacjentami w starszym wieku, "Zdrowie Publiczne i Zarządzanie", 2013; 11(4).

Cudak, H., Zaburzenie struktury rodziny jako konsekwencja makrospołecznych uwarunkowań, "Pedagogika rodziny: Family Pedagogy" 2012, No. 2(4).

Czapiński, J., Panek, T. (ed.) (2013), *Diagnoza społeczna 2013. Warunki i jakość życia Polaków*, Social Monitoring Council, Warszawa.

Frączkiewicz-Wronka, A. (2001), *Reforma systemu opieki zdrowotnej w perspektywie integracji z Unią Europejską. Wybrane aspekty zachodzących zmian*, Wydawnictwo Akademii Ekonomicznej, Katowice.

Kielar, M., Teleopieka u progu starości, "Ogólnopolski Przegląd Medyczny", 2013 (12).

Kozierkiewicz, A. (2004), Zagadnienia zdrowia publicznego Unii Europejskiej, [in:] J.Nosko (ed.), *Zdrowie publiczne w zmieniającej się Europie i w Polsce*, Szkoła Zdrowia Publicznego Instytutu Medycyny Pracy im. Prof. J. Nofera, Łódź.

Mossakowska, M., Więcek, A., Błędowski, P. (eds.) (2012), *Aspekty medyczne, psychologiczne, socjologiczne i ekonomiczne starzenia się ludzi w Polsce*, Termedia Wydawnictwa Medyczne, Poznań.

Polakowski, M., Społeczne i ekonomiczne konsekwencje starzenia się społeczeństw a główne kierunki reform systemów emerytalnych w Europie, "Studia BAS" 2012, No. 2(30), online source http://orka.sejm.gov.pl/wydbas.nsf/0/D047CD44C3AFFD3FC1257A37002AA895/$-File/BAS_30-9.pdf.

Prognoza ludności Polski na lata 2008–2035, GUS, online source http://stat.gov.pl/cps/rde/xbcr/gus/L_prognoza_ludnosci_Pl_2008-2035.pdf; Podstawowe informacje o rozwoju demograficznym Polski do 2013 roku, GUS, http://stat.gov.pl/cps/rde/xbcr/gus/L_podst_inf_o_rozwoju_dem_pl_do_2013.pdf.

Svensson, P. G. (1980), The Concept of Health. Some Comments from a Social Science Perspective, "Scandinavian Journal of Social Medicine", Linkoping.

Szatur-Jaworska, B. (2012), Psychospołeczny wymiar sytuacji ludzi starych – wyniki badania "PolSenior", "Problemy Polityki Społecznej. Studia i Dyskusje", Vol. 18, No. 7.

Szatur-Jaworska, B. (2012), Sytuacja rodzinna i potrzeby opiekuńcze ludzi starszych w Polsce, [in:] *Raport na temat sytuacji osób starszych w Polsce*, Instytut Pracy i Spraw Socjalnych, Warszawa, online source: http://senior.gov.pl/source/raport_osoby%20starsze.pdf.

Szatur-Jaworska, B. (2012), Sytuacja rodzinna i więzi rodzinne ludzi starszych i osób na przedpolu starości, [in:] M. Mossakowska, A. Więcek, P. Błędowski (eds.), *Aspekty medyczne, psychologiczne, socjologiczne i ekonomiczne starzenia się ludzi w Polsce*, Termedia Wydawnictwa Medyczne, Poznań.

Włodarczyk, C. (1988), *Prakseologiczny dylemat polityki ochrony zdrowia w Polsce*, Instytut Medycyny Pracy im. Prof. J. Nofera, Łódź.

Włodarczyk, W. C. (2010), *Wprowadzenie do polityki zdrowotnej*, Oficyna a Wolters Kluwer business, Warszawa.

Zieliński, T. (1994), *Ubezpieczenia społeczne pracowników*, WN PWN Warszawa-Kraków.

Chapter VII

Biotechnology Market in Poland: Selected Overview

Barbara Kozierkiewicz

The Market for Clinical Research in Poland

1. Pharmaceutical and biotechnology sector. Introductory remarks

Research into new, innovative methods of treatment is a very important part of the development of medicine. Today, people live some 30 years longer than they did in the last century, and medicine is able to effectively treat most of the serious diseases that were once considered to be incurable. This, among other factors, can be attributed to progress in the development of new and innovative methods of treatment.

Before a new drug enters the market, it must pass a series of tests, which can be divided into two groups: pre-clinical and clinical.

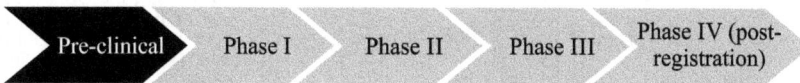

Pre-clinical | Phase I | Phase II | Phase III | Phase IV (post-registration)

Pre-clinical tests are those carried out in the laboratory and on animals. If a substance passes these tests, then clinical trials, in which it is administered to humans, are carried out. Clinical trials are divided into four phases. The first is usually performed in specialized centres and includes administering a substance to a dozen or several dozen healthy volunteers. In the second and third phases the candidate substance is administered to patients in controlled clinical trials in study centres spread throughout the world. While the second phase of research involves up to several hundred patients, the third phase may include several thousand[1].

---

[1] Marcin Walter (ed.), *Badania kliniczne. Organizacja. Nadzór. Monitorowanie*, Warszawa 2004, OINFARMA.

2. Investment and employment in the pharmaceutical R&R industry

Global pharmaceutical and biotechnology R&D investments account for more than 18% of all expenses allocated to research and development activities by all business sectors together. The industry is also a leader in R&D activities and related investments and, as such, is first in the ranking of sectors allocating the greatest share of their revenues to research and scientific activities. The pharmaceutical and biotechnology industries spend more than 14% of their revenue from sales on this type of activity. Ranked second is the IT industry, which spends less than 10% of its income on R&D, and the average expenditure for all industries is valued at only 3.2%[2].

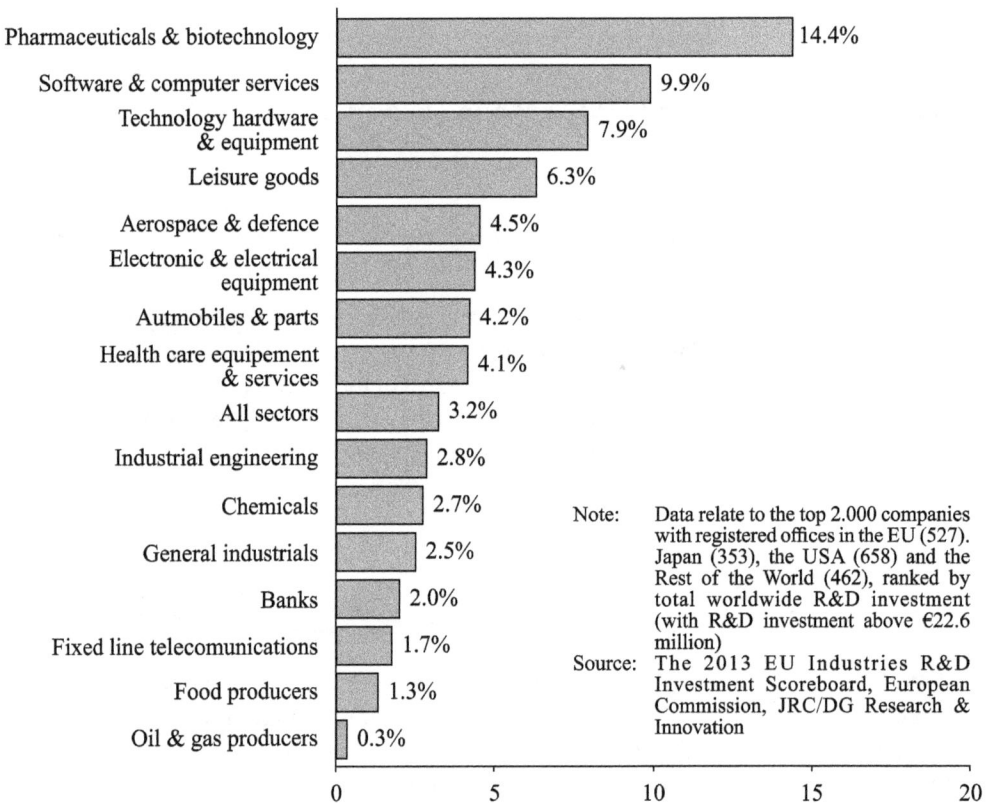

Note: Data relate to the top 2.000 companies with registered offices in the EU (527). Japan (353), the USA (658) and the Rest of the World (462), ranked by total worldwide R&D investment (with R&D investment above €22.6 million)

Source: The 2013 EU Industries R&D Investment Scoreboard, European Commission, JRC/DG Research & Innovation

Figure 1. Ranking of Industrial Sectors by overall sector R&D intensity (R&D as percentage of net sales – 2012)
Source: *The Pharmaceutical Industry in Figures, Key Data*, 2014, European Federation of Pharmaceutical Industries and Associations.

---

[2] *The Pharmaceutical Industry in Figures, Key Data*, 2014, European Federation of Pharmaceutical Industries and Associations.

The rate of investment is fairly stable. In 2008 it was estimated that the pharmaceutical industry was responsible globally for 19.2% of all R&D investments, and the sector ranked highest among those industries, allocating the largest share of their revenue to this activity (16.1% of revenue)[3].

The pharmaceutical and biotechnology R&D sector is also a major employer in Europe among jobs related to innovation and knowledge. In 2013 it was estimated that approximately 115,000 people were employed in this sector in Europe, with an additional 3–4 times more people being indirectly employed[4].

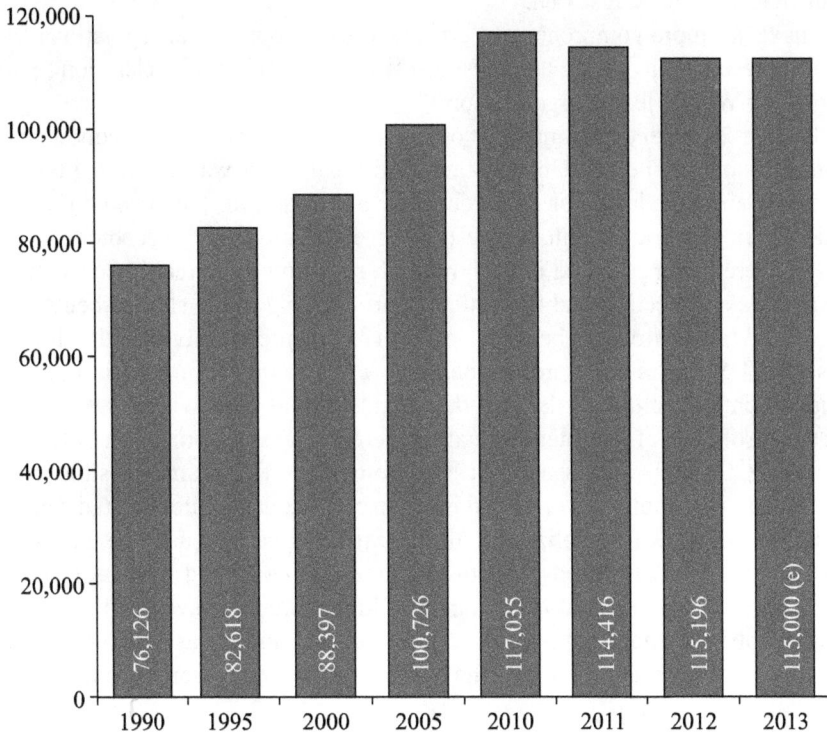

76,126	82,618	88,397	100,726	117,035	114,416	115,196	115,000 (e)
1990	1995	2000	2005	2010	2011	2012	2013

Note: Data include Bulgaria and Turkey (since 2012), Poland (since 2010), Czech Republic, Estonia and Hungary (since 2009), Romania (since 2005) and Slovenia (since 2004). Crotia, Cyprus, Greece, Latvia, Lithuania, Malta, Serbia, Slovakia: data not available.

Source: EFPIA members associations – (e): EFPIA estimate.

Figure 2. Employment in Pharmaceutical R&D (1990–2013)
Source: *The Pharmaceutical Industry in Figures, Key Data*, 2014, European Federation of Pharmaceutical Industries and Associations.

---

[3] *The Pharmaceutical Industry in Figures, Key Data* 2009, Update, EFPIA (The European Federation of Pharmaceutical Industries and Associations).
[4] *The Pharmaceutical Industry in Figures, Key Data*, 2014, European Federation of Pharmaceutical Industries and Associations.

3. History of clinical trials

The first clinical trial was probably carried out in the 16th century. In the 18th century it was already common practice among scientists to carry out clinical trials. The rapid advancements in medicine that occurred in the 19th century led to further improvements in methodology. Clinical trials became better organized and were performed on a larger scale. Following the post-war Nuremberg Trials – and particularly the trials of doctors – the Nuremberg Code was drafted in 1947, and represented the first code of conduct governing the main areas of clinical research.

The next, far more comprehensive document to set out ethical regulations for those carrying out research involving human subjects was the Helsinki Declaration[5], published in 1964 by the World Health Organization.

In the mid-20th century, a number of parallel studies were being conducted in the major markets of Europe, the United States and Japan. This was due to the fact that the requirements and standards for research, their approval and the acceptability of data differed in each market, and thus the results were not universally accepted. As a result, the studies were being repeated in each market, resulting in increased costs, more time required for data collection and the patients participating in the studies being unnecessarily exposed to the products being tested. In 1990, representatives of the three largest markets – the US, Japan and Europe – began to work on the harmonization of standards and requirements for clinical trials, so that results would be universally acceptable. As a result the resolution of the International Conference on Harmonization of Good Clinical Practice (ICH GCP)[6] was issued in 1996. From then on it became possible to conduct clinical trials throughout the world, and make use of the data collected in different parts of the world. The era of globalization of clinical trials had begun. The end of the last century onwards has witnessed a period of increased costs and time required for the introduction of a new drug onto the market. Clinical studies have become an increasingly visible phenomenon in the health care sector and society as a whole, and as such are of interest both to the public and the administrative regulations at both continental and national levels.

4. Current situation of the Global Pharmaceutical R&D Industry

Most publications that deal with the clinical trials sector are based on data available on www.ClinicalTrials.gov. This is a US public register of clinical trials required by the Food and Drug Administration (FDA) since 2002[7], which has now become a global registry of all studies involving humans, following the recommendations of the International

---

[5] Declaration of Helsinki, available online: www.wma.net.
[6] Good Clinical Practice (ICH GCP Guidelines) – Published in Poland by Minister of Health in September 1998.
[7] Guidance for Industry Information Programme on Clinical Trials for Serious or Life-Threatening Diseases and Conditions. Division of Drug Information, Centre for Drug Evaluation and Research, United States Food and Drug Administration, 2002. Available online at fttp://www.fda.gov/cder/guidance/index.htm.

Committee of Medical Journal Editors (ICMJE)[8] in mid-2005. In that year, the ICMJE announced that public disclosure of information regarding phases II-IV is a prerequisite for the publication of study results. As a result, 824 sponsors, including 24 of the top 25 pharmaceutical companies, publish information about their research on www.Clinical-Trials.gov[9]. Similar registers are available at a national level, including registers of trials carried out in Australia, China, India, Germany, Hong Kong, Japan, the Netherlands and Sri Lanka as well as the records of studies in different therapeutic areas, for example, the European Leukaemia Trial register[10]. There is also a European register of clinical trials known as EudraCT[11], but this is not publicly available. Therefore, references to analyses based mainly on data from www.ClinicalTrials.gov will be presented.

Currently, more than 50,000 clinical trials are being performed worldwide in 153 of 192 countries[12]. Each year around 95,000 research centres participate in clinical trials all over the world, recruiting up to 1,300,000 participants. Annual pharmaceutical R&D investment is estimated at 38.5 billion dollars, of which 8.5 billion comprises the manpower costs of the research team, 9.6 billion the administrative costs, with an additional 19.3 billion being spent on laboratory and courier services and other extras[13].

The number of clinical trials being carried out increases each year. In total 21,232 new studies have been registered in the European EudraCT database since 2004[14]. 4,613 studies were registered in this database in 2004. This number has been increasing each year, up to 9,334 new studies registered during the first half of 2009.

5. Globalization

Clinical trials are affected by globalization. The sponsors, mostly pharmaceutical companies, are constantly on the lookout for new study centres all over the world. The most common reason for opening up study centres outside the developed markets of the US, Canada and western Europe are[15]:

- the need to speed up patient recruitment
- ethnic diversity
- access to drug naïve patients
- potential lower costs of research
- potential future markets for marketed medicines

[8] Clinical Trial Registration: a statement from the International Committee of Medical Journal Editors. Available online at http://www.icmje.org/clin_trial.pdf; published: C. De Angelis, J. M. Drazen, F. A. Frizelle *at al.*, "New England Journal of Medicine" 2004; 351:1250–1.

[9] J. P. E. Karlberg, Sponsored Clinical Trial Globalization Trends, "Clinical Trial Magnifier" Feb. 2008; 13–19.

[10] European Leukemia Trial Registry. http://www.leukemia-net.org/content/e58/e3956/e3957/index_eng.htm.

[11] European clinical trials database (EudraCT Database) – not public.

[12] V. Ljubimir, Insider's Tips on Global Clinical Research, "The Monitor", 2008, 22 (2), 51–54.

[13] J. P. E. Karlberg, Industry clinical testing of new medicinal products requires 95,000 study sites and 1,300,000 subjects annually. "Clinical Trial Magnifier" June 2008;101–109.

[14] Statistics based on the studies registered in EudraCT (European clinical trials database) after 1 May 2004 available online: https://eudract.emea.europa.eu/document.html.

[15] V. Ljubimir, Insider's Tips on Global Clinical Research, "The Monitor", 2008, 22 (2), 51–54.

These are the reasons behind the pharmaceutical companies' constant search for new markets, and the opening up of new research centres in different parts of the world, particularly in central and eastern Europe, as well as other countries with large populations such as Brazil, Russia, India and China[16], [17], [18], [19].

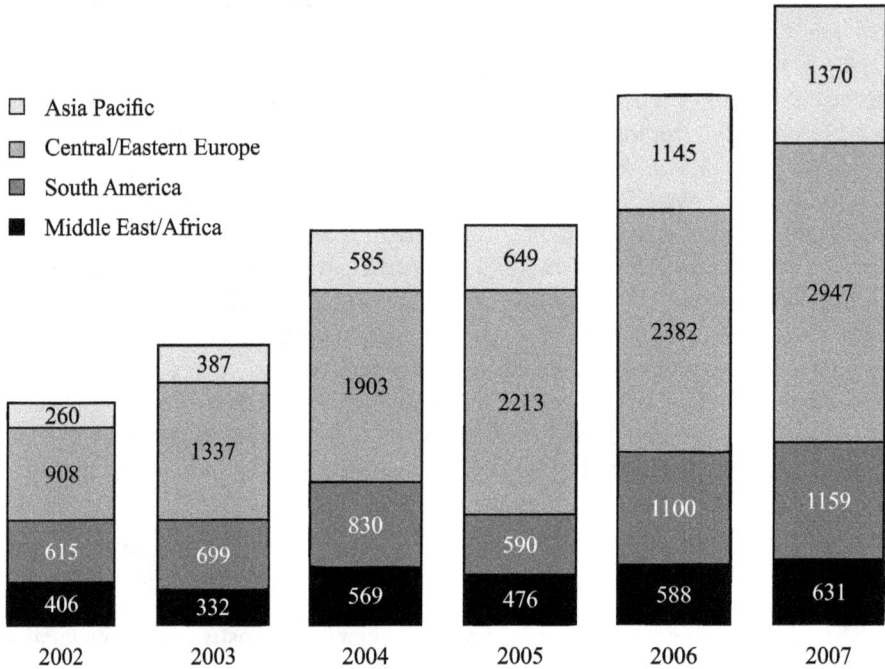

Figure 3. Increase in number of studies performed outside USA and Western Europe
Source: J. V. Farinacci, *Global outsourcing models: Natural selection at work*, GCPj 2009 16 (1), 16–19.

Following the introduction of the ICH GCP in 1996, the countries of central and eastern Europe became a particular focus for clinical trials. In 2004, eight countries in central and eastern Europe, with a population of nearly 74 million, including the largest – Poland – joined the European Union. All of these countries rapidly implemented the European Directives, and proceeded to act in accordance with their guidelines[20].

---

[16] J. V. Farinacci, *Global outsourcing models: Natural selection at work,* GCPj 2009 16 (1), 16–19.

[17] S. Gambrill, Central and Eastern Europe: Growth Opportunities, Growing Pains, Article 562, "The Centerwatch Monthly", 15(8), August 2008.

[18] J. P. E. Karlberg, Sponsored Clinical Trial Globalization Trends, "Clinical Trial Magnifier" Feb 2008; 13–19.

[19] J. P. E. Karlberg, Industry Trials in BRIC Countries – Russia, Moscow and St. Petersburg Stand Out, "Clinical Trial Magnifier", June 2009; 305–320.

[20] I. Cąpała-Szczurko, *Revisiting the European Union, The impact of the EU Clinical Trials Directive on current clinical research practices,* "Applied Clinical Trials", March 1st, 2006; Directive 2001/20/EC of the European Parliament and of the Council of 4 April 2001 on the approximation of the laws, regulations and administrative provisions of the Member States relating to the implementation of good clinical practice in the conduct of clinical trials on medicinal products for human use; Commission Directive 2005/28/EC of 8 April 2005 laying down

An analysis of studies reported on ClinicalTrials.gov between 2005 and 2007 shows that the percentage of research centres conducting clinical trials in the countries of Central and Eastern Europe had increased in this period by a small percentage, and at the same time the share of research centres located in Western Europe and the US showed a slight decrease[21]. A similar analysis based on more recent data for December 2008 reveals that this trend persists.

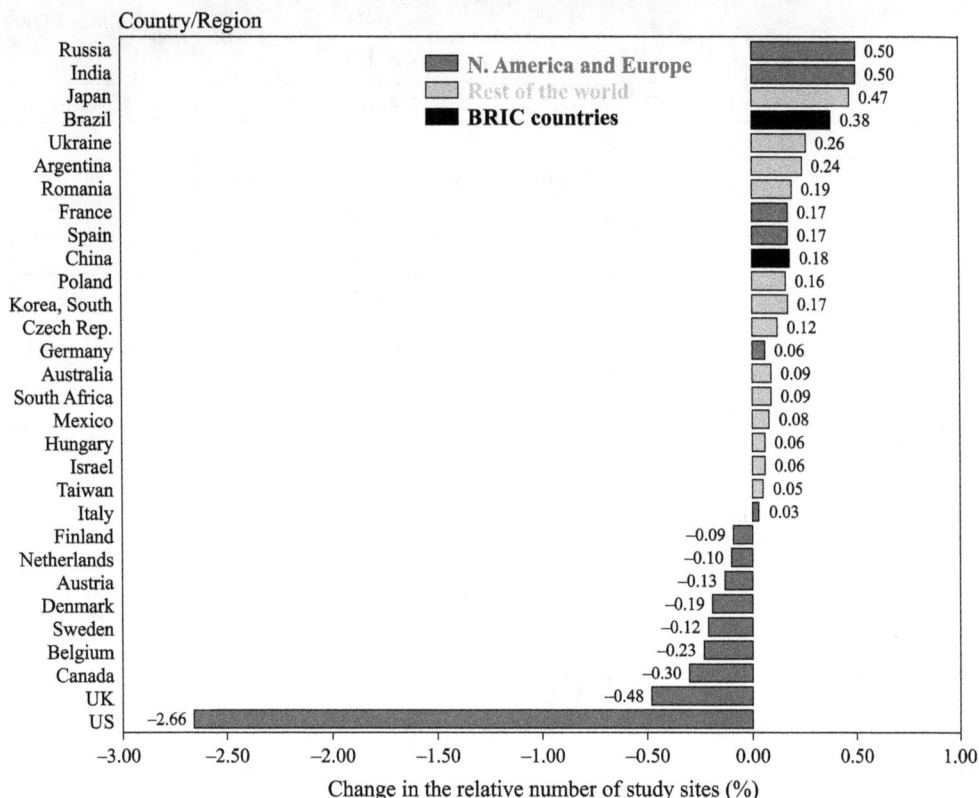

Figure 4. Change in the relative number of phase II–III industry sponsored trial sites (values from Table 1)

Source: J. P. E. Karlberg, Uninterrupted Globalization of Industry Sponsored Clinical Trials, "Clinical Trial Magnifier", February 2009; 79–94.

Poland and Russia are among the top 10 countries with the highest number of active research sites registered from 2005 to 2008. The number of centres registered in Poland (3,245) and Russia (3,513) is comparable with that in the UK (which had 3,592 research sites)[22].

---

principles and detailed guidelines for good clinical practice as regards investigational medicinal products for human use, as well as the requirements for authorization of the manufacturing or importation of such products.

[21] J. P. E. Karlberg, West to East drift in European Sponsored Clinical Trials, "Clinical Trial Magnifier", January 2008;1:1–9.

[22] J. P. E. Karlberg, Uninterrupted Globalization of Industry Sponsored Clinical Trials, "Clinical Trial Magnifier", February 2009; 79–94.

Table 1. The number of industry sponsored phase II–III clinical trial study sites registered with the US trial register for the 60 most active countries for two periods – from 2006.02 for 8 full years and from 2005.10 for two full years. The countries are ranked according to the number of industry sponsored phase II–III clinical trial sites

Country/ Region	From 2006.01 3 full years Rank	Phase II–III Sites	%	From 2005.10 2 full years Rank	Phase II–III Sites	%	Rank Differance	Percentage Differance %
US	1	67,372	44.4	1	492,257	47.1	0	−2.66
Germany	2	9,420	6.2	2	6,438	6.2	0	0.06
Canada	3	6,004	4.0	3	4,456	4.3	0	−0.30
France	4	5,691	3.9	4	3,746	3.6	0	0.17
Japan	5	4,427	2.9	8	2,567	2.5	−3	0.47
Spain	6	4,311	2.8	6	2,792	2.7	0	0.17
Italy	7	3,889	2.6	7	2,648	2.5	0	0.01
UK	8	3,592	2.4	5	2,976	2.8	3	−0.46
Russia	9	3,513	2.3	10	1,904	1.8	−1	0.50
Poland	10	3,245	2.1	9	2,071	2.0	1	0.16
Australia	11	2,413	1.6	12	1,573	1.5	−1	0.09
India	12	2,299	1.5	10	1,066	1.0	−6	0.50
Belgium	13	2,046	1.4	11	1,057	1.6	2	−0.23
Brazil	14	1,991	1.3	20	972	0.9	−6	0.10
Argentina	15	1,971	1.3	17	1,111	1.1	−2	0.24
Czech Republic	16	1,924	1.3	14	1,206	1.2	2	0.12
Netherlands	17	1,823	1.2	13	1,364	1.3	4	−0.10
Hungary	18	1,767	1.2	15	1,152	1.1	3	0.06
Mexico	19	1,543	1.0	19	981	0.9	0	0.06
Ukraine	20	1,533	1.0	23	782	9.7	−3	0.26
South Africa	21	1,401	0.9	21	875	0.8	0	0.09
Sweden	22	1,320	0.9	16	1,126	1.1	6	−0.21
China	23	1,273	0.8	27	687	0.7	−4	0.10
Israel	24	1,186	0.8	25	759	0.7	−1	0.06
Romania	25	1,165	0.8	31	600	0.6	−6	0.19
South Korea	26	1,163	0.8	30	628	0.6	−4	0.17
Austria	27	1,010	0.7	22	835	0.6	5	−0.13
Denmark	28	838	0.6	24	773	0.7	4	−0.19
Finland	29	819	0.5	26	661	0.6	1	−0.09
Taiwan	30	816	0.5	32	512	0.5	−2	0.05
Bulgaria	31	783	0.5	36	416	0.4	−5	0.12

Country/ Region	From 2006.01 3 full years Rank	Phase II–III Sites	%	From 2005.10 2 full years Rank	Phase II–III Sites	%	Rank Differance	Percentage Differance %
Slovakia	32	742	0.5	33	511	0.5	−1	0.00
Greece	33	619	0.4	34	435	0.4	−1	−0.01
Norway	34	582	0.4	29	635	0.6	5	−0.22
Switzerland	35	578	0.4	37	413	0.4	−2	−0.01
Turkey	36	523	0.3	40	256	0.2	−4	0.10
Chile	37	507	0.3	36	262	0.3	−1	0.06
Portugal	38	495	0.3	35	427	0.4	3	−0.06
Philippines	39	424	0.3	39	261	0.2	0	0.03
Peru	40	417	0.3	43	205	0.2	−1	0.06

Source: J. P. E. Karlberg, Uninterrupted Globalization of Industry Sponsored Clinical Trials, "Clinical Trial Magnifier", February 2009; 79–94.

It seems that, out of all the criteria used by sponsors for the selection of research sites, the most important is whether the researchers are able to recruit the required number of patients in a given time and in accordance with the clinical study protocol[23]. This is confirmed by the fact that, among the European countries, the largest drop in the number of active research sites was noted in countries with a small population (Scandinavia), where the potential recruitment base is lower than in bigger countries, and at the same time the potential of commercial market for new medicines is smaller[24]. Lower research costs is certainly an important element; however, the costs associated with the research centres are estimated at only about 25% of the research budget[25].

6. Sponsors of clinical trials

An analysis of the studies registered globally on ClinicalTrials.gov during the period 2005–2008 shows that almost half of the studies registered during this period were sponsored by the pharmaceutical industry (47.6%), with the remaining studies sponsored by government and research institutes (15.1%), other organizations (28%), as well as other organizations in collaboration with the pharmaceutical industry (9,3%). Clinical trials sponsored by the pharmaceutical industry are usually international, multi-centre studies, and are responsible for 77% of registered centres. This shows that the trials are large, involving many more research sites than studies sponsored by other entities. The pharmaceutical industry

[23] J. P. E. Karlberg, West to East drift in European Sponsored Clinical Trials, "Clinical Trial Magnifier", January 2008;1:1–9.
[24] J. P. E. Karlberg, Sponsored Clinical Trial Globalization Trends, "Clinical Trial Magnifier", February 2008; 13–19.
[25] J. P. E. Karlberg, Responding to Emerging Queries on the Legitimacy and Validity of Globalization of Clinical Trials, "Clinical Trial Magnifier", March 2009; 140–152.

conducts research for commercial purposes, leading to new drug registration, or extended registration of already registered medicines. Research sponsored by other bodies, such as governments or academic institutions, is often carried out in a single country. These studies are mostly associated with assessing medical procedures, or other factors affecting health, and seldom lead directly to the development of a new drug[26].

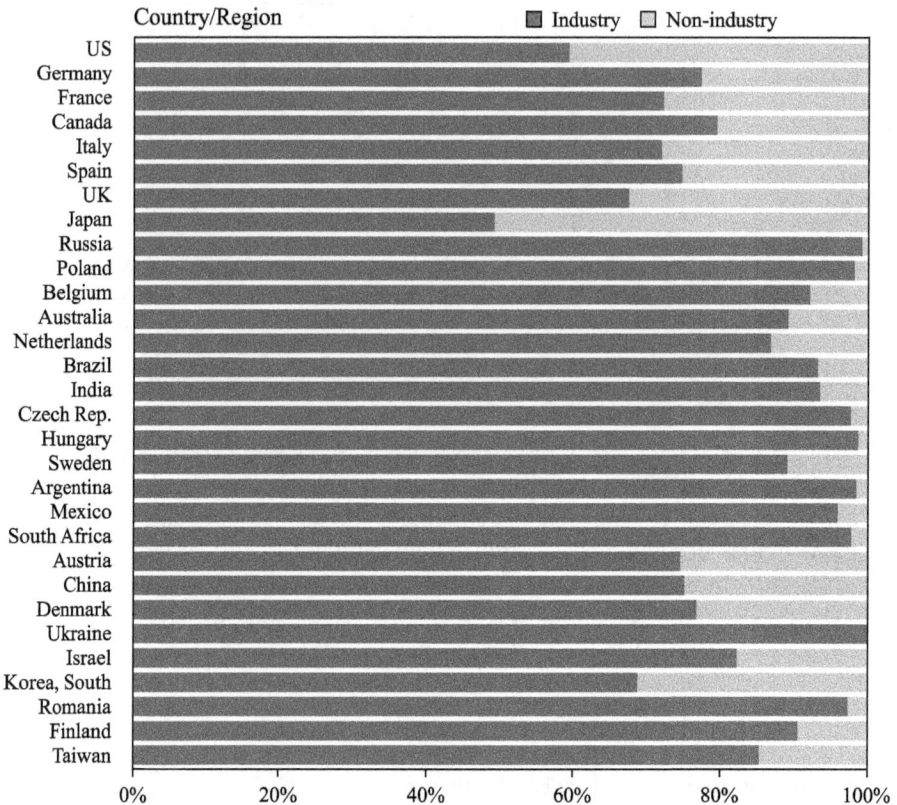

Figure 5. The proportion of industry versus non-industry sponsored phase II–IV trial sites by country/region (values taken from Table 1)

Source: J. P. E. Karlberg, Investigator Initiated Clinical Trials Characteristics, "Clinical Trial Magnifier", October 2008; 208–225.

In Europe, the share of industry sponsored clinical trials in all projects registered in the EudraCT database is even higher, up to 80%, with the remaining 20% including non-commercial research[27].

---

[26] J. P. E. Karlberg, Investigator Initiated Clinical Trials Characteristics, "Clinical Trial Magnifier", October 2008; 208–225.

[27] Statistics based on the studies registered in EudraCT (European clinical trials database) after 1 May 2004, available online: https://eudract.emea.europa.eu/document.html.

7. Time and cost of conducting research

Research into new drugs is expensive and time-consuming. It was estimated that in 2007 the cost of introducing a new drug into the market was more than 1 billion Euro, and required about 12–13 years of research[28],[29],[30].

The time required for developing a new drug has increased significantly in the last 20 years, mostly due to the growing number of requirements imposed by the authorities responsible for the registration of new drugs, as well as the fact that contemporary studies often relate to the chronic diseases, which calls for longer and more complex research projects[31].

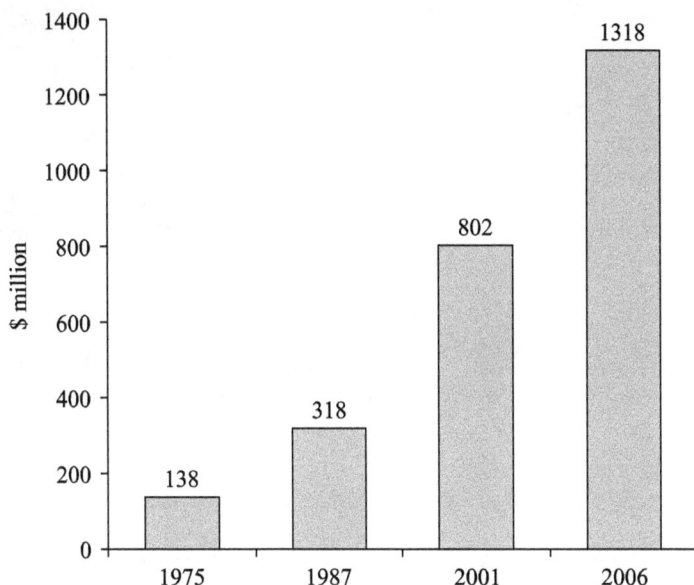

Figure 6. Estimates of the average cost of developing a single new pharmaceutical product from 1975 to present
Source: *The State of Pharmaceutical Innovation in Europe*, EFPIA (The European Federation of Pharmaceutical Industries and Associations).

When a new molecule is being developed, there is no certainty as to whether it will become a new drug in the future. It has been estimated that from the 10,000 particles that

---

[28] *The Pharmaceutical Industry in Figures, Key Data*, 2009 Update, EFPIA (The European Federation of Pharmaceutical Industries and Associations).
[29] *The Innovative Pharmaceutical Industry a key asset to the European Union*, EFPIA (The European Federation of Pharmaceutical Industries and Associations).
[30] *The State of Pharmaceutical Innovation in Europe*, EFPIA (The European Federation of Pharmaceutical Industries and Associations).
[31] M. Dickson, P. Gagnon, Key factors in the rising cost of new drug discovery and development, "Nature Reviews", Drug discovery, 2004, 417–429.

emerge from the earliest phase of the research, only 1–2 molecules will finally be approved as a new medicine[32].

Pharmaceutical industry expenditure on the development of new drugs is constantly increasing. Companies report a 147% increase in their investments between 1993 and 2004, which is not reflected in a similar increase in the number of new drugs registered by the FDA (Food and Drug Administration)[33]. In 2006, R&D investment in new drugs development in the United States was about 55.2 billion, while the FDA registered only 22 new medicines. In comparison, in 1996, when investments for this purpose were half smaller, FDA registered twice as many (53) new medicines[34].

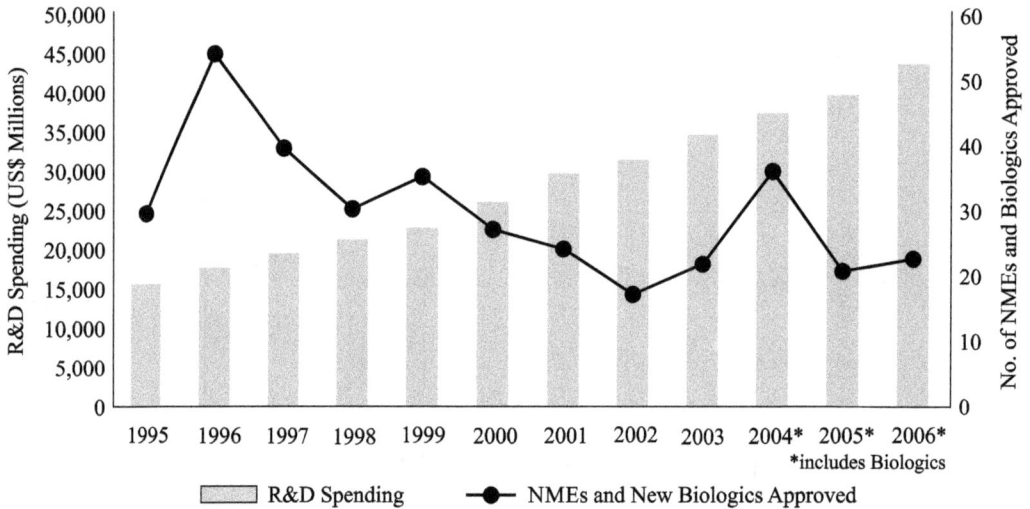

Figure 7. R&D spending has soared but the number of NMEs and biologics approved by the FDA is down

Source: *Pharma 2020. The Vision. Which path will you take?*, PricewaterhouseCoopers.

Note: Data on R&D spending for non-PhRMA companies are not included here, because they are not available for all 11 years.

8. The current situation in Poland

The history of clinical research in Poland dates back to 1984, but most of the growth took place in the mid-1990s[35]. Since 2003, the number of clinical trials registered annually

[32] *The Innovative Pharmaceutical Industry a key asset to the European Union*, EFPIA (The European Federation of Pharmaceutical Industries and Associations); *New Drug Development Science, Business, Regulatory, and Intellectual Property Issues Cited as Hampering Drug Development Efforts*, November 2006.

[33] J. P. E. Karlberg, US FDA New Drug Approval Trends 1999–2008, "Clinical Trials Magnifier", March 2009, 167–170.

[34] *Pharma 2020. The Vision. Which path will you take?*, PricewaterhouseCoopers.

[35] Report from a survey dedicated to clinical trials in Poland performed with pharmaceutical companies, Stowarzyszenie na Rzecz Dobrej Praktyki Badań Klinicznych w Polsce, GCPpl, June 2004.

has remained more or less constant. Each year 400–500 new studies are registered and approved by the Minister of Health, in a more or less constant proportion of Phase I, II, III and IV (I – 10%, II – 30%, III – 55%, IV – 5%) [36].

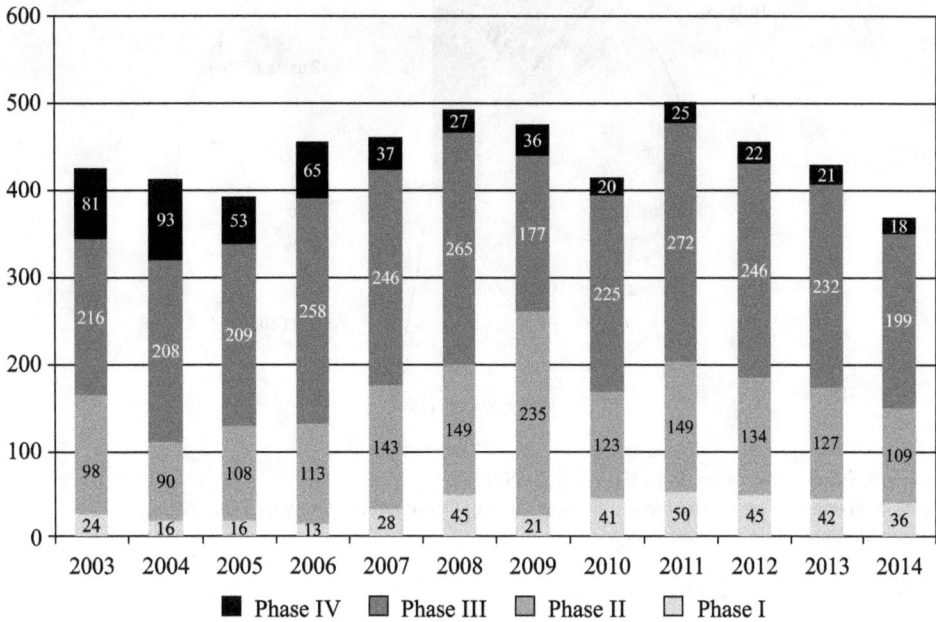

Figure 8. Number of clinical studies registered in Poland per year
Source: Data for 2003–2009: *Badania kliniczne w Polsce – Główne wyzwania*, PWC, November 2010. Data for 2010–14: Office for registration of medical products, medical devices and biocidal products. Average phase distribution: I 10%, II 30%, III 55%, IV 5%).

Poland has a significant market share of the clinical trials in this part of Europe.

Most of the clinical trials performed in Poland are carried out by the pharmaceutical industry. This is particularly apparent in the analysis of international clinical trials that were ongoing from 2005–2008. During this period, 3,643 research sites participated in clinical studies sponsored by the pharmaceutical industry, while only four government sponsored research sites participated in the studies and 21 sites were sponsored by other institutions[37].

Poland is ranked among the second ten on a list of European countries having the highest pharmaceutical industry R&D investments after the majority of major western European countries, but some of the smaller countries also have a higher ranking[38].

---

[36] *Badania kliniczne w Polsce – Główne wyzwania*, PWC, November 2010. Data provided by Office for registration of medical products, medical devices and biocidal products.
[37] J. P. E. Karlberg, Investigator Initiated Clinical Trials Characteristics, "Clinical Trial Magnifier", October 2008; 208–225.
[38] *The Pharmaceutical Industry in Figures, Key Data*, 2014, European Federation of Pharmaceutical Industries and Associations.

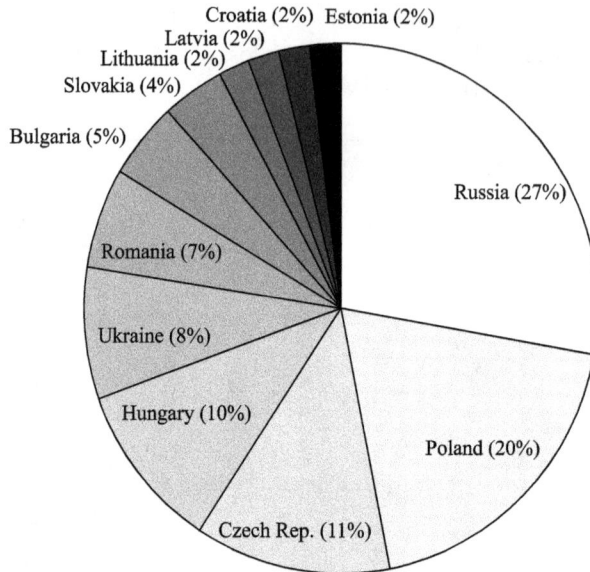

Figure 9. Proportion of trials in CEE 2002–2007
Source: S. Gambrill, Central and Eastern Europe: Growth Opportunities, Growing Pains, Article 562, "The Centerwatch Monthly", 15(8), August 2008.

Table 2. European countries with the highest pharmaceutical industry R&D investment

	EFPIA 2012	€ million		EFPIA 2012	€ million
1	Germany	5 767	14	Romania	200
2	United Kingdom	5 187	15	Ireland	194
3	Switzerland	4 965	16	Slovenia	164
4	France	4 392	17	Hungary	158
5	Belgium	2 343	18	Norway	141
6	Denmark	1 411	19	Portugal	88
7	Italy	1 230	20	Greece	84
8	Spain	997	21	Turkey	83
9	Sweden	942	22	Czech Republic	49
10	Netherlands	642	23	Croatia	40
11	Austria	453	24	Cyprus	14
12	Finland	264		Total	30,035
13	Poland	227			

Source: *The Pharmaceutical Industry in Figures, Key Data*, 2014, European Federation of Pharmaceutical Industries and Associations.

This is not reflected in the number of research centres located in Poland. As described above, the number of research centres in Poland should have placed it much higher in the ranking of European countries. There are various reasons for this.

One might be that the costs of conducting research in Poland are lower than in other, especially western European countries. Another possible explanation is that clinical studies are being performed in Poland, which is why many research sites are registered, but other activities related to the R&D process, such as R&D headquarters or research laboratories, are still located in Western Europe. It has been estimated that the costs associated with research centres account for only about 25% of the research budget while the remaining costs are internal costs of the sponsor (25%) and additional services related to carrying out such research as, for instance, in research laboratories.

Apart from the further development of phase I to III clinical research, Poland might consider the development of those areas of R&D pharmaceutical industry which sponsors have decided not to invest in, such as the above-mentioned R&D headquarters, laboratories or centres for preclinical studies. In recent years, several companies have already begun to invest in such activities in Poland. The first data management centres have already been established, as well as the first global clinical research management centre coordinating clinical trials globally[39].

9. Benefits and risks related to sponsored clinical trials in Poland

There are many benefits associated with the clinical trials conducted in Poland. In addition to the purely financial benefits, non-financial ones include increased knowledge of research methodology, administrative tools required for clinical research, knowledge transfers between researchers from different countries and the opportunity to gain experience while participating in multi-centre, international clinical trials[40].

The opportunity to publish papers based on clinical study results is very important to researchers. The present survey shows that 55% of researchers located outside the US mention the opportunity to publish as having first place among the benefits of participating in sponsored clinical trials[41]. Another study estimates that 40–50% of all articles published in the "New England Journal of Medicine" and the "Lancet" arise from the clinical trial of a new drug[42].

It is possible that a conflict of interest may arise in situations where researchers earn disproportionately more in the clinical trials than in their original place of employment[43].

Insufficiencies in financial accounting of medical procedures performed solely for industry-sponsored clinical trials could lead to a situation where the taxpayer is bearing

---

[39] Warsaw Business Journal's Investment of the Year, "Warsaw Business Journal", 2012 Award.
[40] J. P. E. Karlberg, Investigator Initiated Clinical Trials Characteristics, "Clinical Trial Magnifier", October 2008; 208–225.
[41] J. P. E. Karlberg, Institutional Indirect Fees and Administrative Fees for Industry Sponsored Clinical Trials, Magnifier Subscriber Survey, "Clinical Trial Magnifier", February 2009; 95–100.
[42] J. P. E. Karlberg, Trends of Evidence Based Medicine. "Clinical Trial Magnifier", August 2008; 163–166.
[43] J. V. Farinacci, *Global outsourcing models: Natural selection at work*, GCPj 2009 16 (1), 16–19.

the costs that should be borne by the sponsor of the study. Recently published guidelines for clinical trials cost accounting[44] are a preliminary step towards proper accounting procedures.

References

Cąpała-Szczurko, I. (2006), *Revisiting the European Union, The impact of the EU Clinical Trials Directive on current clinical research practices,* "Applied Clinical Trials", 1 March.

Dickson, M., Gagnon, P. (2004), *Key factors in the rising cost of new drug discovery and development,* Nature Reviews, Drug discovery 417–429.

Farinacci, J. V. (2009), *Global outsourcing models: Natural selection at work,* GCPj 16 (1), 16–19.

Gambrill, S. (2008), *Central and Eastern Europe: Growth Opportunities, Growing Pains,* Article 562, The Centerwatch Monthly, 15(8), August.

Karlberg, J. P. E. (2008), *West to East drift in European Sponsored Clinical Trials.* "Clinical Trial Magnifier", January;1:1–9.

Karlberg, J. P. E. (2008), *Sponsored Clinical Trial Globalization Trends.* "Clinical Trial Magnifier", February; 13–19.

Karlberg, J. P. E. (2008), Industry clinical testing of new medicinal products requires 95,000 study sites and 1,300,000 subjects annually, "Clinical Trial Magnifier", June;101–109.

Karlberg, J. P. E. (2008), *Trends of Evidence Based Medicine,* "Clinical Trial Magnifier", August; 163–166.

Karlberg, J. P. E. (2008), *Investigator Initiated Clinical Trials Characteristics,* "Clinical Trial Magnifier", October; 208–225.

Karlberg, J. P. E. (2009), *Uninterrupted Globalization of Industry Sponsored Clinical Trials,* "Clinical Trial Magnifier", February; 79–94.

Karlberg, J. P. E. (2009), *Institutional Indirect Fees and Administrative Fees for Industry Sponsored,* Clinical Trials Magnifier Subscriber Survey, "Clinical Trial Magnifier", February; 95–100.

Karlberg, J. P. E. (2009), *Responding to Emerging Queries on the Legitimacy and Validity of Globalization of Clinical Trials,* "Clinical Trial Magnifier", March; 140–152.

Karlberg, J. P. E. (2009), *US FDA New Drug Approval Trends 1999–2008,* "Clinical Trial Magnifier", March; 167–170.

Karlberg, J. P. E. (2009), *Industry Trials in BRIC Countries – Russia, Moscow and St. Petersburg Stand Out,* "Clinical Trial Magnifier", June; 305–320.

Ljubimir, V. (2008), *Insider's Tips on Global Clinical Research,* "The Monitor", 22 (2), 51–54.

Walter, M. (2004) (ed.), *Badania kliniczne. Organizacja. Nadzór. Monitorowanie.,* Warszawa 2004, OINFARMA.

Warsaw Business Journal's Investment of the Year, "Warsaw Business Journal", 2012 Award.

Clinical research sector reports

Badania kliniczne w Polsce – Główne wyzwania, PWC, November 2010.

Data provided by Office for registration of medical products, medical devices and biocidal products.

---

[44] Komunikat Departamentu Gospodarki Lekami Narodowego Funduszu Zdrowia: Komunikat w sprawie rozliczeń świadczeń udzielanych pacjentom włączonym do badania klinicznego z dnia 30.04.2009.

Report from a survey dedicated to clinical trials in Poland performed with pharmaceutical companies, Stowarzyszenie na Rzecz Dobrej Praktyki Badań Klinicznych w Polsce GCPpl, June 2004.

Pharma 2020. The Vision. Which path will you take? PriceWaterhouseCoopers.

The Pharmaceutical Industry in Figures, Key Data, 2009 Update, EFPIA (The European Federation of Pharmaceutical Industries and Associations).

The Pharmaceutical Industry in Figures, Key Data, 2014, EFPIA (The European Federation of Pharmaceutical Industries and Associations).

The Innovative Pharmaceutical Industry a key asset to the European Union, EFPIA (The European Federation of Pharmaceutical Industries and Associations).

The State of Pharmaceutical Innovation in Europe, EFPIA (The European Federation of Pharmaceutical Industries and Associations).

Statistic based on the studies registered in EudraCT (European clinical trials database) after 1 May 2004, available online: https://eudract.emea.europa.eu/document.html.

New Drug Development Science, Business, Regulatory, and Intellectual Property Issues Cited as Hampering Drug Development Efforts, November 2006.

Law and regulations

Polish

Komunikat Departamentu Gospodarki Lekami Narodowego Funduszu Zdrowia: Komunikat w sprawie rozliczeń świadczeń udzielanych pacjentom włączonym do badania klinicznego z dnia 30.04.2009.

European

Directive 2001/20/EC of the European Parliament and of the Council of 4 April 2001 on the approximation of the laws, regulations and administrative provisions of the Member States relating to the implementation of good clinical practice in the conduct of clinical trials on medicinal products for human use.

Commission Directive 2005/28/EC of 8 April 2005 laying down principles and detailed guidelines for good clinical practice as regards investigational medicinal products for human use, as well as the requirements for authorization of the manufacturing or importation of such products.

General

Declaration of Helsinki, available online: www.wma.net.

Good Clinical Practice (ICH GCP Guidelines) – Published in Poland by Minister of Health in September 1998.

Guidance for Industry Information Programme on Clinical Trials for Serious or Life-Threatening Diseases and Conditions. Division of Drug Information, Center for Drug Evaluation and Research, United States Food and Drug Administration, 2002. Available online at ftp://www.fda.gov/cder/guidance/index.htm.

Clinical Trial Registration: a statement from the International Committee of Medical Journal Editors. Available online at http://www.icmje.org/clin_trial.pdf; published: C. De Angelis, J. M. Drazen, F. A. Frizelle *at al.*, "New England Journal of Medicine" 2004; 351:1250–1.

Clinical trial registries

US National Institutes of Health and The US National Library of Medicine's Clinical Trial Register. Available online at http://www.clinicaltrials.gov.

Australian New Zealand Clinical Trials Registry (ANZCTR), http://www.anzctr.org.au/Survey/UserQuestion.aspx.

Chinese Clinical Trial Register (ChiCTR), http://www.chictr.org/.

Clinical Trials Registry – India (CTRI), http://www.ctri.in:8080/Clinicaltrials/trials_jsp/index.jsp.

German Clinical Trials Register (DRKS), http://www.germanctr.de/.

Hong Kong Clinical Trials Register, http://www.hkclinicaltrials.com/.

Japan Primary Registries Network, http://rctportal.niph.go.jp/.

The Netherlands Trial Register (NTR), http://www.trialregister.nl/trialreg/index.asp.

Sri Lanka Clinical Trials Registry (SLCTR), http://www.slctr.lk/.

European Leukemia Trial Registry, http://www.leukemia-net.org/content/e58/e3956/e3957/index_eng.htm.

European clinical trials database (EudraCT Database) – not public.

List of contributors

Zbigniew Bochniarz, Prof. Dr Bochniarz is an affiliate professor at the Evans School of Public Policy and Governance, University of Washington. He is also an affiliate faculty of the Microeconomics of Competitiveness programme at Harvard Business School. Earlier, he was a visiting professor and senior fellow at Hubert H. Humphrey Institute of Public Affairs, University of Minnesota, for over 20 years. Prof. Bochniarz founded there the Center for Nations in Transition, which facilitated transformation processes in many central and east European countries. His teaching and research focus on competitiveness, clustering and social capital, strategies for sustainable development, and sustainability of transformation.

Janusz E. Dmochowski, holds PhD in Engineering Science from Warsaw University of Technology; PhD degree in physics from Institute of Physics, Polish Academy of Sciences, and Doctor of Engineering Science in electronics from Institute of Electron Technology in Warsaw. He was a research associate at the Institute of Physics, Polish Academy of Sciences (PAS), where he got awards for research on semiconductor lasers, and for research on donors in ionic semiconductor $CdF2$. He was a research fellow at the Austrian Academy of Sciences and Fonds zur Forderung Wissenschaftlichen Forschung and was twice awarded SERC Visiting Research Fellow at Physics Department, Imperial College of Science, Technology and Medicine in London. For the term 1994–1998 he was also a Member of Parliament of the Capital City of Warsaw, the deputy chairman of Strategy and Development Commission.

Aldona Frączkiewicz-Wronka, PhD, Prof., head of the Department of Public Management and Social Sciences at the University of Economics in Katowice and the Department of Social Work at WSP TWP Warsaw, Faculty of Social and Pedagogical Sciences in Katowice. Her research interests revolve around issues of social policy, management in the public sector, mainly public health and social welfare. She is an expert in the National Foresight Programme "Poland 2000" Technology Foresight development of public services in the GOP, works for many public entities, among others: the Ministry of Science and Higher Education, Ministry of Regional Development, Ministry of Health, the Marshal's Office in Katowice and others.

Christopher G. Gruszczynski, holds a PhD in Public International Law and is Assistant Professor at the College of Management in Warsaw, Faculty of Law and Administration. He cooperates with the Polish Open University established in 1991 as one of the first private universities in Poland, as well as with the Higher School of Safety and Security Services in Cracow and the University of Information Technology and Management in Rzeszów. His recent study includes the analysis of benefits and dangers of sovereign wealth funds in the 21st century, published by the National Defence Academy in Warsaw.

Nicola Grassano, PhD, Junior Analyst at the Joint Research Centre's Institute for Prospective Technological Studies (IPTS) of the European Commission. He holds a PhD in Law and Economics from the University of Bologna and is a visiting fellow at SPRU – Science and Technology Policy Research of the University of Sussex (UK). He joined the Knowledge for Growth Unit at IPTS in November 2013 as post-doc researcher working on Industrial Research and Innovation (IRI). He contributes to the implementation of the Industrial Research and Innovation Monitoring and Analysis (IRIMA) project. His research interests are in economics of innovation, innovation and productivity in the service sector, innovation indicators and measurements problems, R&D and non-R&D based innovations.

Barbara Kos, PhD, Associate Professor working in the Department of Transport of University of Economics in Katowice. Dean of Faculty of Economics, University of Economics in Katowice. She is mainly interested in subjects of transport, shipping, and logistics. Author or co-author of 200 scientific and research papers.

Joanna Kos-Łabędowicz, PhD, Assistant Professor working in the Department of International Economic Relations of University of Economics in Katowice. Her areas of interest are international business and the influence of information and communication technologies on the economy. Author or co-author of 60 scientific and research papers.

Barbara Kozierkiewicz, PhD student in the Koźmiński University in Warsaw. She is also affiliated to a global, science-led biopharmaceutical and innovative medicine research.

Sabina Ostrowska, PhD, Assistant Professor working in the Department of Public Management and Social Sciences at the University of Economics in Katowice. She has won the X edition of the Scientific Paper Competition run by the Committee of Organization and Management of the Polish Academy of Sciences. Winner of an award in the category of doctoral theses: "Mission oriented scorecard implementation in the healthcare management".

Pietro Moncado-Paterno-Castello, Senior Analyst in the Joint Research Centre's Institute for Prospective Technological Studies (IPTS) of the European Commission. He is also Facilitator of the Scientific Cluster of sixteen JRC projects in the area of "Innovation, Knowledge Transfer, Competitiveness and Employment", and member of the "Economics of Research and Innovation" team. Before joining IPTS in 1995 he worked, as Founder and President, in the Agency for Natural Resources Energy and Technology in the Massachusetts Institute of Technology (MIT), Electric Utility Program (USA) and in the EC's Directorate General for Research and Technological Development (BE). His research interests include economics of corporate R&D and innovation, firm dynamics, employment and competitiveness; management of technological change, and research & innovation policy.

Marta Postula, PhD, head of the Department of Corporate Finances at the Faculty of Management, University of Warsaw, professor at the Koźmiński University, member of the research team TIGER. The scope of her professional experiences includes: operation of the public finance system in Poland and worldwide, budget processes and effectiveness of public expenditures. In 2013 she obtained a post-doctoral degree of *doctor habilitowany* of economic sciences in the field of finances. Author and co-editor of book publications devoted to public finances and over 70 other scientific publications.

Małgorzata Runiewicz-Wardyn, PhD, Associate Professor in the Koźmiński University, Transformation, Integration and Globalization Economic Research Centre (TIGER). Her main scientific and research interests include: international competitiveness of regions; knowledge-based economy; industrial economics; industry clusters; technological life-cycle, and regional R&D and innovation policies. She was twice a postdoctoral research fellow at the Center of European Studies of Harvard University, the Institute of Urban and Regional Development at Berkeley University of California; and a visiting lecturer at the Solvay Brussels School of Economics and Management of the Université Libre de Bruxelles (Belgium).

Viktor Shevchuk, PhD, DSc, Professor of Economics in the Institute of Economy, Sociology, and Philosophy of the Cracow University of Technology (since 2004). He teaches courses on macroeconomic policy and managerial economics. He has written extensively on the balance-of-payments adjustment in transformation economies, exchange rate policy and higher education issues, with a focus on its role in economic growth.

Hermann Simon, Prof., PhD, founder and chairman of Simon-Kucher & Partners, the world's leading pricing consultancy. The global strategy and marketing consulting firm has over 750 professionals in 29 offices. Before committing himself entirely to management consulting, Simon was professor of business administration and marketing. In German-speaking countries, Hermann Simon has been acknowledged as the most influential living management thinker (www.hermannsimon.com).

Jerzy Skrzypek, PhD in econometrics and statistics. He is an employee of the Department of Econometrics and Operations Research and director of e-Learning Centre of the University of Economics in Kraków. His research interests revolve around the construction of simulation models that can be used to assess the condition of the company and to draw up comprehensive action plans. Jerzy Skrzypek has extensive experience in preparing business plans and their implementation with the use of e-learning. One of his major publication is the book *Business Plan – a best practice model*, POLTEXT 2012.

Dirk Nicolas Wagner, PhD, Professor at the Faculty of Business Economics & Management, Karlshochschule International University, Professor of Strategic Management, head of Degree Programme "International Business", Dean of Faculty of Business Economics & Management. His research fields and interests include: strategy and organization; project management; new institutional economics; economic order for man and machine and bee-economics. His practical experience includes consulting and analytic work for the VEBA AG: ThyssenKrupp Serv AG, Düsseldorf, and others.

Tomasz Winnicki, PhD, DSc Eng, Professor of Polymer Chemistry and Environmental Engineering, specializing in separation processes. Doctor Honoris Causa of Częstochowa University of Technology, Honorary Professor of Lublin University of Technology, Member of European Academy of Science & Arts and Ukrainian Academy of Technical Sciences, Honorary Member of Polish Membrane Society. Former Chair of the State Environmental Council of Poland, Honorary President of the Rectors' Conference of Public

Colleges in Poland, Rector-Senior of the Karkonsze College of Jelenia Góra. Retired Professor (former Vice-President) of Wrocław University of Technology. Currently Professor of Kalisz University of Applied Sciences.

Lech W. Zacher, PhD, Prof., economist, sociologist and the futurist. He is director of the Centre of Impact Assessment Studies and Forecasting, Koźmiński University in Warsaw; member of the Committee of the Future Studies "Poland 2000 Plus" at the Presidium of the Polish Academy of Sciences; member of the International Studies Association and International Sociological Association, European Association for the Study of Science and Technology; editor-in-chief of the interdisciplinary journal "Transformations" (Polish and English issues; indexed in EBSCO Publishing, Index Copernicus and ERIH). Author of several books and many articles on globalization, science and technology impacts, information society, and the future.

Maria Zrałek, PhD, Prof., Dean of Humanistic Science Faculty at the Humanitas University in Sosnowiec. Her field of research interests is social policy, problems of old and disabled people as well as social pathology. She is a member of team ex-cogitating Strategy of Social Policy of the Silesian Voivodship for years 2006–2020. An expert in projects performed within the Operation Programme on "Innovative Economy" of the European Regional Development Fund (ERDF). Chair of Katowice Department of the Polish Gerontological Association.

Joanna Żyra, PhD, DSc, teaches management courses at the Cracow University of Technology. Her research interests include various aspects of higher education, labour market functioning and university management. In 2008–2010, she was regional director of the HEGESCO (Higher Education as a Generator of Strategic Competences) project for Poland. In 2012–2015, she was project director of the EPAK (Electronic Platform of Competence Analysis) research project. In 2000–2004, she served as vice-rector of the Cracow School of Commerce.

www.ingramcontent.com/pod-product-compliance
Lightning Source LLC
Chambersburg PA
CBHW061803210326
41599CB00034B/6865